Woman, Culture, and Society

Contributors

Joan Bamberger	Sherry B. Ortner
Nancy Chodorow	Lois Paul
Jane Fishburne Collier	Michelle Zimbalist Rosaldo
Bette S. Denich	Karen Sacks
Carol P. Hoffer	Peggy R. Sanday
Louise Lamphere	Carol B. Stack
Nancy B. Leis	Nancy Tanner
Bridget O'Laughlin	Margery Wolf

Woman, Culture, and Society

Edited by Michelle Zimbalist Rosaldo
and Louise Lamphere

Stanford University Press, Stanford, California   1974

Stanford University Press, Stanford, California
© 1974 by the Board of Trustees of the
Leland Stanford Junior University
Printed in the United States of America
Cloth ISBN 0-8047-0850-9   Paper ISBN 0-8047-0851-7
LC 73-89861

Preface

There is no question that the women's liberation movement has stimulated, in recent years, a good deal of interest in understanding and analyzing women's lives. At Stanford, in 1971, a collective of female graduate students in anthropology organized an undergraduate lecture course, "Women in Cross-Cultural Perspective." At more or less the same time anthropologists in other colleges and universities began to prepare similar courses, and to ask themselves what anthropologists might have to say about women and, conversely, how an interest in women might provide a new perspective in their field.

When Rosaldo (who taught that course, along with Jane Collier, Julia Howell, Kim Kramer, Janet Shepherd Fjellman, and Ellen Lewin) showed Lamphere a copy of the Stanford lectures, we both decided that the issues raised, the problems solved, and the questions that remained unasked (and so, unanswered) were of sufficient importance and interest to be shared. The difficulties of bringing an entirely new perspective to bear on anthropological materials had encouraged a good deal of creative thinking, suggestive questioning, and research. How, for example, in a field that had a long tradition of describing men's place in society, could we begin to characterize the interest of women's lives? And then, again, how were we to evaluate the great variation in female activities, roles, and powers that is found in different human groups? What were we to make of the popular claim that women are, biologically, men's inferiors? If we rejected that claim, how then could we begin to explain and understand the fact that women are treated, culturally and socially, as inferior, in virtually all societies in the world? Ultimately, of course, all of these questions revolve around a need to reexamine the ways in which we think about ourselves.

The impetus for this book lies in our conviction that the lack of interest in women in conventional anthropology constitutes a genuine deficiency, that it has led to distorted theories and impoverished ethno-graphic accounts. By focusing on women, and by addressing facts that have conventionally been ignored or taken for granted, we hope to re-appraise old theories and pave the way for future thought. In anthro-pology, it is clear that our conceptions of human social life will be broadened when they address women's lives and strategies along with those of men.

The problem, for us, was how to do it. The anthropological literature tells us relatively little about women, and provides almost no theoretical apparatus for understanding or describing culture from a woman's point of view. Because of our lack of both materials and theories, it seemed more reasonable to collect papers from a number of people working in this area than to attempt a book ourselves. In the last few years, we have found—all of us—that our own thinking about women has become increasingly sophisticated, and this leads us to believe that a number of the papers here will be superseded by later work. In a sense, then, these papers represent a first generation's attempt to integrate an interest in women into a general theory of society and culture. They outline a number of theoretical issues, and illustrate lines of thought that later studies might pursue. The authors vary in their theoretical commit-ments, their politics, and their methods. Some of the papers reflect re-search initiated long before the contemporary women's movement be-came relevant; others represent thinking undertaken specifically for this book. Most of the papers have not been published elsewhere. Taken together, all should serve, minimally, to correct a dominant bias that sees women's lives as lacking in order or in interest. And they illustrate ways in which anthropologists will have to begin to think about women if they are to understand our human world.

M.Z.R.
L.L.

November 1973

Contents

Contents

Contributors

JOAN BAMBERGER received her Ph.D. in anthropology from Harvard University in 1967. Her field research has been among the Northern Kayapó of Central Brazil. A monograph on the subject is forthcoming. She is on the faculty of Brandeis University.

NANCY CHODOROW is Instructor at Wellesley College, with responsibilities concerning the study of women and women's education. She is currently completing a doctoral dissertation in the Department of Sociology at Brandeis University. She works in the fields of psychoanalytic personality theory and the comparative study of women and the family.

JANE FISHBURNE COLLIER received her Ph.D. from Tulane University in 1970 and is now Assistant Professor of Anthropology at Stanford University. Most of her research has been carried out in Zinacantan, a Maya community in southern Mexico, but she has also done limited fieldwork in an Andalusian village in Spain and in a Kpelle community in Liberia. She is the author of *Law and Social Change in Zinacantan.*

BETTE S. DENICH received her Ph.D. from the University of California, Berkeley. She is now Assistant Professor of Anthropology at Barnard College and Columbia University. Her field research in Yugoslavia has focused on industrialization and rural-urban migration, but has also included more traditional ethnological interests. She is the author of several articles based on Yugoslavian research, and is presently completing a monograph on economic and political revolution in a Serbian town.

CAROL P. HOFFER received her Ph.D. from Bryn Mawr College and is presently Assistant Professor and Chairman of the Department of Anthropology at Franklin and Marshall College. She has done fieldwork in the Mende/Sherbro ethnic area of Sierra Leone and ethnohistorical research in Freetown and London. Her previous publications are on West African women in high office.

LOUISE LAMPHERE received her Ph.D. from Harvard University in 1968; she is now Assistant Professor of Anthropology at Brown University. In 1965–66 she conducted research on the Navajo Reservation in New Mexico, and has written several articles on Navajo social organization and a forthcoming monograph, *To Run After Them: The Social and Cultural Bases of Cooperation in a Navajo Community*. In 1971–72 she was a postdoctoral fellow at the London School of Economics, where she conducted a pilot study of working-class women, in both their home and work situations.

NANCY B. LEIS received her Ph.D. from Northwestern University and is now Assistant Professor in the Department of Sociology and Anthropology at Central Michigan University. She has done research in West Africa, both among the Ijaw in Nigeria and among the Nyamnyam in Cameroon. Her interest in studies of women continues, and presently she is involved in research concerning polygyny, divorce, and the socialization of sex roles.

BRIDGET O'LAUGHLIN received her Ph.D. in 1973 from Yale University, and she is now Assistant Professor of Anthropology at Stanford University. Between 1969 and 1971 she did field research in southwestern Tchad on the cooperative labor organization of the Mbum Kpau. Her present research interest is in African modes of production.

SHERRY B. ORTNER received her Ph.D. from the University of Chicago and now teaches at Sarah Lawrence College. Her dissertation research, conducted among the Sherpas of Nepal, focused on village social dynamics and popular Buddhism. She is the author of various articles on Sherpa culture and on the methods of symbolic analysis. She is currently a Member of the Institute for Advanced Study in Princeton (1973–74) and is planning a research project with Sherpa nuns.

LOIS PAUL, currently Research Associate in Anthropology at Stanford University, received training in social science and psychiatric social work at the University of Chicago before accepting a research award to study deviance, child development, and the role of women in the Maya community of San Pedro la Laguna as part of a joint ethnographic enterprise with her anthropologist husband, Benjamin D. Paul. She has returned to this community half a dozen times, most recently in 1973. Between field visits she has done counseling, teaching, and research with families and groups in Newton, Wellesley, and Boston, and published professional papers on the life cycle in Mesoamerica and on changing marriage patterns in San Pedro.

MICHELLE ZIMBALIST ROSALDO received her Ph.D. in social anthropology from Harvard University in 1972 and is presently Assistant Professor at Stanford University. Between 1967 and 1969 she did research with a group of swidden cultivators in northern Luzon, the Philippines, and has since written a number of articles on their magic, oratory, and oral traditions. Her present research interests combine anthropological linguistics, symbolic analysis, and the study of women's social and cultural position in island Southeast Asia.

KAREN SACKS teaches anthropology at Oakland University and received her Ph.D. from the University of Michigan in 1971. Her main interests are in social and economic change, particularly as regards the status of women.

PEGGY R. SANDAY received her Ph.D. from the University of Pittsburgh in 1966. She is currently Associate Professor of Anthropology at the University of Pennsylvania. She is the author of numerous articles in the area of mathematical anthropology, minority groups in the United States, and cognitive anthropology.

CAROL B. STACK received her Ph.D. in anthropology from the University of Illinois, Urbana, in 1972, where she was Assistant Professor in 1971–72, holding a joint appointment in anthropology and child development. She is currently Assistant Professor of Anthropology at Boston University. The author of *All Our Kin: Strategies for Survival in a Black Community*, she is now engaged in research in urban white ethnic communities in the United States.

NANCY TANNER received her Ph.D. from the University of California, Berkeley, was a Fellow of the Committee for the Comparative Study of New Nations and Instructor at the University of Chicago, and is currently Assistant Professor of Anthropology at the University of California, Santa Cruz. She spent four years pursuing field research among the Minangkabau of west Sumatra in 1963–66 and 1972; her published work on the Minangkabau deals primarily with disputing and legal pluralism. She has also written on multilingualism and the role of the national language in Indonesia. During 1973–74 she has a Ford grant for work on Minangkabau women in historical perspective. With Adrienne Zihlman she is completing a book, *Becoming Human: A Model for the Reconstruction of Early Human Social Life*, which deals with the roles of females and males during human evolution.

MARGERY WOLF has no academic degree and is a candidate for none. Her research interests include the dynamics of the Chinese family, with particular emphasis on women and the socialization of children. She has done fieldwork in the rural areas of northern Taiwan. She is the author of *The House of Lim* and *Women and the Family in Rural Taiwan*.

Woman, Culture, and Society

In every known society, the male's need for achievement can be recognized. Men may cook, or weave, or dress dolls or hunt hummingbirds, but if such activities are appropriate occupations of men, then the whole society, men and women alike, votes them as important. When the same occupations are performed by women, they are regarded as less important.

MARGARET MEAD, *Male and Female*

But it will be asked at once: how did all this begin? It is easy to see that the duality of the sexes, like any duality, gives rise to conflict. And doubtless the winner will assume the status of absolute. But why should man have won from the start? It seems possible that women could have won the victory; or that the outcome of the conflict might never have been decided. How is it that this world has always belonged to the men and that things have begun to change only recently? Is this change a good thing? Will it bring about an equal sharing of the world between men and women?

SIMONE DE BEAUVOIR, *The Second Sex*

Introduction

Why is Woman "The Other"? *Are* women universally the "second sex"? Like Simone de Beauvoir (1953), who raised these questions in what must remain one of the most articulate and penetrating essays yet written on women's position in human societies, we ask them not simply out of some sort of abstract, intellectual curiosity, but because we are searching for ways to think about ourselves.

Along with many women today, we are trying to understand our position and to change it. We have become increasingly aware of sexual inequities in economic, social, and political institutions and are seeking ways to fight them. A first step in that direction involves the recognition that in learning to be women in our own society, we have accepted, and even internalized, what is all too often a derogatory and constraining image of ourselves. Contemporary feminists have only begun to uncover the depth and pervasiveness of our inegalitarian sexual ideology—to perceive, and then to question, assumptions about the nature of the female that obtain in everything from psychology to literature to common sense. What once seemed necessary and natural has begun to look arbitrary and unwarranted. What once could be assumed, ignored, or tacitly acknowledged now seems problematic and difficult to explain. And what has been true of common cultural stereotypes has, of course, been true of the view of women implicit in Western social science. For the most part, scholars have taken for granted a view of women as passive sexual objects, as devoted mothers, and as dutiful wives. There have been exceptions—a handful of ethnographies that take a woman's perspective (Chiñas, 1973; Fernea, 1965; Goodale, 1971; Kaberry, 1939, 1952; Landes, 1938, 1947; Leith-Ross, 1952; Strathern, 1972; Wolf, 1972), some theoretical essays (Ardener, 1971; Schlegel, 1972), two collections of articles on women in specific geographic areas (Paulme, 1963; Sweet, 1967), some writings on child rearing, and the suggestive explorations into the relations of culture and sexuality associated with names like DuBois and Mead. Aside from these, however, anthropologists in writing about human culture have followed our own culture's ideological bias in treating women as relatively invisible and describing what are largely the activities and interests of men. In order to correct that bias, to alter our conceptions of the female, and to understand their source, what we need are new perspectives. Today, it seems reasonable to argue that the social world is the creation of both male and female actors, and that any full understanding of human society and any viable program for social change will have to incorporate the goals, thoughts, and activities of the "second sex."

Within the field of anthropology, a concern to understand and to change women's position has generated a number of important questions. Are there societies that, unlike our own, make women the equals or superiors of men? If not, are women "naturally" men's inferiors? Why do women, in our own society and elsewhere, accept a subordinate standing? How, and in what kinds of situations, do women exercise power? How do women help to shape, create, and change the private and public worlds in which they live? New questions demand new kinds of answers. The development of a science depends on discovering, in facts previously taken for granted, a field for serious investigation and research. In recognizing old biases and directing attention to questions previously ignored, we hope to take such a step in this collection. Although the authors writing here have different political and intellectual commitments, all believe that anthropology has suffered from a failure to develop theoretical perspectives that take account of women as social actors. And all feel that our conceptions of human social life will be improved and broadened when they address women's lives and interests along with those of men.

Perhaps the first question that arises in an anthropological study of women is whether there are societies, unlike our own, in which women are publicly recognized as equal to or more powerful than men. This question was addressed in the evolutionary theories of nineteenth-century writers like Bachofen (1861) and L. H. Morgan (1851, 1877), who suggested that in an earlier stage of human development the social world was organized by a principle called matriarchy, in which women had power over men. Although this view has excited the imaginations of several recent feminist writers (Davis, 1972; E. Morgan, 1972), most academic anthropologists have dismissed it out of hand. The matriarchal arguments draw on several kinds of evidence: data from contemporary societies in which women make the major contribution to subsistence; data from societies in which descent is reckoned through women (matriliny), rather than through both parents (bilateral) or from father to son (patriliny); myths of ancient rule by women; archaeological remains suggesting that there have been female goddesses, queens, or a tendency to kill infant males in certain earlier societies. As against this, the current anthropological view draws on the observation that most and probably all contemporary societies, whatever their kinship organization or mode of subsistence, are characterized by some degree of male dominance.

Whereas some anthropologists argue that there are, or have been, truly egalitarian societies (Leacock, 1972), and all agree that there are societies in which women have achieved considerable social recognition and power, none has observed a society in which women have publicly recognized power and authority surpassing that of men (see the papers by Rosaldo and Ortner, this volume). Everywhere we find that women are excluded from certain crucial economic or political activities, that their roles as wives and mothers are associated with fewer powers and prerogatives than are the roles of men. It seems fair to say then, that all contemporary societies are to some extent male-dominated, and although the degree and expression of female subordination vary greatly, sexual asymmetry is presently a universal fact of human social life.

The archaeological data are more problematic, since they have to be interpreted in terms of a set of assumptions based on our knowledge of existing cultures or on some presumed but not presently observed patterns. Elaborate female burials might, for example, indicate a world in which women were the rulers; but they could equally be the remains of wives, mistresses, concubines of male elites, or women who became heads of state in lieu of male heirs in a royal family. Female sculptures may represent goddesses, but there are historically documented and well-studied contemporary societies that manifest female fertility cults while at the same time placing political power in the hands of men. Similarly, myths of primordial female eminence are found today in male-dominated societies, and most anthropologists believe that such myths, rather than reflecting history, are expressions of a culture's dreams or fantasies, or validations of political alignments in the societies in which they are told. The issues involved here are complex, but the evidence of contemporary anthropology gives scant support to an argument for matriarchy. Though our knowledge of the past is sometimes sketchy, there is little reason to believe that early sexual orders were substantially different from those observed around the world today.

Matriarchal accounts of past societies have, of course, the advantage of suggesting that contemporary sexual asymmetry is in no way natural. And one might even argue that the idea of matriarchy constitutes a useful myth, a guide for present action, and that it is important insofar as it enjoins us to imagine a world in which women have real power (Webster and Newton, 1972). At the same time, as Bamberger points out in her contribution to this collection, these accounts often have the disadvantage of highlighting woman's failure as a ruler, and so legitimize a social order dominated by men. As a myth or a utopian vision, the idea of matriarchy has currency today as a source of hope for women. As a recognized fact, however, its status is far from strong. Though the authors writing here follow anthropological consensus in discounting matriarchal theories, they try to provide alternative approaches to the questions of woman's possibilities and woman's past.

What, then, do anthropologists know about our heritage? Does the rejection of matriarchy as an accurate description of early society imply that female subordination is somehow necessary and natural, that it is determined by the biological constitutions of the human species? There are, of course, a number of ways of answering these questions, only some of which are explored in any detail in this book. In order to explain the apparent universality of male dominance, one can, for instance, ask what is its origin and seek evidence for a fixed and given core of "human nature" in biological data, in parallels between the social life of humans and primates, or in reconstructions of the life of early women and men. Or putting aside the questions of origins, one can ask what features of the organization of all known human societies have permitted them to produce and reproduce an inegalitarian sexual order. Since the papers in this book address the second kind of question, it might be helpful to review some of the problems and issues associated with the first.

Surely no one would question that the sexes differ in biological constitution. Women lactate and bear children, and this fact has important consequences for human social life. The sexes differ in reproductive organization, in aspects of hormonal endowments, and probably in size and potential physical strength. (For some recent reviews of the relevant literature, see Maccoby, 1966; Bardwick, 1971; Hutt, 1972; Money and Ehrhardt, 1972.) But the observation of physical differences itself tells us little about the social worlds we live in; for humans, biology becomes important largely as it is interpreted by the norms and expectations of human culture and society. For example, biologists may tell us that men are, on the average, stronger than women; but they cannot tell us why male strength and male activities in general seem to be valued by people in all cultures. Again, it is a biological fact that women lactate, but the behavioral consequences of the fact will differ, depending on the availability of bottles, the amounts and kinds of protein in the diet, or the prevalence of an ideology holding, for example, that children need to be fed every time they cry.

Humans, unlike animals, have the capacity to interpret and perhaps to alter their biological constitutions, to regulate their behavior through the mediation of symbolic forms, like language. Although science has not yet determined the extent to which hormones shape the behavior of humans, it seems likely that humans are not subject to the same sorts of behavioral programming that characterize the lower primates. In fact, it has been argued that human biology requires human culture. In Geertz's words, one striking fact about our "central nervous system is the relative incompleteness with which, acting within the confines of autogenous patterns alone, it is able to specify behavior" (1962: 729). Human activities and feelings are organized, not by biology directly, but by the interaction of biological propensities and those various and culture-specific expectations, plans, and symbols that coordinate our actions and so permit our species to survive. The implication of such an argument for understanding human sex roles is that biological differences between the sexes may not have necessary social and behavioral implications. What is male and what is female will depend upon interpretations of biology that are associated with any culture's mode of life.

Recent investigations of the biological bases of human behavior encourage a similar conclusion. The evidence from primate studies and from examinations of human infants, adult hormones, and the behavior of hermaphrodites and others who have been called "sexual anomalies" (Hutt, 1972; Money and Ehrhardt, 1972) all points to the conclusion that biology constrains but does not determine the behavior of the sexes, and that differences between human males and females reflect an interaction between our physical constitutions and our patterns of social life. So, for example, whereas early theorists sought the origins of human sex roles, and even of the modern Western family, in the activities of certain primates, many researchers today emphasize that primate species differ with respect to extent of sexual dimorphism, male-dominance behavior, aggression, and the like. What is more, the behavior of the sexes within even a single primate species (Rowell, 1972) has been shown to vary from expressions of dominance to relatively egalitarian relations, depending on the environment in which a population is observed. In other words, whatever the biological determinants of their behavior, primates, like humans, seem to have an impressive capacity to adopt new forms of social relationships in new social and physical worlds.

In a similar vein, recent studies of human hormones and of sexually dimorphic patterns of behavior indicate, first, that sex-linked behavioral differences are of a quantitative rather than a qualitative nature, and second, that hormonal levels (which are supposed to govern behaviors) themselves are highly sensitive to changes in one's social environment. In psychological testing, many males behave "like females," and on several measures there is more variation in the performances and capacities of a single sex than there is between the two (Maccoby and Jacklin, 1974). Again, recent evidence that stressful contexts lead to a decrease in testosterone suggests that social contexts and contextually induced behaviors influence the appearance of hormones, rather than the reverse (Kreuz et al., 1972).

In other words, there seems to be increasing evidence that the behavioral possibilities of the sexes are rich and variable, and that even primates adopt new patterns of behavior when confronted with new environments. That human males and females have fixed, significant, and necessarily distinct behavioral propensities is far from clear. Just as foot binding in traditional China created women who were constitutionally incapable of certain kinds of physical exertion, so it seems likely that our culturally specified and different ways of acting themselves influence our physical lives. In short, although we are certain that biological studies will illuminate our understanding of the sexes, we feel that the issues are too complex for definitive treatment in this volume, and furthermore, that they do not *determine* the relations and evaluations of the sexes in contemporary forms of social life.

One other account of the origins of sexual asymmetry deserves our attention. This is the notion that the earliest forms of human society found it adaptive to differentiate the activities of men and women, giving those of men a special value, and that this early adaptation has become part of the sociocultural inheritance of our species. Contemporary evolutionary theorists, perhaps in reaction to earlier ideas of female dominance, have suggested that human social existence originated in the cooperative activities of early men, who were hunters.

The argument has been that hunting large animals demands the coordinated efforts of several individuals, and because it often involves danger and extensive travel, it tends to exclude women, who must produce and care for children, and so are constrained in their movements. A related argument is that male strength and size dictated that men rather than women would adopt the responsibility for intergroup aggression and defense. Hunting, a specifically male activity, is seen as a creative turning point in human evolution; it demanded the first forms of social cooperation and it encouraged the invention of our first "artistic" tools. Washburn and Lancaster sum up the implications of hunting by stating, "In a very real sense our intellect, interests, emotions, and basic social life—all are evolutionary products of the success of the hunting adaptation" (1968: 293).

Whereas those who view evolution in terms of Man the Hunter are aware of the probable importance of female gathering in early social life, they assign the latter only secondary importance. More recently, Linton (1973) has explored the role of Woman the Gatherer and, in redressing the balance, has noted that women contribute the bulk of the diet in contemporary hunting-gathering populations, that small-game hunting practiced by both sexes may have preceded the advent of big-game hunting, and that some early tools (in addition to containers not preserved in the archaeological record) may have been aids in gathering. She also speculates that gathering and the socialization of children, both women's activities, required cooperative and communicative skills as complex as those involved in hunting, and so would have had an important impact on the creation of early social and cultural patterns.

This second reconstruction (further developed in recent work by Tanner and Zihlman, n.d.) emphasizes the role of women as well as that of men, and seems preferable to the Man the Hunter version of human evolution; but whatever account one chooses, it is clear that our knowledge of early human social forms remains speculative. Although it seems likely that the development of big-game hunting and warfare promoted an ethic of male dominance, it is difficult to see why biases associated with man's earliest adaptations should remain with us today. The question then becomes: why, if our social worlds are so different from those of our ancestors, has the relation of the sexes continued to be asymmetrical, and how is it that social groups, which change radically through time, continue to produce and reproduce a social order dominated by men?

This is the question underlying the first three essays in this collection. Each begins with the observation that women everywhere lactate and give birth to children, and are therefore likely to be associated with child rearing and the responsibilities of the home. All three authors argue that the connection between a woman's reproductive system and her domestic role, obvious as it may seem, is not a necessary one; biological factors may make certain sociocultural arrangements highly likely, but with changes in technology, population size, ideas, and aspirations, our social order can change. What is significant, these papers argue, is that insofar as woman is universally defined in terms of a largely maternal and domestic role, we can account for her universal subordination. Elaborations of her reproductive functions shape her social role and her psychology; they color her cultural definition; and they permit us to understand the perpetuation of woman's status without seeing her subordination as entirely determined by her biological propensities or her evolutionary heritage.

Rosaldo argues that an emphasis on woman's maternal role leads to a universal opposition between "domestic" and "public" roles that is necessarily asymmetrical; women, confined to the domestic sphere, do not have access to the sorts of authority, prestige, and cultural value that are the prerogatives of men. She suggests further that, given this imbalance, the exercise of power by women is often seen as illegitimate, and that the avenues by which women gain prestige and a sense of value are shaped and often limited by their association with the domestic world.

Chodorow's paper explores the implications of woman's maternal role for the development of personality in young children. Sex-linked personality differences, she argues, are often the unintentional consequence of the fact that women have the primary responsibility for raising children of both sexes. A mother responds in different ways to her infant sons and daughters, and as they mature, they react differently to her. For the boy, who often has little personal knowledge of adult males and their activities, manhood is typically learned as an abstract set of rights and duties, and its attainment is made possible through an emotional rejection of his mother and the woman's world. Young girls, by contrast, follow in their mother's footsteps and become "little women." Through the ways in which a girl experiences her ties with her mother and learns to deal with the interpersonal demands of the family, feminine personality comes to be founded on relation and connection to other people, in contrast to masculine personality, which seems based on a denial of relation and dependence.

Finally, Ortner shows how the facts of female biology, woman's domestic role, and the so-called "feminine personality" combine to encourage cultural definitions of the female that tend to be degrading. Women, who are excluded from cultural projects of transcendence, and limited to an existence largely dictated by their biology, come to be seen as more "natural" and less "cultural" than men. Ortner takes care to emphasize that this ideology involves arbitrary, and not necessary, connections between women's bodily functions and "nature," which are in turn negatively rather than positively evaluated. In other words, the ease of an association between woman and nonhuman nature provides a cultural rationale for female subordination; woman's biology, social role, and personality encourage cultures to define her as "closer to nature" than man, hence to be subordinated, controlled, and manipulated in the service of "culture's" ends. In short, the three papers speak from a common position in spelling out the ways in which woman's social functions—and in particular her role in child care and reproduction—combine to make women universally the "second sex."

But an account of the factors that contribute everywhere to sexual asymmetry is necessarily incomplete if it leads us to ignore the manifold ways in which women in different social systems achieve power and a sense of personal value. The remaining papers in this collection consider the nature, implications, and extent of female power; they establish that women's role in social processes is far greater than has previously been recognized; and they ask how particular social structures and ideologies enhance or undermine women's attempts to shape and find meanings in their lives.

Because men everywhere tend to have more prestige than women, and because men are usually associated with social roles of dominance and authority, most previous descriptions of social processes have treated women as being theoretically uninteresting. Women who exercise power are seen as deviants, manipulators, or, at best, exceptions. And women's goals and ideologies are assumed to be coordinate with those of men. The papers in the second part of this collection challenge these assumptions from a number of perspectives; the questions they raise provide a direction for future studies of women, and indicate the theoretical importance of such studies for our general understanding of human social life.

To begin with, several papers argue that women, like men, are social actors who work in structured ways to achieve desired ends. Although the formal authority structure of a society may declare that women are impotent and irrelevant, close attention to women's strategies and motives, to the sorts of choices made by women, to the relationships they establish, and to the ends they achieve indicates that even in situations of overt sex role asymmetry women have a good deal more power than conventional theorists have assumed. Collier, for example, argues that it is useful to view women as political strategists who use the resources available to them in support of interests often opposed to those of men. Women's strategies may appear to be deviant and disruptive, yet they are nonetheless important components of the actual processes by which social life proceeds. By causing what have been called domestic tragedies, by seeking divorces, or by using their sons' loyalty and allegiance to undermine family or lineage solidarity, women act in rational ways to achieve personally desired goals. From the point of view of dominant norms, such procedures may appear to be idiosyncratic, disruptive, un-important, or undesirable, but social scientists who ignore them can ex-pect to produce only a partial account of the structure and processes of different forms of social life.

Women's strategies are also the subject of a number of other papers. Lamphere develops a theory of the ways in which structural features of a society interact with women's goals to produce different sorts of align-ments among women in the domestic sphere. Women's strategies are directly related to the power structure of the family. Where power and authority are in the hands of men, women work to influence them, and come into conflict with each other. Where authority is shared by men and women in the family, women do not need to play the game of sub-tle influence and "behind-the-scenes" manipulation; in such societies, women are able to form strong cooperative ties with their female kin and other women in carrying out everyday activities.

Also focusing on domestic relationships, Stack suggests that a charac-terization of the families of American urban Blacks as matrifocal is static and misleading; instead, she views women as strategists and as resilient social actors who cope with the problems of poverty, unem-ployment, and oppression in their everyday lives. The personal histories of a number of Black women in a Midwestern urban area illustrate vividly the ways in which women form alliances and rely on an enduring network of kin among whom goods and services are exchanged.

Women's domestic strategies and power may be reinforced by a strong ideology that stresses the position of women in the family. Tanner sug-gests that matrifocal organization does not depend on the notion of the absent father, but on the culturally valued position of the mother and her effective role as a decision maker. By examining family structure in several Indonesian societies and among the Ibo of Nigeria, she suggests that matrifocality is not a consequence of the kinship system per se—whether bilateral, matrilineal, or patrilineal—but of the cultural defi-nitions and the society-wide structure of male and female roles. This allows Tanner to offer an alternative view of Black urban family struc-ture that focuses, not on the marginal position of Black men, but on the strong role of Black women.

Wolf, in her paper on women in China, does not confine her discus-sion to the realm of the rural, patrilocal domestic group, but also ex-amines women's strategies in the community as a whole. She shows how women coped with their low status as brides in families dominated by men, how they came to influence their husbands and sons indirectly, and how they developed subtle interpersonal skills through socializing children, gossiping with the women's community, and manipulating men through their roles as soul raisers. She then uses her analysis to interpret the positions women were able to assume in a situation of revolutionary change.

Finally, Hoffer treats an example of an African society in which women can become heads of secret societies and even paramount chiefs. Using the case of Madam Yoko, a nineteenth-century Mende female chief, Hoffer examines the sorts of political strategies by which women may obtain real political power. In an era of increasing British colonial hegemony, Madam Yoko was able to make politically astute marriages, become a senior wife, and succeed to her deceased husband's position as paramount chief. Once she had achieved power, she was able to exercise it by using her sex to advantage. Men consolidated political power through marriage alliances; Madam Yoko took wards and married them to men in other lineages, creating alliances in two directions (i.e. with the kin of the ward and with those of the prospective groom). Hoffer's analysis reveals the ways in which women can act as men in a political system, but it also shows how a woman may be able to manipulate political relationships in ways not available to male officeholders.

The papers we have been discussing thus far examine the forms and quality of women's strategies and powers. In doing so they are consistent with recent theoretical developments in anthropology. Theorists like Barth (1959), Leach (1954), and more recently Firth (1962) and Bailey (1969) have argued against static descriptions of social structures that ignore the processes of social and political action through which these structures are produced. By showing that women as well as men are social actors whose goals and strategies are intrinsic to the processes of social life, the papers here extend the work of these theorists into a new area, challenging accepted views of social order and directing our attention to previously unrecognized methods by which the social world is shaped.

Another kind of question, addressed implicitly in some of the papers we have already mentioned (e.g. Tanner, Hoffer), is an explicit focus of several comparative analyses. These ask: What are the factors determining women's social status? How can we account for differences in women's position across societies? Sanday's paper is a statistical treatment of cross-cultural variations in women's status. Arguing that reproduction, subsistence, and defense are crucial aspects of any society's survival, and in particular that women's reproductive role may limit their participation in defense, she suggests that women's contribution to subsistence is a crucial variable in determining their status. In societies where the fruits of production are controlled by men, women may produce most or none of the subsistence goods, but in either case have low status. Women's status, Sanday finds, is highest in those societies where their contribution to subsistence is relatively equivalent to that of men. There women tend to control crucial economic resources, a situation that may lead either to antagonism between the sexes or to recognition of women in ritual and religious spheres.

Sacks, too, suggests that it is *control* of production rather than the sheer amount of foodstuffs produced by women that determines female status. She reinterprets Engels's theory of the origin of the family and private property, emphasizing the historical dynamic by which women are transformed from equal members of society (or social adults) into dependent wives and wards. By examining data from four African societies, she finds that as men become more involved in production for exchange (rather than for immediate use), women's work becomes more domesticated, and women's status correspondingly declines. A reversal of this process, she suggests, is possible only when private domestic work becomes socially valued public work; only when production, consumption, child rearing, and economic decision making all take place in a single sphere will women become the full equals of men.

Leis uses a controlled comparison of two related West African communities in an attempt to identify those features of economy and social structure (such as residence patterns, kinship organization, polygyny, and marriage payments) that encourage or inhibit the formation of women's associations; these, in one community but not the other, provide women with a collective basis for the expression of public power.

Denich's paper, comparing pastoral and agricultural societies in the Balkans, also focuses on the importance of economic and ecological factors in determining women's status. Essentially, she argues that the social adaptations appropriate to a pastoral way of life require solidarity among the male members of a cooperative kin group; women in such a situation are seen as socially disruptive, and much collective effort goes into limiting a woman's effective sphere of power. In agricultural groups, by contrast, small families are the units of productive labor, and there is correspondingly less emphasis on male solidarity at the expense of women, and more emphasis on the cooperation of husbands and wives.

A third kind of question is raised in the three remaining papers. These concentrate on the ways in which cultural ideologies impinge upon women and are used to keep women in their place. Bamberger shows how, in a number of South American societies, myths that tell of women's mythic dominance and future capitulation to masculine rule are used by men to assert their independence from their mothers, to legitimize the present fact of male authority, and to tell women that their ability to exercise power was found wanting in the past and has no place in the future of the group.

Paul and O'Laughlin, working from very different theoretical assumptions, both show how cultural expressions of the vulnerability and mystery of women's reproductive functions give an aura of nature and necessity to women's secondary status. Paul, in her analysis of women's conceptions of their bodies in a Guatemalan community, argues that ideas about the body have two aspects: in work the body is competent and skillful; in sex and reproduction it is changeable, mysterious, and a source of danger. Sex, then, provides a cultural rationale for female subordination; at the same time, the very mystery of a woman's body unites her to conceptions of the cosmos, providing grounds for solidarity with other women, and powers that may be threatening to men.

O'Laughlin's paper, the last in this collection, uses a Marxist framework to explore sexual asymmetry among the Mbum Kpau of Tchad. The key to women's standing in this group lies not in their productive contribution, which equals that of men, but in the ways in which a male lineage organization appropriates surpluses in order to purchase and control the reproductive potential of new wives. Through the complexities of bridewealth payments, women are alienated from their own reproduction; food taboos, whose violation causes reproductive failure, provide a cultural mediation of asymmetries in Mbum society.

Taken together, the papers in this collection do a number of things. First, by providing a critical analysis of the universality of women's subordination, they suggest that sexual asymmetry is not a necessary condition of human societies but a cultural product accessible to change. Second, they show that the observation of sexual asymmetry itself means different things in different places, that women vary in their social roles and powers, their public status, and their cultural definitions, and that the nature, quality, and social significance of women's activities are far more varied and interesting than has often been assumed. Third, the papers in this collection suggest that variations in women's status and power can be accounted for by particular social and economic factors, one important variable being women's contributions to subsistence and their control over those contributions. Finally, they present a challenge to future thinking in anthropology: by focusing on women's roles and actions, they cast a new light on old assumptions about the nature of human society, and they suggest rich fields for future inquiry and research.

We feel that this collection is in many respects only a beginning, but that it has implications both for thinking about ourselves as women and for effecting the kinds of change necessary if women are to realize their hopes and aspirations for an egalitarian world. Although the papers here do not, on the whole, address questions concerning female roles today, they do, in attempting to elucidate a theory of women's secondary status, offer tentative suggestions for the future. If, as we suggest here, women's position is not biologically determined, then it is a cultural product that can be altered. To say that women's secondary status is universal is not to say that it is necessary or right. On the contrary. Biology dictates that women lactate and bear children. But the social and cultural consequences of this fact—that women have been seen as wives, and more particularly as mothers; that their activities have been limited by the responsibilities of child care; that their lives have been defined in terms of reproductive functions; and that their personalities have been shaped by ties with "mothers," who in turn are women—all of these are human products that we feel account for women's secondary status; we suggest, moreover, that they are subject to, and accessible to, change. Surely, the diversity of human cultures and the evidence of societies in which women have achieved considerable recognition and social status might make us optimistic about the possibility of realizing sexual equality in our world today.

The anthropological record provides us with no simple model. Sexual differentiation and sex-role asymmetry seem to have been present in all human societies yet known. Nature, while not dictating women's status, has in the past provided both the conditions and the rationale for female subordination. But, we would argue, just as the particulars of different forms of social and cultural organization have provided women in different places with very different powers and possibilities, so our contemporary situation renders any "natural" ranking or differentiation of the sexes altogether obsolete. What we think of as "men's work" can today be performed by women, and, correspondingly, "women's work" can be performed by men. Change must proceed in two directions. To begin, it would seem imperative to integrate men into the domestic sphere, giving them an opportunity to share in the socialization of children as well as in the more mundane domestic tasks. What is more, the cross-cultural evidence of the importance of female participation in, and control of, the products of economic production indicates that women's status will be elevated only when they participate equally with men in the public world of work.

Before the details of such proposals could be articulated for our own complex society, it would be necessary to go further than we have here in spelling out the role of social class and political hierarchy in female subordination, in challenging a capitalist economic system in which women form a pool of relatively underpaid and surplus labor, and in asking how work and economic success might themselves be redefined. A society in which the sexes are truly equal will have to be a society in which the very terms of our descriptions—power, authority, politics, productivity—forged in order to account for the realities of male-dominated social systems, become irrelevant or change their sense. Lacking models, we cannot say what such a society would be like.

What we *can* do is give direction to our actions, demand public recognition and public power, and, finally, challenge all the complex stereotypes that assume women to be "naturally" what, today, they are. Our own culture (and probably all others) is characterized by an ideology dictating that women's lives are relatively uninteresting; this is a fact that most of social science has failed to examine or explain. By refocusing our attention, then, we are challenging old assumptions. By treating women's lives everywhere as interesting and problematic, we hope to loosen the hold of stereotypes that have, unfortunately, shaped our own lives. Much as the writings of Jane Austen, George Eliot, and Virginia Woolf (among others) have shown that the "insignificant" details of domestic life can be the stuff of novels, we hope to begin, on another level, to alter our assumptions about the sexes by demonstrating the sociological interest and significance of lives previously ignored.

The papers that follow represent a first step in this direction. In demonstrating the importance of women's lives for our understanding of the human record, they point the way to new thinking in social science. And, in touching on issues of human significance universally, they suggest directions for any future worlds we might create.

Woman, Culture, and Society:
A Theoretical Overview

As anthropologists looking at the roles and activities of women, we are confronted, from the outset, with an apparent contradiction. On the one hand, we learn from the work of Mead and others of the extraordinary diversity of sex roles in our own and other cultures. And on the other, we are heirs to a sociological tradition that treats women as essentially uninteresting and irrelevant, and accepts as necessary, natural, and hardly problematic the fact that, in every human culture, women are in some way subordinate to men.

The purpose of this paper is to develop a perspective that at once incorporates earlier observations while at the same time suggesting systematic dimensions within which the social relations of the sexes can be investigated and understood. After a brief discussion of variation, I attempt to document aspects of what I take to be a universal asymmetry in cultural evaluations of the sexes. Women may be important, powerful, and influential, but it seems that, relative to men of their age and social status, women everywhere lack generally recognized and culturally valued authority. The secondary evaluation of women can be approached from a number of perspectives. Here, rather than put forth a single causal explanation, I propose a structural model that relates recurrent aspects of psychology and cultural and social organization to an opposition between the "domestic" orientation of women and the extra-do-

Neither this paper nor this book would have been conceived had I not had the opportunity in 1971, at Stanford University, to teach a course on women with Ellen Lewin, Julia D. Howell, Jane Collier, Janet Shepherd Fjellman, and Kim Kramer. Many of their ideas appear in the collective paper "Power Strategies and Sex Roles" (Lewin et al., 1971) and are echoed in the discussion that follows. Since that time, discussions with Jane Atkinson, Amy Burce, Nancy Chodorow, Jane Collier, Peggy Comstock, Mary Felstiner, Carol Nagy Jacklin, Louise Lamphere, Bridget O'Laughlin, Sherry Ortner, and Ellen Rogat have influenced the development of the ideas presented here. I am indebted to all of them, as well as to Renato Rosaldo, Arthur Wolf, Karl Heider, and Harumi Befu for their comments on this manuscript.

mestic or "public" ties that, in most societies, are primarily available to men. This approach, developed further in some of the other papers in this volume, enables us to make sense of a number of very general characteristics of human sex roles and to identify certain strategies and motivations, as well as sources of value and power, that are available to women in different human groups. As such, it provides an introduction to the various "sources of power" for women that are treated in detail later in this book.

Asymmetries in Cultural Evaluations of the Sexes

The fact that what Westerners take to be the "natural" endowments of men and women are hardly necessary, natural, or universal (as an ethnocentric perspective might lead one to expect) was first emphasized in the work of Margaret Mead. In her words, "If those temperamental attitudes which we have traditionally regarded as feminine—such as passivity, responsiveness, and a willingness to cherish children—can so easily be set up as the masculine pattern in one tribe, and, in another, be outlawed for the majority of women as for the majority of men, we no longer have any basis for regarding aspects of such behavior as sex linked" (1935: 279–80). And to some extent Mead was right. There are, in fact, groups like the New Guinea Arapesh, in which neither sex shows much aggression or assertiveness, and there are societies like our own, in which children of both sexes are more egoistic than boys in other parts of the world (Chodorow, 1971). The same sort of variability attaches to almost every kind of behavior one can think of: there are societies in which women trade or garden, and those in which men do; societies where women are queens and those in which they must always defer to a man; in parts of New Guinea, men are (like Victorian women) at once prudish and flirtatious, fearful of sex yet preoccupied with love magic and cosmetics that will lead the maidens—who take the initiative in courtship—to be interested in them.

But there are also limits to variation. Every known society recognizes and elaborates some differences between the sexes, and although there are groups in which men wear skirts and women wear pants or trousers, it is everywhere the case that there are characteristic tasks, manners, and responsibilities primarily associated with women or with men. Cross-cultural studies of child rearing (Barry, Bacon, and Child, 1957) reveal certain temperamental differences between the sexes, and studies of adults indicate that it is women, and not men, who have the primary responsibility for raising children; this fact seems to make it unlikely that women will be a society's hunters, warriors, or the like (Brown,

1970b). Differences in physical constitution, and especially in endurance and strength, may also lead to characteristic differences in male and female activities.

But what is perhaps most striking and surprising is the fact that male, as opposed to female, activities are always recognized as predominantly important, and cultural systems give authority and value to the roles and activities of men. Contrary to some popular assumptions, there is little reason to believe that there are, or once were, societies of primitive matriarchs, societies in which women predominated in the same way that men predominate in the societies we actually know (see Bamberger, this volume). An asymmetry in the cultural evaluations of male and female, in the importance assigned to women and men, appears to be universal. Mead recognized this in observing that "whatever the arrangements in regard to descent or ownership of property, and even if these formal outward arrangements are reflected in the temperamental relations between the sexes, the prestige values always attach to the activities of men" (1935: 302).

Nor is this difficult to document. We find in some parts of New Guinea, for example, that women grow sweet potatoes and men grow yams, and yams are the prestige food, the food one distributes at feasts. Or again, in the Philippine society I studied, men hunted in groups while women gardened (for the most part) individually; and although a woman's rice became the food supply of her immediate family, its dietary staple, meat was always shared by the community and was the most highly valued food. The same pattern obtains in other hunting societies, where women may help on the hunt but the catch is the men's to distribute, and meat, unlike the nutritious grubs and nuts a woman gathers,[1] is socially valued and shared. Among aboriginal groups in Australia, only the meat, which men distribute, is felt to be a proper "food" (Kaberry, 1939).

Cultural expressions of sexual asymmetry may be associated with economics, but they are often found in other domains of activity as well. Among the Arapesh, studied by Mead (1935, 1971), the roles of men and women were seen as cooperative and complementary, but a wife was felt to be a "daughter" to her husband, and at the time of the dominant male ritual (when men played on secret flutes) she was required to act like an ignorant child. Among the nearby Tchambuli (Mead, 1935), the women were traders, controlling the family economics; yet there the

---

[1] The fact that female gathering rather than male hunting may provide the bulk of a group's nutritional requirements has been suggested by Lee (1968) and others. Linton (1973) uses this, as well as the facts of human newborn development, to criticize the "man the hunter" view of human evolution.

men were artists and ritual specialists, and although the women had little respect for masculine secrets, they still found it necessary to adhere to, and engage in, a ritual order that marked them as inferior—in morality and knowledge—to men. Again, in certain African societies like the Yoruba (Lloyd, 1965), women may control a good part of the food supply, accumulate cash, and trade in distant and important markets; yet when approaching their husbands, wives must feign ignorance and obedience, kneeling to serve the men as they sit. Even the Iroquois, who, according to Murdock, "of all the people of the earth approach most closely to that hypothetical form of society known as the matriarchate" (1934: 302), were not ruled by women; there, powerful women might instate and depose their rulers, but Iroquois chiefs were men.

Still another form of cultural subordination is revealed in the linguistic practices of women of the Merina tribe in Madagascar (Keenan, 1974). There it is felt that in order to be cultured, sophisticated, and respectable, one must learn how to speak indirectly. Rather than being assertive, men are masters of an allusive, formal style in public speech. Women, on the contrary, are said not to know the subtleties of polite language. They are, in effect, cultural idiots, who are expected to blurt out what they mean. And so again, in the public ideology women are inferior. Yet they too have their methods of influence; in public meetings, men cluster together, whispering polite and evasive words of discreet opinion, while women, who are political outsiders, manage to influence public decisions by simply shouting out what they think.

For a final example, consider the Jewish ghetto communities of Eastern Europe (Zborowski and Herzog, 1955). In these communities, women had an extraordinary amount of influence. They were strong and self-confident mothers whose sons were their loyal supporters; as community gossips, they shaped most political events; in the household, a woman kept control of the pocketbook and effectively dictated family spending; and finally, in wealthier families, women and not men were the workers, running the family business, usually a small local store. Yet, in spite of all this, wives would defer to their husbands, and their greatest joy in life was to have a male child. A woman's work was rewarded by having the son become a scholar, a man whose actual activities might have little influence on the everyday life of the community but who stood, nonetheless, as its source of pride and moral value, its cultural ideal.

Taken individually, no one of these examples is surprising, yet a single thread runs through them all. Everywhere, from those societies we might want to call most egalitarian to those in which sexual stratification is most marked, men are the locus of cultural value. Some area of activity is always seen as exclusively or predominantly male, and therefore overwhelmingly and morally important. This observation has its corollary in the fact that everywhere men have some *authority* over women, that they have a culturally legitimated right to her subordination and compliance. At the same time, of course, women themselves are far from helpless, and whether or not their influence is acknowledged, they exert important pressures on the social life of the group. In other words, in various circumstances male authority might be mitigated, and, perhaps rendered almost trivial, by the fact that women (through gossiping or yelling, playing sons against brothers, running the business, or refusing to cook) may have a good deal of informal influence and *power*.[2] While acknowledging male authority, women may direct it to their own interests, and in terms of actual choices and decisions, of who influences whom and how, the power exercised by women may have considerable and systematic effect.

This distinction between power and culturally legitimated authority, between the ability to gain compliance and the recognition that it is right, is crucial to our study of women. Social scientists have by and large taken male authority for granted; they have also tended to accept a male view that sees the exercise of power by women as manipulative, disruptive, illegitimate, or unimportant. But it is necessary to remember that while authority legitimates the use of power, it does not exhaust it, and actual methods of giving rewards, controlling information, exerting pressure, and shaping events may be available to women as well as to men. This point is elaborated in later essays. Here it is necessary simply to note that in acknowledging the universal fact of male authority, we are not denying women importance.

The kinds of power available to women, and the reasons they have been traditionally ignored, will be clarified by examining those features

---

[2] The classic distinction between power, authority, and influence was developed by Weber (1947). M. G. Smith proposes the following definition: "Authority is, in the abstract, the right to make a particular decision and to command obedience.... Power . . . is the ability to act effectively on persons or things, to make or secure favourable decisions which are not of right allocated to the individuals or their roles" (1960: 18–19). Whether power is exercised through influence or force, it is inherently competitive, whereas authority entails a hierarchical chain of command and control. Although the idea of authority implies positive actions and duties, the exercise of power has no positive sanctions, only rules that specify "the conditions of illegality of its operation" (p. 20). Later essays will show that, although women may have neither the right nor the duty to make decisions, they often have a systematic influence on decisions that are made. And although social norms may not acknowledge the positive use of power by women, they often specify the limits or illegality of such power, treating the powerful or influential woman as disruptive, anomalous, and so on. A more technical discussion of power, authority, and influence is given by Lamphere (this volume).

of women's position that present special problems for study. We begin
by asking what to make of the fact of male authority. Why is sexual
asymmetry a universal fact of human societies? What is its importance
and how is it related to other aspects of men's and women's lives? Once
these complex relations are understood, we can ask how and in what
situations male systems of authority are reduced or mitigated in importance, what sources of power are available to women, and what sorts of
social arrangements give what sorts of value to women's lives.

Most available accounts of the asymmetrical relations of the sexes have
attempted to explain them in terms of a universal and necessary cause.
These explanations range from the rather implausible assertion that at
some moment in human history men "took" power away from women
(Engels, 1891)[3] to more suggestive accounts relating sexual asymmetry
to male envy of female reproductive powers (Bettelheim, 1954) or to
aspects of the human biological endowment (Bardwick, 1971). Different
hormonal cycles, infant activity levels, sexual capacities, or emotional
orientations have all been proposed as possible sources of the cultural
subordination of women to men.

But it seems reasonable to ask what the available facts, or the promise
of future information (deriving from, say, advances in biological studies,
or archaeological research), can tell us. Will they explain the constant
factor in the secret flute cults of the Arapesh, the Merina woman's lack
of subtlety, or the bowing and scraping of the Yoruba wife? Although
there is no doubt that biology is important, and that human society is
constrained and directed in its development by facts of a physical kind,
I find it difficult to see how these could possibly lead to moral evaluations. Biological research may illuminate the range in human inclina-
tions and possibilities, but it cannot account for the interpretation of
these facts in a cultural order. It can tell us about the average endowments of groups or of particular individuals, but it cannot explain the
fact that cultures everywhere have given Man, as a category opposed to
Woman, social value and moral worth.

I look, rather, to human social and cultural organization. Paraphrasing Parsons (1964: 58), I would suggest that anything so general as the
universal asymmetry of sex roles is likely to be the result of a constellation of different factors, factors that are deeply involved in the founda-

[3] See also Bachofen (1967) and Davis (1972). Although many societies have myths
that seem to confirm this interpretation (myths in which, for example, men "steal" an
important cultural artifact from the women; see Bamberger, this volume), I would
prefer to see these as cultural reflections of the often tenuous and conflict-ridden
nature of male claims to authority, rather than as historical accounts (see Murphy,
1959).

tion of human societies. Biology may be one of these, but biology becomes significant only as it is interpreted by human actors and associated with characteristic modes of action (De Beauvoir, 1968: 29–33). Because biology dictates that women will be mothers, it seems that an analysis of the balance of forces in human social systems, and of the organization of human families in particular, will give the most promising results. In the discussion that follows, I will suggest that characteristic asymmetries in the experience of men and women—asymmetries ranging from their emotional orientations to the fact that men have public authority—can be understood in terms, not of biology directly, but of a near-universal fact of human experience. The fact that, in most traditional societies, a good part of a woman's adult life is spent giving birth to and raising children leads to a differentiation of domestic and public spheres of activity that can, I think, be shown to shape a number of relevant aspects of human social structure and psychology.[4]

Domestic and Public Orientations

In what follows, it will be seen that an opposition between "domestic" and "public" provides the basis of a structural framework necessary to identify and explore the place of male and female in psychological, cultural, social, and economic aspects of human life.[5] "Domestic," as used here, refers to those minimal institutions and modes of activity that are organized immediately around one or more mothers and their children; "public" refers to activities, institutions, and forms of association that link, rank, organize, or subsume particular mother-child groups. Though this opposition will be more or less salient in different social and ideological systems, it does provide a universal framework for conceptualizing the activities of the sexes. The opposition does not *determine* cultural stereotypes or asymmetries in the evaluations of the sexes, but rather underlies them, to support a very general (and, for women, often demeaning) identification of women with domestic life and of men with

[4] The importance of the woman's role as mother is not a new idea, but it was first suggested to me by Nancy Chodorow as the critical fact in understanding woman's status. See her paper "On Being and Doing" (1971).

[5] It should be stressed that, whereas a number of the empirical observations put forth here might seem to support those theorists who have claimed that men, as opposed to women, have a biological propensity for forming social "groups" (e.g. Tiger, 1969), my point is that what universals can be found in the social organization and position of men and women can be traced to social rather than biological considerations. The universal association of women with young children and its various social, cultural, and psychological implications are seen as likely but not necessary (or desirable) outcomes, and they are more readily derived from organizational factors than from biology.

public life. These identifications, themselves neither necessary nor desirable, can all be tied to the role of women in child rearing; by examining their multiple ramifications, one can begin to understand the nature of female subordination and the ways it may be overcome.

Although the fact that women give birth to and nurse children would seem to have no necessary entailments, it appears to provide a focus for the simplest distinction in the adult division of labor in any human group. Women become absorbed primarily in domestic activities because of their role as mothers. Their economic and political activities are constrained by the responsibilities of child care, and the focus of their emotions and attentions is particularistic and directed toward children and the home. So, for instance, Durkheim was able to speculate that "long ago, woman retired from warfare and public affairs, and consecrated her entire life to her family" (1964: 60). And Simmel points out that woman "because of her peculiar functions was relegated to activities within the limits of her home, confined to devote herself to a single individual and prevented from transcending the group-relations established by marriage [and] family" (1955: 180).

Historical or functional accounts aside, it is striking that, in these two cases as in numerous others, the domestic orientation of woman is felt to be the critical factor in understanding her social position. This orientation is contrasted to the extra-domestic, political, and military spheres of activity and interest primarily associated with men. Put quite simply, men have no single commitment as enduring, time-consuming, and emotionally compelling—as close to seeming necessary and natural—as the relation of a woman to her infant child; and so men are free to form those broader associations that we call "society," universalistic[6] systems of order, meaning, and commitment that link particular mother-child groups. Although I would be the last to call this a necessary arrangement or to deny that it is far too simple as an account of any particular empirical case, I suggest that the opposition between domestic and public orientations (an opposition that must, in part, derive from the nurturant capacities of women) provides the necessary framework for an examination of male and female roles in any society. Obvious as it may seem, its

[6] The use of "universalistic" and "particularistic" here resembles, but is different from, the meanings proposed in Parsons and Shils (1951: 82). Parsons used these terms to differentiate societies in which status is achieved and allocated on the basis of individual attributes, defined and evaluated in generalized terms, from those in which positions of status are determined by kin relations and the like. I speak of the women's world as "relatively particularistic" in all societies because it is governed by informal and personal knowledge of individuals, in contrast to the male world, which is relatively more concerned with formal norms of relationship and publicly recognized characteristics of roles.

ramifications are enormous; it permits us to isolate those interrelated factors that make woman universally the "second sex."

Personality. Chodorow's paper in this volume develops a theory relating adult sex-role behavior to the fact that women raise children, and shows how early involvement with a female figure has characteristic consequences for the development of both boys and girls. A few of her observations seem particularly relevant to the perspective developed here. First, insofar as a young girl has a mother to love and to follow, she also has the option of becoming a "little mother," and consequently of being absorbed into womanhood without effort. Female manners and activities are acquired in a way that seems easy and natural. The young girl's family provides her with an adequate and intelligible picture of most of the possibilities and important relationships that will define her throughout life. This continuity, characteristic of a young girl's development through puberty, is in radical contrast to the experience of boys, who must *learn* to be men. Adult male activities, whether hunting, politics, or farming, are rarely visible or available to young children, and fathers are often away from the home. At some point the boy must break away from his mother and establish his maleness as a thing apart. Therefore, when his sister is learning "to be a mother," he is apt to be restless and assertive and to seek out horizontal ties with male peers.

Three aspects of Chodorow's sophisticated argument seem particularly important. First, girls are most likely to form ties with female kin who are their seniors; they are integrated vertically, through ties with particular people, into the adult world of work.[7] This contrasts with young boys, who, having few responsibilities in late childhood, may create horizontal and often competitive peer groups, which cross-cut domestic units and establish "public" and overarching ties. In this respect, childhood activities and organization are apt to mirror the world of adults.

Second, Chodorow highlights the sense in which a young girl's early development may proceed without conflict or challenge in a group that never questions her membership, where her age rather than her abilities or achievement is likely to define her status. This is both a liability and a privilege. Growing up as a subordinate must be difficult, and if one's mother has accepted a derogatory self-image, identification with the mother can hardly be unproblematic. Such women, confusing themselves with their mothers, often have a weak ego or an uncertain sense of self. At the same time, they may enjoy a sense of ease, love, and accep-

---

[7] The Mae Enga (Meggit, 1964, 1965), who believe that flesh grows "vertically" on the bones of women and "horizontally" on the bones of men, and that this accounts for the fact that girls mature more quickly and easily than men do, seem to have formulated a symbolic statement of the sociological generalization suggested here.

tance in the process of becoming an adult. Male peer groups, by contrast, are difficult to enter; status, power, and sense of worth are often difficult to achieve. The boy's peer group, like adult male associations, is defined in part through its opposition to the family; and to establish himself, to "be a man," the boy is often required to dissociate himself, ritually or in fact, from the home. In this sense, then, a woman's status comes "naturally" (and even in societies that practice female initiation these ceremonies appear to be more a celebration of natural, biological developments than a "proof" of femininity or a challenge to past ties), whereas "becoming a man" is a feat.

Finally, growing up in a family, the young girl probably has more experience of others as individuals than as occupants of formal institutionalized roles; so she learns how to pursue her own interests, by appeals to other people, by being nurturant, responsive, and kind. She develops a "feminine" psychology. Boys, in contrast, are apt to know manhood as an abstract set of rights and duties, to learn that status brings formal authority, and to act in terms of formal roles. Their success or failure is judged in terms of male hierarchies, whereas most women, as wives, mothers, or sisters, gain respect, power, and status through their personal relations with men.

The fact that children virtually everywhere grow up with their mothers may well account for characteristic differences in male and female psychologies, and may also provide a partial psychological motive for men who, in Mead's terms (1949: 168), "need" to achieve an independent sense of worth and identity in order to become full adults.

Authority. A second consequence of the domestic, or familiar, orientation has to do with the ways in which women are perceived by the rest of society. Women are felt to be close to their children; they have access to a kind of certainty, a sense of diffuse belonging, not available to men. Men who are physically and socially distant from their children may well have political and economic claims on them; but their claims tend to be based more on their abstract authority than on personal commitment. In their absence or failure to perform as providers and symbols of status, they may lose their place in the home. This can be seen in our own society, in a father who awkwardly fondles his baby or in the woman-focused families of Blacks (Liebow, 1967; Stack, this volume) and other poor urban groups. In parts of Indonesia, men spend most of their time in long-distance trading, and are treated as outsiders, or guests, in the home (Tanner, this volume).

But distance itself can, and often does, provide interactional support for male claims to authority. In many parts of the world there is a radical break between the life of men—as reflected in their politics, separate sleeping quarters, and rituals—and the life of the domestic group. To the extent that men live apart from women, they of course cannot control them, and women may be able to form informal groups of their own. Yet men are free to build up rituals of authority that define them as superior, special and apart. In New Guinea, for example, men often have collective sleeping quarters, a practice associated with secret rituals and a lore that teaches young men that their health, strength, and beauty are damaged and diminished through their ties to the home. In parts of the Arab world (Fernea, 1965) women interact mostly with women, and men with men; wives meet their husbands briefly when serving dinner and occasionally for a few hours in bed. Interaction is highly structured and limited, subject to the mood of the man. Among the camel-herding Tuareg (Murphy, 1964) of the central Sahara, social roles are often ambiguous and overlapping, because of a preference for endogamy and bilateral reckoning of kin. Furthermore, women enjoy a good deal more freedom and social recognition than they do in most other Islamic societies. For men, it seems likely that the difficult, cooperative work situations of daily life tend to break down social distance; slaves and nobles, women and men, must cooperate in tending the herds. In order to distance themselves from a web of complex social relationships, and to protect their integrity and sense of personal esteem, Tuareg men have adopted the practice of wearing a veil across the nose and mouth. The veil is drawn most tightly when a man confronts a superior. But significantly, high-status men wear their veils more strictly than do slaves or vassals; women have no veils; and to assure his distance, no man is supposed to permit his lover to see his mouth. (In parts of American society, it would seem that men wear their veil of a newspaper in the subways and at breakfast with their wives.)

Such rituals enforce the distance between men and their families; for the individual, they provide a barrier to becoming embedded in an intimate, demanding world. Distance permits men to manipulate their social environment, to stand apart from intimate interaction, and, accordingly, to control it as they wish. Because men can be separate, they can be "sacred"; and by avoiding certain sorts of intimacy and unmediated involvement, they can develop an image and mantle of integrity and worth.

Women, by contrast, would have considerable difficulty in maintaining distance from the people they interact with. They must care for children, feed and clean them, and perform the messy chores. Their social interaction is more difficult for them to structure, being intimate and subject to variation in their own and their children's moods. Women's lives are marked by neither privacy nor distance. They are embedded in, and subject to, the demands of immediate interaction. Women, more than men, must respond to the personal needs of those around them: their public image is more difficult for them to manipulate or control; and where that image is concerned, familiarity may breed contempt. The rituals of authority are not available to woman; only when she is old and free of the responsibility of children, when she is dissociated from child rearing and also from sexuality, can a woman build up the respect that comes with authority.

Achieved and ascribed status. My earlier observations indicated that women's early experience in growing up has continuity. Whatever pain is in fact associated with female socialization, most cultures assume that it is relatively easy for a young girl to become a woman; people in most societies seem to take that process for granted. A man's experience lacks this continuity; he may be wrenched from the domestic sphere in which he spent his earliest years, by means of a series of rituals or initiations that teach him to distrust or despise the world of his mother, to seek his manhood outside the home. A woman becomes a woman by following in her mother's footsteps, whereas there must be a break in a man's experience. For a boy to become an adult, he must prove himself—his masculinity—among his peers. And although all boys may succeed in reaching manhood, cultures treat this development as something that each individual has achieved.

Unlike the two or three generations of a woman's domestic group, the male peer group often has no natural criteria that uniquely determine membership, order relationships, or establish chains of command. Instead, order within male groups, and in the social world in general, is felt to be a cultural product, and men elaborate systems of norms, ideals, and standards of evaluation that permit them to order relationships among themselves. If "becoming a man" is, developmentally, an "achievement," social groups elaborate the criteria for that achievement and create the hierarchies and institutions we associate with an articulated social order. Insofar as achievement in this sense is a prerequisite of manhood, then men create and control a social order in which they compete as individuals. Womanhood, by contrast, is more of a given for the female, and in most societies we find relatively few ways of expressing the differences among women. In Simmel's words, "the most general of her qualities, the fact that she was a woman and as such served the functions proper to her sex, caused her to be classified with all other women under one general concept" (1955: 180). Womanhood is an ascribed status; a woman is seen as "naturally" what she is.

One consequence of this can be seen in those traditional descriptions of social structure that report what are, for the most part, activities of men. Men are, in a real sense, identified with and through those groups of kin or peers that cut across domestic units; ranked in hierarchies of achievement, they are differentiated in their roles. These systems of ranking, grouping, and differentiation comprise the explicit social order that social scientists typically describe. Women, for their part, lead relatively comparable lives, both within a culture and from one culture to the next.[8] Their activities, in comparison with those of men, are relatively uninvolved with the articulation and expression of social differences. Therefore, we find, in most societies, relatively few institutionalized roles for women, and relatively few contexts in which women can legitimately make claims. Women's contributions to extra-domestic relations are rarely made explicit; women are given a social role and definition by virtue either of their age or of their relationship to men. Women, then, are conceived almost exclusively as sisters, wives, and mothers. Whereas men achieve rank as a result of explicit achievement, differences among women are generally seen as the product of idiosyncratic characteristics, such as temperament, personality, and appearance.[9]

Because cultures provide no fine social classification for kinds of women and their interests, women are seen and come to see themselves as idiosyncratic and irrational. Bateson, for example, reports that "structural phrasings" of motives and relations are pronounced among men in Iatmul (New Guinea) culture, whereas "among the women emotional

[8] The wives of herders, agriculturalists, and businessmen lead lives that are conceptualized in remarkably similar terms. Women, who are characterized everywhere as "the other," are often seen by missionaries and colonialists as the easiest people to interact with, convert, or educate; the hispanization of the New World, for example, seems to have depended in large part upon the colonialists' use of native women as lovers and domestics, and therefore as mediators between two worlds (Mary Felstiner, 1973). The fact that sisters can be married off to foreigners (whether in the New Guinea Highlands or the crowned courts of Europe), that women can be "exchanged" (Lévi-Strauss, 1949), corresponds to the fact that cultural conceptions of women's roles are universally very similar; much of what women do in any one society may be seen to have immediately available equivalents in any other.

[9] This generalization has its exceptions; in West Africa (Little, 1951) and in parts of Melanesia (Deacon, 1934), for example, women establish a fine societal classification of ranks among themselves. In general, however, women are not differentiated except in terms of age, relationship to men, or idiosyncratic (and institutionally irrelevant) characteristics. The contrast between categories used for men and women seems to parallel a contrast identified by Cancian (n.d.) between folk statements of what "good" and "bad" men do. "Good" norms are organized in terms of social institutions and provide criteria for ranking achievement in well-articulated social spheres; "bad" norms, by contrast, are only loosely organized, and refer to such considerations as temperament, appearance, sociability—idiosyncratic characteristics that do not lend themselves to organized and public systems of rank.

phrasings of reasons for behaviour are very much more frequent than among the men" (1958: 253). We are also told that Iatmul men are given to histrionic displays of status, whereas women behave in a casual, happy-go-lucky mode. Again, Landes says of the Ojibwa that "only the male half of the population and its activities fall under the traditional regulations, while the female half is left to spontaneous and confused behavior"; successful women may rival men in their achievements, but "they do not pursue these in systematic male fashion" (1971: v). Women's lives appear to be unstructured and "spontaneous" (see also Paul, this volume) in comparison with those of men.

Such perceptions are not, of course, unique to foreign cultures, but seem to be quite general. In the West, thinkers from Durkheim to Parsons have said that women are more "affective" or "expressive," less "intellectual" or "instrumental" than men. The claim has been made that this difference is a functional necessity of the family as a social group (Zelditch, 1955, 1964). Yet increasing evidence belies this assumption and suggests that the "expressive" character of women is as much a cultural interpretation, or cliché, as an accurate reflection of the ways in which women act and think.

If, following Durkheim, we are willing to suppose that the structure and nature of social relationships themselves influence cultural perceptions and modes of thinking, we can now illuminate this long-standing claim of social science. It reflects, not a natural or necessary endowment, but a very general cultural theme. Since women must work within a social system that obscures their goals and interests, they are apt to develop ways of seeing, feeling, and acting that seem to be "intuitive" and unsystematic—with a sensitivity to other people that permits them to survive. They may, then, be "expressive." But it is also important to realize that cultural stereotypes order the observer's own perceptions. It is because men enter the world of articulated social relations that they appear to us as intellectual, rational, or instrumental; and the fact that women are excluded from that world makes them seem to think and behave in another mode.

Nature and culture. There is yet another implication of this discussion. Insofar as men are defined in terms of their achievement in socially elaborated institutions, they are participants, *par excellence*, in the man-made systems of human experience. On a moral level, theirs is the world of "culture." Women, on the other hand, lead lives that appear to be irrelevant to the formal articulation of social order. Their status is derived from their stage in a life cycle, from their biological functions, and, in particular, from their sexual or biological ties to particular men.

What is more, women are more involved than men in the "grubby" and dangerous stuff of social existence, giving birth and mourning death, feeding, cooking, disposing of feces, and the like. Accordingly, in cultural systems we find a recurrent opposition: between man, who in the last analysis stands for "culture," and woman, who (defined through symbols that stress her biological and sexual functions) stands for "nature," and often for disorder.[10]

This point is elaborated in Ortner's paper in this volume. But it may be worth while to review some of its implications here. What is perhaps most striking is the fact that cultural notions of the female often gravitate around natural or biological characteristics: fertility, maternity, sex, and menstrual blood. And women, as wives, mothers, witches, midwives, nuns, or whores, are defined almost exclusively in terms of their sexual functions. A witch, in European tradition, is a woman who sleeps with the devil; and a nun is a woman who marries her god. Again, purity and pollution are ideas that apply primarily to women, who must either deny their physical bodies or circumscribe their dangerous sexuality.

Women as anomalies. The fact that men, in contrast to women, can be said to be associated with culture reflects another aspect of cultural definitions of the female. Recent studies of symbolic culture have suggested that whatever violates a society's sense of order will be seen as threatening, nasty, disorderly, or wrong. Douglas (1966) has called this sort of thing "anomalous." The idea of "order" depends, logically, on "disorder" as its opposite, yet society tries to set such things aside.

Now I would suggest that women in many societies will be seen as something "anomalous." Insofar as men, in their institutionalized relations of kinship, politics, and so on, define the public order, women are their opposite. Where men are classified in terms of ranked, institutional positions, women are simply women and their activities, interests, and differences receive only idiosyncratic note. Where male activities are justified and rationalized by a fine societal classification, by a system of norms acknowledging their different pursuits, women are classified together and their particular goals are ignored. From the point of view

[10] The tendency to associate women rather than men with Nature, and in particular with sexuality, in contemporary Western thought is documented in Ellman's witty observations concerning the popular "association ... between female reproductive organs and the female mind" (1968: 12). Ellman shows how, in literary discussion, there is a stereotyped and "repeated association of women ... with nature and of men with art" (p. 61). De Beauvoir (1953) saw the same thing, as in the nineteenth century did Bachofen (1967), whose claim that modern civilization was preceded by matriarchy is based, in large part, on the notion that nature, and especially fertility (rather than technological prowess), was once highly valued in human societies.

of the larger social system, they are seen as deviants or manipulators; because systems of social classification rarely make room for their interests, they are not publicly understood.

But women defy the ideals of the male order. They may be defined as virgins, yet be necessary to the group's regeneration. They may be excluded from authority, yet exercise all sorts of informal power. Their status may be derived from their male relations, yet they outlive their husbands and fathers. And insofar as the presence of women does introduce such contradictions, women will be seen as anomalous and defined as dangerous, dirty, and polluting, as something to be set apart.

A few examples may clarify this position. In many patrilineal ideologies (see Denich, this volume), women are seen as unnecessary or superfluous, yet at the same time vitally important to men: they are needed as wives, as sisters to be exchanged for wives, and as procreators who produce workers and heirs for the group. Because they are important, they are powerful, yet theirs is a power opposed to formal norms. A woman may, for example, be the mediator between her own kin group and that of the man she has married; her manipulations and choice of male allies may be of crucial importance to her kin. In such situations, cultures may elaborate the idea of her pollution; a woman's activities are circumscribed by calling them dangerous, by making them something to fear. Douglas (1966), for example, says of the Lele of the Kasai in southern Africa that men, who are dependent on women's political manipulations, are afraid to eat food cooked by menstruating women and rigorously abstain from sex, from contact with polluting women, before any important event. An extreme and now classic case is reported by Meggit (1964) in New Guinea. The Mae Enga of the Western Highlands say that they "marry their enemies"; women are pawns in a tenuous political alliance. Yet the in-marrying woman is always, of course, an outsider, and her influence is always feared. So, young Mae Enga boys are taught at an early age to fear the association of women; they learn that sexual indulgence deforms them and that menstrual blood can bring on disease. Pollution ideas are so extreme that marriage itself is seen as extremely dangerous; and to avoid the pollution of childbirth, a man may wait as much as three months before he dares to look at his newborn child.

Elsewhere, of course, women in conventional roles are not threatening. A woman who is a wife and a mother is benign. Danger is perceived only when a woman fails to bear children, or when her husband or children have died. In some societies danger or blame attaches to a woman who lives to mourn the death of her male kin. That many societies give far more cultural elaboration to the role of "widow" than to that of "widower" suggests that such conflicts do arise.[11] Men may take an active part in the rituals of mourning, but it is the women, not the men, who cry longer or louder, or in some other way are forced to show more suffering at death. In Madagascar, for example, women dance with the bones of dead people (Bloch, 1971); in the Mediterranean, women who have lost a close relative are likely to wear black for the rest of their lives. In parts of New Guinea, joints of a young girl's finger are severed when there is a death in the family; high-caste Indian women used to throw themselves on the funeral pyres of their husbands; and in other parts of the world, widows are strangled, commit suicide, or the like.

The sense that the widow is anomalous—that she, rather than the ghost of the dead person or some other close kin, must bear the weight of a loss—seems to be most elaborate in those groups in which a woman is defined exclusively in and through her male relations. Harper (1969) illustrated this in a paper on high-caste Brahmins in southern India. Among members of this group, marriage is seen as a necessary but terrible fact of a woman's maturity. Girls are indulged as little children because their parents pity their imminent fate; before puberty they are married into a group containing none of their kinswomen; they are subordinated to a hostile mother-in-law, and to ensure their purity and exclusive attachment to a single man, they are denied a role in production activities and confined to the house. It is said that a woman should pray to die before her husband. If he dies first, she as an outsider is apt to be suspected as the mystical source of his demise. When these poor women, who have been excluded from any social role of their own, are widowed, they in fact become social anomalies, without meaning or place. Others see them as pariahs, as evildoers and poisoners; they are despised and feared. It is significant that low-caste groups in the same

[11] The belief that extremes in mourning practices reflect the tenuous or anomalous position of the mourner (whose position in relation to a social group is defined solely in and through his or her ties to the deceased) is confirmed by an apparent exception. Fortune (1932) reported extremes in mourning practices among the Dobuans, where widows and widowers alike must spend a year in virtual isolation mourning the lost spouse. Dobuan residence arrangements require that couples spend alternate years in the husband's or wife's matrilineal village. This means that neither spouse has an opportunity to establish regular ties with his or her affines, and neither can be anything but an outsider to the affinal group. When one dies, the sole basis for social ties between spouse and affines is lost and the spouse stands in an "anomalous" relationship—of familiarity without institutional meaning—to the deceased. He or she is then forced to spend a full year grieving at the outskirts of the spouse's village, before their ties can be severed. At the end of mourning, the spouse is barred forever from reentering the village of the deceased.

area have no such beliefs about widows; there women have a role in social life and production, and widows remarry at will.

Finally, women may be "anomalies" because societies that define women as lacking legitimate authority have no way of acknowledging the reality of female power. This difference between rule and reality is reflected in our own society when we speak of powerful women as "bitches"; elsewhere in the world, the powerful woman is often considered a witch. Nadel, in his study of the Nupe of Nigeria (1952), described a situation where, in spite of a male-oriented political and religious system, women had become long-distance traders, thus acquiring a substantial income of their own. What is more, these women had access to contraceptives and illicit sex in faraway markets, defying a dominant norm that made reproduction a husband's prerogative and right. The Nupe, then, came to see societies of female traders as societies of witches. In so doing, they acknowledged the women's real power while labeling it illegitimate and wrong.

Production. A final reflex of the opposition between domestic and public spheres of activity is seen in the relations of production, in the place of men and women in economic life. Here it is particularly difficult to generalize, because female economic activities are truly varied, ranging from the American woman's housework to the African woman's long-distance trade. Yet the economic organization of women does seem to be relatively less public than that of men; women tend to work individually, or in small, loosely organized groups. And the products of female labor tend to be directed to the family and the home. Even when the products of women's labor are distributed in the larger community, it is often in support of male prestige.

Several papers in this volume show the consequences of different modes of female labor as well as the different ways in which a woman's reproductive capacities themselves are integrated into the economic life of a society (see Sanday, Sacks, and O'Laughlin). But whatever the variation, it is clear that the relatively domestic and particularistic orientation of women obtains in the vast majority of social groups. In most hunting bands, for instance, both men and women may hunt and gather, but only gathering is felt to be woman's work. Gathering requires little formal planning or organization; groups of women search the brush together, each doing the same kind of work and each acquiring foodstuffs, which may be shared informally with neighbors but are used primarily to meet individual family needs. Among the Ilongots, the Philippine group I studied, rice is a woman's product and possession; adult women usually have their own gardens and individual granaries in which rice is stored for household use. Hunting, on the other hand, is a responsibility of men as members of the community, and game is distributed through the community as a whole, since it is difficult to store. Even when men hunt individually, and dry and sell their catch, they exchange game for prestige goods, which are used for bride-price payments, gifts, and redress in the case of feuds. Finally, Bateson comments that in Iatmul (New Guinea) society both men and women fish for food, but when women fish "there is none of the excitement which the men introduce into their fishing expeditions. Each woman goes off by herself to do her day's work" (1958: 143).

Although one may find exceptions, then, it is generally the case that woman's economic orientation, like her emotional and social orientation, is relatively more individual and particularistic than that of men. This leads me to restate Engels's suggestive claim (see Sacks, this volume) that women were once involved in "social production" and, with the development of technology and capital, have been relegated to the domestic sphere. Rather, it seems that a domestic/public asymmetry is general in economic forms of human organization as in other forms. Advanced and capitalistic societies, although they are extreme in this regard, are not unique.

Sources of Power and Value

The preceding discussion has suggested that characteristic aspects of male and female roles in social, cultural, and economic systems can all be related to a universal, structural opposition between domestic and public domains of activity. In many ways this claim is far too simple. It is easy—in American society, for example—to identify the domestic sphere of the suburban housewife, and oppose it to the public, social world of industry, finance, and prestige. However, domestic groups themselves are highly varied—ranging from Mbuti lean-tos, which are hardly dissociated from the life of the community, to the famous Iroquois longhouse (Brown, 1970a), which holds several families and is itself a kind of social sphere. In fact, as Lamphere shows in a later paper, variations in domestic group structure are importantly related to variations in the types of female power.

Yet the complexities of particular cases do not undermine our global generalization, which points, not to absolute, but to relative orientations of women and men. Furthermore, by using the structural model as a framework, we can identify the implications for female power, value, and status in various cross-cultural articulations of domestic and public roles. Although the model has no necessary implications for the future, it permits us to identify two sorts of structural arrangements that elevate women's status: women may enter a public world, or men may enter the home.[12] By seeing how women have manipulated, elaborated, or undermined their domestic affiliations, we begin to appreciate women's roles as actors in various social systems, and also to identify the kinds of changes that women might effect in our own.

The model leads me to suggest, first, that women's status will be lowest in those societies where there is a firm differentiation between domestic and public spheres of activity and where women are isolated from one another and placed under a single man's authority, in the home. Their position is raised when they can challenge those claims to authority, either by taking on men's roles or by establishing social ties, by creating a sense of rank, order, and value in a world in which women prevail. One possibility for women, then, is to enter the men's world or to create a public world of their own. But perhaps the most egalitarian societies are those in which public and domestic spheres are only weakly differentiated, where neither sex claims much authority and the focus of social life itself is the home.

To begin (and without specifying particular criteria for reckoning women's status), it is clear that women who are cut off from ties with peers, who are circumscribed in their movements and activities, have an unenviable fate. A good example comes from Campbell's excellent description of the sheepherding Greek Sarakatsani (1964). Men spend their days in the hills, tending animals, while women are strictly confined to the home. An adolescent girl is taught early to limit her movements, to walk modestly, and never to run. Her sex is the stuff of the devil; her body is so feared that she rarely washes her torso; and if she so much as looks eye to eye with a man she is thought to invite assault. Upon marriage, she enters a hostile and distant household, where men and women alike resent any signs that she and her husband are close. For her, the sole joy in life is the son who grows up to support her, guaranteeing comfort when she is old. Yet her son's future status itself depends on her actions, and she must guard her own purity and preserve her husband's good name. She cannot so much as complain of her husband's abuses lest she defame him. Effectively she is his servant, and as Campbell suggests (1964), he is her god (see Denich, this volume).[13]

----

[12] For conceptual purposes, these possibilities are distinguished, although actual societies may be characterized by combinations of the two.

[13] In accord with our emphasis on how women see their lives, it is important to add that a Sarakatsani woman's status is at a low point in late adolescence and the first years of marriage. When her sons marry, they take over their father's position as head of household, and her powers and privileges are heightened, while those of her husband wane.

Other social arrangements, however, accord women more power and value. In some, a woman's opinions and her ability to bring a high bride-price or make ties with particular men are important factors in forging political alliances between groups. In others, her economic contribution and, in particular, her control of foodstuffs permit her to influence men. Where domestic and public spheres are firmly differentiated, women can manipulate men and influence their decisions by strategies as diverse as refusing to cook for their husbands (see Paulme, 1963), winning their sons' loyalties, setting spouse against kinsmen, or instigating what the rest of society may recognize as a "tragedy" in the home (see Wolf, 1972; Collier, 1973 and this volume). Finally, there are societies like our own, in which domestic and public spheres are distinguished, but in which privileged women, by taking on men's roles (becoming doctors, lawyers, or even members of the army), achieve considerable status and power. This seems to be the case with the classic queens and female chieftains of Africa (Lebeuf, 1963; Hoffer, this volume). Among the Lovedu (Krige and Krige, 1943), for instance, a woman may win power, status, and autonomy by taking over her husband's estate or by accumulating capital and marrying wives (the Lovedu have queens who, in the ritual aspects of marriage, perform in the role of a man).

Women in men's roles, however, tend to constitute an elite segment of female humanity; few women in history have achieved a dominant position in the working world, and even fewer have competed with male politicians and become political leaders or queens. More commonly, in those societies where domestic and public spheres are firmly differentiated, women may win power and value by stressing their differences from men. By accepting and elaborating upon the symbols and expectations associated with their cultural definition, they may goad men into compliance, or establish a society unto themselves. Thus, for instance, the traditional American woman can gain power covertly, by playing up to her husband's vanity (privately directing his public life). Or in everything from charities to baking contests, she may forge a public world of her own. Elsewhere, women may form trading societies, church clubs, or even political organizations, through which they force thoughtless men into line. Among the Iroquois (Brown, 1970a), women's power was rooted in a predominantly female organization of domestic life and agricultural labor; men spent long periods away from home hunting or warring, and women worked together, controlled the distribution of foodstuffs, decided on marriages, and generally dominated community concerns. Again, in the prestigious female political and religious societies of West Africa (Lebeuf, 1963; Leis, Hoffer, this volume), women have created fully articulated social hierarchies of their own.

The ideas of purity and pollution, so often used to circumscribe female activities, may also be used as a basis for assertions of female solidarity, power, or value. In the simplest case, we might note that a woman who is feared often has power; many a New Guinea man will observe his wife's wishes for fear that an angry woman will serve him food while she is menstruating, or step over him, letting blood drip, while he sleeps. Again, roles like that of the witch or midwife (see Paul, this volume) seem to be used by women who, by stressing aspects of their special or anomalous position, take on powers uniquely their own. What is more, pollution beliefs can provide grounds for solidarity among women. Women may, for example, gather in menstrual huts, to relax or to gossip, creating a world free from control by men. Or again, as Lewis (1971) has indicated, anomalous and powerless women in many parts of the world may be particularly vulnerable to possession by spirits; on the basis of such possession, women form cult groups that rival the religious organizations of men. Finally, women as both secular and religious prostitutes, as women who never marry yet have intercourse with a wide range of men, may again be making positive use of their "anomalous" sexuality. Because it is both feared and desired, it gives them a real source of power, and in certain situations the brothel and temple may be spheres where women prevail.

If assertions of sexuality can give power to women, so too can its denial. Victorian women won status by denying their own sexuality and treating male sexual drives as a sin. Purity beliefs seem to be particularly attractive to women, who very often elaborate the norms concerned with purity, the rules for strict dress and demeanor, modesty, cleanliness, and prudishness, which they use as a device for contrasting their world and the men's world—establishing grounds for order and status among themselves. So, for example, in a Spanish village I studied, women were vicious in their condemnation of the seductive female; they elaborated a system of strict norms for the period of mourning, and the pure and respectable woman spent most of her life in drab black clothing. Groups of these women gathered during the day at the fountain in the center of the village, defining that center as their own. As is the case elsewhere in the Mediterranean, they saw themselves as purer, more moral and stable, than men, and men, in the fields or the bar or the cities, were rarely in sight. At the fountain, women gossiped and exchanged valuable information. Their dazzlingly white sheets and severe sexless garments testified to their purity; and while men dirtied themselves in work, compromise, and public competition, women had a moral sphere all their own. Perhaps the extreme case of a women's society founded on the idiom of purity, on a lack of involvement with men, is the convent. Brides of Christ need not be tainted by mortal men's foibles. Instead, they establish a pure and moral society, a world wholly their own.

These examples suggest that the very symbolic and social conceptions that appear to set women apart and to circumscribe their activities may be used by women as a basis for female solidarity and worth. When men live apart from women, they in fact cannot control them, and unwittingly they may provide them with the symbols and social resources on which to build a society of their own. Such women's groups, ranging from convents and brothels to informal neighborhood friendships in China (see Wolf, 1972 and this volume) or African political organizations and cults (Leis, Hoffer, this volume), are available to women in men's absence, and they add social and moral value to an otherwise domestic role.

Extra-domestic ties with other women are, then, an important source of power and value for women in societies that create a firm division between public and domestic, or male and female, roles. As suggested above, however, there is another possibility. Societies that do not elaborate the opposition of male and female and place positive value on the conjugal relationship and the involvement of both men and women in the home seem to be most egalitarian in terms of sex roles. When a man is involved in domestic labor, in child care and cooking, he cannot establish an aura of authority and distance. And when public decisions are made in the household, women may have a legitimate public role.

Because none of the other papers in this volume consider this alternative, it might be valuable to treat one example at length. Among the Ilongots, the Philippine society I studied, a man's hunting is more highly valued than the gardening done by women, but the two modes of production are conceived as complementary and the division of labor is not strict. Rituals for hunting and gardening draw on the same complex repertoire of magical objects; in the house when food is being distributed, women cook and allot rice portions, while men cook, cut, and distribute bits of meat. During the day, when women are gardening, men spend long hours with their children, and husband and wife may keep an infant between them while they sleep. A marriage forms a core, an enduring and cooperative social unit; the only Ilongot expression for "family" means "married couple" or "those who have intercourse together."

In fact, there is little in everyday Ilongot life to suggest an asymmetrical relation of the sexes. There are no men's houses or public plazas, no locus for an independent, ranked, and organized hierarchical world of men.[14] Most political confrontations take place in the large one-room households; although men may predominate in such contexts, women are rarely forbidden to speak. The one activity that marks men as special is headhunting. Like male cults and secret rituals elsewhere in the world, this is associated with the attainment of manhood; it is the one activity in which men are definitely set apart. Yet it is particularly interesting to note that headhunting is not felt to be obligatory, nor is it desirable for a man to take a head more than once. The overly anxious killer is thought to be aggressive, and headhunting does not provide a basis on which men readily rank one another or compete among themselves.

In other words, it appears that involvement of men in the domestic sphere and, correspondingly, participation of women in most public events, have a number of related consequences. In an area of the world in which men have traditionally won authority through their competitive success in warfare, Ilongot headhunters seem nonetheless to play down a male ethic of authority and achievement, of systems of ranking among men. Because boys' earliest experiences are shaped by the intimacy of fathers as well as mothers, they are relatively unconcerned with a need to "achieve," or to denigrate women; men involved in domestic tasks demand no submission from their wives. In social and political life, Ilongots evince little stratification, and although sexual asymmetry is certainly present, it is minimized by the fact that women have the right, and the confidence, to speak their minds. Finally, in the home we find relatively egalitarian relations between the sexes, cooperation rather than competition, and a true closeness of husband and wife.

The same point, I think, can be made for other societies considered in the anthropological literature to be "egalitarian." In these, as in Ilongot society, men control prestigious rituals and symbols, but the aura of male authority is minimized through men's involvement in the home. So, for example, the Mbuti pygmies of Africa (Turnbull, 1961) live in groups where domestic units are separated from one another by mere lean-tos and men and women cooperate in both domestic and eco-

---

[14] Recent mission influence has established an institution outside the household, the Church. It has also introduced the explicit Christian idea of the subordination of the wife to her husband. Ilongot women more than men seem open to conversion, but it is significant that leadership roles in the Church (the first formal, institutionalized, important, and explicit leadership roles within Ilongot society) have all been assumed by men.

nomic pursuits. Mbuti men do have a secret flute cult, but it is not used to dominate women or to create rankings among themselves. Another example is the Arapesh, as well as those other New Guinea groups (e.g. Wogeo, described in Hogbin, 1970) that, in a culture area characterized by elaborate and institutionalized expressions of sexual antagonism, seem to have stressed the complementarity of women and men. In these, as opposed to other groups in the area, the "secret" of male flute cults is enforced only weakly. And among the Arapesh, men and women together are said to "give birth to" and "grow" their children; they participate jointly in domestic life. Here again the mutual and complementary involvement of men and women in domestic activities promotes a sense of equality. An egalitarian ethos seems possible to the extent that men take on a domestic role.

Conclusion

I have tried to relate universal asymmetries in the actual activities and cultural evaluations of men and women to a universal, structural opposition between domestic and public spheres. I have also suggested that women seem to be oppressed or lacking in value and status to the extent that they are confined to domestic activities, cut off from other women and from the social world of men. Women gain power and a sense of value when they are able to transcend domestic limits, either by entering the men's world or by creating a society unto themselves. Finally, I suggested that the most egalitarian societies are not those in which male and female are opposed or are even competitors, but those in which men value and participate in the domestic life of the home. Correspondingly, they are societies in which women can readily participate in important public events.

It is interesting to note that American society participates to some extent, especially on the level of ideology (though not, of course, in economic or other forms of organization), in the last complementary ideal. Americans talk about sexual equality, and American rituals from churchgoing to holiday dinners are intended to involve the nuclear family as a whole. Schneider, in an innovative study (1968), has suggested that the idea of "sexual intercourse," of conjugal solidarity, is a central metaphor in American kinship; husband and wife form a core unit, an ordering principle for reckoning relationships, and also a cultural ideal. In a similar way, I indicated that "those who have intercourse together" means "family" for the Ilongots. There too, the union of man and woman is seen as crucial, and again it is associated with an egalitarian sexual ideology.

Unlike the Ilongot, however, American society is in fact organized in a way that creates and exploits a radical distance between private and public, domestic and social, female and male. It speaks, on one level, of the conjugal family, while on another it defines women as domestic (an invisible army of unemployed) and sends its men into the public, working world. This conflict between ideal and reality creates illusions and disappointments for both men and women.

In concluding, I would like to suggest that this conflict is at the core of the contemporary rethinking of sex roles: we are told that men and women should be equals and even companions, but we are also told to value men for their work. So far, women concerned to realize their equality have concentrated on the second half of this paradox, and have sought grounds for female solidarity and opportunities for women in the men's working world. We have conceived of our liberation on the model of women's societies and African queens. Yet as long as the domestic sphere remains female, women's societies, however powerful, will never be the political equivalents of men's; and, as in the past, sovereignty can be a metaphor for only a female elite. If the public world is to open its doors to more than the elite among women, the nature of work itself will have to be altered, and the asymmetry between work and the home reduced. For this, we must, like the Ilongots, bring men into the sphere of domestic concerns and responsibilities. Certainly it is difficult to imagine modeling our society after that of the Ilongot cultivators and hunters. Yet we need today to combine political goals with utopian visions, and to this end the Ilongot example can help. It provides us with an image of a world in which the domestic/public opposition is minimized and dissociated from sexual ascriptions. And it suggests that men who in the past have committed their lives to public achievement will recognize women as true equals only when men themselves help to raise new generations by taking on the responsibilities of the home.

Family Structure and Feminine Personality

I propose here[1] a model to account for the reproduction within each generation of certain general and nearly universal differences that characterize masculine and feminine personality and roles. My perspective is largely psychoanalytic. Cross-cultural and social-psychological evidence suggests that an argument drawn solely from the universality of biological sex differences is unconvincing.[2] At the same time, explanations based on patterns of deliberate socialization (the most prevalent kind of anthropological, sociological, and social-psychological explanation) are in themselves insufficient to account for the extent to which psychological and value commitments to sex differences are so emotionally laden and tenaciously maintained, for the way gender identity and expectations about sex roles and gender consistency are so deeply central to a person's consistent sense of self.

This paper suggests that a crucial differentiating experience in male and female development arises out of the fact that women, universally, are largely responsible for early child care and for (at least) later female socialization. This points to the central importance of the mother-

[1] My understanding of mother-daughter relationships and their effect on feminine psychology grows out of my participation beginning in 1971 in a women's group that discusses mother-daughter relationships in particular and family relationships in general. All the women in this group have contributed to this understanding. An excellent dissertation by Marcia Millman (1972) first suggested to me the importance of boundary issues for women and became a major organizational focus for my subsequent work. Discussions with Nancy Jay, Michelle Rosaldo, Philip Slater, Barrie Thorne, Susan Weisskopf, and Beatrice Whiting have been central to the development of the ideas presented here. I am grateful to George Goethals, Edward Payne, and Mal Slavin for their comments and suggestions about earlier versions of this paper.
[2] Margaret Mead provides the most widely read and earliest argument for this viewpoint (cf., e.g., 1935 and 1949); see also Chodorow (1971) for another discussion of the same issue.

daughter relationship for women, and to a focus on the conscious and unconscious effects of early involvement with a female for children of both sexes. The fact that males and females experience this social environment differently as they grow up accounts for the development of basic sex differences in personality. In particular, certain features of the mother-daughter relationship are internalized universally as basic elements of feminine ego structure (although not necessarily what we normally mean by "femininity").

Specifically, I shall propose that, in any given society, feminine personality comes to define itself in relation and connection to other people more than masculine personality does. (In psychoanalytic terms, women are less individuated than men; they have more flexible ego boundaries.[3]) Moreover, issues of dependency are handled and experienced differently by men and women. For boys and men, both individuation and dependency issues become tied up with the sense of masculinity, or masculine identity. For girls and women, by contrast, issues of femininity, or feminine identity, are not problematic in the same way. The structural situation of child rearing, reinforced by female and male role training, produces these differences, which are replicated and reproduced in the sexual sociology of adult life.

The paper is also a beginning attempt to rectify certain gaps in the social-scientific literature, and a contribution to the reformulation of psychological anthropology. Most traditional accounts of family and socialization tend to emphasize only role training, and not unconscious features of personality. Those few that rely on Freudian theory have abstracted a behaviorist methodology from this theory, concentrating on isolated "significant" behaviors like weaning and toilet training. The paper advocates instead a focus on the ongoing interpersonal relationships in which these various behaviors are given meaning.[4]

[3] Unfortunately, the language that describes personality structure is itself embedded with value judgment. The implication in most studies is that it is always better to have firmer ego boundaries, that "ego strength" depends on the degree of individuation. Gutmann, who recognizes the linguistic problem, even suggests that "so-called ego pathology may have adaptive implications for women" (1965: 231). The argument can be made that extremes in either direction are harmful. Complete lack of ego boundaries is clearly pathological, but so also, as critics of contemporary Western men point out (cf., e.g., Bakan, 1966, and Slater, 1970), is individuation gone wild, what Bakan calls "agency unmitigated by communion," which he takes to characterize, among other things, both capitalism based on the Protestant ethic and aggressive masculinity. With some explicit exceptions that I will specify in context, I am using the concepts solely in the descriptive sense.

[4] Slater (1968) provides one example of such an investigation. LeVine's recent work on psychoanalytic anthropology (1971a,b) proposes a methodology that will enable social scientists to study personality development in this way.

More empirically, most social-scientific accounts of socialization, child development, and the mother-child relationship refer implicitly or explicitly only to the development and socialization of boys, and to the mother-son relationship. There is a striking lack of systematic description about the mother-daughter relationship, and a basic theoretical discontinuity between, on the one hand, theories about female development, which tend to stress the development of "feminine" qualities in relation to and comparison with men, and on the other hand, theories about women's ultimate mothering role. This final lack is particularly crucial, because women's motherhood and mothering role seem to be the most important features in accounting for the universal secondary status of women (Chodorow, 1971; Ortner, Rosaldo, this volume). The present paper describes the development of psychological qualities in women that are central to the perpetuation of this role.

In a formulation of this preliminary nature, there is not a great body of consistent evidence to draw upon. Available evidence is presented that illuminates aspects of the theory—for the most part psychoanalytic and social-psychological accounts based almost entirely on highly industrialized Western society. Because aspects of family structure are discussed that are universal, however, I think it is worth considering the theory as a general model. In any case, this is in some sense a programmatic appeal to people doing research. It points to certain issues that might be especially important in investigations of child development and family relationships, and suggests that researchers look explicitly at female vs. male development, and that they consider seriously mother-daughter relationships even if these are not of obvious "structural importance" in a traditional anthropological view of that society.

The Development of Gender Personality

According to psychoanalytic theory,[5] personality is a result of a boy's or girl's social-relational experiences from earliest infancy. Personality development is not the result of conscious parental intention. The nature and quality of the social relationships that the child experiences are appropriated, internalized, and organized by her/him and come to constitute her/his personality. What is internalized from an ongoing relationship continues independent of that original relationship and is generalized and set up as a permanent feature of the personality. The conscious self is usually not aware of many of the features of personality,

[5] Particularly as interpreted by object-relations theorists (e.g., Fairbairn, 1952, and Guntrip, 1961) and, with some similarity, by Parsons (1964) and Parsons and Bales (1955).

or of its total structural organization. At the same time, these are important determinants of any person's behavior, both that which is culturally expected and that which is idiosyncratic or unique to the individual. The conscious aspects of personality, like a person's general self-concept and, importantly, her/his gender identity, require and depend upon the consistency and stability of its unconscious organization. In what follows I shall describe how contrasting male and female experiences lead to differences in the way that the developing masculine or feminine psyche resolves certain relational issues.

Separation and individuation (preoedipal development). All children begin life in a state of "infantile dependence" (Fairbairn, 1952) upon an adult or adults, in most cases their mother. This state consists first in the persistence of primary identification with the mother: the child does not differentiate herself/himself from her/his mother but experiences a sense of oneness with her. (It is important to distinguish this from later forms of identification, from "secondary identification," which presuppose at least some degree of experienced separateness by the person who identifies.) Second, it includes an oral-incorporative mode of relationship to the world, leading, because of the infant's total helplessness, to a strong attachment to and dependence upon whoever nurses and carries her/him.

Both aspects of this state are continuous with the child's prenatal experience of being emotionally and physically part of the mother's body and of the exchange of body material through the placenta. That this relationship continues with the natural mother in most societies stems from the fact that women lactate. For convenience, and not because of biological necessity, this has usually meant that mothers, and females in general, tend to take all care of babies. It is probable that the mother's continuing to have major responsibility for the feeding and care of the child (so that the child interacts almost entirely with her) extends and intensifies her/his period of primary identification with her more than if, for instance, someone else were to take major or total care of the child. A child's earliest experience, then, is usually of identity with and attachment to a single mother, and always with women.

For both boys and girls, the first few years are preoccupied with issues of separation and individuation. This includes breaking or attenuating the primary identification with the mother and beginning to develop an individuated sense of self, and mitigating the totally dependent oral attitude and attachment to the mother. I would suggest that, contrary to the traditional psychoanalytic model, the preoedipal experience is likely to differ for boys and girls. Specifically, the experience of mothering for a woman involves a double identification (Klein and Rivière, 1937). A woman identifies with her own mother and, through identification with her child, she (re)experiences herself as a cared-for child. The particular nature of this double identification for the individual mother is closely bound up with her relationship to her own mother. As Deutsch expresses it, "In relation to her own child, woman repeats her own mother-child history" (1944: 205). Given that she was a female child, and that identification with her mother and mothering are so bound up with her being a woman, we might expect that a woman's identification with a girl child might be stronger; that a mother, who is, after all, a person who is a woman and not simply the performer of a formally defined role, would tend to treat infants of different sexes in different ways.

There is some suggestive sociological evidence that this is the case. Mothers in a women's group in Cambridge, Massachusetts (see note 1), say that they identified more with their girl children than with boy children. The perception and treatment of girl vs. boy children in high-caste, extremely patriarchal, patrilocal communities in India are in the same vein. Families express preference for boy children and celebrate when sons are born. At the same time, Rajput mothers in North India are "as likely as not" (Minturn and Hitchcock, 1963) to like girl babies better than boy babies once they are born, and they and Havik Brahmins in South India (Harper, 1969) treat their daughters with greater affection and leniency than their sons. People in both groups say that this is out of sympathy for the future plight of their daughters, who will have to leave their natal family for a strange and usually oppressive postmarital household. From the time of their daughters' birth, then, mothers in these communities identify anticipatorily, by reexperiencing their own past, with the experiences of separation that their daughters will go through. They develop a particular attachment to their daughters because of this and by imposing their own reaction to the issue of separation on this new external situation.

It seems, then, that a mother is more likely to identify with a daughter than with a son, to experience her daughter (or parts of her daughter's life) as herself. Fliess's description (1961) of his neurotic patients who were the children of ambulatory psychotic mothers presents the problem in its psychopathological extreme. The example is interesting, because, although Fliess claims to be writing about people defined only by the fact that their problems were tied to a particular kind of relationship to their mothers, an overwhelmingly large proportion of the cases he presents are women. It seems, then, that this sort of disturbed mother inflicts her pathology predominantly on daughters. The mothers Fliess describes did not allow their daughters to perceive themselves as separate people, but simply acted as if their daughters were narcissistic extensions or doubles of themselves, extensions to whom were attributed the mothers' bodily feelings and who became physical vehicles for their mothers' achievement of autoerotic gratification. The daughters were bound into a mutually dependent "hypersymbiotic" relationship. These mothers, then, perpetuate a mutual relationship with their daughters of both primary identification and infantile dependence.

A son's case is different. Cultural evidence suggests that insofar as a mother treats her son differently, it is usually by emphasizing his masculinity in opposition to herself and by pushing him to assume, or acquiescing in his assumption of, a sexually toned male-role relation to her. Whiting (1959) and Whiting et al. (1958) suggest that mothers in societies with mother-child sleeping arrangements and postpartum sex taboos may be seductive toward infant sons. Slater (1968) describes the socialization of precarious masculinity in Greek males of the classical period through their mothers' alternation of sexual praise and seductive behavior with hostile deflation and ridicule. This kind of behavior contributes to the son's differentiation from his mother and to the formation of ego boundaries (I will later discuss certain problems that result from this).

Neither form of attitude or treatment is what we would call "good mothering." However, evidence of differentiation of a pathological nature in the mother's behavior toward girls and boys does highlight tendencies in "normal" behavior. It seems likely that from their children's earliest childhood, mothers and women tend to identify more with daughters and to help them to differentiate less, and that processes of separation and individuation are made more difficult for girls. On the other hand, a mother tends to identify less with her son, and to push him toward differentiation and the taking on of a male role unsuitable to his age, and undesirable at any age in his relationship to her.

For boys and girls, the quality of the preoedipal relationship to the mother differs. This, as well as differences in development during the oedipal period, accounts for the persisting importance of preoedipal issues in female development and personality that many psychoanalytic writers describe.[6] Even before the establishment of gender identity, gender personality differentiation begins.

Gender identity (oedipal crisis and resolution). There is only a slight

[6] Cf., e.g., Brunswick, 1940; Deutsch, 1932, 1944; Fliess, 1948; Freud, 1931; Jones, 1927; and Lampl–de Groot, 1928.

suggestion in the psychological and sociological literature that preoedipal development differs for boys and girls. The pattern becomes explicit at the next developmental level. All theoretical and empirical accounts agree that after about age three (the beginning of the "oedipal" period, which focuses on the attainment of a stable gender identity) male and female development becomes radically different. It is at this stage that the father, and men in general, begin to become important in the child's primary object world. It is, of course, particularly difficult to generalize about the attainment of gender identity and sex-role assumption, since there is such wide variety in the sexual sociology of different societies. However, to the extent that in all societies women's life tends to be more private and domestic, and men's more public and social (Rosaldo, this volume), we can make general statements about this kind of development.

In what follows, I shall be talking about the development of gender personality and gender identity in the tradition of psychoanalytic theory. Cognitive psychologists have established that by the age of three, boys and girls have an irreversible conception of what their gender is (cf. Kohlberg, 1966). I do not dispute these findings. It remains true that children (and adults) may know definitely that they are boys (men) or girls (women), and at the same time experience conflicts or uncertainty about "masculinity" or "femininity," about what these identities require in behavioral or emotional terms, etc. I am discussing the development of "gender identity" in this latter sense.

A boy's masculine gender identification must come to replace his early primary identification with his mother. This masculine identification is usually based on identification with a boy's father or other salient adult males. However, a boy's father is relatively more remote than his mother. He rarely plays a major caretaking role even at this period in his son's life. In most societies, his work and social life take place farther from the home than do those of his wife. He is, then, often relatively inaccessible to his son, and performs his male role activities away from where the son spends most of his life. As a result, a boy's male gender identification often becomes a "positional" identification, with aspects of his father's clearly or not-so-clearly defined male role, rather than a more generalized "personal" identification—a diffuse identification with his father's personality, values, and behavioral traits—that could grow out of a real relationship to his father.[7]

Mitscherlich (1963), in his discussion of Western advanced capitalist

[7] The important distinction between "positional" and "personal" identification comes from Slater, 1961, and Winch, 1962.

society, provides a useful insight into the problem of male development. The father, because his work takes him outside of the home most of the time, and because his active presence in the family has progressively decreased, has become an "invisible father." For the boy, the tie between affective relations and masculine gender identification and role learning (between libidinal and ego development) is relatively attenuated. He identifies with a fantasied masculine role, because the reality constraint that contact with his father would provide is missing. In all societies characterized by some sex segregation (even those in which a son will eventually lead the same sort of life as his father), much of a boy's masculine identification must be of this sort, that is, with aspects of his father's role, or what he fantasies to be a male role, rather than with his father as a person involved in a relationship to him.

There is another important aspect to this situation, which explains the psychological dynamics of the universal social and cultural devaluation and subordination of women.[8] A boy, in his attempt to gain an elusive masculine identification, often comes to define this masculinity largely in negative terms, as that which is not feminine or involved with women. There is an internal and external aspect to this. Internally, the boy tries to reject his mother and deny his attachment to her and the strong dependence upon her that he still feels. He also tries to deny the deep personal identification with her that has developed during his early years. He does this by repressing whatever he takes to be feminine inside himself, and, importantly, by denigrating and devaluing whatever he considers to be feminine in the outside world. As a societal member, he also appropriates to himself and defines as superior particular social activities and cultural (moral, religious, and creative) spheres—possibly, in fact, "society" (Rosaldo, this volume) and "culture" (Ortner, this volume) themselves.[9]

Freud's description of the boy's oedipal crisis speaks to the issues of rejection of the feminine and identification with the father. As his early attachment to his mother takes on phallic-sexual overtones, and his father enters the picture as an obvious rival (who, in the son's fantasy, has apparent power to kill or castrate his son), the boy must radically deny and repress his attachment to his mother and replace it with an

[8] For more extensive arguments concerning this, cf., e.g., Burton and Whiting (1961), Chodorow (1971), and Slater (1968).

[9] The processes by which individual personal experiences and psychological factors contribute to or are translated into social and cultural facts, and, more generally, the circularity of explanations in terms of socialization, are clearly very complicated. A discussion of these issues, however, is not within the scope of this paper.

identification with his loved and admired, but also potentially punitive, therefore feared, father. He internalizes a superego.[10]

To summarize, four components of the attainment of masculine gender identity are important. First, masculinity becomes and remains a problematic issue for a boy. Second, it involves denial of attachment or relationship, particularly of what the boy takes to be dependence or need for another, and differentiation of himself from another. Third, it involves the repression and devaluation of femininity on both psychological and cultural levels. Finally, identification with his father does not usually develop in the context of a satisfactory affective relationship, but consists in the attempt to internalize and learn components of a not immediately apprehensible role.

The development of a girl's gender identity contrasts with that of a boy. Most important, femininity and female role activities are immediately apprehensible in the world of her daily life. Her final role identification is with her mother and women, that is, with the person or people with whom she also has her earliest relationship of infantile dependence. The development of her gender identity does not involve a rejection of this early identification, however. Rather, her later identification with her mother is embedded in and influenced by their ongoing relationship of both primary identification and preoedipal attachment. Because her mother is around, and she has had a genuine relationship to her as a person, a girl's gender and gender role identification are mediated by and depend upon real affective relations. Identification with her mother is not positional—the narrow learning of particular role behaviors—but rather a personal identification with her mother's general traits of character and values. Feminine identification is based not on fantasied or externally defined characteristics and negative identification, but on the gradual learning of a way of being familiar in everyday life, and exemplified by the person (or kind of people— women) with whom she has been most involved. It is continuous with her early childhood identifications and attachments.

[10] The question of the universality of the oedipus complex as Freud describes it is beyond the scope of this paper. Bakan (1966, 1968) points out that in the original Oedipus myth, it was the father who first tried to kill his son, and that the theme of paternal infanticide is central to the entire Old Testament. He suggests that for a variety of reasons, fathers probably have hostile and aggressive fantasies and feelings about their children (sons). This more general account, along with a variety of psychological and anthropological data, convinces me that we must take seriously the notion that members of both generations may have conflicts over the inevitable replacement of the elder generation by the younger, and that children probably feel both guilt and (rightly) some helplessness in this situation.

The major discontinuity in the development of a girl's sense of gender identity, and one that has led Freud and other early psychoanalysts to see female development as exceedingly difficult and tortuous, is that at some point she must transfer her primary sexual object choice from her mother and females to her father and males, if she is to attain her expected heterosexual adulthood. Briefly, Freud considers that all children feel that mothers give some cause for complaint and unhappiness: they give too little milk; they have a second child; they arouse and then forbid their child's sexual gratification in the process of caring for her/him. A girl receives a final blow, however: her discovery that she lacks a penis. She blames this lack on her mother, rejects her mother, and turns to her father in reaction.

Problems in this account have been discussed extensively in the general literature that has grown out of the women's movement, and within the psychoanalytic tradition itself. These concern Freud's misogyny and his obvious assumption that males possess physiological superiority, and that a woman's personality is inevitably determined by her lack of a penis.[11] The psychoanalytic account is not completely unsatisfactory, however. A more detailed consideration of several theorists[12] reveals important features of female development, especially about the mother-daughter relationship, and at the same time contradicts or mitigates the absoluteness of the more general Freudian outline.

These psychoanalysts emphasize how, in contrast to males, the female oedipal crisis is not resolved in the same absolute way. A girl cannot and does not completely reject her mother in favor of men, but continues her relationship of dependence upon and attachment to her. In addition, the strength and quality of her relationship to her father is com-

[11] These views are most extreme and explicit in two papers (Freud, 1925, 1933) and warrant the criticism that has been directed at them. Although the issue of penis envy in women is not central to this paper, it is central to Freud's theory of female development. Therefore I think it worthwhile to mention three accounts that avoid Freud's ideological mistakes while allowing that his clinical observations of penis envy might be correct.

Thompson (1943) suggests that penis envy is a symbolic expression of women's culturally devalued and underprivileged position in our patriarchal society; that possession of a penis symbolizes the possession of power and privilege. Bettelheim (1954) suggests that members of either sex envy the sexual functions of the other, and that women are more likely to express this envy overtly, because, since men are culturally superior, such envy is considered "natural." Balint (1954) does not rely on the fact of men's cultural superiority, but suggests that a little girl develops penis envy when she realizes that her mother loves people with penises, i.e., her father, and thinks that possession of a penis will help her in her rivalry for her mother's attentions.

[12] See, e.g., Brunswick, 1940; Deutsch, 1925, 1930, 1932, 1944; Freedman, 1961; Freud, 1931; Jones, 1927.

pletely dependent upon the strength and quality of her relationship to her mother. Deutsch suggests that a girl wavers in a "bisexual triangle" throughout her childhood and into puberty, normally making a very tentative resolution in favor of her father, but in such a way that issues of separation from and attachment to her mother remain important throughout a woman's life (1944: 205):

> It is erroneous to say that the little girl gives up her first mother relation in favor of the father. She only gradually draws him into the alliance, develops from the mother-child exclusiveness toward the triangular parent-child relationship and continues the latter, just as she does the former, although in a weaker and less elemental form, all her life. Only the principal part changes: now the mother, now the father plays it. The ineradicability of affective constellations manifests itself in later repetitions.

We might suggest from this that a girl's internalized and external object-relations become and remain more complex, and at the same time more defining of her, than those of a boy. Psychoanalytic preoccupation with constitutionally based libidinal development, and with a normative male model of development, has obscured this fact. Most women are genitally heterosexual. At the same time, their lives always involve other sorts of equally deep and primary relationships, especially with their children, and, importantly, with other women. In these spheres also, even more than in the area of heterosexual relations, a girl imposes the sort of object-relations she has internalized in her preoedipal and later relationship to her mother.

Men are also for the most part genitally heterosexual. This grows directly out of their early primary attachment to their mother. We know, however, that in many societies their heterosexual relationships are not embedded in close personal relationship but simply in relations of dominance and power. Furthermore, they do not have the extended personal relations women have. They are not so connected to children, and their relationships with other men tend to be based not on particularistic connection or affective ties, but rather on abstract, universalistic role expectations.

Building on the psychoanalytic assumption that unique individual experiences contribute to the formation of individual personality, culture and personality theory has held that early experiences common to members of a particular society contribute to the formation of "typical" personalities organized around and preoccupied with certain issues: "Prevailing patterns of child-rearing must result in similar internalized situations in the unconscious of the majority of individuals in a culture, and these will be externalized back into the culture again to perpetuate it from generation to generation" (Guntrip, 1961: 378). In a similar vein, I have tried to show that to the extent males and females, respectively, experience similar interpersonal environments as they grow up, masculine and feminine personality will develop differently.

I have relied on a theory which suggests that features of adult personality and behavior are determined, but which is not biologically determinist. Culturally expected personality and behavior are not simply "taught," however. Rather, certain features of social structure, supported by cultural beliefs, values, and perceptions, are internalized through the family and the child's early social object-relationships. This largely unconscious organization is the context in which role training and purposive socialization take place.

Sex-Role Learning and Its Social Context

Sex-role training and social interaction in childhood build upon and reinforce the largely unconscious development I have described. In most societies (ours is a complicated exception) a girl is usually with her mother and other female relatives in an interpersonal situation that facilitates continuous and early role learning and emphasizes the mother-daughter identification and particularistic, diffuse, affective relationships between women. A boy, to a greater or lesser extent, is also with women for a large part of his childhood, which prevents continuous or easy masculine role identification. His development is characterized by discontinuity.

Ariès (1962: 61), in his discussion of the changing concept of childhood in modern capitalist society, makes a distinction that seems to have more general applicability. Boys, he suggests, became "children" while girls remained "little women." "The idea of childhood profited the boys first of all, while the girls persisted much longer in the traditional way of life which confused them with the adults: we shall have cause to notice more than once this delay on the part of the women in adopting the visible forms of the essentially masculine civilization of modern times." This took place first in the middle classes, as a situation developed in which boys needed special schooling in order to prepare for their future work and could not begin to do this kind of work in childhood. Girls (and working-class boys) could still learn work more directly from their parents, and could begin to participate in the adult economy at an earlier age. Rapid economic change and development have exacerbated the lack of male generational role continuity. Few fathers now have either the opportunity or the ability to pass on a profession or skill to their sons.

Sex-role development of girls in modern society is more complex. On the one hand, they go to school to prepare for life in technologically and socially complex society. On the other, there is a sense in which this schooling is a pseudo-training. It is not meant to interfere with the much more important training to be "feminine" and a wife and mother, which is embedded in the girl's unconscious development and which her mother teaches her in a family context where she is clearly the salient parent.

This dichotomy is not unique to modern industrial society. Even if special, segregated schooling is not necessary for adult male work (and many male initiation rites remain a form of segregated role training), boys still participate in more activities that characterize them as a category apart from adult life. Their activities grow out of the boy's need to fill time until he can begin to take on an adult male role. Boys may withdraw into isolation and self-involved play or join together in a group that remains more or less unconnected with either the adult world of work and activity or the familial world.

Jay (1969) describes this sort of situation in rural Modjokuto, Java. Girls, after the age of five or so, begin gradually to help their mothers in their work and spend time with their mothers. Boys at this early age begin to form bands of age mates who roam and play about the city, relating neither to adult men nor to their mothers and sisters. Boys, then, enter a temporary group based on universalistic membership criteria, while girls continue to participate in particularistic role relations in a group characterized by continuity and relative permanence.

The content of boys' and girls' role training tends in the same direction as the context of this training and its results. Barry, Bacon, and Child, in their well-known study (1957), demonstrate that the socialization of boys tends to be oriented toward achievement and self-reliance and that of girls toward nurturance and responsibility. Girls are thus pressured to be involved with and connected to others, boys to deny this involvement and connection.

Adult Gender Personality and Sex Role

A variety of conceptualizations of female and male personality all focus on distinctions around the same issue, and provide alternative confirmation of the developmental model I have proposed. Bakan (1966: 15) claims that male personality is preoccupied with the "agentic," and female personality with the "communal." His expanded definition of the two concepts is illuminating:

I have adopted the terms "agency" and "communion" to characterize two fundamental modalities in the existence of living forms, agency for the existence of an organism as an individual and communion for the participation of the individual in some larger organism of which the individual is a part. Agency manifests itself in self-protection, self-assertion, and self-expansion; communion manifests itself in the sense of being at one with other organisms. Agency manifests itself in the formation of separations; communion in the lack of separations. Agency manifests itself in isolation, alienation, and aloneness; communion in contact, openness, and union. Agency manifests itself in the urge to master; communion in noncontractual cooperation. Agency manifests itself in the repression of thought, feeling, and impulse; communion in the lack and removal of repression.

Gutmann (1965) contrasts the socialization of male personalities in "allocentric" milieux (milieux in which the individual is part of a larger social organization and system of social bonds) with that of female personalities in "autocentric" milieux (in which the individual herself/ himself is a focus of events and ties).[13] Gutmann suggests that this leads to a number of systematic differences in ego functioning. Female ego qualities, growing out of participation in autocentric milieux, include more flexible ego boundaries (i.e. less insistent self-other distinctions), present orientation rather than future orientation, and relatively greater subjectivity and less detached objectivity.[14]

Carlson (1971) confirms both characterizations. Her tests of Gutmann's claims lead her to conclude that "males represent experiences of self, others, space, and time in individualistic, objective, and distant ways, while females represent experiences in relatively interpersonal, subjec-

[13] Following Cohen (1969), I would suggest that the external structural features of these settings (in the family or in school, for instance) are often similar or the same for boys and girls. The different kind and amount of adult male and female participation in these settings accounts for their being experienced by children of different sexes as different sorts of milieux.

[14] Gutmann points out that all these qualities are supposed to indicate lack of adequate ego strength, and suggests that we ought to evaluate ego strength in terms of the specific demands of different people's (e.g. women's as opposed to men's) daily lives. Bakan goes even further and suggests that modern male ego qualities are a pathological extreme. Neither account is completely adequate. Gutmann does not consider the possibility (for which we have good evidence) that the everyday demands of an autocentric milieu are unreasonable: although women's ego qualities may be "functional" for their participation in these milieux, they do not necessarily contribute to the psychological strength of the women themselves. Bakan, in his (legitimate) preoccupation with the lack of connection and compulsive independence that characterizes Western masculine success, fails to recognize the equally clear danger (which, I will suggest, is more likely to affect women) of communion unmitigated by agency—of personality and behavior with no sense of autonomous control or independence at all.

I think this is part of a more general social-scientific mistake, growing out of the tendency to equate social structure and society with male social organization and activities within a society. This is exemplified, for instance, in Erikson's idealistic conception of maternal qualities in women (1965) and, less obviously, in the contrast between Durkheim's extensive treatment of "anomic" suicide (1897) and his relegation of "fatalistic" suicide to a single footnote (p. 276).

tive, immediate ways" (p. 270). With reference to Bakan, she claims that men's descriptions of affective experience tend to be in agentic terms and women's in terms of communion, and that an examination of abstracts of a large number of social-psychological articles on sex differences yields an overwhelming confirmation of the agency/communion hypothesis.

Cohen (1969) contrasts the development of "analytic" and "relational" cognitive style, the former characterized by a stimulus-centered, parts-specific orientation to reality, the latter centered on the self and responding to the global characteristics of a stimulus in reference to its total context. Although focusing primarily on class differences in cognitive style, she also points out that girls are more likely to mix the two types of functioning (and also to exhibit internal conflict about this). Especially, they are likely to exhibit at the same time both high field dependence and highly developed analytic skills in other areas. She suggests that boys and girls participate in different sorts of interactional subgroups in their families: boys experience their family more as a formally organized primary group; girls experience theirs as a group characterized by shared and less clearly delineated functions. She concludes (p. 836): "Since embedded responses covered the gamut from abstract categories, through language behaviors, to expressions of embeddedness in their social environments, it is possible that embeddedness may be a distinctive characteristic of female sex-role learning in this society regardless of social class, native ability, ethnic differences, and the cognitive impact of the school."

Preliminary consideration suggests a correspondence between the production of feminine personalities organized around "communal" and "autocentric" issues and characterized by flexible ego boundaries, less detached objectivity, and relational cognitive style, on the one hand, and important aspects of feminine as opposed to masculine social roles, on the other.

Most generally, I would suggest that a quality of embeddedness in social interaction and personal relationships characterizes women's life relative to men's. From childhood, daughters are likely to participate in an intergenerational world with their mother, and often with their aunts and grandmother, whereas boys are on their own or participate in a single-generation world of age mates. In adult life, women's interaction with other women in most societies is kin-based and cuts across generational lines. Their roles tend to be particularistic, and to involve diffuse relationships and responsibilities rather than specific ones. Women in most societies are *defined* relationally (as someone's wife, mother, daughter, daughter-in-law; even a nun becomes the Bride of Christ). Men's association (although it too may be kin-based and inter-generational) is much more likely than women's to cut across kinship units, to be restricted to a single generation, and to be recruited accord-ing to universalistic criteria and involve relationships and responsibil-ities defined by their specificity.

Ego Boundaries and the Mother-Daughter Relationship

The care and socialization of girls by women ensures the production of feminine personalities founded on relation and connection, with flex-ible rather than rigid ego boundaries, and with a comparatively secure sense of gender identity. This is one explanation for how women's rela-tive embeddedness is reproduced from generation to generation, and why it exists within almost every society. More specific investigation of different social contexts suggests, however, that there are variations in the kind of relationship that can exist between women's role perfor-mance and feminine personality.

Various kinds of evidence suggest that separation from the mother, the breaking of dependence, and the establishment and maintenance of a consistently individuated sense of self remain difficult psychological issues for Western middle-class women (i.e. the women who become sub-jects of psychoanalytic and clinical reports and social-psychological studies). Deutsch (1944, 1945) in particular provides extensive clinical documentation of these difficulties and of the way they affect women's relationships to men and children and, because of their nature, are re-produced in the next generation of women. Mothers and daughters in the women's group mentioned above (p. 47) describe their experiences of boundary confusion or equation of self and other, for example, guilt and self-blame for the other's unhappiness; shame and embarrassment at the other's actions; daughters' "discovery" that they are "really" liv-ing out their mothers' lives in their choice of career; mothers' not com-pletely conscious reactions to their daughters' bodies as their own (over-identification and therefore often unnecessary concern with supposed weight or skin problems, which the mother is really worried about in herself); etc.

A kind of guilt that Western women express seems to grow out of and to reflect lack of adequate self/other distinctions and a sense of ines-capable embeddedness in relationships to others. Tax describes this well (1970: 2; italics mine):

Since our awareness of others is considered our duty, the price we pay when things go wrong is guilt and self-hatred. And things always go wrong. We re-spond with apologies; we continue to apologize long after the event is forgotten

—and *even if it had no causal relation to anything we did to begin with.* If the rain spoils someone's picnic, we apologize. We apologize for taking up space in a room, for living.

As if the woman does not differentiate herself clearly from the rest of the world, she feels a sense of guilt and responsibility for situations that did not come about through her actions and without relation to her actual ability to determine the course of events. This happens, in the most familiar instance, in a sense of diffuse responsibility for everything connected to the welfare of her family and the happiness and success of her children. This loss of self in overwhelming responsibility for and connection to others is described particularly acutely by women writers (in the work, for instance, of Simone de Beauvoir, Kate Chopin, Doris Lessing, Tillie Olsen, Christina Stead, Virginia Woolf).

Slater (1961) points to several studies supporting the contention that Western daughters have particular problems about differentiation from their mother. These studies show that though most forms of personal parental identification correlate with psychological adjustment (i.e. freedom from neurosis or psychosis, *not* social acceptability), personal identification of a daughter with her mother does not. The reason is that the mother-daughter relation is the one form of personal identification that, because it results so easily from the normal situation of child development, is liable to be excessive in the direction of allowing no room for separation or difference between mother and daughter.

The situation reinforces itself in circular fashion. A mother, on the one hand, grows up without establishing adequate ego boundaries or a firm sense of self. She tends to experience boundary confusion with her daughter, and does not provide experiences of differentiating ego development for her daughter or encourage the breaking of her daughter's dependence. The daughter, for her part, makes a rather unsatisfactory and artificial attempt to establish boundaries: she projects what she defines as bad within her onto her mother and tries to take what is good into herself. (This, I think, is the best way to understand the girl's oedipal "rejection" of her mother.) Such an arbitrary mechanism cannot break the underlying psychological unity, however. Projection is never more than a temporary solution to ambivalence or boundary confusion.

The implication is that, contrary to Gutmann's suggestion (see note 3), "so-called ego pathology" may not be "adaptive" for women. Women's biosexual experiences (menstruation, coitus, pregnancy, childbirth, lactation) all involve some challenge to the boundaries of her body ego ("me"/"not-me" in relation to her blood or milk, to a man who penetrates her, to a child once part of her body). These are important and

fundamental human experiences that are probably intrinsically meaningful and at the same time complicated for women everywhere. However, a Western woman's tenuous sense of individuation and of the
firmness of her ego boundaries increases the likelihood that experiences
challenging these boundaries will be difficult for her and conflictive.

Nor is it clear that this personality structure is "functional" for society as a whole. The evidence presented in this paper suggests that
satisfactory mothering, which does not reproduce particular psychological problems in boys and girls, comes from a person with a firm sense
of self and of her own value, whose care is a freely chosen activity rather
than a reflection of a conscious and unconscious sense of inescapable
connection to and responsibility for her children.

Social Structure and the Mother-Daughter Relationship

Clinical and self-analytic descriptions of women and of the psychological component of mother-daughter relationships are not available
from societies and subcultures outside of the Western middle class. However, accounts that are primarily sociological about women in other
societies enable us to infer certain aspects of their psychological situation. In what follows, I am not claiming to make any kind of general
statement about what constitutes a "healthy society," but only to examine and isolate specific features of social life that seem to contribute
to the psychological strength of some members of a society. Consideration of three groups with matrifocal tendencies in their family structure
(see Tanner, this volume) highlights several dimensions of importance
in the developmental situation of the girl.

Young and Willmott (1957) describe the daily visiting and mutual
aid of working-class mothers and daughters in East London. In a situation where household structure is usually nuclear, like the Western
middle class, grown daughters look to their mothers for advice, for aid
in childbirth and child care, for friendship and companionship, and for
financial help. Their mother's house is the ultimate center of the family
world. Husbands are in many ways peripheral to family relationships,
possibly because of their failure to provide sufficiently for their families
as men are expected to do. This becomes apparent if they demand their
wife's disloyalty toward or separation from her mother: "The great triangle of childhood is mother-father-child; in Bethnal Green the great
triangle of adult life is Mum-wife-husband" (p. 64).

Geertz (1961)[15] and Jay (1969) describe Javanese nuclear families in

---

[15] This ethnography, and a reading of it that focuses on strong female kin relations, was brought to my attention by Tanner (1971).

which women are often the more powerful spouse and have primary influence upon how kin relations are expressed and to whom (although these families are formally centered upon a highly valued conjugal relationship based on equality of spouses). Financial and decision-making control in the family often rests largely in the hands of its women. Women are potentially independent of men in a way that men are not independent of women. Geertz points to a woman's ability to participate in most occupations, and to own farmland and supervise its cultivation, which contrasts with a man's inability, even if he is financially independent, to do his own household work and cooking.

Women's kin role in Java is important. Their parental role and rights are greater than those of men; children always belong to the woman in case of divorce. When extra members join a nuclear family to constitute an extended family household, they are much more likely to be the wife's relatives than those of the husband. Formal and distant relations between men in a family, and between a man and his children (especially his son), contrast with the informal and close relations between women, and between a woman and her children. Jay and Geertz both emphasize the continuing closeness of the mother-daughter relationship as a daughter is growing up and throughout her married life. Jay suggests that there is a certain amount of ambivalence in the mother-daughter relationship, particularly as a girl grows toward adulthood and before she is married, but points out that at the same time the mother remains a girl's "primary figure of confidence and support" (1969: 103).

Siegel (1969)[16] describes Atjehnese families in Indonesia in which women stay on the homestead of their parents after marriage and are in total control of the household. Women tolerate men in the household only as long as they provide money, and even then treat them as someone between a child and a guest. Women's stated preference would be to eliminate even this necessary dependence on men: "Women, for instance, envision paradise as the place where they are reunited with their children and their mothers; husbands and fathers are absent, and yet there is an abundance all the same. Quarrels over money reflect the women's idea that men are basically adjuncts who exist only to give their families whatever they can earn" (p. 177). A woman in this society does not get into conflicts in which she has to choose between her mother and her husband, as happens in the Western working class (see above; also Komarovsky, 1962), where the reigning ideology supports the nuclear family.

In these three settings, the mother-daughter tie and other female kin

16 See note 15.

relations remain important from a woman's childhood through her old age. Daughters stay closer to home in both childhood and adulthood, and remain involved in particularistic role relations. Sons and men are more likely to feel uncomfortable at home, and to spend work and play time away from the house. Male activities and spheres emphasize universalistic, distancing qualities: men in Java are the bearers and transmitters of high culture and formal relationships; men in East London spend much of their time in alienated work settings; Atjehnese boys spend their time in school, and their fathers trade in distant places.

Mother-daughter ties in these three societies, described as extremely close, seem to be composed of companionship and mutual cooperation, and to be positively valued by both mother and daughter. The ethnographies do not imply that women are weighed down by the burden of their relationships or by overwhelming guilt and responsibility. On the contrary, they seem to have developed a strong sense of self and self-worth, which continues to grow as they get older and take on their maternal role. The implication is that "ego strength" is not completely dependent on the firmness of the ego's boundaries.

Guntrip's distinction between "immature" and "mature" dependence clarifies the difference between mother-daughter relationships and women's psyche in the Western middle class and in the matrifocal societies described. Women in the Western middle class are caught up to some extent in issues of infantile dependence, while the women in matrifocal societies remain in definite connection with others, but in relationships characterized by mature dependence. As Guntrip describes it (1961: 291): "*Mature dependence* is characterized by full differentiation of ego and object (emergence from primary identification) and therewith a capacity for valuing the object for its own sake and for giving as well as receiving; a condition which should be described not as independence but as mature dependence." This kind of mature dependence is also to be distinguished from the kind of forced independence and denial of need for relationship that I have suggested characterizes masculine personality, and that reflects continuing conflict about infantile dependence (Guntrip, 1961: 293; my italics): "Maturity is not equated with independence though it includes a certain capacity for independence. . . . The independence of the mature person is simply that he does not collapse when he has to stand alone. It is not an independence of needs for other persons with whom to have relationship: *that would not be desired by the mature.*"

Depending on its social setting, women's sense of relation and connection and their embeddedness in social life provide them with a kind of security that men lack. The quality of a mother's relationship to her children and maternal self-esteem, on the one hand, and the nature of a daughter's developing identification with her mother, on the other, make crucial differences in female development.

Women's kin role, and in particular the mother role, is central and positively valued in Atjeh, Java, and East London. Women gain status and prestige as they get older; their major role is not fulfilled in early motherhood. At the same time, women may be important contributors to the family's economic support, as in Java and East London, and in all three societies they have control over real economic resources. All these factors give women a sense of self-esteem independent of their relationship to their children. Finally, strong relationships exist between women in these societies, expressed in mutual cooperation and frequent contact. A mother, then, when her children are young, is likely to spend much of her time in the company of other women, not simply isolated with her children.

These social facts have important positive effects on female psychological development. (It must be emphasized that all the ethnographies indicate that these same social facts make male development difficult and contribute to psychological insecurity and lack of ease in interpersonal relationships in men.) A mother is not invested in keeping her daughter from individuating and becoming less dependent. She has other ongoing contacts and relationships that help fulfill her psychological and social needs. In addition, the people surrounding a mother while a child is growing up become mediators between mother and daughter, by providing a daughter with alternative models for personal identification and objects of attachment, which contribute to her differentiation from her mother. Finally, a daughter's identification with her mother in this kind of setting is with a strong woman with clear control over important spheres of life, whose sense of self-esteem can reflect this. Acceptance of her gender identity involves positive valuation of herself, and not an admission of inferiority. In psychoanalytic terms, we might say it involves identification with a preoedipal, active, caring mother. Bibring points to clinical findings supporting this interpretation: "We find in the analysis of the women who grew up in this 'matriarchal' setting the rejection of the feminine role less frequently than among female patients coming from the patriarchal family culture" (1953: 281).

There is another important aspect of the situation in these societies. The continuing structural and practical importance of the mother-daughter tie not only ensures that a daughter develops a positive personal and role identification with her mother, but also requires that the close psychological tie between mother and daughter become firmly grounded in real role expectations. These provide a certain constraint and limitation upon the relationship, as well as an avenue for its expression through common spheres of interest based in the external social world.

All these societal features contrast with the situation of the Western middle-class woman. Kinship relations in the middle class are less important. Kin are not likely to live near each other, and, insofar as husbands are able to provide adequate financial support for their families, there is no need for a network of mutual aid among related wives. As the middle-class woman gets older and becomes a grandmother, she cannot look forward to increased status and prestige in her new role.

The Western middle-class housewife does not have an important economic role in her family. The work she does and the responsibilities that go with it (household management, cooking, entertaining, etc.) do not seem to be really necessary to the economic support of her family (they are crucial contributions to the maintenance and reproduction of her family's class position, but this is not generally recognized as important either by the woman herself or by the society's ideology). If she works outside the home, neither she nor the rest of society is apt to consider this work to be important to her self-definition in the way that her housewife role is.

Child care, on the other hand, is considered to be her crucially important responsibility. Our post-Freudian society in fact assigns to parents (and especially to the mother[17]) nearly total responsibility for how children turn out. A middle-class mother's daily life is not centrally involved in relations with other women. She is isolated with her children for most of her workday. It is not surprising, then, that she is likely to invest a lot of anxious energy and guilt in her concern for her children and to look to them for her own self-affirmation, or that her self-esteem, dependent on the lives of others than herself, is shaky. Her life situation leads her to an overinvolvement in her children's lives.

A mother in this situation keeps her daughter from differentiation and from lessening her infantile dependence. (She also perpetuates her son's dependence, but in this case society and his father are more likely to interfere in order to assure that, behaviorally, at least, he doesn't *act* dependent.) And there are not other people around to mediate in the mother-daughter relationship. Insofar as the father is actively involved in a relationship with his daughter and his daughter develops some identification with him, this helps her individuation, but the formation

---

[17] See Slater (1970) for an extended discussion of the implications of this.

of ego autonomy through identification with and idealization of her father may be at the expense of her positive sense of feminine self. Unlike the situation in matrifocal families, the continuing closeness of the mother-daughter relationship is expressed only on a psychological, interpersonal level. External role expectations do not ground or limit it.

It is difficult, then, for daughters in a Western middle-class family to develop self-esteem. Most psychoanalytic and social theorists[18] claim that the mother inevitably represents to her daughter (and son) regression, passivity, dependence, and lack of orientation to reality, whereas the father represents progression, activity, independence, and reality orientation.[19] Given the value implications of this dichotomy, there are advantages for the son in giving up his mother and identifying with his father. For the daughter, feminine gender identification means identification with a devalued, passive mother, and personal maternal identification is with a mother whose own self-esteem is low. Conscious rejection of her oedipal maternal identification, however, remains an unconscious rejection and devaluation of herself, because of her continuing preoedipal identification and boundary confusion with her mother.

Cultural devaluation is not the central issue, however. Even in patrilineal, patrilocal societies in which women's status is very low, women do not necessarily translate this cultural devaluation into low self-esteem, nor do girls have to develop difficult boundary problems with their mother. In the Moslem Moroccan family, for example,[20] a large amount of sex segregation and sex antagonism gives women a separate (domestic) sphere in which they have a real productive role and control, and also a life situation in which any young mother is in the company of other women. Women do not need to invest all their psychic energy in their children, and their self-esteem is not dependent on their relationship to their children. In this and other patrilineal, patrilocal societies, what resentment women do have at their oppressive situation is more often expressed toward their sons, whereas daughters are seen as allies against oppression. Conversely, a daughter develops relationships of attachment to and identification with other adult women.

18 See, e.g., Deutsch, 1944, *passim*; Erikson, 1964: 162; Klein and Rivière, 1937: 18; Parsons, 1970, *passim*; Parsons and Bales, 1955, *passim*.

19 Their argument derives from the universal fact that a child must outgrow her/ his primary identification with and total dependence upon the mother. The present paper argues that the value implications of this dichotomy grow out of the particular circumstances of our society and its devaluation of relational qualities. Allied to this is the suggestion that it does not need to be, and often is not, relationship to the father that breaks the early maternal relationship.

20 Personal communication from Fatima Mernissi, based on her experience growing up in Morocco and her recent sociological fieldwork there.

Loosening her tie to her mother therefore does not entail the rejection of all women. The close tie that remains between mother and daughter is based not simply on mutual overinvolvement but often on mutual understanding of their oppression.

Conclusion

Women's universal mothering role has effects both on the development of masculine and feminine personality and on the relative status of the sexes. This paper has described the development of relational personality in women and of personalities preoccupied with the denial of relation in men. In its comparison of different societies, it has suggested that men, while guaranteeing to themselves sociocultural superiority over women, always remain psychologically defensive and insecure. Women, by contrast, although always of secondary social and cultural status, may in favorable circumstances gain psychological security and a firm sense of worth and importance in spite of this.

Social and psychological oppression, then, is perpetuated in the structure of personality. The paper enables us to suggest what social arrangements contribute (and could contribute) to social equality between men and women and their relative freedom from certain sorts of psychological conflict. Daughters and sons must be able to develop a personal identification with more than one adult, and preferably one embedded in a role relationship that gives it a social context of expression and provides some limitation upon it. Most important, boys need to grow up around men who take a major role in child care, and girls around women who, in addition to their child-care responsibilities, have a valued role and recognized spheres of legitimate control. These arrangements could help to ensure that children of both sexes develop a sufficiently individuated and strong sense of self, as well as a positively valued and secure gender identity, that does not bog down either in ego-boundary confusion, low self-esteem, and overwhelming relatedness to others, or in compulsive denial of any connection to others or dependence upon them.

SHERRY B. ORTNER

Is Female to Male as Nature Is to Culture?

Much of the creativity of anthropology derives from the tension between two sets of demands: that we explain human universals, and that we explain cultural particulars. By this canon, woman provides us with one of the more challenging problems to be dealt with. The secondary status of woman in society is one of the true universals, a pan-cultural fact. Yet within that universal fact, the specific cultural conceptions and symbolizations of woman are extraordinarily diverse and even mutually contradictory. Further, the actual treatment of women and their relative power and contribution vary enormously from culture to culture, and over different periods in the history of particular cultural traditions. Both of these points—the universal fact and the cultural variation—constitute problems to be explained.

My interest in the problem is of course more than academic: I wish to see genuine change come about, the emergence of a social and cultural order in which as much of the range of human potential is open to women as is open to men. The universality of female subordination, the fact that it exists within every type of social and economic arrangement and in societies of every degree of complexity, indicates to me that we are up against something very profound, very stubborn, something

The first version of this paper was presented in October 1972 as a lecture in the course "Women: Myth and Reality" at Sarah Lawrence College. I received helpful comments from the students and from my co-teachers in the course: Joan Kelly Gadol, Eva Kollisch, and Gerda Lerner. A short account was delivered at the American Anthropological Association meetings in Toronto, November 1972. Meanwhile, I received excellent critical comments from Karen Blu, Robert Paul, Michelle Rosaldo, David Schneider, and Terence Turner, and the present version of the paper, in which the thrust of the argument has been rather significantly changed, was written in response to those comments. I, of course, retain responsibility for its final form. The paper is dedicated to Simone de Beauvoir, whose book *The Second Sex* (1953), first published in French in 1949, remains in my opinion the best single comprehensive understanding of "the woman problem."

we cannot rout out simply by rearranging a few tasks and roles in the social system, or even by reordering the whole economic structure. In this paper I try to expose the underlying logic of cultural thinking that assumes the inferiority of women; I try to show the highly persuasive nature of the logic, for if it were not so persuasive, people would not keep subscribing to it. But I also try to show the social and cultural sources of that logic, to indicate wherein lies the potential for change.

It is important to sort out the levels of the problem. The confusion can be staggering. For example, depending on which aspect of Chinese culture we look at, we might extrapolate any of several entirely different guesses concerning the status of women in China. In the ideology of Taoism, *yin*, the female principle, and *yang*, the male principle, are given equal weight; "the opposition, alternation, and interaction of these two forces give rise to all phenomena in the universe" (Siu, 1968: 2). Hence we might guess that maleness and femaleness are equally valued in the general ideology of Chinese culture.[1] Looking at the social structure, however, we see the strongly emphasized patrilineal descent principle, the importance of sons, and the absolute authority of the father in the family. Thus we might conclude that China is the archetypal patriarchal society. Next, looking at the actual roles played, power and influence wielded, and material contributions made by women in Chinese society—all of which are, upon observation, quite substantial—we would have to say that women are allotted a great deal of (unspoken) status in the system. Or again, we might focus on the fact that a goddess, Kuan Yin, is the central (most worshiped, most depicted) deity in Chinese Buddhism, and we might be tempted to say, as many have tried to say about goddess-worshiping cultures in prehistoric and early historical societies, that China is actually a sort of matriarchy. In short, we must be absolutely clear about *what* we are trying to explain before explaining it.

We may differentiate three levels of the problem:

1. The universal fact of culturally attributed second-class status of woman in every society. Two questions are important here. First, what do we mean by this; what is our evidence that this is a universal fact? And second, how are we to explain this fact, once having established it?

2. Specific ideologies, symbolizations, and socio-structural arrangements pertaining to women that vary widely from culture to culture. The problem at this level is to account for any particular cultural com-

---

[1] It is true of course that *yin*, the female principle, has a negative valence. Nonetheless, there is an absolute complementarity of *yin* and *yang* in Taoism, a recognition that the world requires the equal operation and interaction of both principles for its survival.

plex in terms of factors specific to that group—the standard level of anthropological analysis.

3. Observable on-the-ground details of women's activities, contributions, powers, influence, etc., often at variance with cultural ideology (although always constrained within the assumption that women may never be officially preeminent in the total system). This is the level of direct observation, often adopted now by feminist-oriented anthropologists.

This paper is primarily concerned with the first of these levels, the problem of the universal devaluation of women. The analysis thus depends not upon specific cultural data but rather upon an analysis of "culture" taken generically as a special sort of process in the world. A discussion of the second level, the problem of cross-cultural variation in conceptions and relative valuations of women, will entail a great deal of cross-cultural research and must be postponed to another time. As for the third level, it will be obvious from my approach that I would consider it a misguided endeavor to focus only upon women's actual though culturally unrecognized and unvalued powers in any given society, without first understanding the overarching ideology and deeper assumptions of the culture that render such powers trivial.

The Universality of Female Subordination

What do I mean when I say that everywhere, in every known culture, women are considered in some degree inferior to men? First of all, I must stress that I am talking about *cultural* evaluations; I am saying that each culture, in its own way and on its own terms, makes this evaluation. But what would constitute evidence that a particular culture considers women inferior?

Three types of data would suffice: (1) elements of cultural ideology and informants' statements that *explicitly* devalue women, according them, their roles, their tasks, their products, and their social milieux less prestige than are accorded men and the male correlates; (2) symbolic devices, such as the attribution of defilement, which may be interpreted as *implicitly* making a statement of inferior valuation; and (3) social-structural arrangements that exclude women from participation in or contact with some realm in which the highest powers of the society are felt to reside.[2] These three types of data may all of course be interrelated

---

[2] Some anthropologists might consider this type of evidence (social-structural arrangements that exclude women, explicitly or de facto, from certain groups, roles, or statuses) to be a subtype of the second type of evidence (symbolic formulations of inferiority). I would not disagree with this view, although most social anthropologists would probably separate the two types.

in any particular system, though they need not necessarily be. Further, any one of them will usually be sufficient to make the point of female inferiority in a given culture. Certainly, female exclusion from the most sacred rite or the highest political council is sufficient evidence. Certainly, explicit cultural ideology devaluing women (and their tasks, roles, products, etc.) is sufficient evidence. Symbolic indicators such as defilement are usually sufficient, although in a few cases in which, say, men and women are equally polluting to one another, a further indicator is required—and is, as far as my investigations have ascertained, always available.

On any or all of these counts, then, I would flatly assert that we find women subordinated to men in every known society. The search for a genuinely egalitarian, let alone matriarchal, culture has proved fruitless. An example from one society that has traditionally been on the credit side of this ledger will suffice. Among the matrilineal Crow, as Lowie (1956) points out, "Women ... had highly honorific offices in the Sun Dance; they could become directors of the Tobacco Ceremony and played, if anything, a more conspicuous part in it than the men; they sometimes played the hostess in the Cooked Meat Festival; they were not debarred from sweating or doctoring or from seeking a vision" (p. 61). Nonetheless, "Women [during menstruation] formerly rode inferior horses and evidently this loomed as a source of contamination, for they were not allowed to approach either a wounded man or men starting on a war party. A taboo still lingers against their coming near sacred objects at these times" (p. 44). Further, just before enumerating women's rights of participation in the various rituals noted above, Lowie mentions one particular Sun Dance Doll bundle that was not supposed to be unwrapped by a woman (p. 60). Pursuing this trail we find: "According to all Lodge Grass informants and most others, the doll owned by Wrinkled-face took precedence not only of other dolls but of all other Crow medicines whatsoever.... This particular doll was not supposed to be handled by a woman" (p. 229).[3]

In sum, the Crow are probably a fairly typical case. Yes, women have certain powers and rights, in this case some that place them in fairly high positions. Yet ultimately the line is drawn: menstruation is a threat to warfare, one of the most valued institutions of the tribe, one that is central to their self-definition; and the most sacred object of the tribe is taboo to the direct sight and touch of women.

[3] While we are on the subject of injustices of various kinds, we might note that Lowie secretly bought this doll, the most sacred object in the tribal repertoire, from its custodian, the widow of Wrinkled-face. She asked $400 for it, but this price was "far beyond [Lowie's] means," and he finally got it for $80 (p. 300).

Similar examples could be multiplied ad infinitum, but I think the onus is no longer upon us to demonstrate that female subordination is a cultural universal; it is up to those who would argue against the point to bring forth counterexamples. I shall take the universal secondary status of women as a given, and proceed from there.

Nature and Culture[4]

How are we to explain the universal devaluation of women? We could of course rest the case on biological determinism. There is something genetically inherent in the male of the species, so the biological determinists would argue, that makes them the naturally dominant sex; that "something" is lacking in females, and as a result women are not only naturally subordinate but in general quite satisfied with their position, since it affords them protection and the opportunity to maximize maternal pleasures, which to them are the most satisfying experiences of life. Without going into a detailed refutation of this position, I think it fair to say that it has failed to be established to the satisfaction of almost anyone in academic anthropology. This is to say, not that biological facts are irrelevant, or that men and women are not different, but that these facts and differences only take on significance of superior/inferior within the framework of culturally defined value systems.

If we are unwilling to rest the case on genetic determinism, it seems to me that we have only one way to proceed. We must attempt to interpret female subordination in light of other universals, factors built into the structure of the most generalized situation in which all human beings, in whatever culture, find themselves. For example, every human being has a physical body and a sense of nonphysical mind, is part of a society of other individuals and an inheritor of a cultural tradition, and must engage in some relationship, however mediated, with "nature," or the nonhuman realm, in order to survive. Every human being is born (to a mother) and ultimately dies, all are assumed to have an interest in personal survival, and society/culture has its own interest in (or at least momentum toward) continuity and survival, which transcends the lives and deaths of particular individuals. And so forth. It is in the realm of such universals of the human condition that we must seek an explanation for the universal fact of female devaluation.

I translate the problem, in other words, into the following simple question. What could there be in the generalized structure and conditions of existence, common to every culture, that would lead every culture to place a lower value upon women? Specifically, my thesis is that

4 With all due respect to Lévi-Strauss (1969a,b, and *passim*).

woman is being identified with—or, if you will, seems to be a symbol of—something that every culture devalues, something that every culture defines as being of a lower order of existence than itself. Now it seems that there is only one thing that would fit that description, and that is "nature" in the most generalized sense. Every culture, or, generically, "culture," is engaged in the process of generating and sustaining systems of meaningful forms (symbols, artifacts, etc.) by means of which humanity transcends the givens of natural existence, bends them to its purposes, controls them in its interest. We may thus broadly equate culture with the notion of human consciousness, or with the products of human consciousness (i.e., systems of thought and technology), by means of which humanity attempts to assert control over nature.

Now the categories of "nature" and "culture" are of course conceptual categories—one can find no boundary out in the actual world between the two states or realms of being. And there is no question that some cultures articulate a much stronger opposition between the two categories than others—it has even been argued that primitive peoples (some or all) do not see or intuit any distinction between the human cultural state and the state of nature at all. Yet I would maintain that the universality of ritual betokens an assertion in all human cultures of the specifically human ability to act upon and regulate, rather than passively move with and be moved by, the givens of natural existence. In ritual, the purposive manipulation of given forms toward regulating and sustaining order, every culture asserts that proper relations between human existence and natural forces depend upon culture's employing its special powers to regulate the overall processes of the world and life.

One realm of cultural thought in which these points are often articulated is that of concepts of purity and pollution. Virtually every culture has some such beliefs, which seem in large part (though not, of course, entirely) to be concerned with the relationship between culture and nature (see Ortner, 1973, n.d.). A well-known aspect of purity/pollution beliefs cross-culturally is that of the natural "contagion" of pollution; left to its own devices, pollution (for these purposes grossly equated with the unregulated operation of natural energies) spreads and overpowers all that it comes in contact with. Thus a puzzle—if pollution is so strong, how can anything be purified? Why is the purifying agent not itself polluted? The answer, in keeping with the present line of argument, is that purification is effected in a ritual context; purification ritual, as a purposive activity that pits self-conscious (symbolic) action against natural energies, is more powerful than those energies.

In any case, my point is simply that every culture implicitly recognizes and asserts a distinction between the operation of nature and the operation of culture (human consciousness and its products); and further, that the distinctiveness of culture rests precisely on the fact that it can under most circumstances transcend natural conditions and turn them to its purposes. Thus culture (i.e. every culture) at some level of awareness asserts itself to be not only distinct from but superior to nature, and that sense of distinctiveness and superiority rests precisely on the ability to transform—to "socialize" and "culturalize"—nature.

Returning now to the issue of women, their pan-cultural second-class status could be accounted for, quite simply, by postulating that women are being identified or symbolically associated with nature, as opposed to men, who are identified with culture. Since it is always culture's project to subsume and transcend nature, if women were considered part of nature, then culture would find it "natural" to subordinate, not to say oppress, them. Yet although this argument can be shown to have considerable force, it seems to oversimplify the case. The formulation I would like to defend and elaborate on in the following section, then, is that women are seen "merely" as being *closer* to nature than men. That is, culture (still equated relatively unambiguously with men) recognizes that women are active participants in its special processes, but at the same time sees them as being more rooted in, or having more direct affinity with, nature.

The revision may seem minor or even trivial, but I think it is a more accurate rendering of cultural assumptions. Further, the argument cast in these terms has several analytic advantages over the simpler formulation; I shall discuss these later. It might simply be stressed here that the revised argument would still account for the pan-cultural devaluation of women, for even if women are not equated with nature, they are nonetheless seen as representing a lower order of being, as being less transcendental of nature than men are. The next task of the paper, then, is to consider why they might be viewed in that way.

Why Is Woman Seen as Closer to Nature?

It all begins of course with the body and the natural procreative functions specific to women alone. We can sort out for discussion three levels at which this absolute physiological fact has significance: (1) woman's *body and its functions*, more involved more of the time with "species life," seem to place her closer to nature, in contrast to man's physiology, which frees him more completely to take up the projects of culture; (2) woman's body and its functions place her in *social roles* that in turn are considered to be at a lower order of the cultural process than man's;

and (3) woman's traditional social roles, imposed because of her body and its functions, in turn give her a different *psychic structure*, which, like her physiological nature and her social roles, is seen as being closer to nature. I shall discuss each of these points in turn, showing first how in each instance certain factors strongly tend to align woman with nature, then indicating other factors that demonstrate her full alignment with culture, the combined factors thus placing her in a problematic intermediate position. It will become clear in the course of the discussion why men seem by contrast less intermediate, more purely "cultural" than women. And I reiterate that I am dealing only at the level of cultural and human universals. These arguments are intended to apply to generalized humanity; they grow out of the human condition, as humanity has experienced and confronted it up to the present day.

    1. Woman's physiology seen as closer to nature. This part of my argument has been anticipated, with subtlety, cogency, and a great deal of hard data, by de Beauvoir (1953). De Beauvoir reviews the physiological structure, development, and functions of the human female and concludes that "the female, to a greater extent than the male, is the prey of the species" (p. 60). She points out that many major areas and processes of the woman's body serve no apparent function for the health and stability of the individual; on the contrary, as they perform their specific organic functions, they are often sources of discomfort, pain, and danger. The breasts are irrelevant to personal health; they may be excised at any time of a woman's life. "Many of the ovarian secretions function for the benefit of the egg, promoting its maturation and adapting the uterus to its requirements; in respect to the organism as a whole, they make for disequilibrium rather than for regulation—the woman is adapted to the needs of the egg rather than to her own requirements" (p. 24). Menstruation is often uncomfortable, sometimes painful; it frequently has negative emotional correlates and in any case involves bothersome tasks of cleansing and waste disposal; and—a point that de Beauvoir does not mention—in many cultures it interrupts a woman's routine, putting her in a stigmatized state involving various restrictions on her activities and social contacts. In pregnancy many of the woman's vitamin and mineral resources are channeled into nourishing the fetus, depleting her own strength and energies. And finally, childbirth itself is painful and dangerous (pp. 24–27 *passim*). In sum, de Beauvoir concludes that the female "is more enslaved to the species than the male, her animality is more manifest" (p. 239).

    While de Beauvoir's book is ideological, her survey of woman's physiological situation seems fair and accurate. It is simply a fact that proportionately more of woman's body space, for a greater percentage of her lifetime, and at some—sometimes great—cost to her personal health, strength, and general stability, is taken up with the natural processes surrounding the reproduction of the species.

De Beauvoir goes on to discuss the negative implications of woman's "enslavement to the species" in relation to the projects in which humans engage, projects through which culture is generated and defined. She arrives thus at the crux of her argument (pp. 58–59):

Here we have the key to the whole mystery. On the biological level a species is maintained only by creating itself anew; but this creation results only in repeating the same Life in more individuals. But man assures the repetition of Life while transcending Life through Existence [i.e. goal-oriented, meaning-ful action]; by this transcendence he creates values that deprive pure repetition of all value. In the animal, the freedom and variety of male activities are vain because no project is involved. Except for his services to the species, what he does is immaterial. Whereas in serving the species, the human male also re-models the face of the earth, he creates new instruments, he invents, he shapes the future.

In other words, woman's body seems to doom her to mere reproduction of life; the male, in contrast, lacking natural creative functions, must (or has the opportunity to) assert his creativity externally, "artificially," through the medium of technology and symbols. In so doing, he creates relatively lasting, eternal, transcendent objects, while the woman creates only perishables—human beings.

This formulation opens up a number of important insights. It speaks, for example, to the great puzzle of why male activities involving the destruction of life (hunting and warfare) are often given more prestige than the female's ability to give birth, to create life. Within de Beau-voir's framework, we realize it is not the killing that is the relevant and valued aspect of hunting and warfare; rather, it is the transcendental (social, cultural) nature of these activities, as opposed to the naturalness of the process of birth: "For it is not in giving life but in risking life that man is raised above the animal; that is why superiority has been accord-ed in humanity not to the sex that brings forth but to that which kills" (*ibid.*).

Thus if male is, as I am suggesting, everywhere (unconsciously) asso-ciated with culture and female seems closer to nature, the rationale for these associations is not very difficult to grasp, merely from considering the implications of the physiological contrast between male and female. At the same time, however, woman cannot be consigned fully to the category of nature, for it is perfectly obvious that she is a full-fledged human being endowed with human consciousness just as a man is; she is half of the human race, without whose cooperation the whole enterprise would collapse. She may seem more in the possession of nature than man, but having consciousness, she thinks and speaks; she generates, communicates, and manipulates symbols, categories, and values. She participates in human dialogues not only with other women but also with men. As Lévi-Strauss says, "Woman could never become just a sign and nothing more, since even in a man's world she is still a person, and since insofar as she is defined as a sign she must [still] be recognized as a generator of signs" (1969a: 496).

Indeed, the fact of woman's full human consciousness, her full involvement in and commitment to culture's project of transcendence over nature, may ironically explain another of the great puzzles of "the woman problem"—woman's nearly universal unquestioning acceptance of her own devaluation. For it would seem that, as a conscious human and member of culture, she has followed out the logic of culture's arguments and has reached culture's conclusions along with the men. As de Beauvoir puts it (p. 59):

> For she, too, is an existent, she feels the urge to surpass, and her project is not mere repetition but transcendence towards a different future—in her heart of hearts she finds confirmation of the masculine pretensions. She joins the men in the festivals that celebrate the successes and victories of the males. Her misfortune is to have been biologically destined for the repetition of Life, when even in her own view Life does not carry within itself its reasons for being, reasons that are more important than life itself.

In other words, woman's consciousness—her membership, as it were, in culture—is evidenced in part by the very fact that she accepts her own devaluation and takes culture's point of view.

I have tried here to show one part of the logic of that view, the part that grows directly from the physiological differences between men and women. Because of woman's greater bodily involvement with the natural functions surrounding reproduction, she is seen as more a part of nature than man is. Yet in part because of her consciousness and participation in human social dialogue, she is recognized as a participant in culture. Thus she appears as something intermediate between culture and nature, lower on the scale of transcendence than man.

2. *Woman's social role seen as closer to nature.* Woman's physiological functions, I have just argued, may tend in themselves to motivate[5] a view

---

[5] Semantic theory uses the concept of motivation of meaning, which encompasses various ways in which a meaning may be assigned to a symbol because of certain objective properties of that symbol, rather than by arbitrary association. In a sense,

of woman as closer to nature, a view she herself, as an observer of herself and the world, would tend to agree with. Woman creates naturally from within her own being, whereas man is free to, or forced to, create artificially, that is, through cultural means, and in such a way as to sustain culture. In addition, I now wish to show how woman's physiological functions have tended universally to limit her social movement, and to confine her universally to certain social contexts which *in turn* are seen as closer to nature. That is, not only her bodily processes but the social situation in which her bodily processes locate her may carry this significance. And insofar as she is permanently associated (in the eyes of culture) with these social milieux, they add weight (perhaps the decisive part of the burden) to the view of woman as closer to nature. I refer here of course to woman's confinement to the domestic family context, a confinement motivated, no doubt, by her lactation processes.

Woman's body, like that of all female mammals, generates milk during and after pregnancy for the feeding of the newborn baby. The baby cannot survive without breast milk or some similar formula at this stage of life. Since the mother's body goes through its lactation processes in direct relation to a pregnancy with a particular child, the relationship of nursing between mother and child is seen as a natural bond, other feeding arrangements being seen in most cases as unnatural and makeshift. Mothers and their children, according to cultural reasoning, belong together. Further, children beyond infancy are not strong enough to engage in major work, yet are mobile and unruly and not capable of understanding various dangers; they thus require supervision and constant care. Mother is the obvious person for this task, as an extension of her natural nursing bond with the children, or because she has a new infant and is already involved with child-oriented activities. Her own activities are thus circumscribed by the limitations and low levels of her children's strengths and skills:[6] she is confined to the domestic family group; "woman's place is in the home."

Woman's association with the domestic circle would contribute to the view of her as closer to nature in several ways. In the first place, the sheer fact of constant association with children plays a role in the issue; one can easily see how infants and children might themselves be considered part of nature. Infants are barely human and utterly unsocial-

---

this entire paper is an inquiry into the motivation of the meaning of woman as a symbol, asking why woman may be unconsciously assigned the significance of being closer to nature. For a concise statement on the various types of motivation of meaning, see Ullman (1963).

[6] A situation that often serves to make her more childlike herself.

ized; like animals they are unable to walk upright, they excrete without
control, they do not speak. Even slightly older children are clearly not
yet fully under the sway of culture. They do not yet understand social
duties, responsibilities, and morals; their vocabulary and their range of
learned skills are small. One finds implicit recognition of an association
between children and nature in many cultural practices. For example,
most cultures have initiation rites for adolescents (primarily for boys;
I shall return to this point below), the point of which is to move the
child ritually from a less than fully human state into full participation
in society and culture; many cultures do not hold funeral rites for children who die at early ages, explicitly because they are not yet fully social
beings. Thus children are likely to be categorized with nature, and
woman's close association with children may compound her potential
for being seen as closer to nature herself. It is ironic that the rationale
for boys' initiation rites in many cultures is that the boys must be purged
of the defilement accrued from being around mother and other women
so much of the time, when in fact much of the woman's defilement may
derive from her being around children so much of the time.

The second major problematic implication of women's close association with the domestic context derives from certain structural conflicts
between the family and society at large in any social system. The implications of the "domestic/public opposition" in relation to the position of women have been cogently developed by Rosaldo (this volume),
and I simply wish to show its relevance to the present argument. The
notion that the domestic unit—the biological family charged with repro-
ducing and socializing new members of the society—is opposed to the
public entity—the superimposed network of alliances and relationships
that *is* the society—is also the basis of Lévi-Strauss's argument in the
Elementary Structures of Kinship (1969a). Lévi-Strauss argues not only
that this opposition is present in every social system, but further that
it has the significance of the opposition between nature and culture.
The universal incest prohibition[7] and its ally, the rule of exogamy
(marriage outside the group), ensure that "the risk of seeing a biological
family become established as a closed system is definitely eliminated;
the biological group can no longer stand apart, and the bond of alliance
with another family ensures the dominance of the social over the biological, and of the cultural over the natural" (p. 479). And although
not every culture articulates a radical opposition between the domestic

<hr />

[7] David M. Schneider (personal communication) is prepared to argue that the
incest taboo is not universal, on the basis of material from Oceania. Let us say at
this point, then, that it is virtually universal.

and the public as such, it is hardly contestable that the domestic is always subsumed by the public; domestic units are allied with one another through the enactment of rules that are logically at a higher level than the units themselves; this creates an emergent unit—society—that is logically at a higher level than the domestic units of which it is composed.

Now, since women are associated with, and indeed are more or less confined to, the domestic context, they are identified with this lower order of social/cultural organization. What are the implications of this for the way they are viewed? First, if the specifically biological (reproductive) function of the family is stressed, as in Lévi-Strauss's formulation, then the family (and hence woman) is identified with nature pure and simple, as opposed to culture. But this is obviously too simple; the point seems more adequately formulated as follows: the family (and hence woman) represents lower-level, socially fragmenting, particularistic sort of concerns, as opposed to interfamilial relations representing higher-level, integrative, universalistic sorts of concerns. Since men lack a "natural" basis (nursing, generalized to child care) for a familial orientation, their sphere of activity is defined at the level of interfamilial relations. And hence, so the cultural reasoning seems to go, men are the "natural" proprietors of religion, ritual, politics, and other realms of cultural thought and action in which universalistic statements of spiritual and social synthesis are made. Thus men are identified not only with culture, in the sense of all human creativity, as opposed to nature; they are identified in particular with culture in the old-fashioned sense of the finer and higher aspects of human thought—art, religion, law, etc.

Here again, the logic of cultural reasoning aligning woman with a lower order of culture than man is clear and, on the surface, quite compelling. At the same time, woman cannot be fully consigned to nature, for there are aspects of her situation, even within the domestic context, that undeniably demonstrate her participation in the cultural process. It goes without saying, of course, that except for nursing newborn infants (and artificial nursing devices can cut even this biological tie), there is no reason why it has to be mother—as opposed to father, or anyone else—who remains identified with child care. But even assuming that other practical and emotional reasons conspire to keep woman in this sphere, it is possible to show that her activities in the domestic context could as logically put her squarely in the category of culture.

In the first place, one must point out that woman not only feeds and cleans up after children in a simple caretaker operation; she in fact is the primary agent of their early socialization. It is she who transforms newborn infants from mere organisms into cultured humans, teaching them manners and the proper ways to behave in order to become full-fledged members of the culture. On the basis of her socializing functions alone, she could not be more a representative of culture. Yet in virtually every society there is a point at which the socialization of boys is transferred to the hands of men. The boys are considered, in one set of terms or another, not yet "really" socialized; their entrée into the realm of fully human (social, cultural) status can be accomplished only by men. We still see this in our own schools, where there is a gradual inversion in the proportion of female to male teachers up through the grades: most kindergarten teachers are female; most university professors are male.[8]

Or again, take cooking. In the overwhelming majority of societies cooking is the woman's work. No doubt this stems from practical considerations—since the woman has to stay home with the baby, it is convenient for her to perform the chores centered in the home. But if it is true, as Lévi-Strauss has argued (1969b), that transforming the raw into the cooked may represent, in many systems of thought, the transition from nature to culture, then here we have woman aligned with this important culturalizing process, which could easily place her in the category of culture, triumphing over nature. Yet it is also interesting to note that when a culture (e.g. France or China) develops a tradition of *haute cuisine*—"real" cooking, as opposed to trivial ordinary domestic cooking—the high chefs are almost always men. Thus the pattern replicates that in the area of socialization—women perform lower-level conversions from nature to culture, but when the culture distinguishes a higher level of the same functions, the higher level is restricted to men.

In short, we see once again some sources of woman's appearing more intermediate than man with respect to the nature/culture dichotomy. Her "natural" association with the domestic context (motivated by her natural lactation functions) tends to compound her potential for being viewed as closer to nature, because of the animal-like nature of children, and because of the infrasocial connotation of the domestic group as against the rest of society. Yet at the same time her socializing and cooking functions within the domestic context show her to be a powerful agent of the cultural process, constantly transforming raw natural resources into cultural products. Belonging to culture, yet appearing to have stronger and more direct connections with nature, she is once again seen as situated between the two realms.

[8] I remember having my first male teacher in the fifth grade, and I remember being excited about that—it was somehow more grown-up.

3. Woman's psyche seen as closer to nature. The suggestion that woman has not only a different body and a different social locus from man but also a different psychic structure is most controversial. I will argue that she probably *does* have a different psychic structure, but I will draw heavily on Chodorow's paper (this volume) to establish first that her psychic structure need not be assumed to be innate; it can be accounted for, as Chodorow convincingly shows, by the facts of the probably universal female socialization experience. Nonetheless, if we grant the empirical near universality of a "feminine psyche" with certain specific characteristics, these characteristics would add weight to the cultural view of woman as closer to nature.

It is important to specify what we see as the dominant and universal aspects of the feminine psyche. If we postulate emotionality or irrationality, we are confronted with those traditions in various parts of the world in which women functionally are, and are seen as, more practical, pragmatic, and this-worldly than men. One relevant dimension that does seem pan-culturally applicable is that of relative concreteness vs. relative abstractness: the feminine personality tends to be involved with concrete feelings, things, and people, rather than with abstract entities; it tends toward personalism and particularism. A second, closely related, dimension seems to be that of relative subjectivity vs. relative objectivity: Chodorow cites Carlson's study (1971), which concludes that "males represent experiences of self, others, space, and time in individualistic, objective, and distant ways, while females represent experiences in relatively interpersonal, subjective, immediate ways" (this volume, p. 56, quoting Carlson, p. 270). Although this and other studies were done in Western societies, Chodorow sees their findings on the differences between male and female personality—roughly, that men are more objective and inclined to relate in terms of relatively abstract categories, women more subjective and inclined to relate in terms of relatively concrete phenomena—as "general and nearly universal differences" (p. 43).

But the thrust of Chodorow's elegantly argued paper is that these differences are not innate or genetically programmed; they arise from nearly universal features of family structure, namely that "women, universally, are largely responsible for early child care and for (at least) later female socialization" (p. 43) and that "the structural situation of child rearing, reinforced by female and male role training, produces these differences, which are replicated and reproduced in the sexual sociology of adult life" (p. 44). Chodorow argues that, because mother is the early socializer of both boys and girls, both develop "personal identification" with her, i.e. diffuse identification with her general personality, behavior traits, values, and attitudes (p. 51). A son, however, must ultimately shift to a masculine role identity, which involves building an identification with the father. Since father is almost always more remote than mother (he is rarely involved in child care, and perhaps works away from home much of the day), building an identification with father involves a "positional identification," i.e. identification with father's male role as a collection of abstract elements, rather than a personal identification with father as a real individual (p. 49). Further, as the boy enters the larger social world, he finds it in fact organized around more abstract and universalistic criteria (see Rosaldo, this volume, pp. 28–29; Chodorow, p. 58), as I have indicated in the previous section; thus his earlier socialization prepares him for, and is reinforced by, the type of adult social experience he will have.

For a young girl, in contrast, the personal identification with mother, which was created in early infancy, can persist into the process of learning female role identity. Because mother is immediate and present when the daughter is learning role identity, learning to be a woman involves the continuity and development of a girl's relationship to her mother, and sustains the identification with her as an individual; it does not involve the learning of externally defined role characteristics (Chodorow, p. 51). This pattern prepares the girl for, and is fully reinforced by, her social situation in later life; she will become involved in the world of women, which is characterized by few formal role differences (Rosaldo, p. 29), and which involves again, in motherhood, "personal identification" with *her* children. And so the cycle begins anew.

Chodorow demonstrates to my satisfaction at least that the feminine personality, characterized by personalism and particularism, can be explained as having been generated by social-structural arrangements rather than by innate biological factors. The point need not be belabored further. But insofar as the "feminine personality" has been a nearly universal fact, it can be argued that its characteristics may have contributed further to the view of women as being somehow less cultural than men. That is, women would tend to enter into relationships with the world that culture might see as being more "like nature"— immanent and embedded in things as given—than "like culture"— transcending and transforming things through the superimposition of abstract categories and transpersonal values. Woman's relationships tend to be, like nature, relatively unmediated, more direct, whereas man not only tends to relate in a more mediated way, but in fact ultimately often relates more consistently and strongly to the mediating categories and forms than to the persons or objects themselves.

It is thus not difficult to see how the feminine personality would lend weight to a view of women as being "closer to nature." Yet at the same time, the modes of relating characteristic of women undeniably play a powerful and important role in the cultural process. For just as relatively unmediated relating is in some sense at the lower end of the spectrum of human spiritual functions, embedded and particularizing rather than transcending and synthesizing, yet that mode of relating also stands at the upper end of that spectrum. Consider the mother-child relationship. Mothers tend to be committed to their children as individuals, regardless of sex, age, beauty, clan affiliation, or other categories in which the child might participate. Now any relationship with this quality—not just mother and child but any sort of highly personal, relatively unmediated commitment—may be seen as a challenge to culture and society "from below," insofar as it represents the fragmentary potential of individual loyalties vis-à-vis the solidarity of the group. But it may also be seen as embodying the synthesizing agent for culture and society "from above," in that it represents generalized human values above and beyond loyalties to particular social categories. Every society must have social categories that transcend personal loyalties, but every society must also generate a sense of ultimate moral unity for all its members above and beyond those social categories. Thus that psychic mode seemingly typical of women, which tends to disregard categories and to seek "communion" (Chodorow, p. 55, following Bakan, 1966) directly and personally with others, although it may appear infracultural from one point of view, is at the same time associated with the highest levels of the cultural process.

The Implications of Intermediacy

My primary purpose in this paper has been to attempt to explain the universal secondary status of women. Intellectually and personally, I felt strongly challenged by this problem; I felt compelled to deal with it before undertaking an analysis of woman's position in any particular society. Local variables of economy, ecology, history, political and social structure, values, and world view—these could explain variations within this universal, but they could not explain the universal itself. And if we were not to accept the ideology of biological determinism, then explanation, it seemed to me, could only proceed by reference to other universals of the human cultural situation. Thus the general outlines of the approach—although not of course the particular solution offered —were determined by the problem itself, and not by any predilection on my part for global abstract structural analysis.

I argued that the universal devaluation of women could be explained by postulating that women are seen as closer to nature than men, men being seen as more unequivocally occupying the high ground of culture. The culture/nature distinction is itself a product of culture, culture being minimally defined as the transcendence, by means of systems of thought and technology, of the natural givens of existence. This of course is an analytic definition, but I argued that at some level every culture incorporates this notion in one form or other, if only through the performance of ritual as an assertion of the human ability to manipulate those givens. In any case, the core of the paper was concerned with showing why women might tend to be assumed, over and over, in the most diverse sorts of world views and in cultures of every degree of complexity, to be closer to nature than men. Woman's physiology, more involved more of the time with "species of life"; woman's association with the structurally subordinate domestic context, charged with the crucial function of transforming animal-like infants into cultured beings; "woman's psyche," appropriately molded to mothering functions by her own socialization and tending toward greater personalism and less mediated modes of relating—all these factors make woman appear to be rooted more directly and deeply in nature. At the same time, however, her "membership" and fully necessary participation in culture are recognized by culture and cannot be denied. Thus she is seen to occupy an intermediate position between culture and nature.

This intermediacy has several implications for analysis, depending upon how it is interpreted. First, of course, it answers my primary question of why woman is everywhere seen as lower than man, for even if she is not seen as nature pure and simple, she is still seen as achieving less transcendence of nature than man. Here intermediate simply means "middle status" on a hierarchy of being from culture to nature.

Second, intermediate may have the significance of "mediating," i.e. performing some sort of synthesizing or converting function between nature and culture, here seen (by culture) not as two ends of a continuum but as two radically different sorts of processes in the world. The domestic unit—and hence woman, who in virtually every case appears as its primary representative—is one of culture's crucial agencies for the conversion of nature into culture, especially with reference to the socialization of children. Any culture's continued viability depends upon properly socialized individuals who will see the world in that culture's terms and adhere more or less unquestioningly to its moral precepts. The functions of the domestic unit must be closely controlled in order to ensure this outcome; the stability of the domestic unit as an institution must be placed as far as possible beyond question. (We see some aspects of the protection of the integrity and stability of the domestic group in the powerful taboos against incest, matricide, patricide, and fratricide.[9]) Insofar as woman is universally the primary agent of early socialization and is seen as virtually the embodiment of the functions of the domestic group, she will tend to come under the heavier restrictions and circumscriptions surrounding that unit. Her (culturally defined) intermediate position between nature and culture, here having the significance of her *mediation* (i.e. performing conversion functions) between nature and culture, would thus account not only for her lower status but for the greater restrictions placed upon her activities. In virtually every culture her permissible sexual activities are more closely circumscribed than man's, she is offered a much smaller range of role choices, and she is afforded direct access to a far more limited range of its social institutions. Further, she is almost universally socialized to have a narrower and generally more conservative set of attitudes and views than man, and the limited social contexts of her adult life reinforce this situation. This socially engendered conservatism and traditionalism of woman's thinking is another—perhaps the worst, certainly the most insidious—mode of social restriction, and would clearly be related to her traditional function of producing well-socialized members of the group.

Finally, woman's intermediate position may have the implication of greater symbolic ambiguity (see also Rosaldo, this volume). Shifting our image of the culture/nature relationship once again, we may envision culture in this case as a small clearing within the forest of the larger natural system. From this point of view, that which is intermediate between culture and nature is located on the continuous periphery of culture's clearing; and though it may thus appear to stand both above and below (and beside) culture, it is simply outside and around it. We can begin to understand then how a single system of cultural thought can often assign to woman completely polarized and apparently contradictory meanings, since extremes, as we say, meet. That she often represents both life and death is only the simplest example one could mention.

For another perspective on the same point, it will be recalled that the psychic mode associated with women seems to stand at both the bottom and the top of the scale of human modes of relating. The tendency in that mode is to get involved more directly with people as individuals and not as representatives of one social category or another; this mode can be seen as either "ignoring" (and thus subverting) or "transcending"

---

[9] Nobody seems to care much about sororicide—a point that ought to be investigated.

(and thus achieving a higher synthesis of) those social categories, depending upon the cultural view for any given purpose. Thus we can account easily for both the subversive feminine symbols (witches, evil eye, menstrual pollution, castrating mothers) and the feminine symbols of transcendence (mother goddesses, merciful dispensers of salvation, female symbols of justice, and the strong presence of feminine symbolism in the realms of art, religion, ritual, and law). Feminine symbolism, far more often than masculine symbolism, manifests this propensity toward polarized ambiguity—sometimes utterly exalted, sometimes utterly debased, rarely within the normal range of human possibilities.

If woman's (culturally viewed) intermediacy between culture and nature has this implication of generalized ambiguity of meaning characteristic of marginal phenomena, then we are also in a better position to account for those cultural and historical "inversions" in which women are in some way or other symbolically aligned with culture and men with nature. A number of cases come to mind: the Sirionó of Brazil, among whom, according to Ingham (1971: 1098), "nature, the raw, and maleness" are opposed to "culture, the cooked, and femaleness";[10] Nazi Germany, in which women were said to be the guardians of culture and morals; European courtly love, in which man considered himself the beast and woman the pristine exalted object—a pattern of thinking that persists, for example, among modern Spanish peasants (see Pitt-Rivers, 1961; Rosaldo, this volume). And there are no doubt other cases of this sort, including some aspects of our own culture's view of women. Each such instance of an alignment of women with culture rather than nature requires detailed analysis of specific historical and ethnographic data. But in indicating how nature in general, and the feminine mode of interpersonal relations in particular, can appear from certain points of view to stand both under and over (but really simply outside of) the sphere of culture's hegemony, we have at least laid the groundwork for such analyses.

In short, the postulate that woman is viewed as closer to nature than man has several implications for further analysis, and can be interpreted in several different ways. If it is viewed simply as a *middle* position on a scale from culture down to nature, then it is still seen as lower than culture and thus accounts for the pan-cultural assumption that woman is lower than man in the order of things. If it is read as a *mediating*

---

10 Ingham's discussion is rather ambiguous itself, since women are also associated with animals: "The contrasts man/animal and man/woman are evidently similar... hunting is the means of acquiring women as well as animals" (p. 1095). A careful reading of the data suggests that both women and animals are mediators between nature and culture in this tradition.

element in the culture-nature relationship, then it may account in part for the cultural tendency not merely to devalue woman but to circumscribe and restrict her functions, since culture must maintain control over its (pragmatic and symbolic) mechanisms for the conversion of nature into culture. And if it is read as an *ambiguous* status between culture and nature, it may help account for the fact that, in specific cultural ideologies and symbolizations, woman can occasionally be aligned with culture, and in any event is often assigned polarized and contradictory meanings within a single symbolic system. Middle status, mediating functions, ambiguous meaning—all are different readings, for different contextual purposes, of woman's being seen as intermediate between nature and culture.

Conclusions

Ultimately, it must be stressed again that the whole scheme is a construct of culture rather than a fact of nature. Woman is not "in reality" any closer to (or further from) nature than man—both have consciousness, both are mortal. But there are certainly reasons why she appears that way, which is what I have tried to show in this paper. The result is a (sadly) efficient feedback system: various aspects of woman's situation (physical, social, psychological) contribute to her being seen as closer to nature, while the view of her as closer to nature is in turn embodied in institutional forms that reproduce her situation. The implications for social change are similarly circular: a different cultural view can only grow out of a different social actuality; a different social actuality can only grow out of a different cultural view.

It is clear, then, that the situation must be attacked from both sides. Efforts directed solely at changing the social institutions—through setting quotas on hiring, for example, or through passing equal-pay-for-equal-work laws—cannot have far-reaching effects if cultural language and imagery continue to purvey a relatively devalued view of women. But at the same time efforts directed solely at changing cultural assumptions—through male and female consciousness-raising groups, for example, or through revision of educational materials and mass-media imagery—cannot be successful unless the institutional base of the society is changed to support and reinforce the changed cultural view. Ultimately, both men and women can and must be equally involved in projects of creativity and transcendence. Only then will women be seen as aligned with culture, in culture's ongoing dialectic with nature.

JANE FISHBURNE COLLIER

Women in Politics

Both natives and ethnographers tend to view politics as a male pastime. With the exception of a few queens, powerful matriarchs, or talented courtesans, women are seldom seen as political actors, but rather as pawns to be used in the political maneuvers of men: hoarded for their productive, reproductive, and prestige-enhancing value, or traded to create and cement alliances. This view has a surface validity, for male informants often speak of women as pawns, and women are usually excluded from political gatherings, ineligible for political office, and occupied with child-rearing and domestic tasks. But the men who compete for political prizes operate in a world where women are also seeking to maximize desired ends.[1] Women may never achieve political offices or hold recognized authority, but their actions constrain the choices open to politically active men. Although male informants may treat women as politically irrelevant, the anthropologist who seeks a deeper understanding of political processes cannot ignore women's goals and strategies.

Women's participation in the political life of any group is patterned, but regularities may be hard to detect because native models of social structure tend to discount women's political role. Whereas native informants usually explain conflicts between men in terms of culturally recognized rules, women's quarrels are often attributed to personal idiosyn-

[1] In several anthropological studies of kinship or politics it is implied, if not explicitly stated, that throughout history women have been so preoccupied with child-rearing and domestic tasks that they have been content to let the men decide issues affecting the wider social group. Though it may be true that "the sheer physiological facts of existence make her (woman's) role secondary to that of the male in the decision-making process in any level higher than the purely domestic" (Fox, 1967: 32), it cannot be lightly assumed that women have not cared about wider political issues. The argument in this paper rests on the assumption that women everywhere have been interested in "political" decisions and have rationally sought to influence outcomes.

crasies or to particularistic circumstances. Barth (1966) has argued that anthropologists seeking to understand observable regularities in behavior must look beyond moral injunctions to the wider set of constraints and incentives that channel individual choices, but this approach has seldom been applied to women because both natives and ethnographers have failed to perceive regularities in their actions. In this paper I shall argue that ethnographers should use Barth's approach both to find and to account for patterns of feminine political behavior. I shall try to show that societies with patrilocal extended households, where political power rests on size and cohesiveness of the co-resident kin group, exhibit a standard range of household quarrels and share a common conception of "woman's nature." Such regularities cannot be explained by looking at moral injunctions or jural rules, both of which stress woman's duty to obey her male relatives, but become intelligible only if women are seen as actors whose efforts to control the social environment are channeled by cultural rules, by available resources, and by the choices of others within the social system.

It would be unfair to suggest that anthropologists have entirely overlooked the patterning in women's conflicts. Domestic quarrels and marital instability have been attributed to women's desire to escape oppressive male dominance (Cohen, 1971), to their conflicting lineage loyalties in a system with patrilineal descent (Fallers, 1969), to a lack of clear guides for behavior in a system where the norms governing marriage are neither explicit nor enforced (Gibbs, 1963), and to the contradictory position of women within a patrilineage where they must bear children to strengthen the lineage while inevitably creating the lines of cleavage that lead to lineage fission (Gluckman, 1965). But these approaches have limited utility, because they treat women as actors seeking to minimize unpleasantness instead of as actors trying to maximize gains; and, once unpleasantness has been minimized, there is no further basis for prediction. The model woman of my argument, therefore, is not the affectionate daughter, hard-working wife, or loving mother who gets into trouble while trying to make the best of a difficult situation, but the cold, calculating female who uses all available resources to control the world around her. My model woman seeks power: the capacity to determine her own and others' actions (Runciman, 1968).

The political behavior of women is patterned because political competition tends to be orderly and predictable. Bailey has compared a political structure to a game. Both operate "within limits set by agreed rules, which specify prizes, say how teams may be formed and led, lay down lawful and unlawful tactics," and give procedures to be followed when a rule is broken (Bailey, 1969: 33). Although women may be ineligible to win prizes, or even to form part of the teams that compete for them, they, like men, regard political prizes as important and worth having. They use what power they can appropriate to affect the distribution of prizes among those eligible to receive them.

Although the alert ethnographer can discern patterning in women's political participation, native informants seldom recognize such regularities and may be unwilling to admit their existence once they are pointed out. There are two reasons for this: politics concerns relations between groups usually represented by men and can therefore be discussed in terms of relations between men without reference to women; and political competition involving women takes place within domestic groups where relationships are defined in ethical rather than contractual terms. Women, because of their child-rearing activities, are conceptually confined to the home and are only linked to wider social networks through relationships with men (see Rosaldo, this volume). Because almost every woman is perceived to be under the authority of some man (Schneider, 1961) who sponsors her participation in social and political life, women's efforts to control their own and others' actions necessarily disrupt men's efforts to exercise their socially legitimated authority. Men thus have every reason to discount women's roles in political life and to attribute women's disruptive behavior to personal idiosyncrasies or to the general inferiority of the female sex. But there is a deeper reason why natives resist seeing women's conflicts as a structured and recurring aspect of social life. Because women are confined to the domestic sphere, their efforts to achieve power necessarily bring them into competition with close kin and affines: with those to whom they are bound by moral and ethical ties. Conflicts in such relationships are universally perceived as tragedies (see Bailey, 1969: 38). Those who are involved in a dispute know every cruel word and nasty deed that led to the outbreak and naturally find it hard to attribute such quarrels to the mechanistic workings of society.

Women are always at a disadvantage in competing for power and prestige (Dahrendorf, 1968), but their handicap is least in those political systems where leadership rests on ability and where there is little separation between the domestic and public spheres (see Rosaldo, also Lamphere, this volume). In such fluid systems, women's efforts to achieve power and to influence decisions may even be recognized as recurring and acceptable aspects of political life. But in political systems where decisions are made outside the home and where leadership rests on control of resources available primarily to men, women are often excluded from direct political participation. Confined to the home and defined as legal minors, women must work in concealed ways to gain their ends. In such systems women's efforts to achieve power are regarded as most disruptive, and overt ideology most consistently denies the wider implications of domestic disturbances.

In societies with patrilocal extended households, where positions of overt prestige and authority can be held only by men, a woman who seeks power must latch onto a man and try to control the world through him. The most available male for the role of political front man is a woman's son. Although she must wait years for him to mature, her patient labor in his behalf will pay off in the end: she can use the period of his immaturity to bind him to her by teaching him that he owes life, security, and position to her efforts. Husbands are much more difficult to control: by the time a man marries, he is already tied to his mother and has been taught to put the interests of his natal family before those of his stranger-bride.

Wives are the worms within the apple of a patrilocal domestic group. They work to advance the fortunes of particular individuals—their sons or husbands—in a social system where men are taught to put group interests before private ones. In a world where men gain political power by having a large and cohesive body of co-resident kin, young women gain power by breaking up domestic units. Men work to bind lineage mates together; women work to tear them apart. This inevitable conflict between male and female strategies seems to give rise to similar perceptions of women's nature. A recurring theme in the literature on societies with patrilocal extended households is the belief that women in general are irresponsible and sexually threatening, whereas mothers are idealized as warm and self-sacrificing (Campbell, 1964; Fallers, 1969; Wolf, 1972; Michaelson and Goldschmidt, 1971). Christian tradition provides a particularly vivid image for describing this belief in suggesting that there are two types of women in the world: those who take after Eve and tempt men away from God, and those who follow Mary and devote themselves to their sons. In reality, Eve and Mary are the same woman, for she who would be Mary to her son must inevitably be Eve to her husband.

The Eve-Mary distinction provides a very apt description of feminine behavior in such societies. Women's lives follow a characteristic pattern as they move from the loneliness of early marriage, through competent motherhood, to domineering old age. The several women who must live together in an extended patrilocal household also exhibit a characteristic pattern of domestic quarrels, and these quarrels affect wider political alignments by causing a redistribution of the people who form the core of a leader's following.

Marriage in a society with patrilocal extended households is a traumatic affair for everyone, but particularly for a bride. She must leave her natal home to take up residence among strangers who rightfully regard her coming as a threat to their solidarity and who expect her to make up for her inevitable defects by working hard and producing children to strengthen the group. A bride has no cause to settle happily into her new home; she is at the bottom of the domestic status hierarchy and knows it. But as a woman bears children, her interests change. She now has something to work for, because her future power will depend on the status of her sons. The ambitious woman will use all her political knowledge to increase her sons' inheritance and all her feminine wiles to persuade her husband to set up a separate household where she may have more control over family resources. An adult woman thus works to separate her husband from his family at the same time that she seeks to bind her own sons securely to her. She promotes the disintegration of one extended household—the lifetime creation of her mother-in-law—to ensure the solidarity of her own offspring. Old matriarchs and young mothers are doomed enemies. And so the cycle continues, for the man who is blessed with Mary for a mother must regard her enemy—his own wife—as Eve the temptress.

The quarrels that plague a patrilocal extended household can be predicted from a knowledge of women's life cycles. Brides are unhappy and want to go home to mother, wife-beating is a common occurrence, mother-in-law and daughter-in-law compete for the loyalty of their son/husband, while sisters-in-law and co-wives squabble over household resources. The usual cultural explanation for such tense domestic relations places the blame on women. They are seen as selfish and naturally quarrelsome. Whereas many men can cooperate and live together in peace, women are inherently unstable and immature. This explanation provides a justification for treating women as legal minors and also allows individuals and society as a whole to ignore the deeper political consequences of domestic disputes.

Many anthropologists have followed their informants in believing that marital disputes and the quarrels among women in a patrilocal extended household are "domestic tragedies" without major consequences for the wider political system. Even I was slow to realize that such "domestic tragedies" are neither wholly domestic nor very tragic. In studying the legal system of Zinacantan, a Maya community in the highlands of Chiapas, Mexico (Collier, 1973), I followed most ethnographers of law in treating marital disputes as routine and uninteresting. Like others, I focused my attention on the "big" cases—the land disputes and witchcraft accusations—that led to a redefinition of important relations. But as I worked with my field data, I began to realize that an appalling amount of legal time and energy was being spent on domestic quarrels. In simple economic terms, more working time was lost and more bottles of liquor were bought to calm women's angry hearts than for all other kinds of disputes combined. It might have been easy to overlook the wider social consequences of any single marital dispute, but the cumulative result of all marital disputes could hardly be ignored. Further thought led me to see that the high divorce rate in Zinacantan, combined with the fact that most young couples (at the wife's instigation) manage to move out of the husband's father's house after three years of marriage, causes lineages to be shallow and means that in most cases a political following (described by informants as an agnatic descent group) actually consists of a motley group of relatives gathered around a rich and influential man.

Having realized that Zinacanteco women play an important, if unrecognized, role in local-level political alignments, I began to consider other ways in which women's actions affect the public world ostensibly dominated by men. I soon saw that women's quarrels provide occasions for focusing attention on critical issues. "Issue recognition" is the first of five stages in the development of a political decision listed by Clark (1968). Women may not have the authority to make certain types of decisions, but they can prod men into action at a time when other factors favor the outcome they desire. Many ethnographers who have noted the unhappiness of brides in a patrilocal extended household have attributed their sadness solely to their traumatic change of residence and role. But it is also true that brides have far more to gain by sulking than by playing Pollyanna. The bride who works hard and strives to please can be safely ignored, but the one who cries or threatens to leave must be heeded and placated. Where women are denied a legitimate voice in family councils, they may affect decisions by causing an uproar that forces others to pay attention to their wishes.

In societies like Zinacantan, where political power rests on size and cohesiveness of the co-resident kin group, fights between mothers and daughters-in-law take on the aura of political power struggles. The daughter-in-law who succeeds in breaking up a household can undermine the power of an important leader, while the aging mother who keeps her adult sons together may have real, though unacknowledged, power in the community (Campbell, 1964). Women in such households may ostensibly fight over trivialities, but the real stakes are political—the capacity to determine the actions of others.

Analyses of political dynamics in matrilineal societies have stressed women's roles in the building of cohesive political followings. Turner has described how aspiring Ndembu leaders try to attract their sisters at the same time that they seek to prevent their wives from leaving. Divorce is frequent, and villages grow and dissolve, as women, with their attendant children, move in and out (Turner, 1957). Similar political processes seem to occur in many patrilineal societies, but are harder to detect because informants describe political alignments in the idiom of agnatic kinship. Zinacanteco informants who are asked to account for a leader's co-resident followers use agnatic kinship to explain the presence of brothers, sons, or nephews, but explain the presence of adult sisters, daughters, or aunts by recounting the unique series of events that led each woman to violate the normative rule of patrilocality. These colorful and diverse accounts effectively mask the coherent pattern that underlies the behavior of all such "stray" females. Zinacanteco women regularly fight with their husbands and beg their fathers or brothers for asylum. If the father or brother happens to be a wealthy man with land to spare, he can afford to offer his kinswoman a place to live in return for her loyalty and that of her sons. Zinacanteco political followings may be described as agnatic descent groups, but wealth, not kinship, is the crucial factor. Those who have land can attract "kin"; those without land lose their relatives to others.

A similar pattern seems to underlie political alignments among the Nuer, a tribe famous for its emphasis on agnatic descent. Gough, in a reexamination of Nuer kinship, concluded from the analysis of a Nuer village census that "just under half the women of child-bearing age are under the legal guardianship of no man" (Gough, 1971: 109), and she attributed the autonomy of women to the situation created by rapid Nuer expansion through conquest. She also noted a tendency for the women born into aristocratic, conquering lineages to adopt male roles through woman marriage or to marry men of lesser lineages who agreed to live with the wife's kin group, while the women born to conquered lineages but married to aristocratic men lived in the husband's homestead and remained faithful wives (pp. 110–12). This pattern is easily explained if women are perceived as political actors seeking to maximize power. Nuer women gain power by attaching themselves to men of aristocratic lineages: both daughters and wives of such lineages are reluctant to leave. Wealthy Nuer, like wealthy Zinacantecos, have large and cohesive kin groups.

Gough's analysis of Nuer society in transition underlines the importance of perceiving women as social actors. If women are seen as passive creatures under the control of men, it becomes impossible to explain why so many Nuer women lack male guardians. Although it may be possible to ignore women's contribution to political alignments in a stable society (or in one defined as stable for analytical purposes), a knowledge of women's goals and strategies is indispensable for understanding the processes of social change. As new resources enter a political field, both men and women seek advantage from expanded opportunities, and the course of change necessarily reflects the complex interplay of male and female tactics.

In this brief paper I have argued that women are social actors whose choices affect the options open to politically active men. If we, as anthropologists, are to develop models of social reality capable of generating both the normative rules of a system and the pragmatic strategies actually followed by people (Whitten and Whitten, 1972; Buchler and Nutini, 1970), we must accommodate in our analyses the behavior of *all* human participants. Previous analyses of political systems that treat men as social actors (Firth, 1951; Barth, 1959; Bailey, 1969) have shown how normative rules and patterned deviations from these rules are inextricably linked, but we will gain an even deeper understanding of political processes if we look for patterns of feminine behavior. Such patterns may be hard to find, because they are obscured by informants who voice only normative rules, and because ethnographers seldom look for them, but they do exist and must be found if we are to develop models of social processes with wide applicability. The adult woman in pre-industrial, pre-birth-control society may indeed be "above all a wife, whose life is centered in her home and family" (Evans-Pritchard, 1963: 46), but she is also a human being whose strivings and failings affect the lives of those around her. To the degree that her sisters share her experiences and aspirations, their cumulative choices will have far-reaching effects.

LOUISE LAMPHERE

Strategies, Cooperation, and Conflict Among Women in Domestic Groups

In most societies the world of the domestic and familial is the world of women, and that of the public and political the world of men. We might expect, then, that women within the same domestic group would share common interests and unite in solving problems arising out of such daily activities as child rearing, food preparation, the making of clothing, and even the cultivation or gathering of foodstuffs. In fact, ethnographic reports show that many kinds of domestic groups are ridden with conflict and competition between women. Accounts of jealousy among co-wives, of the dominance of mother-in-law over daughter-in-law, and of quarrels between sisters-in-law provide some of the most common examples. In this paper I shall discuss family life in a variety of societies in order to isolate the factors that promote cooperation and common interests among women, in contrast to those that account for conflict and competing interests.

The anthropological literature on the family and domestic group centers on two themes, both of which appear to derive from a male perspective. First, in order to understand the changes that take place in family structure throughout the lifetime of any individual, anthropologists have viewed the domestic group in terms of a developmental cycle (Fortes, 1949; Goody, 1958). With this framework, families and domestic units have been treated primarily in terms of their formation, development, and fission. Most discussions, though not ignoring the position of women, have treated processes within the family from a male ego's point of view.[1] Authors such as Fortes and Goody emphasize the continuity

[1] For example, Leach describes changes in residence, marriage, and political alliances in the Trobriands only from the perspective of the Trobriand male (Goody, 1958: 120–45). Goody suggests that the wife's access to grain among the LoDagaba is a male strategy of keeping inheritable possessions for his dependent wife and children, rather than allowing them to be allocated to his matrilineal male kin at his death. How the women in each of these societies operate within the system is largely overlooked (Goody, 1958: 53–91).

of domestic groups and the transmission of property and authority roles. Since both are often in the hands of males, the focus is on men rather than on women. The ways in which women view the male domestic power structure and how they operate within it are topics usually not treated.

Second, in the analysis of marriage, the approach developed by Radcliffe-Brown (1950) and other British anthropologists (Leach, 1955; Gluckman, 1950) stresses the rights and duties transferred at marriage from the kin group of one spouse to that of the other and/or the rights and duties created by the marriage itself. A woman is viewed in terms of the rights her kin have to her domestic labor, to the property she might acquire, to her children, and to her sexuality. In many societies, the marriage ceremony and the payment of bridewealth give these rights to the husband and residually to his kin. Rights to the male's services, property, and procreative power also can be transferred at marriage, but even in analysis of matrilineal societies (Schneider and Gough, 1961), the emphasis is on the rights in the woman that are retained by her kin group and consequently not given to the husband. The control over women by male-dominated kin groups is an important theme, whereas the ways in which women resist or acquiesce in this control are not discussed.

Thus, neither of these approaches—one focusing on the family or domestic group and the other on marriage—considers the woman's point of view. If we are to better understand the position of women in our own and other cultures, we can no longer fail to analyze carefully how half of the population views and responds to the norms and institutions governing family life.

An Alternative Perspective

The following pages present an alternative approach that does emphasize the woman's perspective. This approach entails three elements. First, rather than discussing rights and duties per se, I shall frame my analysis around the political aspects of family life—specifically, the distribution of power and authority within the family—in order to learn which aspects are in the hands of men and which are in the hands of women. Second, I shall retain the concept of the developmental cycle of domestic groups and show how the structure of the domestic group changes, authority roles shift, and property is transferred over a period of time. These topics will be discussed not only in relation to men, who may hold positions of authority and inherit the economic goods of a domestic group, but with particular attention to women's roles, and how any particular woman's relationship to the allocation of power and authority changes as she grows older and her children mature. Third, I shall analyze the strategies women employ in attaining their ends, whether this entails making decisions themselves, exercising influence over those who make decisions, or circumventing the domestic power structure.

The distribution of power and authority in the family, the developmental cycle of the domestic group, and women's strategies are all related. Power and authority are concepts that characterize the way in which decisions are made and carried out. Power, according to Weber, "is the probability that one actor within a social relationship will be in a position to carry out his own will despite resistance, regardless of the basis on which this probability rests" (1947: 152). When power rests on legitimacy (that is, on the notion that an individual has the "right" to impose his will), and when it is exercised within a hierarchy of roles, it is defined as authority. Authority, in other words, "is the aspect of a status in a system of social organization . . . by virtue of which the incumbent is put in a position legitimately to make decisions which are binding, not only on himself but on the collectivity" (Parsons, 1963a). Most systems, of course, contain unassigned power, so that an individual or group not in authority may, in some circumstances, make decisions and gain compliance from those in authority. For instance, in domestic groups where men hold the authority positions and have the legitimate right to make decisions binding on others, women may hold unassigned power, that is, the means of gaining compliance with their actions through withholding food and sexual services.

An individual's relationship to the distribution of power and authority in a domestic group is best conceptualized in terms of the strategies a person uses to achieve his or her own ends. The notion that individuals employ strategies to achieve particular goals has been utilized in the analysis of political systems (Bailey, 1969; Barth, 1959; Leach, 1954), but it also has validity, I believe, in understanding relationships within the domestic group.

Women's strategies are a response to the distribution of power and authority and will differ, I suggest, depending on whether women are able to make decisions or whether decisions are made by men. Since women are often not in positions of authority, a key concept in understanding their strategies is that of influence, one of the most important forms of persuasion (Parsons, 1963b). A woman exercises influence when she is able to bring about a decision on another's part to act in a certain way, because it is felt to be good for the other person, independent of changes in his or her situation and for positive reasons, not because of sanctions that might be imposed (Parsons, 1963b: 38, 48). Influence might also be exercised by appeal to one particular norm rather than another within a context of equally appropriate norms. Where men hold positions of authority, a woman (in her role as wife, mother, or sister) may be able to influence a man's decision (to press for partition of a joint estate, for example) by persuading him that such a decision is in his own interests or perhaps in the interests of his children or other kin.

Women's goals are of course defined by their position in the society as a whole and by their place in the developmental cycle of the family with its concomitant power structure. Thus, a woman may have no access to land or to a leadership position, but may work to make it possible for her son to acquire greater control over economic resources, more political power, or a ritual position. For herself, she may want enough of her husband's land to provide food for herself and her children, enough cash to begin a trading venture, security in her old age, or someone to mourn for her. In using various strategies to reach these goals, a woman may be brought into cooperation or conflict with the women in her own domestic group, or she may find solidarity with women in other domestic groups.

As Rosaldo suggests (this volume), one dimension that affects family authority structure is the relative integration or separation of political and domestic spheres.[2] As the following data show, societies where domestic and political spheres are integrated are among those in which authority within the domestic group is shared by both men and women. Women's strategies focus on cooperation for everyday activities and are "economic" in nature. Furthermore, even though there is a division of labor between the sexes so that different classes of kin are recruited depending on the sex of the individual and the type of task, strategies for recruiting aid do not differ between men and women. In contrast, in many societies where domestic and political spheres are separated and where extended family structures are found, power and authority are built around a hierarchy of males. Women's strategies are centered on "political" goals, i.e. on influencing the men who hold authority.

In order to contrast strategies for recruiting aid with those for gaining power or influence, I will first examine domestic groups in societies where domestic and political spheres are integrated, and then compare these cases with societies that are more stratified and where political and domestic contexts are distinct. Examples in the latter case are drawn

[2] My use of the term "political sphere" is similar to Rosaldo's concept of "public sphere." However, I have retained the more narrow term "political" since I am comparing women's strategies in various systems with particular reference to decision making, power, and authority.

from (1) peasant communities in state societies, (2) African tribal societies, and (3) modern industrial societies. Within each type of society the relative effect of economic factors is examined, specifically a woman's contribution to household resources and how this contribution tends to shape her strategies within the domestic group.

Women, Strategies, and Cooperation Among the Navajo

The first example comes from data collected on domestic groups and patterns of cooperation among the Navajo Indians of New Mexico and Arizona (Lamphere, 1974). The Navajo, a loosely organized American Indian population, migrated to the Southwest as hunter-gatherers and subsequently came to depend on pastoralism and agriculture. Under present-day reservation conditions they are increasingly involved in a wage and welfare economy. The pre-conquest political organization consisted of leadership by "headmen" who had very little authority but who settled disputes and gave advice. These leaders (as well as other public officials such as raid leaders and medicine men) were male. Even today, with a full-fledged modern tribal government, most political offices are held by men, though women are not excluded.

The reservation system has imposed a political superstructure on Navajo life, but most important decisions are still made in the domestic group or by individuals. Property is individually owned; there is an emphasis on autonomy. Requests for help are made indirectly, and Navajos expect generosity from others in response to any indication of need (Lamphere, 1971). All of these circumstances allow for the relative equality of men and women, particularly in the family, and indicate that political and domestic spheres are rather undifferentiated.

Navajo domestic groups often take the form of "matrilocal grand-families" and are structured around female bonds, backed by a positive cultural valuation of the role of the mother (Witherspoon, 1970). These dispersed extended families have the following developmental cycle. Upon marriage, a couple may live with either the wife's mother or the husband's mother. In practice, the mother-daughter bond is stronger, so that the pull is toward uxorilocal rather than virilocal residence. Soon after marriage, a young couple set up a separate dwelling within the camp.

In the extended family, the parents or the widowed mother hold positions of authority. In Navajo terms, "it's up to them to decide" in matters that concern sheepherding, shearing, dipping, or agricultural work, although each household retains a great deal of autonomy. Rather than being hierarchical, Navajo concepts of authority are egalitarian, as in Parsons' definition of authority mentioned above. An individual's decision is not binding on another person or on a group. Instead, a Navajo makes a decision and requests a similar one from another Navajo. If they are in agreement, they are both obligated to participate in joint activities (Lamphere, 1971: 97).

Navajo parents or a widowed mother, thus, do not impose their decisions on other households but serve as a focus of communication and of organizing cooperation. Requests for aid are made directly between parents and children, though the father may use the mother as an intermediary with his daughters. In-married affines are in a peripheral position, especially a son-in-law living uxorilocally (Aberle, 1961). He and his wife in the early years of marriage do not form a team; rather, his wife is a buffer between him and her parents. Navajo marriages are brittle, especially in the early years, partly because of the strains created by the wife's loyalty to her kin and the husband's obligations to his own parents and siblings, who usually reside in another camp. If a marriage endures, the couple become more and more of a unit. Eventually they found a new camp in the same neighborhood as the wife's or the husband's parents. A son-in-law gains in moving, because he becomes a decision maker in a wider range of situations and is no longer at the beck and call of his in-laws.

Also, as the parental couple increase in age, and especially after the death of the mother (who is more of a focus of communication and dispute settlement than the father), tensions between siblings and their spouses in the same camp increase. Brothers and sisters quarrel over livestock. There are accusations that one sibling has not contributed enough goods toward a ceremony. By moving apart, tensions are decreased and daily cooperation is changed to more occasional requests.

Thus, during the final phase of the developmental cycle of a residence group, a couple are head of their own camp, which contains married children and grandchildren. Ties with the husband's and wife's siblings are maintained for help in ceremonies.

Cooperation beyond the residence group is recruited on an ego-centered basis. In obtaining help for ceremonies, both men and women use what I have termed a "proximity strategy." For the organizer, residence-group members are the "closest" and most easily recruited participants; next to be activated are people with ties to primary and secondary kin[3] in other residence groups, with those in the same neighborhood being the most likely to participate. Then, neighbors with whom an individual has clan ties are recruited. Finally, distant clan relatives are likely to

[3] Primary kin are those one genealogical link from ego (i.e. parents, siblings, and children), and secondary kin are two genealogical links in distance (parents' siblings, siblings' children, and grandchildren).

participate only in funerals or very large ceremonies. Since there are usually two individuals who organize a ceremony (such as a husband and wife), more members of one person's set of kin may be activated if one person has few kin, or if his or her kin are residentially distant from the camp where the ceremony is held (Lamphere, 1973).

To summarize, among the Navajo, domestic and political spheres are relatively undifferentiated and most crucial decisions are taken within the domestic group rather than in a wider political arena. Authority within domestic groups is egalitarian, with the emphasis on individual autonomy. Under these conditions, Navajo women have a great deal of control over their lives. They do not need to wrest power from others who hold positions of authority or attempt to influence decisions that are not theirs to make.

At no time do a Navajo woman's interests conflict with those of her close female kin. The mother-daughter coalition is strongest during the early years of a woman's life and until a marriage is stabilized. The husband-wife coalition increases in strength as a woman reaches middle age, and may become the basis for a new camp that she and her husband head, though the conjugal relationship never completely overrides the mother-daughter one. Finally, the strategies women use in recruiting aid are not substantially different from those of men. Women rarely "work through" men, but are themselves mediators between men, as, for instance, between a young husband and his father-in-law.

Among hunter-gatherer groups where the band is the largest social unit, political and domestic spheres are even more integrated than among the Navajo. Material from the Bushman (Marshall, 1959, 1960; Lee, 1972) and Eskimo (Briggs, 1970; Damas, 1968; Spencer and Jennings, 1965; and Hoebel, 1954) confirms the relationship I have suggested between the distribution of power and authority and women's strategies. Authority is also egalitarian; decisions are by consensus, and individual autonomy is maximized.[4] In contrast with the Navajo, the nuclear family is the major domestic unit for both the Bushman and the Eskimo, and the husband-wife dyad is stable throughout a woman's life. The developmental cycle of the nuclear family does not bring about changes in women's interests or allies. Rather than a gradual shift in emphasis from cooperation with natal kin (mainly females) to that with a husband and children, Eskimo and Bushman women work independently or with the husband throughout their adult lives. At the same

---

[4] Leadership positions are held by men, but at least in the Bushman case (Lee, 1972: 129) leaders do not control rights to resources; these rights reside with the whole group. Furthermore, unlike Radcliffe-Brown's model of the patrilocal horde, membership in Bushman bands is flexible and is based on ties between siblings of either sex.

time, they have a continuing network of occasional cooperators among other women in the band, the closest of whom are sisters, mothers, cousins, and possibly sisters-in-law.[5]

Bushman and Eskimo women see their goals as primarily coinciding with those of their husbands. The husband-wife relationship among the Eskimo (Briggs, 1970) is definitely a dominant/subordinate one, in marked contrast to the Bushman situation, perhaps because of the Bushman woman's contribution to subsistence that amounts to providing two-thirds of the diet (Lee, 1968). Despite the differences in family structure and the extent of husband dominance that emerge in comparing the Eskimo, Bushman, and Navajo, it is still apparent that women's strategies revolve around recruiting help in primarily economic tasks. Although men and women may work separately and are likely to cooperate with kin of the same sex, women's strategies of recruitment do not differ from those of men. Women have positive ties with female kin and other women in the two-band societies where the nuclear family is important, and Navajo women have very close ties with female kin in a system where uxorilocal extended families are important.

The Patricentered Peasant Family

What happens to relationships between women of the same family in societies in which domestic and political spheres are highly differentiated and when authority is hierarchical and in the hands of male members of the group? The question is complicated by the variety of political systems found cross-culturally (ranging from acephalous tribal societies and preindustrial states, on the one hand, to modern industrial societies and third-world nations, on the other). The authority structure of the domestic group itself is affected by economic and power relations within the larger society. Strategies available to women are in turn related to rules of descent and inheritance, marriage, and access to economic resources. The interaction of these factors can be seen by examining examples of domestic group structure and women's strategies in three different kinds of societies where political and domestic spheres are differentiated: (1) peasant communities in state societies, (2) tribal societies in Africa, and (3) modern industrial societies.

In analyzing family structure and sex roles in forty-six peasant com-

---

[5] The data presented by Briggs, Lee, and Marshall are not detailed enough to draw definitive conclusions, but I suspect that recruitment for aid follows a "proximity strategy" based on ties within a bilateral kindred. In contrast, Navajo strategies seem more skewed toward matrilateral kin, because of the importance of uxorilocal residence.

munities,[6] Michaelson and Goldschmidt (1971) find that in both patrilineal and bilateral household types, economic control is in the hands of men. Polygyny is rare, and clans or corporate descent groups are either weak or absent. Wolf's material on Taiwanese family life (1968, 1972, and this volume) gives a detailed view of women's responses to the patrilineal extended family patterns summarized by Michaelson and Goldschmidt (1971: 330). Women enter patrilocal households as strangers, legitimize their place through the birth of male offspring, and spend their lives in domestic chores and the socialization of children. Wolf's hypothesis is that a woman builds a uterine family (i.e. a family based on ties with children and excluding the husband) as a means of counteracting her isolation and as a way of establishing security for her old age. But, of course, this process interferes with the uterine family already established by the young wife's mother-in-law. While raising her children, a woman is likely to invest a great deal of effort in securing the loyalty of her son. Thus, a young bride is seen as a threat, someone who can undermine that loyalty. The son, of course, is "in the middle" in the conflicts that arise over each woman's attempt to build her uterine family.

Outside the family, the young wife creates relationships in the women's community. She meets other brides who become her allies. In these extra-domestic neighborhood groups, women exercise a good deal of influence over men's decisions (Wolf, 1972: 40) through subtle manipulation of opinion and by creating rumors that will damage reputations or "lose face" for the menfolk.

The authority structure of the patrilocal, patrilineal extended family, where father has authority over son and husband over wife, brings about conflict rather than cooperation between women in these groups. The developmental cycle of extended families, in contrast to the Navajo and hunter-gatherer examples, brings sharp changes in the status of women. As a young bride a woman enters the group in the lowest status, but as her children grow she gains influence with her husband and builds loyalty in her sons. As a mother-in-law, she has authority over her daughters-in-law but also sees them as competing for what little influence she has been able to achieve. Women's strategies revolve around "working through men," either their husbands or their sons. Women's interests never coincide; competition and conflict are to be expected.

---

[6] The authors define peasants as those populations which consist mainly of agricultural producers who have rights in their land, produce primarily for their own subsistence, though also for exchange, and are part of a state-organized political system (Goldschmidt and Kunkel, 1971: 1058).

Competition may reach its highest proportions in a joint patrilocal family (as found in India: Minturn and Hitchcock, 1966) after the father has died and before the partition of an estate among brothers. At this point, the failure of cooperation among brothers is often blamed on quarrels between women (see Denich, this volume). But it is also true that disputes that do arise between women reflect real conflicts of interest and may be instrumental in the breakup of the domestic group. Cooperation and alliance with other women is usually limited to the less intense relationships outside the domestic group. These informal women's groups, through gossip, exert another kind of informal pressure on men.

Strategies women use, especially in attempting to influence men, differ in bilateral households in peasant societies where the nuclear family, rather than the extended family, is important. Bilateral inheritance and nuclear family structure are, like the patrilineal, patrilocal households, a response to factors generated outside the peasant community; for example, (1) legal arrangements with a landowner, which keep landholdings small and create a rural proletariat (as in Latin America and Italy), and (2) urban opportunities and the commercialization of agriculture (in most parts of modern Europe) and the existence of a frontier situation (as in some areas of Southeast Asia) (Goldschmidt and Kunkel, 1971). In bilateral peasant households the increased economic power of women tends to make for brother-sister rivalry, and where male authoritarian roles are expected, this rivalry seems to create a machismo syndrome (Michaelson and Goldschmidt, 1971: 330).

A good example comes from Ernestine Friedl's study of a Greek village (1967). Men hold power and authority in the public sphere and are also the official decision makers in the home. But women have an effective voice in many domestic decisions because of the dowries they bring to their marriages. In other words, nuclear family structure means that there is no male hierarchy within the domestic group, and the wife, through control of economic resources, is able to counteract her husband's dominance. She exercises influence over him, but in doing so she is not brought into competition with other women.

Extended Families in African Societies

Tribal societies contrast with peasant societies and allow us to examine additional factors that affect the structure of domestic groups, the distribution of power and authority, and women's strategies. In tribal societies, corporate kin groups are the "building blocks" of the political structure (regardless of whether it is acephalous or centralized;

Fortes and Evans-Pritchard, 1940). The importance of these extra-domestic kin groups in turn suggests that wives might retain ties with their own groups after marriage and that divorce might be frequent. These ties would give women more leverage against men in the domestic group into which they married, and matrilineal rather than patrilineal descent could also enhance the power of women. Finally, polygyny will affect the structure of domestic groups, reduce the unassigned power of each wife, and alter the strategies of women. In order to examine these factors, as well as the importance of a woman's control over economic resources, I will discuss examples from several African societies.

Polygyny itself tends to be associated with societies where women do the bulk of the agricultural work and where land can be obtained for successive wives (Goldschmidt and Kunkel, 1971: 1061). Political or socially stratified divisions within a society also favor the emergence of polygyny, since economic rights to women can be acquired, and since marriages can be used to create political alliances between unequal groups (Clignet, 1970: 21). Finally, polygyny is associated with the predominance of male orientations, as indicated by the fact that 84 percent of African peoples who practice polygyny are also patrilocal (Clignet, 1970: 23). Thus, in polygynous African societies the common form of the extended family at its most fully developed stage is that of a male head of household with two or more wives (each with her own hut) and their children. Since these domestic groups are most often two-generational and not three-generational units, the dominance of the husband over the wife is structurally more important and the competition of co-wives is more critical than conflict between mother-in-law and daughter-in-law.

These tensions are clearly illustrated in Cohen's study of marriage and divorce among the Kanuri of Bornu, part of a centralized Muslim state (1971). The typical Kanuri compound is composed of a patrilocal, polygynous family. Women are married very young, often to middle-aged men. A woman's ability to control a husband's dominance depends on her ability to withdraw food and sexual services. A second wife is a considerable threat to her, resulting in less attention for her as well as for her children, and she loses some of her ability to gain compliance from her husband.

Within the polygynous extended family, then, there is conflict between co-wives, since women compete for goods and services from the husband and since each wife attempts to build a uterine family at the expense of her co-wives' children. The high divorce rate indicates that divorce itself is a strategy for achieving independence for Kanuri women.

Where influence over the husband fails, a woman may force a divorce through insubordination and return to her father's or brother's compound until remarriage. If subsequent marriages are equally unbearable, there is always the knowledge that her son or other male kinsmen will provide a place to live after her final divorce where she will have a fair amount of respect and influence.

There are examples of polygynous extended families where co-wife conflict is minimized, often by a set of rules that carefully govern how often a husband sleeps with each wife and how often she is obligated to cook for him (see Leis, this volume, for one instance).

As in peasant societies, a woman's control over economic resources (a factor absent in the Kanuri case) may give her more control over decisions within the domestic group. Furthermore, in many African polygynous societies women gain economic autonomy through trading. Trading not only gives de facto independence from the husband's authority (and may ease tensions between co-wives), but also brings women together in extra-domestic cooperative groups such as trading associations (G. Marshall, 1964; Leis, this volume).

A final factor may be the rule of descent and inheritance. For instance, among the Ashanti, matrilineal descent and inheritance, the ability of women to acquire land, and the lack of polygyny all coincide to maximize the common interests of women and minimize a husband's dominance. Both men and women can be heads of extended families. Marriage ties are brittle, and women often live with their mothers or maternal uncles instead of with their husbands (Fortes, 1950). Women have equal rights to matrilineage land, and occasionally become wealthy, owning more property than their menfolk. Ashanti women may be subordinate to their husbands in early married life, but they are always able to acquire the beginnings of an independent livelihood from their own matrilineal kin. An Ashanti woman has two possible strategies: either she can build a uterine family which, since it is also the core of a matrilineage, can become a viable household with her at the head, or she can live with a brother with whom she has considerable influence.

The preceding examples from African societies confirm the conclusions reached with patricentered peasant families, but they highlight the effects on women's strategies of polygynous marriage, ties to a natal kin group, access to economic resources, and rules of descent and inheritance. As in peasant societies, political and domestic spheres are differentiated (though tribal political systems are very different from peasant systems). Domestic power and authority are in the hands of men, so that women are in a position of using influence or "working through men," either sons or husbands. Women's interests never coincide, and the co-wife relationship is particularly full of conflict. As in the case of bilateral peasant families, where women have access to economic resources, their ability to influence those in authority is increased.

Three patterns emerge that contrast the tribal with the peasant examples. First, since a woman usually retains ties with her own kin, she may use the support of her male relatives against her husband, or sever the marriage tie altogether. Second, women's access to land or cash may make possible the formation of extra-domestic women's groups, which have economic functions and which wield considerable political power, in contrast to the Taiwanese neighborhood groups, where women seek influence through gossip.[7] Finally, a woman's position in a system of matrilineal descent and inheritance is such that she is likely to have more access to economic resources and domestic authority, making it possible for her to achieve economic independence and the headship of a household in her own right.

Women's Strategies in Modern Industrial Societies

My first examples of the Navajo, Bushman, and Eskimo suggested that where authority was egalitarian, women's interests would coincide; they would have autonomy or a great deal of influence in many domestic decisions, and their strategies for cooperation would be similar to those of men. Cooperation could be built around ties to other female kin, or extended in a bilateral fashion, with spatial and genealogical "proximity" being an important factor. These latter characteristics are also found in contemporary Western society among subgroups that exhibit family and kinship patterns usually labeled female-centered or "matrifocal."

An example is the working-class English family, from the early part of the century until the 1950's. Here nuclear families existed in poor urban neighborhoods. Men were absent from the home for long hours during the week, when they were engaged in semiskilled manual work. When they were present, however, they were dominant; men controlled

---

[7] Jane Collier (personal communication) suggests that a necessary condition for the formation of women's groups is a dense rather than scattered settlement pattern (e.g. villages or towns). If domestic power and authority are in the hands of men, women's interests within the domestic group are in conflict and women are unlikely to form groups. Extra-domestic groups would be likely only where women with common interests are living fairly close together. This implies that the formation of women's groups and "female bonding" depend on a combination of economic and social factors and not on biological propensities, as Tiger (1969) suggests (see Leis, this volume, for a more complete analysis).

the household finances and provided their wives with a weekly allowance. Mother-daughter ties were a focus for a network of kin, between whom goods and services could be exchanged to cope with domestic problems and stretch the meager wages of the men (Young and Willmott, 1957; Bott, 1968).

The strength of mother-daughter ties and the importance of the bonds between a woman and her female kin are also themes in the literature on Black families, particularly those in low-income neighborhoods in cities in the United States (Ladner, 1971). The Moynihan report (Rainwater and Yancey, 1967) and other studies have underemphasized the proportion of male-headed nuclear families, have viewed female-headed households as pathological, and have engaged in "blaming the victim," i.e. seeking the causes of social problems in individual psychology and family patterns rather than examining the ways in which racism and inequality are an inherent part of our major institutions. Black sociologists are beginning to formulate an alternative analysis of the Black family (Billingsley, 1968; Ladner, 1973) that emphasizes the strengths of individual adaptations to poverty and the resilience of Black men and women. It seems clear that the formation of woman-centered domestic groups is related to external economic and political factors. The effects of economic racism on Black males, access to welfare, and even poorly paid unskilled work on the part of Black females and the instability of housing contribute to the fact that households are constantly forming and breaking up, usually around women who can provide needed child care.

Stack (1972, also this volume) suggests that the kindred is the pool from which households are formed. "Households have shifting membership, but on the average they maintain a steady state of three generations of kin: adult males, and females beyond childbearing age; a middle generation of mothers raising their own children or children of close kin; and their children" (Stack, 1972: 164). Unlike English working-class women, who are part of male-dominated nuclear family households and whose ties with female kin form an extra-domestic network, Black women are often co-resident with female as well as male members of their kin network. There is an ideology of male dominance in the Black community (Liebow, 1967), but since females have access to economic resources, they are able to maintain self-sufficient domestic units without men or with only their occasional support.

Superficially, many elements of women's authority and women's strategies may resemble those found among the Navajo and hunter-gatherer groups. Women make important decisions within the domestic sphere, women's interests often coincide, there is high cooperation between female kin, and strategies of recruitment are similar for both men and women. However, it is important to examine the structure of these societies as a whole and to discuss class relationships in the modern industrial cases. In the Navajo and hunter-gatherer examples, domestic and political spheres are fused and authority is egalitarian. However, in Black urban communities and among English working-class populations the domestic sphere is totally separated from the political, and neither men nor women have power or authority in this latter sphere. In spite of a domestic ideology of male dominance, English working-class men are removed from the home as a consequence of the long hours they work, and Black men who can find only occasional unskilled work often cannot fill the role of husband-provider. The domestic authority of women comes only at the expense of men, and at the same time working-class and Black women (along with their men) do not have access to the centers of power or to an equal place in the labor force.

Conclusion

I began this paper with a critique of the literature on the family that treats domestic group structure, marriage, descent, and inheritance from a male point of view. In examining family relationships in a variety of cultures I have taken a female perspective, treating women as political actors who employ strategies to achieve ends. Women's strategies are directly related to the structure of power and authority in the domestic group and to a woman's position with relation to the developmental cycle.

In societies like the Navajo, Eskimo, and Bushman, where domestic and political spheres are integrated, women's strategies focus on cooperation for everyday activities. They are "economic" in the sense that they center on the exchange of goods and services. In contrast, many societies where domestic and political spheres are separated are also those where the extended family structure is built around a hierarchy of males. Women's strategies here are centered on "political" goals, that is, on influencing the men who hold authority. Thus, wives have subtle methods of changing the minds of husbands, mothers build loyalty in their sons, neighborhood groups of women use gossip to affect the decisions of community males, and wives play male kinsmen against their husbands in settling grievances. Access to economic resources, the ability to withdraw goods and services, and even sheer defiance give women unassigned power, or increase their influence over husbands, sons, and brothers.

Women's strategies in working- and lower-class families exhibit an important paradox. Women exercise de facto control, and their strategies also focus on "economic" activities (e.g. the exchange of goods and services among a network of kin). But unlike Navajo, Eskimo, and Bushman women, who have decision-making ability in societies where authority is shared and where politics becomes domestic, working-class and Black women operate autonomously only in the domestic and not in the political sphere.

Women quarrel with or dominate other women when it is in their interest to do so; they share and exchange with other women when it suits their own goals. Cooperation and conflict among women in families or kin groups cannot be understood without reference to domestic power structure, to women's place within it, and to the factors that shape the relationship between the family and the larger society.

CAROL B. STACK

Sex Roles and Survival Strategies in an Urban Black Community

The power and authority ascribed to women in the Black ghettos of America, women whose families are locked into lifelong conditions of poverty and welfare, have their roots in the inexorable unemployment of Black males and the ensuing control of economic resources by females. These social-economic conditions have given rise to special features in the organization of family and kin networks in Black communities, features not unlike the patterns of domestic authority that emerge in matrilineal societies, or in cultures where men are away from home in wage labor (Gonzalez, 1969, 1970). The poor in Black urban communities have evolved, as the basic unit of their society, a core of kinsmen and non-kin who cooperate on a daily basis and who live near one another or co-reside. This core, or nucleus, has been characterized as the basis of the consanguineal household (Gonzalez, 1965) and of matrifocality (Tanner, this volume; Abrahams, 1963; Moynihan, 1965; Rainwater, 1966).

The concept of "matrifocality," however, has been criticized as inaccurate and inadequate. Recent studies (Ladner, 1971; Smith, 1970; Stack, 1970; Valentine, 1970) show convincingly that many of the negative features attributed to matrifocal families—that they are fatherless, unstable, and produce offspring that are "illegitimate" in the eyes of the folk culture—are not general characteristics of low-income Black families in urban America. Rather than imposing widely accepted defi-

This article is adapted for the most part from Chapter 7 of the book *All Our Kin: Strategies for Survival in a Black Community*, by Carol B. Stack (Harper & Row, 1974). I am grateful to Harper & Row for permission to use most of the material from that chapter. I should like to thank Professors Louise Lamphere, Michelle Rosaldo, Robert Weiss, Nancie Gonzalez, and Eva Hunt for helpful suggestions in the analysis and organization of this paper, and William W. Carver, of Stanford University Press, for his thoughtful editorial advice.

nitions of the family, the nuclear family, or the matrifocal family on the ways in which the urban poor describe and order their world, we must seek a more appropriate theoretical framework. Elsewhere I have proposed an analysis based on the notion of a domestic network (Stack, 1974). In this view, the basis of familial structure and cooperation is not the nuclear family of the middle class, but an extended cluster of kinsmen related chiefly through children but also through marriage and friendship, who align to provide domestic functions. This cluster, or domestic network, is diffused over several kin-based households, and fluctuations in individual household composition do not significantly affect cooperative arrangements.

In this paper I shall analyze the domestic network and the relationships within it from a woman's perspective—from the perspective that the women in this study provided and from my own interpretations of the domestic and social scene. Many previous studies of the Black family (e.g. Liebow, 1967, and Hannerz, 1969) have taken a male perspective, emphasizing the street-corner life of Black men and viewing men as peripheral to familial concerns. Though correctly stressing the economic difficulties that Black males face in a racist society, these and other studies (Moynihan, 1965; Bernard, 1966) have fostered a stereotype of Black families as fatherless and subject to a domineering woman's matriarchal rule. From such simplistic accounts it is all too easy to come to blame juvenile delinquency, divorce, illegitimacy, and other social ills on the Black family, while ignoring the oppressive reality of our political and economic system and the adaptive resiliency and strength that Black families have shown.

My analysis will draw on life-history material as well as on personal comments from women in The Flats, the poorest section of a Black community in the Midwestern city of Jackson Harbor.[1] I shall view women as strategists—active agents who use resources to achieve goals and cope with the problems of everyday life. This framework has several advantages. First, because the focus is on women rather than men, women's views of family relations, often ignored or slighted, are given prominence. Second, since households form around women because of their role in child care, ties between women (including paternal aunts, cousins, etc.) often constitute the core of a network; data from women's

[1] This work is based on a recent urban anthropological study of poverty and domestic life of urban-born Black Americans who were raised on public welfare and whose parents had migrated from the South to a single community in the urban North (Stack, 1972). Now adults in their twenties to forties, they are raising their own children on welfare in The Flats. All personal and place names in this paper are fictitious.

lives, then, crucially illuminate the continuity in these networks. Finally, the life-history material, taken chiefly from women, also demonstrates the positive role that a man plays in Black family life, both as the father of a woman's children and as a contributor of valuable resources to her network and to the network of his own kin.

I shall begin by analyzing the history of residential arrangements during one woman's life, and the residential arrangements of this woman's kin network at two points in time, demonstrating that although household composition changes, members are selected or self-selected largely from a single network that has continuity over time. Women and men, in response to joblessness, the possibility of welfare payments, the breakup of relationships, or the whims of a landlord, may move often. But the very calamities and crises that contribute to the constant shifts in residence tend to bring men, women, and children back into the households of close kin. Newly formed households are successive recombinations of the same domestic network of adults and children, quite often in the same dwellings. Residence histories, then, are an important reflection of the strategy of relying on and strengthening the domestic kin network, and also reveal the adaptiveness of households with "elastic boundaries." (It may be worth noting that middle-class whites are beginning to perceive certain values, for their own lives, in such households.)

In the remainder of the paper, the importance of maximizing network strength will be reemphasized and additional strategies will be isolated by examining two sets of relationships within kin networks—those between mothers and fathers and those between fathers and children. Women's own accounts of their situations show how they have developed a strong sense of independence from men, evolved social controls against the formation of conjugal relationships, and limited the role of the husband-father within the mother's domestic group. All of these strategies serve to strengthen the domestic network, often at the expense of any particular male-female tie. Kin regard any marriage as a risk to the woman and her children, and the loss of either male or female kin as a threat to the durability of the kin network. These two factors continually augment each other and dictate, as well, the range of socially accepted relationships between fathers and children.

Residence and the Domestic Network

In The Flats, the material and cultural support needed to sustain and socialize community members is provided by cooperating kinsmen. The individual can draw upon a broad domestic web of kin and friends—

some who reside together, others who do not. Residents in The Flats characterize household composition according to where people sleep, eat, and spend their time. Those who eat together may be considered part of a domestic unit. But an individual may eat in one household, sleep in another, contribute resources and services to yet another, and consider himself or herself a member of all three households. Children may fall asleep and remain through the night wherever the late-evening visiting patterns of the adult females take them, and they may remain in these households and share meals perhaps a week at a time. As R. T. Smith suggests in an article on Afro-American kinship (1970), it is sometimes difficult "to determine just which household a given individual belongs to at any particular moment." These facts of ghetto life are, of course, often disguised in the statistical reports of census takers, who record simply sleeping arrangements.

Households in The Flats, then, have shifting memberships, but they maintain for the most part a steady state of three generations of kin: males and females beyond child-bearing age; a middle generation of mothers raising their own children or children of close kin; and the children. This observation is supported in a recent study by Ladner (1971: 60), who writes, "Many children normally grow up in a three-generation household and they absorb the influences of a grandmother and grandfather as well as a mother and father." A survey of eighty-three residence changes among welfare families, whereby adult females who are heads of their own households merged households with other kin, shows that the majority of moves created three-generation households. Consequently, it is difficult to pinpoint structural beginning or end to household cycles in poor Black urban communities (Buchler and Selby, 1968; Fortes, 1958; Otterbein, 1970). But it is clear that authority patterns within a kin network change with birth and death; with the death of the oldest member in a household, the next generation assumes authority.

Residence changes themselves are brought on by many factors, most related to the economic conditions in which poor families live. Women who have children have access to welfare, and thus more economic security than women who do not, and more than all men. Welfare regulations encourage mothers to set up separate households, and women actively seek independence, privacy, and improvement in their lives. But these ventures do not last long. Life histories of adults show that the attempts by women to set up separate households with their children are short-lived: houses are condemned; landlords evict tenants; and needs for services among kin arise. Household composition also expands or contracts with the loss of a job, the death of a relative, the beginning or end of a sexual partnership, or the end of a friendship. But fluctuations in household composition rarely affect the exchanges and daily dependencies of participants. The following chronology of residence changes made by Ruby Banks graphically illuminates these points:

Age	Household composition and context of household formation
Birth	Ruby lived with her mother, Magnolia, and her maternal grandparents.
4	To be eligible for welfare, Ruby and Magnolia were required to move out of Ruby's grandparents' house. They moved into a separate residence two houses away, but ate all meals at the grandparents' house.
5	Ruby and Magnolia returned to the grandparents' house and Magnolia gave birth to a son. Magnolia worked and the grandmother cared for her children.
6	Ruby's maternal grandparents separated. Magnolia remained living with her father and her (now) two sons. Ruby and her grandmother moved up the street and lived with her maternal aunt Augusta and maternal uncle. Ruby's grandmother took care of Ruby and her brothers, and Magnolia worked and cooked and cleaned for her father.
7–16	The household was now composed of Ruby, her grandmother, her grandmother's new husband, Augusta and her boyfriend, and Ruby's maternal uncle. At age sixteen Ruby gave birth to a daughter.
17	Ruby's grandmother died and Ruby had a second child, by Otis, the younger brother of Ruby's best friend, Willa Mae. Ruby remained living with Augusta, Augusta's boyfriend, Ruby's maternal uncle, and her daughters.
18	Ruby fought with Augusta and she and Otis moved into an apartment with her two daughters. Ruby's first daughter's father died. Otis stayed with Ruby and her daughters in the apartment.
19	Ruby broke up with Otis. Ruby and her two daughters joined Magnolia, Magnolia's "husband," and her ten half-siblings. Ruby had a miscarriage.
19½	Ruby left town and moved out of state with her new boyfriend, Earl. She left her daughters with Magnolia and remained out of state for a year. Magnolia then insisted she return home and take care of her children.
20½	Ruby and her daughters moved into a large house rented by Augusta and her mother's brother. It was located next door to Magnolia's house, where Ruby and her children ate. Ruby cleaned for her aunt and uncle, and gave birth to another child, by Otis, who had returned to the household.

Age	Household composition and context of household formation
21	Ruby and Otis broke up once again. She found a house and moved there with her daughters, Augusta, and Augusta's boyfriend. Ruby did the cleaning, and Augusta cooked. Ruby and Magnolia, who now lived across town, shared child care, and Ruby's cousin's daughter stayed with Ruby.
21½	Augusta and her boyfriend have moved out because they were all fighting, and the two of them wanted to get away from the noise of the children. Ruby has a new boyfriend.

Ruby's residential changes, and the residences of her own children and kin, reveal that the same factors contributing to the high frequency of moving also bring men, women, and children back into the households of close kin. That one can repeatedly do so is a great source of security and dependence for those living in poverty.

A look in detail at the domestic network of Ruby's parents, Magnolia and Calvin Waters, illustrates the complexity of the typical network and also shows kin constructs at work both in the recruitment of individuals to the network and in the changing composition of households within the network, over less than three months:

Household	Domestic arrangements, April 1969	Domestic arrangements, June 1969
1	Magnolia, her husband Calvin, their eight children (4–18).	Unchanged.
2	Magnolia's sister Augusta, Augusta's boyfriend, Ruby, Ruby's children, Ruby's boyfriend Otis.	Augusta and boyfriend have moved to #3 after a quarrel with Ruby. Ruby and Otis remain in #2.
3	Billy (Augusta's closest friend), Billy's children, Lazar (Magnolia's sister Carrie's husband, living in the basement), Carrie (from time to time—she is an alcoholic).	Augusta and boyfriend have moved to a small, one-room apartment upstairs from Billy.
4	Magnolia's sister Lydia, Lydia's daughters Georgia and Lottie, Lydia's boyfriend, Lottie's daughter.	Lottie and her daughter have moved to an apartment down the street, joining Lottie's girl friend and child. Georgia has moved in with her boyfriend. Lydia's son has moved back into Lydia's home #4.
5	Ruby's friend Willa Mae, her husband and son, her sister, and her brother James (father of Ruby's daughter).	James has moved in with his girl friend, who lives with her sister; James keeps most of his clothes in household #5. James's brother has returned from the army and moved into #5.

Household	Domestic arrangements, April 1969	Domestic arrangements, June 1969
6	Eloise (Magnolia's first son's father's sister), her husband, their four young children, their daughter and her son, Eloise's friend Jessie's brother's daughter and her child.	Unchanged.
7	Violet (wife of Calvin's closest friend Cecil, now dead several years), her two sons, her daughter Odessa, and Odessa's four children.	Odessa's son Raymond has fathered Clover's baby. Clover and baby have joined household #7.

These examples do indeed indicate the important role of the Black woman in the domestic structure. But the cooperation between male and female siblings who share the same household or live near one another has been underestimated by those who have isolated the female-headed household as the most significant domestic unit among the urban Black poor. The close cooperation of adult siblings arises from the residential patterns typical of young adults (Stack, 1970). Owing to poverty, young women with or without children do not perceive any choice but to remain living at home with their mothers or other adult female relatives. Even when young women are collecting welfare for their children, they say that their resources go further when they share food and exchange goods and services daily. Likewise, the jobless man, or the man working at a part-time or seasonal job, often remains living at home with his mother—or, if she is dead, with his sisters and brothers. This pattern continues long after such a man becomes a father and establishes a series of sexual partnerships with women, who are in turn living with their own kin or friends or are alone with their children. A result of this pattern is the striking fact that households almost always have men around: male relatives, affines, and boyfriends. These men are often intermittent members of the households, boarders, or friends who come and go—men who usually eat, and sometimes sleep, in these households. Children have constant and close contact with these men, and especially in the case of male relatives, these relationships last over the years. The most predictable residential pattern in The Flats is that individuals reside in the households of their natal kin, or the households of those who raised them, long into their adult years.

Welfare workers, researchers, and landlords in Black ghetto communities have long known that the residence patterns of the poor change frequently and that females play a dominant domestic role.

What is much less understood is the relationship between household composition and domestic organization in these communities. Household boundaries are elastic, and no one model of a household, such as the nuclear family, extended family, or matrifocal family, is the norm. What is crucial and enduring is the strength of ties within a kin network; the maintenance of a strong network in turn has consequences for the relationships between the members themselves, as demonstrated in the following discussion of relationships between mothers and fathers and between fathers and their children.

Mothers and Fathers

Notwithstanding the emptiness and hopelessness of the job experience in the Black community, men and women fall in love and wager buoyant new relationships against the inexorable forces of poverty and racism. At the same time, in dealing with everyday life, Black women and men have developed a number of attitudes and strategies that appear to mitigate against the formation of long-term relationships. Even when a man and woman set up temporary housekeeping arrangements, they both maintain primary social ties with their kin. If other members of a kin network view a particular relationship as a drain on the network's resources, they will act in various and subtle ways to break up the relationship. This is what happened in the life of Julia Ambrose, another resident of The Flats.

When I first met Julia, she was living with her baby, her cousin Teresa, and Teresa's "old man." After several fierce battles with Teresa over the bills, and because of Teresa's hostility toward Julia's boyfriends, Julia decided to move out. She told me she was head over heels in love with Elliot, her child's father, and they had decided to live together.

For several months Julia and Elliot shared a small apartment, and their relationship was strong. Elliot was very proud of his baby. On weekends he would spend an entire day carrying the baby around to his sister's home, where he would show it to his friends on the street. Julia, exhilarated by her independence in having her own place, took great care of the house and her baby. She told me, "Before Elliot came home from work I would have his dinner fixed and the house and kid clean. When he came home he would take his shower and then I'd bring his food to the bed. I'd put the kid to sleep and then get into bed with him. It was fine. We would get in a little piece and then go to sleep. In the morning we'd do the same thing."

After five months, Elliot was laid off from his job at a factory that hires seasonal help. He couldn't find another job, except part-time work for a cab company. Elliot began spending more time away from the house with his friends at the local tavern, and less time with Julia and the baby. Julia finally had to get back "on aid" and Elliot put more of his things back in his sister's home so the social worker wouldn't know he was staying with Julia. Julia noticed changes in Elliot. "If you start necking and doing the same thing that you've been doing with your man, and he don't want it, you know for sure that he is messing with someone else, or don't want you anymore. Maybe Elliot didn't want me in the first place, but maybe he did 'cause he chased me a lot. He wanted me and he didn't want me. I really loved him, but I'm not in love with him now. My feelings just changed. I'm not in love with no man, really. Just out for what I can get from them."

Julia and Elliot stayed together, but she began to hear rumors about him. Her cousin, a woman who had often expressed jealousy toward Julia, followed Elliot in a car and told her that Elliot parked late at night outside the apartment house of his previous girl friend. Julia told me that her cousin was "nothing but a gossip, a newspaper who carried news back and forth," and that her cousin was envious of her having an "old man." Nevertheless, Julia believed the gossip.

After hearing other rumors and gossip about Elliot, Julia said, "I still really liked him, but I wasn't going to let him get the upper hand on me. After I found out that he was messing with someone else, I said to myself, I was doing it too, so what's the help in making a fuss. But after that, I made him pay for being with me!

"I was getting a check every month for rent from welfare and I would take the money and buy me clothes. I bought my own wardrobe and I gave my mother money for keeping the baby while I was working. I worked here and there while I was on aid and they were paying my rent. I didn't really need Elliot, but that was extra money for me. When he asked me what happened to my check I told him I got off and couldn't get back on. My mother knew. She didn't care what I did so long as I didn't let Elliot make an ass out of me. The point is a woman has to have her own pride. She can't let a man rule her. You can't let a man kick you in the tail and tell you what to do. Anytime I can make an ass out of a man, I'm going to do it. If he's doing the same to me, then I'll quit him and leave him alone."

After Elliot lost his job, and kin continued to bring gossip to Julia about how he was playing around with other women, Julia became embittered toward Elliot and was anxious to hurt him. There had been a young Black man making deliveries for a local store who would pass her house every day, and flirt with her. Charles would slow down his truck and honk for Julia when he passed the house. Soon she started running

out to talk to him in his truck and decided to "go" with him. Charles
liked Julia and brought nice things for her child.

"I put Elliot in a trick," Julia told me soon after she stopped going
with Charles. "I knew that Elliot didn't care nothing for me, so I made
him jealous. He was nice to the kids, both of them, but he didn't do
nothing to show me he was still in love with me. Me and Elliot fought
a lot. One night Charles and me went to a motel room and stayed there
all night. Mama had the babies. She got mad. But I was trying to hurt
Elliot. When I got home, me and Elliot got into it. He called me all
kinds of names. I said he might as well leave. But Elliot said he wasn't
going nowhere. So he stayed and we'd sleep together, but we didn't do
nothing. Then one night something happened. I got pregnant again by
Elliot. After I got pregnant, me and Charles quit, and I moved in with
a girl friend for a while. Elliot chased after me and we started going
back together, but we stayed separate. In my sixth month I moved
back in my mother's home with her husband and the kids."

Many young women like Julia feel strongly that they cannot let a
man make a fool out of them, and they react quickly and boldly to
rumor, gossip, and talk that hurts them. The power that gossip and
information have in constraining the duration of sexual relationships
is an important cultural phenomenon. But the most important single
factor affecting interpersonal relationships between men and women
in The Flats is unemployment. The futility of the job experience for
street-corner men in a Black community is sensitively portrayed by
Elliot Liebow in *Tally's Corner*. As Liebow (1967: 63) writes, "The job
fails the man and the man fails the job." Liebow's discussion (p. 142)
of men and jobs leads directly to his analysis of the street-corner male's
exploitive relationships with women: "Men not only present themselves as economic exploiters of women but they expect other men to
do the same." Ghetto-specific male roles that men try to live up to at
home and on the street, and their alleged round-the-clock involvement
in peer groups, are interpreted in *Soulside* (Hannerz, 1969) as a threat
to marital stability.

Losing a job, then, or being unemployed month after month debili-
tates one's self-importance and independence and, for men, necessitates
sacrificing a role in the economic support of their families. Faced with
these familiar patterns in the behavior and status of men, women call
upon life experiences in The Flats to guide them. When a man loses
his job, that is the time he is most likely to begin "messing around."

And so that no man appears to have made a fool of them, women
respond with vengeance, out of pride and self-defense. Another young
woman in The Flats, Ivy Rodgers, told me about the time she left her

two children in The Flats with her mother and took off for Indiana with Jimmy River, a young man she had fallen in love with "the first sight I seen." Jimmy asked Ivy to go to Gary, Indiana, where his family lived. "I just left the kids with my mama. I didn't even tell her I was going. My checks kept coming so she had food for the kids, but I didn't know he let his people tell him what to do. While he was in Gary, Jimmy started messing with another woman. He said he wasn't, but I caught him. I quit him, but when he told me he wasn't messing, I loved him so much I took him back. Then I got to thinking about it. I had slipped somewhere. I had let myself go. Seems like I forgot that I wasn't going to let Jimmy or any man make an ass out of me. But he sure was doing it. I told Jimmy that if he loved me, he would go and see my people, take them things, and tell them we were getting married. Jimmy didn't want to go back to The Flats, but I tricked him and told him I really wanted to visit. I picked out my ring and Jimmy paid thirty dollars on it and I had him buy my outfit that we was getting married in. He went along with it. What's so funny was when we come here and he said to me, 'You ready to go back?' and I told him, 'No, I'm not going back. I never will marry you.' "

Forms of social control in the larger society also work against successful marriages in The Flats. In fact, couples rarely chance marriage unless a man has a job; often the job is temporary, low-paying, and insecure, and the worker is arbitrarily laid off whenever he is not needed. Women come to realize that welfare benefits and ties within kin networks provide greater security for them and their children. In addition, caretaker agencies such as public welfare are insensitive to individual attempts for social mobility. A woman may be immediately cut off the welfare rolls when a husband returns home from prison or the army, or if she gets married. Unless there is either a significant change in employment opportunities for the urban poor or a livable guaranteed minimum income, it is unlikely that urban low-income Blacks will form lasting conjugal units.

Marriage and its accompanying expectations of a home, a job, and a family built around the husband and wife have come to stand for an individual's desire to break out of poverty. It implies the willingness of an individual to remove himself from the daily obligations of his kin network. People in The Flats recognize that one cannot simultaneously meet kin expectations and the expectations of a spouse. Cooperating kinsmen continually attempt to draw new people into their personal network; but at the same time they fear the loss of a central, resourceful member in the network. The following passages are taken from the detailed residence life history of Ruby Banks. Details of her story were substantiated by discussions with her mother, her aunt, her daughter's father, and her sister.

"Me and Otis could be married, but they all ruined that. Aunt Augusta told Magnolia that he was no good. Magnolia was the fault of it, too. They don't want to see me married! Magnolia knows that it be money getting away from her. I couldn't spend the time with her and the kids and be giving her the money that I do now. I'd have my husband to look after. I couldn't go where she want me to go. I couldn't come every time she call me, like if Calvin took sick or the kids took sick, or if she took sick. That's all the running I do now. I couldn't do that. You think a man would put up with as many times as I go over her house in a cab, giving half my money to her all the time? That's the reason they don't want me married. You think a man would let Aunt Augusta come into the house and take food out of the icebox from his kids? They thought that way ever since I came up.

"They broke me and Otis up. They kept telling me that he didn't want me, and that he didn't want the responsibility. I put him out and I cried all night long. And I really did love him. But Aunt Augusta and others kept fussing and arguing so I went and quit him. I would have got married a long time ago to my first baby's daddy, but Aunt Augusta was the cause of that, telling Magnolia that he was too old for me. She's been jealous of me since the day I was born.

"Three years after Otis I met Earl. Earl said he was going to help pay for the utilities. He was going to get me some curtains and pay on my couch. While Earl was working he was so good to me and my children that Magnolia and them started worrying all over again. They sure don't want me married. The same thing that happened to Otis happened to many of my boyfriends. And I ain't had that many men. I'm tired of them bothering me with their problems when I'm trying to solve my own problems. They tell me that Earl's doing this and that, seeing some girl.

"They look for trouble to tell me every single day. If I ever marry, I ain't listening to what nobody say. I just listen to what he say. You have to get along the best way you know how, and forget about your people. If I got married they would talk, like they are doing now, saying, 'He ain't no good, he's been creeping on you. I told you once not to marry him. You'll end up right back on aid.' If I ever get married, I'm leaving town!"

Ruby's account reveals the strong conflict between kin-based domestic units and lasting ties between husbands and wives. When a mother in The Flats has a relationship with an economically nonproductive man, the relationship saps the resources of others in her domestic network. Participants in the network act to break up such relationships, to maintain kin-based household groupings over the life cycle, in order to maximize potential resources and the services they hope to exchange. Similarly, a man's participation is expected in his kin network, and it is understood that he should not dissipate his services and finances to a sexual or marital relationship. These forms of social control made Ruby afraid to take the risks necessary to break out of the cycle of poverty. Instead, she chose the security and stability of her kin group. Ruby, recognizing that to make a marriage last she would have to move far away from her kin, exclaimed, "If I ever get married, I'm leaving town!" While this study was in progress, Ruby did get married, and she left the state with her husband and her youngest child that very evening.

Fathers and Children

People in The Flats show pride in all their kin, and particularly new babies born into their kinship networks. Mothers encourage sons to have babies, and even more important, men coax their "old ladies" to have their babies. The value placed on children, the love, attention, and affection children receive from women and men, and the web of social relationships spun from the birth of a child are all basic to the high birthrate among the poor.

The pride that kinsmen take in the children of their sons and brothers is seen best in the pleasure that the mothers and sisters of these men express. Such pride was apparent during a visit I made to Alberta Cox's home. She introduced me to her nineteen-year-old son Nate and added immediately, "He's a daddy and his baby is four months old." Then she pointed to her twenty-two-year-old son Mac and said, "He's a daddy three times over." Mac smiled and said, "I'm no daddy," and his friend in the kitchen said, "Maybe going on four times, Mac." Alberta said, "Yes you are. Admit it, boy!" At that point Mac's grandmother rolled back in her rocker and said, "I'm a grandmother many times over, and it make me proud." A friend of Alberta's told me later that Alberta wants her sons to have babies because she thinks it will make them more responsible. Although she usually dislikes the women her sons go with, claiming they are "no-good trash," Alberta accepts the babies and asks to care for them whenever she has a chance.

Although Blacks, like most Americans, acquire kin through their mothers and fathers, the economic insecurity of the Black male and the availability of welfare to the mother-child unit make it very difficult for an unemployed Black husband-father to compete with a woman's kin for authority and control over her children. As we have seen, women seek to be independent, but also, in order to meet everyday needs, they act to strengthen their ties with their kin and within their domestic network. Though these two strategies, especially in the context of male joblessness, may lead to the breakup of a young couple, a father will maintain his ties with his children. The husband-father role may be limited, but, contrary to the stereotype of Black family life, it is not only viable but culturally significant.

Very few young couples enter into a legal marriage in The Flats, but a father and his kin can sustain a continuing relationship with the father's children if the father has acknowledged paternity, if his kin have activated their claims on the child, and if the mother has drawn these people into her personal network. Widely popularized and highly misleading statistics on female-headed households have contributed to the assumption that Black children derive nothing of sociological importance from their fathers. To the contrary, in my recent study of domestic life among the poor in a Black community in the Midwest (Stack, 1972), I found that 70 percent of the fathers of 1,000 children on welfare recognized their children and provided them with kinship affiliations. But because many of these men have little or no access to steady and productive employment, out of the 699 who acknowledged paternity, only 84 (12 percent) gave any substantial financial support to their children. People in The Flats believe a father should help his child, but they know that the mother cannot count on his help. Community expectations of fathers do not generally include the father's *duties* in relation to a child; they do, however, assume the responsibilities of the father's kin. Kinship through males in The Flats is reckoned through a chain of acknowledged genitors, but social fatherhood is shared by the genitor with his kin, and with the mother's husband or with her boyfriends.

Although the authority of a father over his genealogical children or his wife's other children is limited, neither the father's interest in his child nor the desire of his kin to help raise the child strains the stability of the domestic network. Otis's kin were drawn into Ruby's personal network through his claims on her children, and through the long, close friendship between Ruby and Otis's sister, Willa Mae. Like many fathers in The Flats, Otis maintained close contact with his children, and provided goods and care for them even when he and Ruby were not on speaking terms. One time when Otis and Ruby separated, Otis stayed in a room in Ruby's uncle's house next door to Ruby's mother's house. At that time Ruby's children were being kept by Magnolia each day while Ruby went to school to finish working toward her high school diploma. Otis was out of work, and he stayed with Ruby's uncle over six months helping Magnolia care for his children. Otis's kin were proud of the daddy he was, and at times suggested they should take over the raising of Otis and Ruby's children. Ruby and other mothers know well that those people you count on to share in the care and nurturing of your children are also those who are rightfully in a position to judge and check upon how you carry out the duties of a mother. Shared responsibilities of motherhood in The Flats imply both a help and a check on how one assumes the parental role.

Fathers like Otis, dedicated to maintaining ties with their children, learn that the relationship they create with their child's mother largely determines the role they may assume in their child's life. Jealousy between men makes it extremely difficult for fathers to spend time with their children if the mother has a boyfriend, but as Otis said to me, "When Ruby doesn't have any old man then she starts calling on me, asking for help, and telling me to do something for my kids." Between such times, when a man or a woman does not have an ongoing sexual relationship, some mothers call upon the fathers of their children and temporarily "choke" these men with their personal needs and the needs of the children. At these times, men and women reinforce their fragile but continuing relationship, and find themselves empathetic friends who can be helpful to one another.

A mother generally regards her children's father as a friend of the family whom she can recruit for help, rather than as a father failing his parental duties. Although fathers voluntarily help out with their children, many fathers cannot be depended upon as a steady source of help. Claudia Williams talked to me about Harold, the father of her two children. "Some days he be coming over at night saying, 'I'll see to the babies and you can lay down and rest, honey,' treating me real nice. Then maybe I don't even see him for two or three months. There's no sense nagging Harold. I just treat him as some kind of friend even if he is the father of my babies." Since Claudia gave birth to Harold's children, both of them have been involved in other relationships. When either of them is involved with someone else, this effectively cuts Harold off from his children. Claudia says, "My kids don't need their daddy's help, but if he helps out then I help him out, too. My kids are well behaved, and I know they make Harold's kinfolk proud."

Conclusions

The view of Black women as represented in their own words and life histories coincides with that presented by Joyce Ladner: "One of the chief characteristics defining the Black woman is her [realistic approach] to her [own] resources. Instead of becoming resigned to her fate, she has always sought creative solutions to her problems. The ability to utilize her existing resources and yet maintain a forthright determination to struggle against the racist society in whatever overt and subtle ways necessary is one of her major attributes" (Ladner, 1971: 276–77).

I have particularly emphasized those strategies that women can employ to maximize their independence, acquire and maintain domestic authority, limit (but positively evaluate) the role of husband and father, and strengthen ties with kin. The last of these—maximizing relationships in the domestic network—helps to account for patterns of Black family life among the urban poor more adequately than the concepts of nuclear or matrifocal family. When economic resources are greatly limited, people need help from as many others as possible. This requires expanding their kin networks—increasing the number of people they hope to be able to count on. On the one hand, female members of a network may act to break up a relationship that has become a drain on their resources. On the other, a man is expected to contribute to his own kin network, and it is assumed that he should not dissipate his services and finances to a marital relationship. At the same time, a woman will continue to seek aid from the man who has fathered her children, thus building up her own network's resources. She also expects something of his kin, especially his mother and sisters. Women continually activate these lines to bring kin and friends into the network of exchange and obligation. Most often, the biological father's female relatives are also poor and also try to expand their network and increase the number of people they can depend on.

Clearly, economic pressures among cooperating kinsmen in the Black community work against the loss of either males or females—through marriage or other long-term relationships—from the kin network. The kin-based cooperative network represents the collective adaptations to poverty of the men, women, and children within the Black community. Loyalties and dependencies toward kinsmen offset the ordeal of unemployment and racism. To cope with the everyday demands of ghetto life, these networks have evolved patterns of co-residence; elastic household boundaries; lifelong, if intermittent, bonds to three-generation households; social constraints on the role of the husband-father within the mother's domestic group; and the domestic authority of women.

NANCY TANNER

Matrifocality in Indonesia and Africa and Among Black Americans

From time to time, at points scattered widely over the globe, ethnographers have encountered societies with kinship systems that cannot be comfortably summarized in terms of the usual categories of residence and descent. Not only is some quality that is distinctive to the particular culture reflected in the kinship system, but the women are more important in the system—and, indeed, in the society at large—than would have been anticipated. In fact, the women are more important than we tend to expect women to be in *any* kinship system.[1] Such systems have been termed "matricentric" or, more commonly, "matrifocal." More precisely, matrifocality is not itself a "kinship system" in the usual structural sense; it is, rather, an *attribute* of any of several kinship system types. But because this distinction is in many cases no more than semantic or technical, I shall often speak of "matrifocal kinship systems."

This essay explores (1) the nature of matrifocality and (2) the special social and cultural features that characterize societies in which it occurs. My approach is inductive and purposely avoids premature hypotheses— and for a reason: I assume Western cultural biases have profoundly affected kinship theory. It is almost impossible for this not to be so.

I would like to thank the people who gave me extensive and thoughtful comments and suggestions, as well as moral support, during the various stages of writing this paper. In addition to Michelle Rosaldo and Louise Lamphere, they include J. Herman Blake, Carolyn Clark, Marta J. Devins, Lloyd Fallers, Hildred Geertz, Richard Henderson, Diane K. Lewis, John Ogbu, Richard Randolph, James Siegel, and Sjamsir Sjarif. I would also like to acknowledge the generous support of the Ford Foundation, under Grant #739–0003–200, and of the Faculty Research Committee, University of California, Santa Cruz, for making this project possible.

[1] In a recent article, Raymond T. Smith aptly summarizes this state of affairs (1973: 129): "In all the reports of matrifocal family structure that I have cited there is the suggestion that it is somehow anomalous. It is rarely made clear whether the anomaly exists for the people being studied or for the investigator."

Kinship deals with intimate aspects of life and is based on cultural constructs that are very deep and rarely examined.

We come from a society that deals oddly with women, a society that categorizes women as a distinct (mostly lower) type of person. Consider the dualism that pervades American sex-role concepts—e.g. blue-pink, strong-weak, aggressive-passive, independent-dependent. Think also of our images of male and female within the family—the male instrumental (the provider, making decisions), the female nurturant; the man linked to the wider political and economic structure, the woman a "housewife." Then remember these are *our* dichotomies, not universals.

In contrast, many societies do not arbitrarily allot half of the whole range of human potentialities to women and half to men. There are societies where an angry woman can cut you with a knife or where a man can cry.[2] Personal characteristics are primary in some societies, rather than traits assigned by sex.[3]

In the present essay I discuss the Javanese, Atjehnese, and Minangkabau (all Indonesian groups), the Igbo of West Africa, and the Black Americans. My purpose here is not only to record what the ethnographers have noted and how it differs from middle-class Anglo-American expectations concerning the kin roles of women and men, but also to ascertain in what respects these societies are similar to each other. Although the kinship systems of these groups contrast along a number of dimensions, the roles of women in the kinship systems show important similarities. Moreover, these commonalities in women's kin roles appear to be related to similarities in their status in the societies at

[2] Among the Minangkabau, for example, men (in the context of an intimate discussion with a close friend or relative) refer unashamedly and unselfconsciously to instances when they have cried. In most situations overtly violent behavior is not valued for Minangkabau men *or* women. But the disapproval a woman encounters if she aggressively wields a long heavy cleaver (used for cracking open coconuts) is a generalized disapproval that any person would face in that society; there is no special horror or surprise because she is a woman.

[3] Among Black Americans personality attributes are highly individualized, not bimodally distributed by sex (Lewis, 1973). Boys and girls are socialized similarly (Young, 1970) and sex-role identity is primarily based on sexuality per se (Lewis, 1973). For Black adults sexuality remains an aspect of sex-role identity. Beyond and superseding sexuality per se, however, becoming a mother is perhaps the major distinguishing feature of Black *womanhood*: having a child signifies the transition from girlhood to womanhood; becoming a mother also marks off a woman from a man. The act of procreation itself demonstrates that a person is a woman, not whether or not one embodies a cluster of obscure "feminine" qualities such as those presented by the white advertising establishment (e.g. fragile, blonde, passive, scatterbrained, and perfumed). Black women, along with Black men, are active participants in the public economic realm. They are assertive and have strong self-concepts. But there is no danger anyone will think they are men; do men have babies?

large. Specifically, in each society the mother role is the central one within the domain of kinship, and women are relatively equal participants in the economic and ritual realms.

The fascinating quality shared by these societies is a relative egalitarianism between the sexes. In each case both women's and men's roles are significant and important. Within the kinship systems of these societies the mother's role is central, but the contributions of men are highly valued.

Since the term was first coined (Smith, 1956), numerous examples of societies having "matrifocal" kinship systems have been found. Doubtless there is much discussion ahead of us concerning the distinctive features of matrifocality.[4] Nonetheless, let me specify what I, at present, mean by the term. The term's literal meaning, "mother-focused," serves as my point of departure. Beyond that, and more precisely, I am concerned with two constructs: (1) *kinship systems* in which (a) the role of the mother is structurally, culturally, and affectively central and (b) this multidimensional centrality is legitimate; and (2) the *societies* in which these features coexist, where (a) the relationship between the sexes is relatively egalitarian and (b) both women and men are important actors in the economic and ritual spheres.[5]

By *structurally central* I mean that the mother has some degree of control over the kin unit's economic resources and is critically involved in kin-related decision-making processes. The structural component of

[4] Once we look seriously at women's kin roles, we are embarrassed to find how often they are significant and how frequently this has been overlooked. As we begin to investigate women's roles in earnest, we shall find that in *all* societies they are more interesting and important than previously assumed (as articles in this book attest). The question of how to distinguish societies with matrifocal kinship systems from other societies in which women's kin roles are also important will become increasingly problematic. That question cannot yet be answered definitively. Conceivably it is not terribly important—it may prove more interesting to explore in which respects and to what extent kinship systems are matrifocal than to argue about whether a particular one is or is not matrifocal.

[5] The extent of women's political participation is left for future investigation. From a conceptual standpoint, this is an important issue, but it cannot be resolved without painstaking historical reconstruction. (For two recent attempts, both concerning West African societies, see Hoffer, this volume, and Richard Henderson's discussion of Onitsha Ibo queens and their female counselors, 1972: 309–14; see also Lebeuf, 1963.) The investigation of female political roles in most non-Western societies is complicated by the fact that the beginnings of data accumulation on such societies coincided with the onset of Western colonial expansion. This expansion was carried out by Western males who assumed it was "natural" for them to deal with other males in trade, warfare, or negotiations. A pervasive male bias was thereby built into the historical documentation of the contact period; and there was a male-skewed impact on the political structures of the peoples themselves.

matrifocality relates to economic and political power within the kin group. *Cultural centrality*, by contrast, derives from questions of *valuation*. The basic questions here are: (1) What is the image of "mother"? Is it a role that is culturally elaborated and valued? And, specifically, what is the cultural content of the role itself? (2) Are girls socialized for such a future role? Do they grow up with images of the self appropriate to an active, decisive, strong, central kin role? (3) Is the centrality of the mother's role legitimate for the society in question?

The mother occupies an emotionally central position in far more societies than those in which her role is culturally and structurally central. With regard to questions of affect (of the emotional linkages to the mother), I am concerned with kinship systems in which this affect is culturally valued and patterned, and particularly with those where it is utilized as the appropriate motivating force for culturally and structurally defined matrifocality. Anglo-American "momism" does not qualify.

The contrast between Anglo-American "momism" and the role of the mother in the matrifocal kinship systems we are about to examine is instructive. Among middle-class whites, women create affectively central roles for themselves within the household as a counterbalance to their economic and emotional dependence on their husbands; women can gain considerable power over their offspring, but this must be seen in the context of their powerlessness in the wider society. The questionable legitimacy of this emotionally based maternal power is evident in the fact that an adult is conceptualized as one who has "cut the apron strings." "Momism" and matrifocality contrast in almost every possible way. "Momism" flows from extreme sex-role dichotomization,[6] is affectively based, and is of dubious legitimacy. Matrifocality is based on minimal differentiation between the sexes, is a matter of both cultural and structural centrality, and is normal and expected for the societies in which it occurs.

Matrifocality is found within a variety of kinship types. A bilateral, patrilineal, matrilineal, or other type of kinship system may or may not be matrifocal. Descent and matrifocality vary independently. Furthermore, there is no one-to-one correlation between the usual designation used to describe residence rules (e.g. patrilocal, matrilocal, neolocal, etc.) and matrifocality. The societies discussed below differ with respect to the *structural level* that is matrifocal—for the patrilineal Igbo

---

[6] For further elaboration of this concept as it applies to whites, as well as for a discussion of distinctive Black American cultural conceptualizations and how they relate to sex roles, see Lewis (1973).

it is the elemental family, for the Minangkabau it is the matrilineally extended household.

Similarly, matrifocality can occur in a wide range of social and economic contexts. Whether the society or ethnic group in question is generally in comfortable circumstances or poverty-stricken, powerful or powerless, is not the issue. Rather, I am interested in those groups where the culturally defined role of "mother" (not always the genealogical mother, but sometimes the senior woman of a kinship unit, e.g. a MoMo or MoOSi or MoMoSi) is a powerful, economically significant, and culturally central one within the kinship group.

Matrifocality is not to be defined in negative terms. It is not, for example, characterized by the absence of, say, the husband/father, for he may be physically present and/or have a well-defined and culturally significant role, and the kin unit may nonetheless be matrifocal.[7] In a matrifocal kin unit—whether an elemental mother-child unit, the nuclear family, or a large unit such as the extended family—the role of the mother is ideologically and structurally central.[8]

[7] Matrifocality is a more inclusive concept than either "consanguineal household" (Gonzalez, 1969) or "female-headed household" (a U.S. census category), two terms that are sometimes confused with "matrifocal family." Consanguineal households (lit., households made up of "blood kin," but generally related through the mother in Gonzalez's usage) and female-headed households (which for the U.S. census merely means households without a resident husband/father) are likely to be focused around the mother. However, matrifocality is by no means limited to these types of households, but also occurs in contexts where the husband/father and/or kin related through the father are present. Furthermore, whereas the "female-headed" household, the mother-child household, or the "consanguineal" household is defined in terms of household composition, matrifocality relates to both cultural emphasis and structural centrality. Matrifocality is far more than a residence category; it is a feature that pervades multiple dimensions of the kinship system.

[8] When matrifocality is defined in terms of the *role of the mother* rather than the presence or absence of various types of male roles, much of the controversy of the past 15 years can be seen in proper perspective. I *identify* matrifocal kinship systems by examining mother roles; if the mother role is culturally and structurally central, the kinship system is matrifocal. We can then go on to discriminate *subtypes* among matrifocal kinship systems by examining the total constellation of female-male kinship roles.

In this context Randolph's (1964) correction to Kunstadter (1963) becomes significant. Kunstadter based his work on the presumption that the absence of a husband/father is a defining characteristic of the matrifocal family. He then went on to compare the matrilineal Nayar of India with several bilateral societies—e.g. various Black American (mostly Caribbean) groups and the Mescalero Apache. For none of these groups does he provide sufficient information to determine whether they have matrifocal kinship systems under the criteria I suggest. The Nayar, for example, may or may not be matrifocal. If we go beyond Kunstadter to look at the literature on the Nayar, we find it tells us a great deal about their form of ritual marriage, the controversy over whether they have nuclear families or not, the role of the mother's brother, the functioning of their matrilineages, and the caste role of Nayar men. The

To illustrate these points I shall describe the matrifocal emphasis in the kinship systems of three Indonesian ethnic groups—the Javanese, Atjehnese, and Minangkabau—and one African group, the Igbo. This cross-cultural perspective will then be brought to bear on Black America. I shall discuss the negative view of matrifocality found in many Anglo-American writings about Black Americans and show that this can be understood as a product of Anglo-American attitudes concerning women's roles and family structure, as well as of Anglo-American racial ethnocentrism.

Most of the American literature on matrifocality concerns Black Americans. Much of it was written from a "social pathology" perspective or, at the very least, with a sense of Black Americans being "different" from the Anglo-American "mainstream." It is difficult for members of a dominant portion of society to write objectively concerning the culture and social structure of members of a subjugated segment of that same society. Difficulties are compounded for intimate value-laden topics such as the family. When values differ, the whole question of the nature of matrifocality becomes obfuscated by speculations concerning why it should exist at all.

In order to approach the question of the nature of matrifocality, we need a fresh perspective. We must attempt to develop the concept by examining societies further afield, societies for which we have no ready stereotypes.

Java

The Javanese homeland is east and central Java, Indonesia. The Javanese are the nation's most populous ethnic group; their members are found at every level of political and economic life. Neither the basic structure of their kinship system nor its underlying values differ significantly with class, although there are some minor variations. At all levels the system, like that of Anglo-Americans, is bilateral and the

Nayar may or may not be matrifocal in the sense I propose; we simply do not have enough information on the mother's role to decide. Randolph's critique points out that within the limits of Kunstadter's approach (i.e. attempting to identify matrifocality by looking at what men do or do not do) he has omitted an important consideration: Kunstadter discusses the absence of the husband/father but not the presence of the retired brother of the Nayar mother. Just as the mother's brother is important, so too may the father's brother play an important role in some kinship systems (see the discussion of the patrilineal Igbo, below). This again relates to differentiating the particular type of matrifocal kinship system, *not* to determining whether or not a system is matrifocal.

Investigating male roles can never tell us whether a kinship system is matrifocal; but for systems that we know to be matrifocal because of the nature of the mother's role, it is possible to differentiate subtypes according to how other roles (male and female) relate to the mother role.

nuclear family is the most important unit. Residence is neolocal after the family is established; for the first year or so the young couple may live with whichever set of parents has room.

Rural families depend on wet-rice (*sawah*) agriculture; urban families are primarily involved in small-scale entrepreneurship and in white-collar work; some are laborers. Javanese predominate in the political elite and in the army, and dominate the Indonesian bureaucracy. Most national enterprises (e.g. Dutch colonial businesses nationalized after independence) are managed by Javanese.[9]

Hildred Geertz, studying the family in a central Javanese town of about 20,000 during the early 1950's, found that it was not sufficient to describe the Javanese kinship system as bilateral and nucleating. Such a description, although accurate as far as it goes, would have omitted one of the most interesting features of the system, its matrifocal emphasis in the areas of dominance and solidarity. In other words, the special characteristics of the Javanese kinship system demanded conceptualization.

The manner in which Geertz utilizes the concept of matrifocality to illuminate and organize her Javanese data is suggestive of how we might further elaborate the concept itself (1961: 78–79):

There are two spheres of [Javanese] kinship to which the term matrifocal might be applied. The first is within the nuclear family. . . . The second is the kindred . . . For the nuclear family to be matrifocal means that the woman has more authority, influence and responsibility than her husband, and at the same time receives more affection and loyalty. The concentration of both of these features on the female role leaves the male role relatively functionless in regard to the internal affairs of the nuclear family. In such circumstances it is unimportant whether or not the male role in the family is actually filled, or whether or not it is always occupied by the same man. For the kindred to be matrifocal means that the persons of greatest influence are women, and that the relationships of greatest solidarity are those between women or between persons related through women. Correspondingly, the relationships with the least amount of influence and solidarity are those between men or persons related through men.

Note that both cultural/structural qualities (authority, influence, responsibilities, solidarity) and matters of affect (affection, loyalty) are discussed. When all of these features are centered in the mother role, the role of husband/father is somewhat peripheral to the effective functioning of the system.

A number of factors contribute to Javanese matrifocality: the relative equality of women and men in general societal role systems, an empha-

[9] The larger domestic enterprises are in the hands of immigrant Chinese, Indians, and Arabs, and occasionally of members of other Indonesian ethnic groups. A number of foreign enterprises (Japanese, American, and others) exist as well.

sis on the mother-child bond, and the specifically Javanese personality
make-up (H. Geertz, 1961: 80, 81).

Javanese men and women are relatively equal participants in the
society at large. Neither sex is confined to the household; both engage
in earning money, can have prestige, and can participate both as ordinary followers and as important functionaries in religious and political
activities. Most occupations are open to women—including agricultural
work, trade, and civil service jobs such as teaching. Indeed women dominate the small-scale agricultural trade in the indigenous markets (Dewey, 1962: 117). Even upper-class women may be traders; for example
they often sell expensive batiks.

Women are also very much involved in ceremonial life, e.g. in weddings, circumcisions, birth. Much of the work necessary for these celebrations is done by the kinswomen of the woman holding the ceremony. Rituals are also a context in which the mother's role is high-
lighted. As part of the wedding ceremony, for instance, the bride's
mother offers a sip of water from a dipper to the bride and groom; a
shawl (used to cradle babies) is also circled around the mother of the
bride, the bride, and her new husband in this same ceremony. The
first wedding is an elaborate affair; one of its functions is the celebration of a girl's formal entry into adulthood. A number of ritual activities and prohibitions also center around pregnancy, birth, and the post-
partum period. Ritual meals (selamatan) are often given during pregnancy to ward off evil spirits. A ritual meal for the baby is given on the
day of the birth; the new mother's participation is essential, for it is she
who receives the guests. After birth the midwife bathes and massages
the mother and her baby and uses her mystical knowledge to ensure
their health.

Divorce is readily available, and mothers with children can and do
live alone; the occupational structure makes it possible for single women
to earn a living. It is also quite common for divorced women to live with
their parents; in contrast, "a divorced or widowed man is loath to return to his parental home, and usually seeks another wife quite quickly"
(H. Geertz, 1961: 46). Despite a high turnover (about 50 percent of marriages end in divorce), at any one moment most adults are married.

The mother-child bond is strong and persistent.[10] Until about five,

[10] During the nursing period the child is usually fed on demand; the baby is carried in a shawl and is with the mother constantly the first few months. Older babies
whose mothers are traders may be fed more or less according to a schedule, with the
person caring for the baby bringing it to the market to be nursed. Weaning is relatively late, usually after the child can walk.

the youngster is often also quite close to its father, but after that the child must stay respectfully away from him and speak circumspectly and softly; the closeness has been replaced by formality. "The relationship with the mother remains as strong and secure as before—and lasts throughout the individual's life. . . . The mother is seen as a bulwark of strength and love to whom one can always turn" (H. Geertz, 1961: 107). Mothers may divorce and remarry several times; children remain with their mothers. Although this is not a sufficient condition of matrifocality, a strong mother-child bond is obviously a necessary component of it.

The "Javanese personality make-up" is not discussed in detail, but the data indicate that a constellation of features is involved: the recurrent interpersonal tensions between Javanese husbands and wives, which lead to frequent divorce, are probably culturally patterned; the Javanese are socialized into patterns of formality and semiavoidance between brothers and between fathers and sons; and positive affect and practical interdependence among female kin and kin linked by females are encouraged.

These three points—relatively egalitarian participation of females and males in non-kin aspects of society, a cultural emphasis on the mother-child tie, and a cultural patterning of affect and of interpersonal relations that promotes kin ties to and through women—may well prove to be basic prerequisites of matrifocality.

Atjeh

At the northern tip of Sumatra another Indonesian ethnic group exhibits similar patterns. The Atjehnese, like the Javanese, have a bilateral kinship system. However, residence is uxorilocal and matrilocal. Husbands move to the households and villages of their wives. There may be more than one house per house yard; all are owned by women related through women. As in Java the nuclear family is the basic unit, but because of residential contiguity, the extended family (through the female line) takes on greater importance. Structurally, the Atjehnese kinship system is intermediate between the Javanese and the Minangkabau.

We are fortunate in having data from the early colonial period (Snouck-Hurgronje, 1906). This historical information, predating the economic impact of Dutch colonialism on Atjeh, indicates that Atjehnese kinship structure has remained essentially the same for at least 70 years. Siegel (1969: 51–55, 145) summarizes the Atjehnese family system as follows:

Atjehnese children are born in the house of their mother. The idiomatic expression for wife is, in fact, "the one who owns the house." Girls grow up in their mother's house and remain there or nearby for the rest of their lives. . . . A typical village consists of clusters of houses owned by sisters and . . . mother's sisters, with the compounds often sharing a well and a fence. After marriage, men had [financial] obligations both to their wives and to their wives' parents; . . . although men tried to create a role as husbands and, especially, as fathers, women thought of them as essentially superfluous. They allowed men no part in raising children and tolerated them only so long as they paid their own way and contributed money for goods that a woman could not obtain through her own resources. Most resources [except houses], however, are owned by men. . . . [But] regardless of ownership of land, control of it is given to women, and this underlies their expectations that men properly should not provide rice, which the women can obtain themselves, but money. . . . Thus (in the past) most men had to leave the rice-growing areas for the pepper regions in order to fulfill their duties as husbands. [And today men also spend little time in the village; they are often involved in urban trade.] . . . Women get houses and sometimes rice land at marriage, or shortly thereafter, whereas men are usually without resources in the village until their parents die or until they earn enough through trade to buy rice land. . . . It is not, however, only young or poor men who are powerless in their families. Even wealthy men have little ability to make decisions involving their wives.

Why even wealthy, successful Atjehnese men should be peripheral to the nuclear families in which they are husbands and fathers was a question that puzzled Siegel—and well it might, for such a situation runs counter to our own ethnocentric assumptions. Yet the peripheral quality of men's relationships to the families they enter into at marriage should not be misconstrued; as husbands and fathers they are peripheral, but not functionless or unimportant. At the very least, a woman views her husband as a financial resource. Men, who have ways to earn money outside the village subsistence economy, can provide cash that women value as a useful supplement to their own resources (houses, rice). That Atjehnese women look with disfavor on husbands who do not contribute financially to the household economy should not surprise us: to a woman with children, a resident nonproductive male would be a clear liability.

Sawah, or wet-rice agriculture, forms the subsistence base of Atjehnese villages. As Clifford Geertz has emphasized with regard to Java (1963), irrigated rice agriculture as practiced in Indonesia is one of the most labor-intensive techniques in the world. Atjehnese *sawah* techniques are not as labor-intensive as the Javanese wet-rice cultivation Geertz describes; nonetheless a constant input of labor is required. Most of this agricultural labor is carried out by the women; men work sporadically, contributing to the preparation of the fields (by clearing land, building irrigation systems, plowing) and at harvest time. But the women's involvement in *sawah* agriculture is continuous. The subsistence economy depends on them, and by and large, they control its produce.

The cash needs of the villagers are largely met by men's earnings in the *rantau* (migration areas). Men control their earnings while in the *rantau* and pay for their own livelihood when living away from the village; on their return they are expected to turn over a portion of their earnings to their wives, who handle the household economy and provide for the husbands while they are in the village.

Atjehnese matrifocality and the peripheral role of the husband/father are, in part, a result of the residential and economic facts. The women stay in the village, control the subsistence economy, and manage their households. Children observe that it is their mothers who feed them, instruct them, and indulge them. They see their mothers as responsible and important figures who work hard, are respected in the village at large, and take care of most family affairs. Mothers' kinfolk are nearby; but father's relatives are farther away. Fathers are simply not present very much, and when they are, they may not be actively involved in the important and necessary affairs of daily life. (The men most regularly return to the village for a holiday and rest during the Islamic fasting month and the subsequent festivities.)

Structurally, the tie between a mother and her child persists, while the marital link is readily broken. For the village Siegel lived in, 39 percent of marriages ended in divorce. (For the district as a whole, the rate was even higher, 50 percent.) Fourteen of the 22 divorce cases in the village studied involved conflicts over money, and in each instance it was the woman who instigated the action leading to divorce. Siegel summarizes women's attitudes (1969: 117):

> They feel that their husbands' contributions entitle them to be fed and deferred to while they pay for it, but when the money is gone, they should go too. They do not feel that men are entitled to share in the larger decisions of the family.
>
> From the women's point of view the family consists of the people who occupy the house compound—themselves, their sisters, mothers, and children. Their husbands have no place, and hence no right to make decisions.

Husbands are treated as guests, but as Siegel so aptly points out, guests can outstay their welcome (p. 179). When husbands do not succeed in the *rantau*, they do sometimes stay in the village. It is not always a happy solution. For example, in a fight between one such husband and his wife—a fight engendered by the husband's interference with his wife's domain—she kicked him, tried to stab him, and slashed at him with a cleaver as well as reportedly exclaimed, "What do I need you for?" (p. 168). During the fight the husband hit his wife. Subsequently she moved his mattress out of the bedroom, and whenever she recalled that he hit her, she would slap him or rip his shirt. Of such incidents Siegel says, "He stands there and takes it" (p. 168). Although Siegel acknowledges that neighbors may have exaggerated details of the quarrel, he points out that this is the sort of "situation villagers imagine a man confronts if he does not provide what his wife wants" (p. 169).

Atjehnese men have played significant economic and political roles both with regard to Atjehnese society and also in the broader Indonesian context, during the colonial period as well as since independence. In the nineteenth century the men of the village Siegel studied worked in the pepper gardens on the east coast of Atjeh (i.e. in northeastern Sumatra). These gardens, managed by Atjehnese *uleebelang* (who were both political figures and pepper entrepreneurs), provided pepper for world markets. Today many Atjehnese village men have small firms in Medan, Sumatra's largest city, also on the east coast. In general, then, most Atjehnese men are successful enough to contribute to their families. They are nonetheless only minimally involved in family decision making; they do not control the family purse strings, nor are they active participants in child rearing. These functions are centered on the women.

Siegel was concerned with trying to understand male kinship marginality. Since economic factors were insufficient to explain the phenomena, he looked for—and found—convincing cultural reasons for the peripheral kin role of the husband/father. His cultural argument is based on the Atjehnese male's understanding of how the Islamic concepts of *hawa nafsu* (instinctive nature) and *akal* (rationality) relate to a series of dichotomies: boy-man; mother-son; wife-husband; village–migration area; indulgence–self-denial. The young boy lives in his mother's home in the village, is indulged, and spends his time in play. By and large, instinctive nature characterizes this part of his life, although as he begins religious instruction, an activity that takes place outside the home, he also begins to learn rationality. The adult man spends most of his time in the migration area. In his life away from the village he must consistently exercise rationality in his business dealings. Men feel that living and working in the migration area requires considerable self-denial.

What then happens when men go home? A man no longer resides in his mother's house, but rather returns to the home of his wife, bringing money earned away from the village. In her home he is indulged, rather as his mother indulged him as a child. This a man accepts as his due, for he has worked hard and been away a long time. His wife, on the other hand, finds the extra work onerous. Although her husband regards himself as a rational, self-denying adult because of his activities away from the village, a woman notes that in the village he does little, and adds to her own responsibilities. Whereas most of the year she must work in the fields and care for her children, when he is home she not only continues with her usual work but also must care for him as well.

For men, returning home for an extended period is likely to produce a conflict in their image of themselves as adults with rationality. At home they can satisfy instinctive nature both sexually and by being cared for and indulged. But this places them in a relatively childish position vis-à-vis their wives. It is in this context that Siegel understands husbands' lack of authority in their wives' homes.

His cultural argument explains male kin marginality but does not delineate the cultural foundation for female centrality. Nonetheless, although Siegel does not focus on or analyze the cultural basis *for* matrifocality in the Atjehnese kinship system, he provides tantalizing clues that such a cultural basis does indeed exist. In a chapter entitled "Men and Boys in Atjehnese Families," he describes a complex series of rituals that characterize a woman's first pregnancy and birth.[11]

The rituals prior to birth serve to announce the pregnancy; not surprisingly the prime actors are the mothers of the bride and groom. During the rituals and the birth the attending specialists—the midwife and the specialist in Islamic and customary lore—are women. Although

[11] Subsequent odd-numbered pregnancies had the same set; the rituals were abbreviated for even-numbered pregnancies. The rituals begin in the fifth month, when a female Islamic and customary lore specialist (*teungku ineong*) performs a ritual "in which the husband and wife are 'cooled off'" (Siegel, 1969: 156). As part of the ritual, the mother of the pregnant woman brings glutinous rice cakes to the mother of the groom; she also presents the groom or his mother with a gift of money. In the sixth month the groom's mother returns the call, taking rice to the bride's mother and, after a few days, rice cakes to the bride. Then, in the seventh month, the groom's mother brings rice, spices, a new sarong, soap, and dusting powder to the bride. On this visit she is accompanied by a lore specialist from her village to bathe the bride. Also in the seventh month a lore specialist performs an important ritual during which she makes a special salad from unripe fruit. The lore specialist inspects each piece of fruit and lights incense as an invitation for souls of dead family members and important spirits to come and eat; then the women eat some of the fruit and the rest is given to whatever men and boys are around. A female midwife, who not only is a medical specialist but also has been visited by a female spirit named Nek Rabi, supervises the birth. After birth the mother is "baked" on a platform over hot bricks for 44 days. For the first seven days she is frequently rubbed with coconut oil. Her activities and, after the first week, her diet are severely restricted. At the end of this period there is another ceremony, *putran aneuk*, or "bringing down the child" from the house.

both the bride and groom receive presents during pregnancy, the focus is on the "bride." During much of the pregnancy, the bride is given a great deal of solicitous care. She then enters a period of rigorous self-denial, said to result in a healthy, trim body and the strength to care for her child. In view of the importance of the ideas of self-denial and indulgence for men, it is interesting to ask whether similar themes may not also be significant to the ways in which women conceptualize their experience.

Clearly birth is a tremendously significant occasion in the life of Atjehnese women. It is a transforming event for the young mother and is preceded and followed by an extended ritual sequence in which older women are the prime movers and the specialists. Significantly, married women are "brides" before the birth of their first child; then they are "mothers." The role of mother supersedes and has more cultural weight than that of wife. Becoming a mother is a culturally emphasized role transformation with practical consequences, for at that time a woman becomes an adult and gets legal possession of her house.

The rituals of pregnancy, birth, and the post-partum period stem largely from the indigenous pre-Islamic cultural tradition (adat). In addition, a cultural rationale and legitimization for female centrality in the Atjehnese kinship system might conceivably be found in the Atjehnese interpretation of Islam.[12] In this regard it is interesting to note that husbands and fathers do not figure in women's image of the hereafter. Women conceive of paradise as a place of abundance where they are reunited with their children and mothers.

In rural Atjeh, like Java, women have important economic roles and are in even more frequent contact with their kinswomen. Most decisions within the family appear to be made by mothers, and the mother-child tie is very strong. The role of mother is culturally emphasized, with the first birth marking a critical transition for women.

Minangkabau

The particular form that matriliny takes among the Minangkabau (an Indonesian ethnic group whose home area is the highlands of west

---

[12] The cultural support of Atjehnese matrifocality, however, probably stems largely from basic and ancient Atjehnese cultural assumptions concerning the nature of women and men and from their conceptions of what family life is like, and is transmitted to children during the socialization process. Explicit statements of such deep assumptions are rare, but sayings, homilies, proverbs, and allusions are likely sources of data. Hopefully future research on Atjeh will investigate such matters. The adat ritual complex surrounding birth provides a strong indication that a search for further cultural underpinnings for Atjehnese matrifocality will prove fruitful.

Sumatra)[13] involves a patterning of sex role differentiation and associated attitudes and values such that the woman, as mother, is focal in terms both of affect and of effective power within the minor lineage, the matrilineally extended family, and the nuclear family.

The Minangkabau social system is highly centrifugal, sending its members (especially but not exclusively men) to other areas of Indonesia. Minangkabau men *marantau*, or "go out," for trade or education; this tradition has been intensified by urbanization.

They are entrepreneurs par excellence, and have made contributions to Indonesian national life in fields as diverse as literature, politics, religion, business, and education far in excess of their small numbers. On the national scene the Minangkabau, as an ethnic group, are heavily represented in the emergent urban middle class. In all these respects the similarities between the Minangkabau and Igbo are striking (see below, on the Igbo; also Ottenberg, 1959).

Structural features of Minangkabau matrifocality include women's important economic roles, women's extensive participation in decision making, and a residential pattern that enhances ties among kinswomen. Kinswomen form the permanent co-resident structural core of Minangkabau kin groups. This structural solidarity places women in a strong position vis-à-vis men, whose kin positions (both as lineage males and as in-married males) are more peripheral. In most Minangkabau homes in west Sumatra, urban as well as rural, there are more adult females residing in the household than adult males. In one household, for example, there was a great-grandmother (MoMoMo), a grandmother (MoMo), a mother, two married daughters, one in-married male (DaHsb), an unmarried daughter, and two daughters' children. A man may have more than one wife; if so he commutes between his wives' households. Divorce and separation are frequent.

Notwithstanding the initial fragility of the marital bond, or the fact that for many Minangkabau the strongest cross-sex ties are those of mother-son and sister-brother, deeply affectionate relations can and do develop between women and their husbands and between children and their fathers. There are many types of satisfying human relationships available. Ties among consanguineal kin are more important among the Minangkabau, as among the other societies discussed here, than among Anglo-Americans; perhaps this fact has so impressed some observers that they have failed to note the intimate and lasting ties that can occur between marital partners or between partners in consensual unions.

[13] I did anthropological research among the Minangkabau from 1963 to 1966 and during the fall of 1972; see Tanner (1969, 1970, 1972).

Among the Minangkabau the early years of any marriage tend to be unstable; most marry more than once. But genuine fondness, mutual respect, and interdependency can be observed in many marriages that have persisted over the years.

Minangkabau women, like Atjehnese women, do much of the agricultural labor. In addition, many are involved in home industries (weaving cloth, mats, and purses; embroidering, etc.). Many sell agricultural goods in the tiny village markets (eggs, tomatoes, onions, chili peppers, etc.) to earn small sums for their daily needs. Some sell agricultural and craft products in the larger urban markets; there is a market cycle in the highlands and women traders may make a weekly circuit of the major markets, traveling by bus, with their goods piled on the bus top. A few women have shops in town. As in Java, women also work in civil service jobs as clerks, teachers, judges, etc. There are female Islamic teachers and women who are politically active.

The ideology of kin decision making among the Minangkabau is one of communal deliberation and consensus. In fact, however, mothers make most of the day-to-day decisions; sometimes they consult informally with other family members, sometimes not. These decisions involve land use, household management and expenditures, the education of children, lending and borrowing, and sale of handicrafts or agricultural produce. Decisions concerning ceremonies (a wedding, for example) or matters involving the lineage as a whole are made in the context of formal consultations in the lineage house; the senior women invite the lineage males (and sometimes husbands, depending on the topic) to attend these consultations. They sit on the floor and discuss the matter in a relatively formal manner. One of the young women usually serves the men coffee and a snack; the senior woman or women generally sit informally on the floor a bit apart from the men, perhaps leaning against a wall near the door to the kitchen. She listens to the discussion; if it does not go as she wishes she interjects her opinion. When she feels the need to comment, she does not stand on formality. Her opinion and its reasons are stated briefly and succinctly. The men then discuss her suggestion at length. Her position often prevails. In addition to the respect the men have for her views, she also controls the rice necessary for any ceremony.

The lineage as a whole is brought into play in the selection of lineage headmen (here again the decision-making scenario portrayed above is played out). Although many headmen are elderly men, it is not uncommon for a prominent woman to promote her son as a candidate for lineage headman.

Women are the central actors *within* Minangkabau kin groups, particularly within the minimal family unit and the matrilineally extended family (*sarumah*, "one house"). The minimal family unit (*sapariuek nasi*, "one rice pot") may consist of mother and children; mother, father, and children; or one of these units plus daughters' children and sometimes a daughter's husband as well. This unit is basically an economic one. It is usually a smaller unit than the household, although sometimes a large household (a matrilineally extended family) pools its economic resources. Women not only do most of the daily work and make most day-to-day decisions with regard to their *sapariuek nasi*, but initiate the broader communal consultations within the minor or major lineage, provide the setting for that consultation (space and refreshments), and keep track of and directly influence the course of the consultation itself.

Male lineage members represent the kin group to the outside and contribute to it materially. The two major features of the male role in Minangkabau are those of (1) economic resource and (2) ritual, political, and legal representation. These dual features were once largely united in the role of the mother's brother, but today they are increasingly split between the role of mother's brother (representation) and that of husband/father (economic contribution).

Minangkabau matriliny is based not only on the structurally focal position of the Minangkabau mother described above but also on a wide range of cultural beliefs. The mother is considered a source of wisdom. In contrast to the situation described by Siegel for Atjeh, the Minangkabau mother can give advice as well as indulgence to her son. Bundo Kandueng, literally "Own Mother," is the mythical queen mother of Minangkabau. Her importance is celebrated in women's ceremonial dress, in weddings, parades, etc. Even a local bus was named Bundo Kandueng.

Bundo Kandueng had no husband, and her brother is never mentioned; her son, on the other hand, plays an important role in a traditional tale. This suggests, as does other traditional literature, that the mother-son dyad is exceedingly significant in Minangkabau culture and symbolizes the relationship of women and men within the Minangkabau matrilineage. The cultural image of the mother as simultaneously strong, nurturant, and wise is found throughout Minangkabau drama and literature (Iljas Pajakumbuh, n.d.; Johns, 1958; Tulis St. Sati, 1963). However, the mother's nurturance and solicitousness are conditional upon her children's moral performance: the successful son in the migration area must not forget his poor village mother or he may lose all he has. This is attested to by a popular folk drama, entitled Malin Kundang. In the story Malin Kundang goes away to the migration area and becomes exceedingly rich. He sends nothing home to his mother who is old and very poor. When finally he sails back to Minangkabau with a ship laden with riches, a storm sinks his ship and all is lost. That is how the offshore island came into existence. The island is still there, serving to remind young men who leave home of their responsibility to their mothers. The Minangkabau world view is such that heaven is said to be beneath the sole of mother's foot. Moral virtue—even God himself—is allied with women, and human affect also focuses on them.

The cultural base for matrifocality is of long-standing and continuing significance; the mother's power position grows stronger and her sphere of influence expands as her brother's economic contribution (and therefore his ability to influence decisions) decreases, while the husband remains an honored but relatively insecure guest in his wife's home.

Despite major differences in kinship structure, there are important commonalities in the role of women in Java, Atjeh, and Minangkabau. In all three of these Indonesian societies women are producers and control economic resources. Kinswomen are in frequent contact and often assist one another. Women are decisive and are at least as assertive as men. In addition to these general similarities, in each society women occupy central kin positions. Mothers' roles are ritually elaborated. A woman's role as mother is more important than her role as wife. Furthermore, although the financial contribution of men—husbands, brothers, sons—is valued by women, when necessary women can effectively support and care for their children for long periods with very little input from men. Help is available from kinswomen; and mothers are farmers, craftswomen, and traders, or have jobs.

Igbo

The Igbo of eastern Nigeria,[14] West Africa, are of special interest, for although their kinship system is both patrilineal and patrilocal, they have matrifocal minimal units.[15] To Victor Chikenzie Uchendu, an Igbo anthropologist, this is quite unremarkable. He takes it so for granted, in fact, that he relegates his discussion to a footnote: "Some-

[14] I follow Uchendu in using Igbo rather than Ibo (a name commonly found in the ethnographic literature) to characterize this group. The Igbo are far from homogeneous. Although they are a distinct cultural and linguistic grouping, prior to the colonial period they consisted of more than 200 independent territorial groups (Ottenberg, 1959).

[15] Among societies having a matrifocal emphasis, the Igbo probably fall close to one end of a continuum. Structurally, within the kinship system, matrifocality is *primarily* although not exclusively expressed in the context of the mother-child unit (e.g. the minimal kinship unit for that society). And within the society at large, although women are relatively equal participants in the economic and ritual spheres

times called a matricentric family, it is a mother-centered segment of the polygynous family. Two or more matrifocal units 'linked' to or sharing a husband (who may be male or female) result in a polygynous family. . . . A matrifocal household consists of a mother, her children, and other dependents. Among the Igbo it is essentially a cooking unit and an eating unit" (Uchendu, 1965: 55).

Within an Igbo village are a number of compounds. A large compound consists of several brothers, their wives and children, plus some sisters (or daughters)[16] and their "wives" and children. A rich man or woman may have several wives and many children. Each wife has her own quarters and the children live with her; the husband has separate quarters.

The basic structural unit of this patrilineal society—the residential, economic, and socialization unit—is that of a woman and her children. On the cultural level, there is no doubt that this is a legitimate and expected arrangement. The mother-child tie is strong and persistent and is *supposed* to be that way. Igbo patrilineages segment along maternal lines.[17] Competition between co-wives is a matter of course and solidarity among the children of one mother is expected. The role of mothers in founding myths is of particular interest. Dual divisions within villages are accounted for by claims that the founder had two wives. Similarly a group of villages said to be founded by brothers is referred to as a village group with "one mother" (Green, 1947). It is

(with a political-economic-kin elaboration in traditional Onitsha; see R. Henderson, 1972), Igbo women are probably not as prominent in public affairs as the women in certain other African societies, such as Dahomey (Herskovitz, 1967) or Lovedu (Lebeuf, 1963).

[16] A woman who separates from her husband—a not uncommon occurrence—returns to her natal home or to the home of her maternal grandparents. This pattern doubtless is an expression of the durability and strength of the mother-child and sibling bonds. One wonders whether a woman would choose to return to her maternal grandparents' home only when her mother has already returned to *her* natal home, or whether this pattern reflects the importance of an additional (and more extended) bond between a woman and her mother's mother, and between a woman and her mother's siblings. "It is said that brothers or parents of . . . a wealthy trader may well be eager to repay her bridewealth and help her maintain her trade from a base in her natal home. . . . Onitsha people . . . think of their women as strongly trade-oriented and independent-minded; . . . villages expect to have a core of daughters in residence and to provide them with houses. Trade in village marketplaces appears to be organized largely by its daughters" (R. Henderson, 1972: 234–35).

[17] The significance of the mother's role is built into the conceptual categories of their kinship system. With regard to the Onitsha Ibo, R. Henderson states, "Kinship terminology is . . . based on a set of rules which include a basic assumption about motherhood and, . . . the most generalized sibling term is an allusion to motherhood" (personal communication; see also R. Henderson, 1967).

almost as if Igbo social structure, both genealogical and territorial, were symbolically accounted for by a generational alteration in the determining role of men and women.[18]

As in the other societies described above, the women have economic resources. They plant their own marketable garden crops on land adjacent to their houses and they are active traders. Indeed they control the local markets,[19] while the men, for their part, engage in long-distance trading (Uchendu, 1965).

In the Onitsha region, where traditional political organization was more complex and stratified than among most other Igbo groups, women developed political institutions that were directly related to their economic role. "The queen and her councillors directly control the activities of the great market. Trade cannot begin before they have arrived and occupied their stalls. In public women's meetings ... they regulate what products may be sold ... by whom, and at what price. They ... handle market violations in their court. ... They receive regular tribute ... from all trading women in the market" (R. Henderson, 1972: 312–13).[20] It is the women who have kin ties outside the village; they have an important mediating function between disputing groups from different villages (Green, 1947; R. Henderson, 1972). Women organize themselves into groups centered around (1) their place of birth[21] and (2) their place of marriage. Female deities exist, as do female ritual specialists. Thus, among the Igbo, as among the Javanese, Atjehnese, and

[18] The role of the mother-child unit in polygynous African societies, the importance of the sibling bond (e.g. the children of one mother) in African segmentary lineage systems, reference to the sibling bond/one-mother relationship in kinship terminology, the significance of the network of ties through women for linking African patrilineal descent groups and villages, and the importance of matrifiliation for ritual purposes, have all been noted elsewhere. What is suggested here is that the full significance of *the total constellation* of such features among the Igbo (and possibly among other African groups as well) has not been realized.

[19] "Symbolically, the marketplace is defined as outside the sphere of assertion by males, whether human or animal; any cock that crows there during trading hours must become the property of the queen" (R. Henderson, 1972: 311).

[20] Interestingly, these institutions were developed out of the kinship system and were grounded in it—but in a manner that emphasized women's ties to their natal kin groups rather than to their husband's kin groups. This may be related to the role that women who return to their natal groups play in the trade sector (see note 16).

[21] This is not to imply that men do not also participate in organizations that serve to tie them to kin related through their mothers. Indeed, for both women *and* men such ties are so significant, particularly for ritual matters, that one can speak of an Igbo ideology of matrifiliation. This ideology is expressed both in terms of the traditional religious system and in marriage patterns. For example, people related through "one-mother" (even if the tie is a distant one) should not marry unless a special ritual is performed to break that bond (R. Henderson, 1972).

Minangkabau, women are relatively equal participants in the society at large (H. Henderson, 1969).

Uchendu, in writing of his own family background, tells of his mother's life and of his own youth; he mentions his father, his father's older brother, and his mother's "wives." In so doing he provides an invaluable inside account of female and male kin roles among the Igbo. The details Uchendu presents about his mother show her to be a decisive, assertive woman with a strong sense of initiative in ideological, practical, and personal matters (pp. 5, 6):

> In my mother's youth, the Christian churches were preaching a radical doctrine. Challenging the Igbo practice of killing twins, they protected these infants. With the feverish enthusiasm of a convert, my mother carried in her arms twins who had been isolated in a hut outside the village limits. . . . The news that my mother, then an unmarried girl, had carried twins in her arms . . . was disconcerting to my mother's mother. . . . Life became unbearable for my mother. . . . My mother made a desperate decision. . . . She decided to marry in a non-Igbo community.

His mother's long trip to the offshore island of Okrika, where she became the "love wife" of a wealthy man, is then described. After about three years the author's mother's mother died, his mother returned home and subsequently divorced her first husband, married the author's father, and had a son (the author). He grew up in a big compound, which was dominated by his father's oldest brother, Ogbonna (p. 7):

> Ogbonna never agreed with my mother because of her defiant attitude and uncompromising demand that he share with his brothers while he was still alive the "family property" (which was my father's mother's property). . . . Ogbonna loved me . . . I carried his medicine bag and listened to his stories. . . . He told me what he could remember about our lineage, *the wealth of his mother*, the feuds in our lineage, and the coming of the white man [emphasis mine].

Although the Igbo, like every known human society, do differentiate somewhat between the roles of females and males, the system is very flexible. Little boys may have responsibilities more commonly assigned to little girls and adult women can be "husbands," that is, they can pay a bride-price in order to gain rights in the labor of women. Uchendu's account indicates that doing something unusual for one's *age* (e.g. a young boy having a wife) may be considered more inappropriate and worthy of teasing commentary than doing something unusual for one's *sex* (a woman having a "wife") (pp. 7, 8):

> Since my mother had female children late in her life, she forced me to perform the chores normally done by girls. "You are my own daughter," she would

insist. . . . I survived schooling through the intervention of my mother . . .
Though I was spared the teacher's cane, I had the taunts of my schoolmates to
combat. They told everyone that I had a wife. . . . My mother was then a "big"
trader and she needed someone to help in our house and so she "married" one
wife after another. . . . By the time I finished grade school, my father had
plunged into debt. . . . My father ran off to Okrika, where he did odd jobs. . . .
Although he was able to pay his debts, my father did not prosecute his own
debtors; my mother exploited this weakness whenever they quarreled. Financially unable to afford a high school education, I became a grade school teacher.
. . . I was admitted to a four year teacher's training college after I had taught in
grade school for five years.

He had already married a young girl, and his family supported him (at
college), his wife (in grade school), and his younger brother during this
period. After college he taught high school in his own town for four
years (p. 9):

This was a period of great responsibility for me. My town regarded me as one
of the emergent elite. . . . My family expected me to justify the investment my
education represented. . . . My town demanded leadership of me. But this leadership is a trying as well as a thankless experience. My town has a passionate
desire to "get up." There is nothing unique about this; every Igbo community
wants to "get up."

He later graduated from the University of Ibadan, Nigeria, and received
a B.S. from London University and a Ph.D. in anthropology from Northwestern University. The Igbo, like the Minangkabau, are noted for their
entrepreneurial skills and have been particularly active and successful
in the field of education.

Uchendu's account gives us insight into a number of characteristics
of Igbo society. Although the kinship system is patrilineal, the patrilineal segments are founded by women (e.g. mothers). The wealth of
these founding mothers forms an important part of the segment's history; subsequent generations are told of it. Once the founding mother
dies, her property passes to her children, and its control and division
may become a matter of dispute. Role activities are not rigidly allocated
by sex; both men and women are assertive and initiating. Achievement
is highly valued, but brings many family and community responsibilities. Both women and men have important roles in the kinship system
and in the community at large. This is the social context in which Igbo
matrifocality is expressed.

Black Americans

A cross-cultural perspective on matrifocality, particularly one that
stresses cultural as well as structural features, should enable us to look

at matrifocality among Black Americans in less biased terms. The Black American family system has been the subject of so much speculation and so little actual investigation that a precise description is impossible at this time. However, it is clear that extended and flexible kin networks are characteristic of the system (Jack, 1973; Stack, 1970, 1973, and this volume), that socialization is similar for male and female children (Young, 1970; Lewis, 1973), and that women's kin roles are of special significance (Ladner, 1971). Ladner, in *Tomorrow's Tomorrow*, a study of young Black women, describes the central role of women in the family (pp. 127, 131):

> The strongest conception of womanhood that exists among all preadult females is that of how the woman has to take a strong role in the family. . . . All of these girls had been exposed to women who played central roles in their households. . . . The symbol of the *resourceful* woman becomes an influential model in their lives. . . . Most of the girls viewed the duties of the woman as those associated with keeping the home intact. . . . In sum, women were expected to be strong, and parents socialized their daughters with this intention.

Ladner's work illustrates the positive cultural factors underlying the central position of Black women in the Black American family. There is a clear conception of what a woman should be: a strong, resourceful mother with a structurally central position. Girls are socialized for such roles.

Let us contrast Ladner's conclusions, which were the product of intensive long-term research, with the views of Moynihan. In a U.S. Government report entitled *The Negro Family: The Case for National Action* (1965), Moynihan used U.S. census data on marriage and residence indicating that among women who had ever married, more Black women than white women were not residing with their husbands at the time of the census. I shall not deal with the very considerable problems of the census material itself, nor with the well-recognized fact that census material does not in and of itself tell us anything about the structure of a kinship system (Valentine, 1968). From this census material and without field investigation, Moynihan went on to discuss what he called the "breakdown of the Negro family." (This "breakdown" refers to census figures of 9 percent to 23 percent of "absent or divorced husbands" for "non-whites.") Moynihan then used this presumed "breakdown"—one of whose features he terms "matriarchy"—to "explain" among other things the higher arrest and welfare rates among "non-whites," as well as lower school-performance rates.[22] The Moyni-

[22] See also "The Negroes," in Glazer and Moynihan (1963: 50–53).

han Report thus presents us with a classic example of ethnocentrism
in the social sciences: the report a priori assumes that there is no distinctive Black American kinship system, and that whatever there is, is
an imperfect and disorganized variant of the white middle-class family
system.[23] However, the particular form ethnocentrism takes in this instance is peculiarly white middle-class American, for it is sexist as well
as racist. Statistics showing the participation of Black women in the
labor force and their educational attainments are utilized by Moynihan
as further "evidence" of the "breakdown" of the Black family. Thus
the Moynihan Report has entered American folk culture as a scholarly
legitimization of a popular (and of course racist) stereotype of the Black
man as somehow less a man because the Black woman is a strong and
resourceful woman.

Matrifocality can and does coexist with the socialization of men and
women with strong achievement motivation and entrepreneurial orientation. The Atjehnese and Minangkabau of Indonesia, in addition to
producing women with crucial kin and economic roles, also produce
men who are highly mobile both geographically and in terms of socioeconomic position; so too do the Igbo of Nigeria. The cross-cultural
materials examined here give no indication of any causal link between
matrifocality and low status or achievement for men. Indeed, if anything, the Atjehnese, Minangkabau, and Igbo material might be interpreted to suggest a positive correlation between matrifocality and male
achievement orientation.

If, among Black Americans, arrest rates are high and school-performance rates are low, this may indicate something about the structure
of opportunities in the society at large, or about the police and schools.
It says nothing about the nature of the Black American kinship system.

The mother's role in the Black American kinship system is exceedingly significant and of central importance. It is in this sense that the
Black American kinship system has a matrifocal emphasis.[24] The mother's role functions in the context of a wide and flexible range of kin ties.

        [23] For a more detailed critique of the Moynihan Report and subsequent contro-
versy, see Schneider (1968).
        [24] In the literature on Black America there has been considerable confusion in the
use of the term "matrifocal." Most often it has simply referred to a structural entity—
the mother-child unit. That is *not* what I mean by the term. I refer, let me repeat,
to a quality of a kinship system that has *both* cultural and structural aspects. A kinship system with a matrifocal emphasis is one in which the role of the mother is central in terms of cultural values, family finances and patterns of decision making, and
affective ties. It is a system in which girls are socialized to become strong and active
women and mothers. Roles of men can vary rather widely in mother-focused kinship
systems.

Although co-residence with maternal kin is probably more common than with paternal kin, ties to and through the father are available and utilized (Stack, 1971). When studied as a system in its own terms, as anthropologists routinely attempt to study the kinship systems of all peoples, it is evident that Moynihan's label of "breakdown" is inappropriate and seriously misleading.

Matrifocality presumes an emphasis on the mother-child bond and implies the capacity for mother-child units to function effectively on their own. In *all* cases discussed, including that of Black America, the mother-child unit is ordinarily embedded in larger kin networks. However, in some instances the mother-child unit may be only minimally dependent on such wider kin networks.[25] In societies with matrifocal kinship systems, when the mother-child unit functions relatively independently, it is able to do so effectively. It can be more effective than its counterpart in societies that are not matrifocal, because women have been socialized to be the backbone of the family.

Historically, the matrifocal emphasis among Black Americans may be related to African patterns. To check this out, comparative work on West African groups plus historical research, perhaps following up on some of the early suggestions of Herskovits (1941), would be necessary. What are the common cultural features of West African kinship systems and conceptions of women and men that facilitated the transformation of these structurally distinct systems into one common system in the New World?[26] How and why did these commonalities among various West African groups predispose them toward the type of system that eventually came into being in North America and the West Indies?

Whatever its historical origins, matrifocality clearly worked well for Africans in the New World, where their lineages could not be reconstituted and where even small units such as nuclear and polygynous families were disrupted by the conditions of slavery. The Black American kinship system, as it developed in the United States, has put a premium on flexibility. This has meant maintaining a wide range of bilateral kin ties that can be activated as need arises. Kin often reside together or care for one another's children. Extended kin networks may reach from the

[25] For example, a successful Javanese woman trader who is divorced might have her own household composed of herself, her children, and one or two related adolescents for whom she takes responsibility and who also help her with housework and child care.

[26] Features common to West African societies, regardless of whether they are matrilineal or patrilineal, clearly include (1) broadly extended kinship ties, (2) a cultural emphasis on the mother-child and sibling bonds, and (3) a strong economic role for women.

rural south to northern cities (Jack, 1973; Shimkin, Louie, and Frate, 1973). These flexible kin ties are an important and historically persistent component of the Black American kinship system. Equally significant is the matrifocal emphasis that has been maintained from very early times to the present, in both rural and urban, Northern and Southern, contexts. Black women have always been socialized to be strong and resourceful and to know that motherhood—although an important and expected role—is not mutually exclusive to working outside the home. This means that mother-child units in Black society can survive and the next generation be socialized effectively. This is not to deny, of course, that mother-child family units—whether white or Black—face certain disadvantages in a sexist society or that Black family units face the additional disadvantages engendered by racism.

However, to assume that Black women will cease having strong self-images, will cease regarding themselves and being regarded as in some sense the backbone of the family, and will retire from their jobs and their participation in religious and political activities if and when Black men no longer face economic and political discrimination, is to ignore the positive cultural factors supporting the various roles of Black women. Interestingly, among Black professional people, although the female-male ratio is very low, as in all professions, there are proportionately more Black women than white women in the professions. "In 1960, six percent of white physicians were women, . . . but ten percent of black physicians were women. Black women made up eight percent of black lawyers, white women made up only three percent of white lawyers" (Epstein, 1973: 58). Epstein, who interviewed 31 Black professional women in New York, reports that the Black women seemed less ambivalent about combining their careers with roles as wives and mothers than did white women; they also relied more than white women on help from relatives for child care, etc. Epstein also stressed that "From early childhood on, the women I talked to all had the image of *woman as doer* fixed in their minds" (1973: 60).

Summary

Matrifocality as used here refers to the *cultural elaboration and valuation*, as well as the *structural centrality, of mother roles within a kinship system*. This can occur in matrilineal and patrilineal systems as well as in bilateral systems. It is useful, however, to distinguish which units within the kinship system are matrifocal. Thus matrifocality may be limited to the elemental mother-child unit (as among the patrilineal Igbo of Nigeria), or it may be a feature of the nuclear family and more inclusive kin units, such as the loose bilateral kindred (as among the

Javanese and Black Americans) or the matrilineally extended family (as among the Minangkabau).

Among all the groups discussed, the children usually feel especially close to their mother, and there is a cultural emphasis on the mother role; these are necessary but not sufficient conditions of matrifocality. In Atjeh and Minangkabau there is a residential core of related women; men often work outside the village. Kinswomen maintain strong ties among the Javanese and Black Americans, although residence may be neolocal. And even among the patrilineal, patrilocal Igbo, solidarity among women is valued, and contact between kinswomen is maintained. There are, for example, women's organizations based on place of birth and on place of marriage. The former serve to bring together women and their sisters and mothers, the latter to maintain ties among the women living in one community.

In all the above societies, there is little difference between women and men with regard to initiative, assertiveness, autonomy, decisiveness. In none of these societies are women socialized to find their identity in intimate dependence on men. Instead, they are socialized to become relatively independent, active women and mothers. In all these societies men and women have relatively similar economic resources. Some degree of control over available economic resources by women may be a structural prerequisite of matrifocality; certainly in all of the societies discussed women have important resources such as houses, rice, or money. But this sort of observation is not new. Equally important, but seldom pointed out, are the cultural dimensions of matrifocality (Tanner, 1971).[27] Raymond T. Smith in a recent discussion of his findings among Black families in the West Indies comes to similar conclu-

---

[27] Schneider and Smith differentiate two levels of culture—"pure cultural conceptions in the domain of kinship" (1973: 103) and "the norms which provide rules for the formation of real families and for the proper behavior of family members towards each other" (1973: 105). The coexistence of (1) a commonality of certain very general kinship categories throughout American culture regardless of class or ethnicity, but yet (2) the evident contrasts in the structure and functioning of Black and white American kinship systems, combined with (3) the differences between Blacks and whites in their valuation of (and manner of thinking about) *certain* kin roles, bonds, and activities, have long posed a dilemma for students of American kinship. The Schneider-Smith formulation provides an ingenious restatement of this conceptual dilemma, but does not fully resolve the issues. Their recent formulation stresses class at the expense of ethnicity, which is problematic for two reasons: (1) Americans of African and European ancestry appear to differ with regard to basic cultural assumptions, some of which influence modes of sex-role socialization (Lewis, 1973); and (2) class differences probably do not have the same "depth" of meaning among Black Americans as among Anglo-Americans because of the precariousness of middle- and upper-class status for Blacks. This precariousness of class status, although fostering the use of external signals of class membership, also permits and encourages considerable inter-class (but intra-ethnic) communication and interaction.

sions (1973: 140–41): "What we find is *priority of emphasis* placed upon the mother-child and sibling relationship, while the conjugal relationship is *expected to be* less solidary and less affectively intense. It is this aspect of familial relations which is crucial in producing matrifocal family structure" (emphasis mine).[28]

Matrifocality is *not* limited to lower-class, economically marginal groups (Gonzalez, 1969: 242–43) or to rapidly changing societies (Bell, 1971), although it *can* enhance survival for groups in difficult circumstances. However, the fact that matrifocality has frequently been discussed with reference to Black Americans in the United States and the Caribbean has led to a focus on economic and social marginality as determinants of the phenomenon. Cultural factors have rarely been examined. In this article I have suggested that positive cultural conceptions of women's kin roles (and particularly of the mother's role), an absence of extreme cultural dichotomization[29] of role expectations for women and men (Lewis, 1973), and therefore relatively equal participation of women and men in general societal role systems form a constellation of features critical to the effective functioning of matrifocality. Together they support a matrifocal emphasis in a variety of kinship structures and economic and social contexts.

[28] There is some question in my mind whether this exceedingly important generalization about the relative *valuation* of these two types of kinship bonds can be adequately subsumed under (without being obscured by) the conceptual schema used elsewhere by Schneider and Smith (1973) and Smith (1970).

[29] "Dichotomization" is not to be confused with "separation." In some of the societies described here, females and males have separate spheres, and this may be one source of strength for women.

Chinese Women: Old Skills in a New Context

For the Westerner, the enigmatic nature of all things Chinese is confirmed by the contradictory stereotypes we are given of the character of women in traditional China. From the translations of old Chinese novels and memoirs, we have charming pictures of daintily selfless mothers, happily spending their lives in the women's apartments behind the high walls of their husbands' compounds, gracefully ignorant of the turmoil outside their gates. From the writings of family reformists in the 1920's and 1930's, we have a less pleasant view: silent, colorless drudges, sold without protest by fathers to unknown husbands, subject to beatings by all. Another description found in the reports of missionaries, Western travelers, and ethnographers is that of the village shrew or her town counterparts, "the women who curse the street." These women, usually but not always middle-aged, are reputed to terrorize the men of their households and their neighbors with their fierce tempers, searing tongues, and indomitable wills. And then, as if to totally confound our thinking, we have the Communist version: ignorant country women who met the social revolution and overnight were transformed into intelligent activists, skilled village diplomats, and molders of progressive (male and female) opinion.

We could account for some of these discrepancies by identifying their source in romanticism, Western misunderstanding of class differences, or the excesses of propaganda, but we would still be left with two seemingly inconsistent truisms. All observers seem to agree that (1) the jural position of women in China has always been low, and (2) women were effective participants (not merely grateful recipients) in the social revolution that swept across China in 1949 with the Communist army. Using my observations of Chinese women in rural Taiwan and gleanings from missionary accounts and village studies of other provinces of China, I will try in the pages that follow to give the reader a picture of the way in which traditional Chinese women coped with their low status. Hopefully, this exposition will also make intelligible the facility with which Chinese women adjusted themselves to change and the capacity they revealed for controlling the direction of those changes. Nearly all of my observations will be about the women who lived on the farms and in the villages of China, not only because I am more familiar with the life-styles of country women but also because they account for the majority of the female population in China and were the backbone of the revolution. I am well aware of the dangers in making generalizations about a country known for its cultural variation. An even graver danger would be risked in making no attempt to identify the patterns of behavior the Chinese find characteristic of themselves as a people.

The birth of a female infant always caused some degree of dismay in China. She was not a member of her father's lineage and could not (except under unusual circumstances) provide even her father's descent line with descendants. By the time she was old enough to be of even minimal labor value she had to be sent to another family as a bride. Given the narrow margin between survival and starvation within which many Chinese peasants existed, the high rate of female infanticide in traditional China should not be surprising. Although at marriage a girl's parents were usually given a cash payment by the family of her husband, much of it had to be returned to the groom's family in the form of a dowry (or, more accurately for peasants, a trousseau). After her marriage all rights to a woman's labor and progeny belonged to her husband's family. Her natal family had some obligation to see that she was not excessively ill-treated, but unless they could afford to negotiate a divorce and assume the responsibility for housing and feeding her, there was little they could do beyond expressing their dissatisfaction to the other family. Thus a woman was not only irrelevant to her father's descent group but once married retained only fragile ties to the domestic group in which she grew up. Marriage gave her automatic membership in her husband's domestic group, but her relationship to his descent group was more ambiguous. She had no place in the lineage genealogy unless she produced sons for it, and formal acknowledgment of her contribution to the lineage was not made until after her death. Without sons, the record of her existence was limited to a tablet on the family altar and eventual anonymity. Hence, the lineage and its male ideology held little practical value for women. The male descent lines, nonetheless, were dependent on women for their continuation.[1]

[1] I am guilty here of furthering a common misconception. The form of marriage described above is the ideal from which many farm families in China were forced to

Given this kind of structural analysis, it is easy to accept the stereotype of Chinese women as so many uterine pawns in a male system. The Confucian values dominating Chinese social behavior (from that of the emperor to that of the poorest farm laborer) certainly codified such attitudes. Illiterate Taiwanese women, in talking to me about "good" daughters-in-law, often quoted the "three obediences" expected of a woman—to her father before marriage, to her husband after marriage, and to her son as a widow—and the "four virtues"—propriety in behavior, speech, demeanor, and employment. Yet many of these same women were very much in control of their own fates and often of their husbands', and were expecting and receiving the obedience of their adult sons. Arthur Smith, a missionary writing in 1899, had remarkable (if not always sympathetic) insights into Chinese character. Of women he wrote (1899: 303–5):

To defend herself against the fearful odds which are often pitted against her, a Chinese wife has but two resources. One of them is her mother's family, which, as we have seen, has no real power . . .

The other means of defense which a Chinese wife has at her command is—herself. If she is gifted with a fluent tongue, especially if it is backed by some of the hard common sense which so many Chinese exhibit, it must be a very peculiar household in which she does not hold her own. Real ability will assert itself, and such light as a Chinese woman possesses will assuredly permeate every corner of the domestic bushel under which it is of necessity hidden. If a Chinese wife has a violent temper, if she is able at a moment's notice to raise a tornado about next to nothing, and to keep it for an indefinite period blowing at the rate of a hundred miles an hour, the position of such a woman is almost certainly secure. The most termagant of mothers-in-law hesitates to attack a daughter-in-law who has no fear of men or of demons and who is full equal to any emergency. A Chinese woman in a fury is a spectacle by no means uncommon. But during the time of the most violent paroxysms of fury, Vesuvius itself is not more unmanageable by man.

. . . If a Chinese woman has the heaven-bestowed gift of being obstreperous to such a degree . . . this is unquestionably her surest life-preserver. . . . But if such an endowment has been denied her, the next best resource is to pursue a course exactly the opposite, in all circumstances and under all provocations *holding her tongue*. To most Chinese women, this seems to be a feat as difficult as aerial navigation, but now and then an isolated case shows that the difficult is not always the impossible.

Angry women are a threat to more than domestic tranquillity, according to Francis L. K. Hsu. In his ethnographic study of a village in Yunnan, Hsu tells us that a man who comes upon a furious woman will

---

depart owing to the exigencies of poverty, lack of male progeny, and other factors. In a recent paper Arthur Wolf has pointed out that these apparently distinct forms of marriage are simply compromises with this ideal (1973: 2).

quickly leave the scene, for a quarrel with an unrelated woman is "a bad omen for them" (1948: 207). He also describes an instance in which a woman made use of this semimystical power in order to reform her husband (pp. 65–66):

> Not long before I went to West Town the following incident occurred. A man was so addicted to gambling that he was always found at a certain den. His wife, in desperation, went to the den one night while the gamblers, including her husband, were at their hottest. She made a big row with her husband then and there.
>
> Quarrels among gamblers were not uncommon. As soon as such quarrels were patched up, the whole affair was at an end. But if a man and woman quarreled in someone else's home, the owner of the latter was doomed. It was one of the worst omens possible. In this case the owner not only permanently banned the husband from his den but also resorted to the use of witchcraft for revenge.

Hsu goes on to say that, although the woman was beaten by her husband for this act, her authority in the home and the shop (he was a small shopkeeper) increased sharply.

At the opposite end of China, in Shantung, householders sometimes pasted paper charms on their doorways to protect themselves from "violent females" (Johnston, 1910: 198). Writing in 1910, R. F. Johnston, a British magistrate in the Chinese port of Weihaiwei in eastern Shantung province, makes the following observations about Chinese women (p. 197):

> Sometimes a high-spirited and obstinate young woman will become absolute ruler of the household—including her husband and his parents—before she has lived a month in her new home, though her tenure of authority will always be somewhat precarious until she has given birth to her first son. . . . The number of such women (village shrews) in China is much larger than might be supposed by many Europeans, who regard the average Chinese wife as the patient slave of a tyrannical master. The fact is that Chinese women, in spite of their compressed feet and mincing gait, rule their households quite as effectually as women do in countries further west, and in the lower classes they frequently extend the sphere of their masterful activity to their neighbors' houses as well.

Johnston's observations are interesting beyond the evidence they give for the less than submissive personality usually attributed to women in China. They come from his experience as a magistrate in an essentially Chinese judicial system. For the people in the district with which he was charged, the system was innovative in offering truly free access to his services. Usually Chinese avoided contact with the courts if at all possible because the amount of money required to bribe the various court officials (and the judges themselves) could impoverish them, and if they were already in that condition, there was little hope of a fair hearing.

In a very short time, the rural women of Weihaiwei evaluated the advantages of the new judicial practices and put them to full use. Johnston, indeed, complains that "noisy and unreasonable women add no slight burden to the labours of an English magistrate" (1910: 103). There is an interesting similarity here between these illiterate country women who in 1910 readily sized up the advantages a new judicial system had for them and another generation of illiterate country women in the 1950's who shrewdly analyzed the advantages and disadvantages Communist policies had for them.

Harking back to the stereotypes of Chinese women described on the first pages of this essay, it is hard to reconcile a picture of women living in physical and social seclusion with that of the "noisy and unreasonable women" in Johnston's court in Weihaiwei. The source of our confusion is a common enough fallacy. Peasant women did not live threadbare versions of urban upper-class women's lives. In traditional China (and for many conservative families that period extended well into the first half of this century) the mothers, wives, and daughters of wealthy men lived in virtual purdah. They had little association with unrelated women (other than servants), limited contact with even the male members of their family, and very little information about events outside their living quarters, including the income-producing activities on which they were dependent.

Peasant families could not afford the luxury of secluding their women. A man and his sons worked in the fields from dawn to dusk in order to provide barely enough to eat. They could not then carry water, do laundry, gather firewood, make purchases at the village store, or carry out the innumerable other outdoor tasks a simple technology requires. They could at best make gestures toward this particular aspect of "gentility." As late as 1970 in Taiwan I found farm families in which the women I was talking to would all sidle out of the room and recongregate just outside the doors to it when one of the older men in the family walked in and engaged me in conversation. And at village feasts (for weddings or gods' birthdays) the women guests were served at separate tables, usually in one of the back rooms. Women stayed out of sight when suspicious strangers were around, but the rest of the time they were very much involved in interactions with their neighbors and fellow villagers. Marion J. Levy describes the settings of women's lives in mainland China in a way that sounds very familiar to one who has lived in Taiwan (1949: 80):

The peasants lived in small separate houses, or sometimes several families shared one of the old gentry houses. In any case, their living quarters afforded them much less seclusion than was afforded gentry families. Light inside their houses was poor, and peasant women frequently sat on their doorsteps or along the street to do sewing and similar jobs. They did their washing along the banks of local streams or canals, and several groups of women were generally busy with their work at the same time. Since they had no servants to shop and market for them, the peasant women and their daughters who accompanied them came into more contact with local shopkeepers and peddlers than did their gentry counterparts.

Martin Yang says of the women in the village of Taitou in Shantung (1945: 153):

Women of neighboring families gather before their front doors to talk and gossip. Especially in the summer time, when the men are eating at home, the women come out to have a breath of fresh air under the trees. A spontaneous and informal group is formed and the talk ranges from discussion of the daily work to gossip about the marriage of a family at the other end of the village.

From my observations of women's informal gatherings in rural Taiwan, I doubt that the activities of these groups were always as superficial as Levy and Yang suggest. A young woman whose mother-in-law was treating her with a harshness that exceeded village standards for such behavior told her woes to a work group, and if the older members of the group felt the complaint was justified, the mother-in-law would be allowed to overhear them criticizing her, would know that she was being gossiped about, and would usually alter her behavior toward her daughter-in-law. Every woman valued her standing within the women's circles because at some time in her life she might also need their support. The concept of "face" has immediacy for men in village society, and their "face" was in danger when unfavorable aspects of their behavior were being talked about. If a woman brought her complaints against a brother-in-law or son to the women's community, each woman would bring the topic up at home, and before long it was also being discussed by the men, with considerable loss of face for the culprit. In the Taiwanese village I knew best, some women were very skilled at forming and directing village opinion toward matters as apparently disparate as domestic conflicts and temple organization. The women who had the most influence on village affairs were those who worked through the women's community.

Traditionally in China any changes introduced by the government came to the villages by decree and were implemented by coercion. The Communists, however, used the villagers' own problem-solving technique, a technique in which women were both competent and confident. An injustice (or problem) was revealed; all details were discussed at length; everyone's opinion was expressed; gradually a consensus, often one subtly guided by interested parties, emerged. In *Fanshen*, Hinton describes the first campaign against the landlords, led by young cadres Fu-yuan, T'ien-ming, and Kuei-ts'ai (1968: 132–34). A Peasants' Association was formed of the thirty poorest families.

Fu-yuan posed to them the question of "who lives off whom?" He urged each member to tell his or her life story and to figure out for himself the root of the problem.

Once again Kuei-ts'ai led off. In order to move the others he told his own history....

This reminded poor peasant Shen T'ien-hsi of the loss of his home....

Then poor peasant Ta-hung's wife spoke up....

Story followed story. Many wept as they remembered the sale of children, the death of family members, the loss of property. The village cadres kept asking "What is the reason for all this? Why did we all suffer so? Was it the 'eight ideographs' that determined our fate or was it the land systems and the rents we had to pay? Why shouldn't we now take on the landlords and right the wrongs of the past?"

T'ien-ming finally challenged them to action...

The committee of the Peasants' Association decided to tackle Kuo Ch'ung-wang first.... The cadres... held small group meetings ahead of time in order to gather opinions against Ch'ung-wang. Those with serious grievances were encouraged to make them known among their closest neighbors and were then mobilized to speak out at the village-wide meetings to come.

The major difference between the technique described by Hinton and that familiar to Chinese women is the requirement that women speak out for themselves and before men. Chinese women learn as children (and have known from time immemorial) that if their opinion is to be valued, it must be spoken by a man. Jan Myrdal quotes an old man who disapproved of opinions expressed in a public meeting by a woman. "We should not listen to women when it is a question of serious business. They understand nothing. After all, they are only women and ought not to disturb our discussions. We do not need to concern ourselves with what they have said" (1964: 222). Such attitudes, and the fact that many women were conscious of the advantages in not having to take responsibility for the opinions men expressed for them, must have retarded full female participation in many places. Hinton, although lacking in insight into the reasons for women's silence, gives an interesting account of the influence of the Women's Association in Long Bow (1968: 157).

A few poor peasant women in Long Bow, the wives of leading revolutionary cadres, early organized a Women's Association where brave wives and daughters-in-law, untrammeled by the presence of their menfolk, could voice their own bitterness against traitors (in the war against Japan), encourage their poor sisters to do likewise, and thus eventually bring to the village-wide gatherings the strength of "half of China," as the more enlightened women, very much in earnest, liked to call themselves. By "speaking pains to recall pains," the women found that they had as many if not more grievances than the men and that once given a chance to speak in public they were as good at it as their fathers and husbands.

Sophia H. Chen Zen, writing in 1931 on the status of women, made the following statement about the Chinese family: "It is a government with all the paraphernalia of all other state governments, such as intrigue, diplomacy, treason, and so forth. And no woman who is not a born or a trained politician may hope to find a decent place in such a government, no matter how well educated and honourable she may be" (1931: 1076–77). Dr. Zen might well have added that it is also in the setting of this domestic "government" that each girl receives her training in politics, a training that starts very early. Nearly every Chinese girl, often as early as four or five years of age, is burdened with the care of a younger sibling. If she is to join the play group of her peers, many of whom have similar unwelcome appendages, she must develop techniques for convincing baby brother that whatever she wants to do is what he wants to do. By the time she is ten years old, an intelligent girl has a strikingly varied repertoire of promises, threats, evasions, and diversions. Along the way she develops a number of other skills, such as putting her words in baby brother's mouth ("He is crying because the rice-cake peddler is coming and he wants money to buy some"), taking an accurate reading of adult moods to evaluate which orders must be obeyed promptly and which can be ignored, and, by careful observation of adult females, identifying what kinds of conflicts can only be resolved by histrionic loss of temper. In general, little boys are not presented with these learning situations, and those few who are required to mind a younger sibling are relieved of their responsibilities as soon as their mothers can find a female substitute.

I do not mean to imply that male peasants are lacking in the skills of diplomacy, but their talents are developed later in life, in a different setting, and are less crucial to the quality of their everyday existence. Women learn to assess moods and evaluate the consequences of their own and others' actions in the domestic setting and, having refined these skills, continue to practice them in their interactions with people outside the domestic unit. Within the family, boys are so valued that they can simply demand, and insofar as possible their demands are met. As adults their position of authority within the family puts little strain on their diplomatic talents. It is outside the family that they must learn and use the subtler techniques, and in the comparatively simple world of the peasant few situations require them. The rules of proper behavior are well defined and the penalties for departing from them are well known. Men in Taiwan, incidentally, often say that women are inept in dealing with the world "outside," by which they mean women do not follow the rules that they as men must in order to preserve their dignity and "face." Women improvise and hence are difficult to deal with. The consternation women's participation in public affairs can lead to is amusingly illustrated in the following explanation by a village-level Communist official of why women had not been recruited into the party. "We felt that the militant women weren't virtuous and the virtuous women weren't militant. So though we knew we ought to recruit some women members into the branch we couldn't find any who seemed suitable" (Crook and Crook, 1959: 108).

There are two occupations, one amateur and one professional, that serve as good examples of the ways in which women used their heightened sensitivity to human motivation. Even though marriage is considered, by men at least, to be the means by which the men's descent lines are continued, the delicate and complicated negotiations that precede it are usually handled by women. It is the mother who hears of likely candidates, often through friends or her natal family, chooses the woman who will be the go-between, and conveys her evaluation of the prospective spouse to her husband. The go-between with much tact and patience must convince both families to compromise their demands. Moreover, she must be prepared to be recalled for years after to mediate marital disputes. It would seem to me a thankless task, but it is one that many women in Taiwan relish—so much so that it becomes almost a full-time occupation among many older women.

A more frankly income-producing occupation that depends on the social talents of women is that of soul raising. A. J. A. Elliott, who studied spirit-medium cults in Singapore, found only a few Chinese women performing as mediums in the major cults, but discovered that they held a virtual monopoly in the practice of soul raising. In a seance-like situation the soul raiser calls upon Kuan Yin (the goddess of mercy) to help her locate the soul of a deceased member of the family that has hired her. Once located, the soul enters the body of the soul raiser and answers the questions put by the still living members of his family. As Elliott describes the performance (1955: 138–39):

Little by little during the course of the performance a clear picture of the family's background and problems are brought to light, until it becomes a relatively easy task for the soul raiser to persuade all who are present that everything about them is known as intimately as if it were the ghost himself speaking. Some of the more susceptible members ask the ghost about particular problems that are worrying them. Some of these problems may involve personal antagonisms within the family or questions of rights to property. In each case the ghost gives a judgment, which must be observed by those who hear it. In all his conversations, the ghost resumes what would have been his rightful status in the kinship circle were he still living, and adds to it a certain occult wisdom derived from his period of residence in another world.

Elliott was profoundly impressed by the skill of the practitioners (p. 140).

The simplest explanation would be that the soul raiser is in some sort of telepathic communication with the circle in which she is performing. But any such judgment is outside the scope of the present study. On whatever powers the soul raiser may depend, it must be admitted that a competent performance requires very great skill. The feelings of the audience must be perfectly judged in order to establish a maximum credulity among all those who are present. Special pains must be taken with those who tend towards disbelief, and the seance must be led forward step by step until a sufficient knowledge of the family's background has been acquired for all pronouncements to be made with the certainty of acceptance. Further, the soul raiser can never deviate from the religious symbolism to which her listeners are familiar, or make mistakes in the manner in which a member of a kinship circle would address his superiors or inferiors. Whatever the psychical content of her performance may be, a good soul raiser at work is a revelation in the skilful use of sociological knowledge.

A Chinese woman trained from childhood to be sensitive to attitude change, to understand and make use of the kin and emotional relations between people, and, in a sense, to "live by her wits" clearly comes equipped with the basic essential skills of the soul raiser.[2]

C. K. Yang, in his study *The Chinese Family in the Communist Revolution*, gives some perspective on the adaptability of such talents as those of the soul raisers. He quotes the following anecdote from the newspaper *Shing-tao jih-pao* (April 18, 1951) (1959: 132):

In a visit to my home village after a prolonged absence the most unimaginable thing I found is how progressive the women folk have become in this old culturally a-century-behind place. When I first arrived I heard the woman representative for the village was none other than the female sorcerer, the "spirit-worshiping Ti." Immediately, an ugly, laughable, and contemptible face

---

[2] In conversation, Dr. Michael Saso, anthropologist *cum* Taoist priest, told me that in southern Taiwan soul raisers were often sinicized women from the nearby aborigine tribes and it was his understanding that this was frequently the case in other areas of China. Dr. Saso and Arthur Wolf suggest that the high frequency of women in this particular occupation is due to "face." Men would find it intolerable for other men in their social group to know so much about their domestic affairs, but they can dismiss such intimate knowledge in low-status women. I am inclined to reject this hypothesis, for it is commonly believed that practitioners have no recall of what they hear or say while in trance and hence the information should be as safe with men as with women.

appeared in my memory of things ten years ago. In the past this poverty stricken female feigned the incarnation of gods and spirits, talked of mysticism to the ignorant women in the village. She threatened, she bluffed, she swindled, she aroused excitement. She used every trick to gain money. I thought, "It couldn't be a fact!" If such a person could become the village's woman representative, the appointment of public officers would be too indiscriminate. But she was no longer the picture in my memory; she has become a vanguard of the new age. When she spoke before the women audience of the village, she talked fluently and systematically on the new political line.

Yang comments on this:

Female sorcery was an occupation for the poverty stricken when there was no other alternative to making a living. Here again, in conformity with Communist stated policy the poor are being brought in as the core of the new local government. In this case, the skill in human relations and facility of speech so necessary in her former trade became invaluable assets for this woman in her present position of power.

This woman may very well have refined her skills beyond those of other women, but, of more importance, she had had the experience of using them publicly and in her own right. Unlike economically more fortunate women, she had apparently not had a man to speak for her and thus had overcome *before* the revolution one of the traditional patterns of "proper" behavior that restrained women from direct action.

Isabel and David Crook provide another example of a woman whose harsh early life taught her to speak for herself and equipped her well for leadership under the new regime (1959: 106):

When the peasant women's association was set up under the direction of the sub-county, Wang Hsiang found herself pushed to the fore by the rather shy and timid members of the new organization because she was one of the few poor peasant women who never feared to speak her mind. Her gruff manner and the sharp tongue which she had acquired in thirty years of family oppression became one of the weapons in the armoury of the peasant women's association.

One of the first hard lessons a young Chinese bride learns when she enters her new family is that the stranger who is her husband is not the man she can count on to speak for her. He is primarily his mother's son and spokesman, and she can expect harsh and unpleasant treatment at the hands of her mother-in-law for any precipitous moves that come between them. A young husband will rarely side with his bride in a conflict with his mother, and since it is with the older woman that she must spend most of her time, a bride soon discovers (if she did not know at the outset) that she must create a place for herself without offending her mother-in-law or depending on her husband. Chinese marriage ritual is dominated by fertility symbols that make the bride's function in her new family abundantly clear. She is to provide them with descendants, male descendants, and until the first signs of pregnancy appear, her mother-in-law will find numerous occasions to remind her of her purpose. In this goal the young woman and the family are united, although for different reasons. A son will not only give her more status in the family; he will give her the nucleus of what I have called elsewhere a uterine family. In the midst of this family of strangers a young wife builds her own small circle of security, binding her children, in particular her sons, to her with the emotional ties that only a mother can weave. By herself a woman is dependent upon the largesse of her husband's family for her daily rice, but through her sons she has at least use-rights to their share of the family estate. If her husband dies or is incapacitated, his family's obligations to her as the mother of their descendants do not change, but if she has no son, her position is ambiguous at best.

Simply giving birth to a son, however, is not sufficient. The formal and informal education in a young man's world teaches him his obligations to his father's line of descent (and lineage in regions where they are important), but his obligations to his mother are included under the general precepts of filial piety. Chinese women have a fairly jaundiced view of what they can expect at the mercies of an androcentric society. They rely instead on the skills they learned in their childhood, and behave, as Dr. Zen observed they must, as "politicians." Chinese parents believe that children will not respect and obey them as adults if they are too "intimate" with them after they reach the age of reason (about six years old in Taiwan). If a man is to raise his son properly, he must withdraw from him, no longer allow him to fall asleep on his lap, no longer express amusement at his naughtiness. Where once he ignored a disobedient act, he must now punish it coolly and harshly. Mothers say that they too must not continue to be affectionate with their young sons and must dispassionately insist on obedience, but in practice they do not. A woman makes full use of her husband's isolation from his children to strengthen their bonds to her. She becomes their confidante, and they hers; she interprets their father's behavior, and if her relations with him are bad, her interpretation is not to his advantage; she negotiates with him to get them off punishments, punishments for which she may also have set them up. For the children, the final evidence of the unity of their uterine family, in opposition to the family defined by their father, may well be the fact that father beats not only them but mother as well.

In describing traditional parent-child relations in Shantung, Martin

Yang verifies the strength of the bonds between women and their sons (1945: 58).

When father and son do work together, they have nothing to say, and even at home they speak only when there is business to discuss. At street gatherings or in places of amusement, they mutually avoid each other. . . . The relationship between mother and son, on the other hand, is comparatively close. Although a boy who reaches the age of ten is dependent entirely upon his father's authority and teaching, this does not interfere with his intimacy with his mother. Because of the lack of female companions and the meager possibilities for recreation, a young man spends much time talking to his mother during his formative years. After supper, when the father is absent and she is busy with household chores, he talks with her freely of the things which concern him. . . . At this time the son may also complain of his father's harshness or confide that he would like to learn some trade other than farming, or that he would like to continue to study. In her turn, the mother may tell him what she and his father think of him. A son at this time has no one, except his mother, to whom he can tell his thoughts freely, and this provides an unshakable foundation for the long-lasting mother-son relationship.

Yang goes on to describe a scene that must pass through every Chinese woman's mind as she looks at her infant son and dreams of the future (pp. 58–59).

When the son and his wife are middle-aged parents, the mother-son relationship comes to include the son's family. In the winter, when the men are not busy in the fields and supper is usually finished earlier, sons, wives, and grandchildren will gather in the old mother's room and the grandmother will play with her youngest grandchildren, while the wives and older grandchildren and the sons talk about what they have seen and heard outside. The father may take part in this gathering if he likes, but he usually keeps himself aloof in order to maintain his patriarchal status. If he attempts to disrupt the free atmosphere, he will be chased out by his old wife.

The revolution in China at first asked nothing of women that posed any real threat to what they took to be their most trustworthy source of security. For centuries women accepted the fact that ideologies, ethics, and "official promulgations" might benefit men but women must work out their own problems. They had done so, with individual degrees of success, but nearly always after securing a base of power in crucial family relationships. So long as official Communist campaigns for change concentrated on land reform, the eradication of landlords, and the equalization of women's status, most women could enthusiastically contribute their talents. The right to own land in their own names seemed to many women (and a good many cadres) the solution to most of their problems. For example, Hinton quotes the following anecdote from a training conference for cadres (1968: 397).

In Chingtsun the work team found a woman whose husband thought her ugly
and wanted to divorce her. She was very depressed until she learned that under
the Draft Law she could have her own share of land. Then she cheered up immediately. "If he divorces me, never mind," she said. "I'll get my share and
the children will get theirs. We can live a good life without him."

This woman was carrying the traditional emotional exclusion of unsatisfactory husbands from the uterine family one step further into economic exclusion. Here indeed was liberation.

On May 1, 1950, the new Marriage Law was promulgated, requiring
the free choice of marital partners, monogamy, the right of widows to
remarry, and an end to child betrothals and bride-prices. The law also
assured women as well as men of the right to divorce, and of equal rights
in the children produced by the marriage. In the propaganda campaign
that followed, large numbers of women found themselves threatened for
the first time by an aspect of the revolution. More precisely, for the first
time they were being asked to destroy their traditional source of security
and put their faith in the new social order. Older women should encourage their sons and daughters to choose their own mates, to live
separately, to pledge their primary loyalty to the state. Younger women
should refuse the marriages arranged by their parents, resist overbear-
ing mothers-in-law, and divorce (rather than tolerate and eventually
isolate) husbands who were unsatisfactory. One might expect the older
women to be hesitant, but interestingly enough, the younger women
seemed no more enthusiastic than their mothers. If they honored the
Marriage Law and rejected the marital partner chosen by their parents,
on what basis would they choose their own, and who would they turn
to if their choice was a bad one? Ideological guidelines were put out to
help identify a good mate, and the newspapers described exemplary
couples, but rural youth apparently were content to marry in the old
way, giving lip service to the revolution by appearing at the registration
office and swearing that the marriage was one of their own choice. Older
women may have extended their diplomacy to include their dealings
with their daughters-in-law, but I doubt that they were innovative in
their relations with their sons. The only examples they had of old women
without loyal sons were not enviable.

In 1951 and 1952, when the propaganda campaign for marriage and
family reform was at its height, the newspapers were full of optimistic
statistics describing the number of free-choice marriages. There were
also reports of high divorce rates from some areas, statistics concerning
which the government expressed somewhat more ambivalence. Another
set of statistics accumulating in district offices, but which the govern-

ment did not reveal until 1953, described a shocking increase in female suicides. Something was going wrong. In late 1952 and early 1953, directives were circulated "readjusting" the campaign; in the spring of 1953 marriage reform was described as a "long-term slow task"; in November in an official report published in the *People's Daily*, the Vice-Chairman for the Regulation of the Marriage Law Movement admitted that 15 percent of the population accepted marriage and family reform, 60 percent were reluctant, and 20 percent had not been touched at all by the propaganda campaigns. (The remaining 5 percent were not accounted for.) At this point the marriage reform campaign dropped into the phase China watchers call "low-ebb," not abandoned but with little energy being expended on it.

Only a specialist on Communist China, drawing together all the bits and pieces appearing in official reports and newspapers, could give a completely satisfactory picture of what went wrong in the marriage reform campaign. Some analysts blame the failure almost entirely on the cadres who used the violent methods so effective in class struggle and expected the same quick results.[3] Others also blame the cadres, but for being unwilling to implement the government policy—finding their own old-fashioned values regarding the proper relations between the sexes and the structure of authority in the family too deeply embedded to be overcome. The fact that women, supposedly the primary beneficiaries of the campaign, resisted it cannot help having had some influence on the social planners' decision to turn aside for a while. Reform in this area must come more slowly. New forms of marriage, new patterns of interaction between the generations, and new styles of family accommodation have been introduced. For them to be totally accepted, a new generation of women must appear, women whose horizons extend beyond the confines of home and village, women who see evidence that they can find security and satisfaction in life without using a male as spokesman and shield.

My purpose in this paper has been to dispel some stereotypes about the nature of women in traditional China and to share my conviction that women in modern China are not shiny new models turned out especially for the new society. A silent, oppressed population of women did not overnight turn into an energetic, astute body politic. In fact, the family system that ignored them for so many centuries also equipped them well to participate in the revolution and the new society. They

[3] See, for example, *China News Analysis* #83, May 13, 1955.

were far more experienced than their brothers at shaping opinions, sensing changes in attitude, evaluating personal advantage and disadvantage in sets of circumstances. It is not their skills that are new but the appreciation of these skills. Women now use them openly, speaking in their own voices rather than the voices of their sons or husbands. They are not yet ready to abandon the family system that provides their security (as evidenced by their resistance to the marriage and family reform campaign), for experience has taught them to view with caution any changes that lessen their personal control. But neither are they ever likely to be again content with the limited security their manipulation of family relationships can provide.

CAROL P. HOFFER

Madam Yoko: Ruler of the Kpa Mende Confederacy

There is a tendency in Western culture to define women as weak and needing protection, since they bear children. In West Africa the same biological facts are given a different cultural interpretation. The bearing of children demonstrates that women are strong and active agents in a society, capable of holding political office.[1]

In the Mende ethnic area of Sierra Leone, women produce a scarce resource: offspring for their husbands' patrilineages. Their nurturing role is also consciously valued in this geographical area of high infant mortality (Dow, 1971: 157). As children of both sexes mature to adulthood, they continue to look upon their biological and classificatory mothers as strong supportive figures. Women paramount chiefs within this context are seen as mothers writ large, calling into question any theoretical dichotomy in women's influence between the domestic and the juro-political domains.

Mende women are not to begin their procreative role until they have been initiated at puberty into Sande, the pervasive women's secret society.[2] Procreation and marriage are linked by payment of bridewealth,

This essay is based upon ten months' fieldwork in the Moyamba District of Sierra Leone in 1969–70, an additional six weeks' fieldwork in 1971–72, and archival work in Freetown and London in 1972–73. The National Science Foundation, Franklin and Marshall College, and the American Philosophical Society have generously financed this research.

[1] Both oral tradition and written historical documents suggest that for centuries women in this ethnic area have enjoyed high office, as lineage heads, heads of secret societies, and chiefs (Alldridge, 1901: 166, 181; Fyfe, 1962: 3, 19; Little, 1967: 195–96). A 1914 listing of paramount chiefs in Sierra Leone indicated that 15 percent of the Mende chiefdoms were ruled by women (Sierra Leone, 1914), and in 1970 9 percent were ruled by women (Sierra Leone, 1970).

[2] Sande sometimes appears in the anthropological literature by its Temne name, Bundu. As many as 95 percent of the women in the provinces of Sierra Leone are Sande women (Margai, 1948: 228).

which affiliates a child to his father's patrilineage. The laws of both Sande and Poro, the men's initiation society, discourage a man from marrying an uninitiated woman. Therefore, Sande, a women's social institution, enjoys a monopoly on transforming girls into marriageable women, a fact of political significance (Hoffer, 1973).

Women who are officials of Sande collect fees for their initiation services and fines from those who transgress against the secret society's laws that protect women's rights. In addition to their religious power and influence in Sande, women also have economic power as wives, especially if they are head wives in large polygynous households. The head wife organizes co-wives, children, clients, wards, and, in the past, slaves, into an agricultural work force. She also stores and markets economic surpluses. Because of these roles, Mende head wives are seen as authority figures, and occasionally a chief's head wife will succeed him in office even though she resides virilocally in his chiefdom and has no genealogical right to rule in the villages of his kin.

As the following case study illustrates, Mende women—especially if they are born of chiefly lineage, have intelligence, charm, and strength of character—can use their womanliness in a positive way to achieve significant political power. However, many of the political strategies women employ are used by both women and men seeking high office. Candidates of both sexes stress the loyalty due to them from kin, clients, and friends. They seek to impress their supporters with the influence they command in high places, reminding them of their own achievements, and they stress their nearness to consanguines, affines, and friends in positions of authority. They intimate that with such powerful connections they will surely be able to assist their followers in time of need. If they are of chiefly lineage, they remind others of the power of their ancestors, the "owners of the land," to bring blessings to all. They are people of influence in one or more secret societies, they often control "medicine," and sometimes possess a talisman or enjoy the services of a Muslim ritual specialist, who links them to cosmic power.

Both men and women give gifts to supporters, the gift being a tangible symbol of a special relationship in which the political aspirant may later ask for a reciprocal favor. Women candidates may give, or at least suggest the bestowal of, sexual favors to a key figure, a political ploy more useful to women than to men. In some cases a woman may bear a child fathered by an influential person, and as the woman ages and diminishes in physical attractiveness, the child remains as a focus to bind the affective alliance.

Occasionally a strong-willed woman of a ruling descent group will make alliances with men of her choosing, refusing to have bridewealth given for her. Her children in this patrilineal society then adhere to her and support her as they mature. Most commonly, however, a woman with political aspirations marries a man of influence and begins to build a base of political support as the wife in an influential household filled with many kin, guests, wards, and clients.

An undercurrent in Madam Yoko's life was the tragedy of a barren woman with no descendants to keep her memory alive. But during her life, biological inadequacy could easily be compensated for through the taking of wards. Yoko played the mothering role fully, having many wards, especially Sande initiates, whom she used with great skill in making political alliances. She also utilized her consanguineal kinship network, her marriage alliances, and friendship relationships, even with colonial officials, to expand the base of political support until she became the ruler of a vast confederacy.

Background

Madam Yoko came to power in the latter part of the nineteenth century, a period of rapid social and political change in the Mende ethnic area of Sierra Leone. The Mende, of the Mande-speaking language group, originated in the western Sudan, and within historic times have migrated into forested areas of Sierra Leone from the east (Kup, 1962: 124, 146). Yoko, at the height of her power, unified and led a confederacy of Kpa Mende, a splinter group of Mende that migrated westward from the Gorama Chiefdom area in an expansionary burst during the first half of the nineteenth century.

Yoko was a child of that pioneering movement, maturing in a milieu of warfare and diplomacy, coming to chiefly power in Senehun, a town on the leading edge of the Mende advance into Temne and Sherbro country. She was a central figure in the drama that ensued when Mende expansion was halted by an even more formidable power, the British Empire.

In 1663 the first British trading company was established in Sierra Leone. In 1787 treaties with local chiefs created the Sierra Leone colony for repatriated slaves on the Freetown peninsula, and a firm West African base for continued British trade. However, by the latter part of the nineteenth century, British plans for smooth and abundant trade had been continually frustrated. War chiefs who led the abrasive expansion of inland tribes often compounded disorder in the country by becoming involved in wars of the coastal trading families that contested with each other for control of trading spheres. Therefore, in 1896, extensive coastal

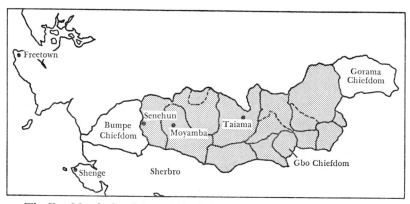

The Kpa Mende Confederacy (shaded area) in west-central Sierra Leone

and hinterland areas were declared a British Protectorate in order to impose the *pax Britannica* upon them, and stabilize the area politically. Relative peace came in time, but only after the sudden and violent insurrection in 1898 against British political officials, their taxes, their police, their traders and missionaries. See Denzer (1971) for an account of this rebellion.

Through all this, Madam Yoko charted a steady course, enhancing her own power with each adjustment in the changing political structure. She was recognized a paramount chief in 1884 by the British colonial government, having succeeded her husband in office. But she extended the area under her hegemony far beyond that controlled by her war-chief husband until she was paramount over all the Kpa Mende, ruling an area that, 13 years after her death in 1906, broke down into 14 separate chiefdoms.

Madam Yoko became paramount chief over a set of subchiefs who ruled the areas conquered by their fathers or grandfathers, the first generation of Kpa Mende warriors. She was as skillful in diplomacy with them as she was with the British. With the latter she won the cooperation of key colonial officials, some of whom, despite their ethnocentric notions of natural British superiority, looked upon her with admiration. Sir Harry Luke, aide-de-camp to the governor of Sierra Leone in 1908, wrote of her (1953: 182–83):

> By sheer ability and force of character this resolute little woman had built up in the formative years of the country the biggest chiefdom in the whole Protectorate. Madam Yoko was not only a sagacious chief but a woman of a mentality unusual in members of a primitive race. At the height of her authority she deliberately committed suicide because, as she told her attendants just after

drinking poison, she had enjoyed to the full all that life had to give—power and love—and, now that old age had approached, found it had nothing further to offer her.

Today in the section of Moyamba town where Madam Yoko ruled at the height of her power, her grave lies unattended. People walk by on their way to the market, taking no notice of the concrete marker covered by weeds, where wash is spread to dry and goats come looking for green leaves and household leavings. Who was this woman who acquired such vast political power and why is she nearly forgotten now?

Acquisition of Power

Yoko was born about 1849 in Gbo Chiefdom.[3] Through her mother she was linked to a leader in Gorama Chiefdom, the nuclear area from which the Mende expanded, and her father was a warrior in the outward movement. She had three brothers, Ali Kongo, Lamboi, and Goba.[4]

As a child, Yoko was known by her baby name, Soma. At puberty she was initiated into the Sande society. She and her co-initiates were ritually set apart in the sacred grove of the society, where they were instructed in singing, dancing, medicine, child-bearing and -rearing, and other traditional knowledge pertaining to the roles of wife and mother. Yoko especially distinguished herself as a graceful dancer (Easmon, 1958: 166).

After a few months of training in the Bundu bush, she took an oath of secrecy, swearing never to improperly divulge the women's secrets she had learned. Following this ritual of status transformation, she was reincorporated into society as an adult with a woman's name: Yoko. She was eligible for marriage.

Yoko's first husband was a warrior named Gongoima, "who wore a belt of large pealing bells around his waist, in order to frighten the enemy in war" (Abraham, 1971: 125). He has been described as "a near relative" to Yoko (Yoko MS), and may have been her father's sister's son, since matrilateral cross-cousin marriage is the preferred type of marriage for a Mende man to contract (Little, 1967: 146). Gongoima became an increasingly jealous and suspicious husband, and Yoko left him, her kinsmen presumably returning the bridewealth that had been given for her (Abraham, 1971: 125; Yoko MS).

---

[3] In 1885 the Reverend Thomas H. Carthew described Yoko in a letter to the *United Methodist Free Churches' Magazine*, estimating her age to be 35 (Fyfe, 1964: 238).

[4] This account is based upon a manuscript by Ngolotamba Lamboi, Yoko's classificatory grandson, quoted in Abraham (1971), and a second manuscript, whose author is unknown, henceforth to be cited as Yoko MS.

Yoko's second marriage was to Gbenje, a son of another of the migrating Kpa Mende pioneer-warriors, Kori. They resided in Taiama, Kori Chiefdom, where Yoko went to Gbenje's household as a junior wife, subordinate to the authority of his first wife (Abraham, 1971: 126; Yoko MS).

A husband chooses his first wife with care, since she is responsible for training all subsequent wives and organizing them, older children, wards, clients, and slaves into an agricultural work force. The senior wife is responsible for producing the agricultural wealth of the household, and if her warrior husband is absent or preoccupied for long periods of time, it is she who often functions as the effective head of household. Even though a husband may marry younger, more beautiful wives, he continues to regard his "big wife" with great respect and consideration. In Gbenje's case, however, the junior wife, Yoko, was so able and responsible that he elevated her to the rank of senior wife (Abraham, 1971: 126; Yoko MS).

After marriage, a Mende woman always remains a member of her patrilineal descent group. Even while residing virilocally in marriage, she maintains close relationships with her consanguineal kinsmen (Hoffer, 1972: 154). While she was Gbenje's wife, Yoko received gifts from her kinsmen, notably a lion-tongue talisman that her elder brother, Ali Kongo, had acquired in a raid. It had originally been fashioned by a Muslim elder to give its possessor fame, wealth, and power (Abraham, 1971: 126). Thus Yoko's innate intelligence and charm were augmented by this link to cosmic power.

During the 1860's and 1870's a "nephew" of Gbenje named Gbanya settled in the upper Bumpe River area, at Senehun, and became widely known as a powerful warrior in the area. When Yoko's husband Gbenje died after a brief illness, Gbanya left Senehun and went to Taiama for Gbenje's mortuary ceremonies. Yoko and her widowed co-wives mourned, then underwent purification ceremonies that ritually severed them from the deceased and prepared them for remarriage.

Customarily, for the patrilineal Mende, a widow of child-bearing age will enter a leviratic marriage with her deceased husband's brother, son by a different mother, or (classificatory) brother's son. Each widow chooses the eligible man she prefers. The man, meanwhile, "shows himself" to the widow of his choice by making small gifts to her parents (Little, 1967: 150).

Yoko chose Gbanya, who was possibly her husband's classificatory brother's son. She went to him in Senehun in the style of an important woman, accompanied by her younger brother Lamboi and a contingent that probably included some of her junior kinsmen and domestic slaves (Easmon, 1958: 166).

Gbanya's fame as a warrior spread until he was considered the chief leader in the upper Bumpe River area. Even the British colonial officials in Freetown knew of him and hired his services. In 1861 when Temne warriors raided an area newly ceded to the British colony, the Governor retaliated by calling out 300 militia from the colony and hiring several hundred Mende warriors from Gbanya. In 1873 Gbanya sent his warriors to the Gold Coast (Ghana), at the government's request, to assist the British in a conflict with the Ashanti (Fyfe, 1962: 310–11, 396).

Gbanya's relationship with the British was not always smooth, however. In 1875 he incurred their wrath by sending two of his subchiefs, with their warriors, to the coast in order to assist John Caulker in a dispute with his kinsman, Chief George Stephen Caulker II, at Shenge. The warriors, as was the custom, plundered the countryside first, then attacked Chief Caulker at Shenge (Caulker MS, part II, p. 13).

This was the very kind of disruption that diminished British-fostered trade, and Governor Rowe personally left Freetown in command of forces to settle the matter. He went into the Senehun area, sent for Gbanya, and detained him in the town of Taiamawaro (Great Britain, 1875, no. 52). As a Mende manuscript narrates, Gbanya's junior wife sought to free him by direct appeal to the Governor (Yoko MS):

Yoko, meanwhile, worked for the release of her husband. She took presents to the Governor and his officers, on behalf of her husband. She left Senehu for Taiamawaro, with a beautiful girl she had just taken out of Bundo [Sande]. The girl carried a bag of rice. A ram was also taken as a gift. Yoko was also accompanied by one of her brothers, Lamboi, who, when they were approaching the encampment, deserted her with the apprehension that he too might be taken prisoner. She proceeded confidently alone, arriving at the gate, and asking the sentry for admission and an interview with the Governor. Impressed by the courage and the beauty of the woman, the sentry and the officers granted her request.

On being introduced to Sir Samuel Rowe, she presented her gifts and meekly pleaded the innocence of her husband, Banya, in the recent outbreak and promised that if His Excellency would release him she would immediately direct the capture of the ring leaders of the upheaval. Sir Samuel Rowe was touched by this woman's valiant attitude and courage, and acceded to the request.

Gbanya and some of his subchiefs were flogged, warriors' towns were destroyed, and the people were fined 10,000 bushels of rice. Three Sherbro war leaders were publicly hanged, and the Caulker chiefs ceded the right to collect customs to the colonial government (Great Britain, 1875, no. 51). Yoko now had firsthand experience with the power of the British and her own skill in dealing with them. Gbanya encouraged her in developing her own reputation as a political figure, sending her on diplomatic missions over a wide area of the interior, and to the colonial capital (Easmon, 1958: 167). He also elevated her to the status of head wife. For a chief of Gbanya's stature the "household" (*mawe*) of kin, wards, clients, and slaves would extend to the limits of the town and beyond to satellite villages. The head wife, if she possessed organizational skills, might produce considerable agricultural surpluses. From those stores that she controlled, she could feed her own kin and clients, such people constituting a political wealth of supporters residing with her in her husband's town. Gbanya would be appreciative of any surplus wealth Yoko might achieve, since he was obliged to offer hospitality to subchiefs and other notables. He could also feed more warriors and give gifts, the necessary ingredient in all alliance-making transactions.

When Gbanya became fatally ill, Yoko cared for him attentively. For this and the above reasons, she is remembered and praised for being a good wife who deserved to achieve respect and power in full measure (Kandeh, 1969).

Before Gbanya died in 1878, he called his kinsmen to tell them that he wished to be succeeded by his wife Yoko. He further instructed them to inform Governor Rowe of his wish that she be recognized as a chief (Easmon, 1958: 167; Yoko MS; Leigh, 1969). However, the colonial officials seemed far more interested in seeing a person friendly to their commercial interests established as chief at Senehun than in honoring Gbanya's dying wish (Sierra Leone, 1878–82: Rowe to Kebekeh, Sept. 9, 1878). It was not until 1884 that Yoko was recognized as the "Principal Lady at Sennehoo" and later as the "Queen of Sennehoo" (Sierra Leone, 1882–86: Havelock to Yoko, May 6, 1884).

Although a formal Protectorate was not declared until 18 years after Gbanya's death, Madam Yoko was well aware that the British had become the overriding power in the upper Bumpe River area, and she set about winning their favor. When disputes threatened to become petty wars, she mediated them in the style of a chief, at the same time keeping the government in Freetown informed of developments and asking their assistance when necessary.[5]

5 The following is a sample of Sierra Leone relevant documents: Rowe to Yoko, Dec. 1, 1885, and Feb. 14, 1886 (1882–86); Hay to Yoko, Jan. 8 and Feb. 14, 1887 (1886–87); Parkes to Yoko, May 11, 1889 (1887–89); Parkes to Yoko, April 26, 1890 (1890); Parkes to Yoko, Nov. 22, 1895 (1895–96); and Parkes to Yoko, Sept. 7, 1897 (1889–98).

The following is a description of Madam Yoko written by a traveling missionary in 1885, a year after she was officially recognized as a chief (Carthew in Fyfe, 1964: 238):

In the evening we paid a visit to the most wealthy and influential native in town, named Yoko, the widow of the late chief of Sennehoo. She is about 35 years of age, has a good appearance, is very reserved in manners, shrewd, thoughtful, and dignified, and has all the semblance of superiority to her surroundings, befitting her for her elevated position. As is customary in these places, she is the possessor of many slaves, who live in small towns owned by her, near and around Sennehoo. These work her farms, and she is supported solely by their labor and industry. About her person is a train of female attendants—about twenty in number, all slaves—who are her ladies-in-waiting, and ministers to her wants and wishes.

To summarize, Yoko acquired power through traditional avenues as well as displaying innovative behavior in the incipient colonial period. She had some claim to aristocratic descent, and enjoyed support from her brothers and other consanguines, even while living in the towns of her three husbands. As a wife she created wealth through farming and received gifts of goods and slaves from her appreciative husbands and kinsmen. She was becoming prominent in the Sande society, a source of ritual authority and wealth in goods and loyal supporters, as well as having power in her lion-tongue talisman. Finally, she was intelligent and charming and actively sought power for herself.

Exercise of Power

Where the role of earlier Kpa Mende chiefs had been one of warrior-leaders expanding into alien territory, Madam Yoko correctly assessed the new colonial realities and abandoned any attempts to encourage further migrations. Her political task was to consolidate the gains and unify the Kpa Mende under her authority. She did this primarily by making alliances and secondarily by using judicious force, even using troops under British orders.

When Gbanya died in 1878, Madam Yoko was about 29 years of age. She had not borne a child. Never marrying again, she did have consorts, perhaps so that any child she might bear would be her successor rather than being affiliated to the father's patrilineage. However, Madam Yoko remained childless and was succeeded in office by Lamboi, her younger brother.

She was a most attractive woman by all accounts and did make direct friendship alliances with several figures, notably with the Governor's native interpreters in Freetown (Easmon, 1958: 167; Fyfe, 1962: 256). Even today the interpreter serving an official in that multilingual country has great latitude in presenting a petitioner's case in a favorable or unfavorable light (Jambai, 1970).

A woman chief like Madam Yoko has an advantage in that she can make alliances, which might include the gift of sexuality, with men directly. A man making an alliance with another man must do it indirectly through a woman, the sister or daughter he gives as a wife. Any children born of such a union remain a focus of interest and responsibility for both biological parents, binding the aging woman and her ally together in an on-going alliance.

As important as alliances of this quality are, a chief, in order to effectively bind subjects and allies to herself or himself, must make alliances in quantity as well. If Madam Yoko were a male chief in Mende society at that time, she might take daughters from 100 or more leading families as wives. All would benefit from the alliance. The women enjoy the status of a chief's wife in a large, important household, and their parents and extended kin, in the role of in-laws to the chief, can expect such privileges as a favorable decision following litigation in the chief's court. Reciprocally, the chief expects to receive special loyalty and assistance from his affines, and the children his wives bear make his lineage grow strong.

Being a woman, Madam Yoko used the Sande society to augment her alliance-making potential. Since her initiation she had been distinguished in the womanly art of Sande dancing. As Gbanya's wife she may have functioned as the chief patron of Sande in the Senehun area (Yoko MS). Later in her life, when she moved to Moyamba, she established a chapter of the women's society there. An aged informant, who had been initiated into Sande by Madam Yoko and had remained in her household as a ward, related that after Yoko was made chief she proclaimed a law that Sande leaders in all the country around should not initiate women in their localized chapters but bring them to the initiation bush that she sponsored: "That would increase her fame" (Kandeh, 1969).

Following initiation, after the young women had been discharged from the Sande bush they were presented to their parents. According to Hannah Kandeh, the parents would refuse them, saying: " 'No, Madam, we have given these children to you; you are the owner of these girls. You may give them in marriage to anyone you please.' She gave them to husbands, to constables and noble men of the country." Easmon also relates that families strove to get their daughters into Madam Yoko's Sande bush: "She selected all the best young girls for her bush and then disposed of them in marriage to the leading men who would help in her own advancement" (1958: 167). Women chiefs today continue to utilize Sande in their political careers (Hoffer, 1972: 159–61).

Where a male chief makes alliances in one direction by receiving a wife from a family, Madam Yoko made alliances in two directions, by receiving a young woman through initiation and wardship, and then giving her out later as a wife into another family. Yoko had a special relationship with the young woman's family, acting as their daughter's "mother" in a society where fosterage is a widespread institution. Later she would be mother-in-law to the influential man who received the ward as his wife.

Ideally, a male chief is obliged to keep his wife for life; therefore there is a limit to the number of women his household can accommodate. Madam Yoko made a double alliance with each ward, and since she did not keep a ward for long, she could make far more alliances through the exchange of women than a male chief could. Only one thing was lacking in this arrangement. She did not actually "marry" her wards by giving bridewealth to their families. Therefore the children they bore during wardship were never affiliated to Madam Yoko's lineage. Indeed, she died without having a single direct heir.

Madam Yoko's alliance with the British, and with Sierra Leoneans under British command in the Frontier Police and civil services, was many-faceted. An elderly Mende recounted how Madam Yoko would invite British officials to her town and stage a dance with Sande dancers; the white men would "dash" the dancers by placing a pound note on their perspiration-covered foreheads (Leigh, 1969). Also, Madam Yoko had many wards to give as wives to native officers of the Frontier Police and to helpful civil servants in Freetown.

Her relationship with the British was part of her mystique of power. "She was feared because she could call upon the British, but she was also feared and respected for her own power. Disputes were brought to her from far away. If the headman or chief could not reach a decision, she was asked to decide" (Leigh, 1969). Unfortunately the historical account, written largely as a by-product of British imperial interests, records far more of her dealings with colonial officials than with her own people.

As an example of her political skill in the colonial milieu, Madam Yoko used the British to rid herself of the Kpa Mende chief, Kamanda, who was her rival for supremacy in the upper Bumpe River area. She told the Governor, through her friend the Government Interpreter, that Kamanda was allied with a group of raiding Temne warriors. The colonial government put the Temne down by burning towns and rice fields and deporting six leaders: five Temne warriors and Kamanda (Fyfe, 1962: 475–76; 1964: 242–43).

Madam Yoko's success at manipulating British colonial power for her own ends eventually caught her up in a conflict of interests. Since 1892, contingents of the Frontier Police had been established in outposts beyond the limits of the colony. In the hospitable tradition of a Mende chief, Madam Yoko looked after the personal comfort and routine needs of those stationed at Senehun (Little, 1967: 45; Ranson, 1968: 13).[6] However, the Frontier Police were poorly supervised and were predisposed to flout the traditional authority of chiefs, the "owners of the land." The Frontier Police were recruited in Freetown, where many had gone as escaped slaves or young men evading the authority of elders. Posted up country, they were blamed for "spoiling the country": taking fowls, goats, slaves, and even chiefs' wives for themselves in a high-handed fashion. The phrase "to spoil the country" has deep meaning, connoting any act that violates the laws ordained by the ancestors and guarded by the authority of the secret societies. Since Madam Yoko was accredited, more than anyone else, with making way for the intrusion of colonial institutions into Mende land, some chiefs began to grumble that it was Madam Yoko herself who had "spoilt the country" (Leigh, 1969; Sierra Leone, 1899: 241–42).

In 1896 all the hinterland areas that constitute the present nation of Sierra Leone were declared a British Protectorate. Soon after, an ordinance was sent out to all chiefs requiring them to collect a 5-shilling tax on every house in the land. The financial burden fell most heavily on chiefs, since their houses might constitute an entire town of 200 people, and even outlying villages. Madam Yoko agreed to pay the tax and directed her subchiefs to pay as well. Some of the chiefs grumbled that if they paid for what they already "owned," they would no longer be masters of their own land. In this unsettled situation the District Commissioner, on two occasions, requisitioned large numbers of laborers from Madam Yoko and her subchiefs to build administrative centers in the Protectorate (Sierra Leone, 1899: 234–35).

Some of Madam Yoko's subchiefs held secret meetings, blaming her for abuses of the Frontier Police, taxes, and requisitioned labor. They also felt that the tax money was "measured out in baskets and given to her" but not to them (Sierra Leone, 1899: 234–35). They spoke of her as a "little girl," a towering insult in a society structured upon age-status respect relationships (Kandeh, 1969). It asserted that she was a small child with no training and no sense. That insult extended to her parents

---

[6] Madam Yoko accepted police from the colony as early as 1884. See Sierra Leone, 1882–86: Havelock to Yoko, May 19, 1884; and 1887–89: Parkes to Yoko, May 27, 1889.

and entire family, implying that they had not been responsible enough to see that she was properly reared, initiated into Sande, and made knowledgeable about womanly matters. An insult of that magnitude could easily be a declaration of war in Mende land.

After the last directive for laborers, Madam Yoko narrated: "I sent some, and sent word to the other Chiefs to send some. The people said: 'Our labourers will turn into warriors....' And that was the time the outbreak began" (Sierra Leone, 1899: 234–35). Some of her subchiefs remained loyal. Biriwa, son of the late chief of Taiama, later testified: "Madam Yoko is the Paramount Chief: I look on her as my mother" (p. 241). But Chief Furi Vong, also of Taiama, said: "I have become an instrument of Madam Yoko. The respect that is due to us as Chief of the country has been taken away from us and given to policemen" (p. 241). Madam Yoko, warned of the impending war, went to the newly constructed barracks, which received reinforcements from the colony, and withstood the attack.

The Hut Tax War encompassed the entire Sierra Leone Protectorate, coordinated secretly by the men's Poro society in much of the country (Fyfe, 1962: 556ff; 1964: 247; Mannah-Kpaka, 1953: 36). It occurred suddenly, a simultaneous rising throughout the country. All police and English-speaking people who could be seized—administrators, traders, missionaries—were killed.

"When the war was over the young boys and girls captured as prisoners were rescued and given to Madam Yoko" (Yoko MS). Warriors were tried under British law, and after a commission of inquiry into the rebellion was held, Madam Yoko was commended and "awarded a large silver medal by Her Most Gracious Majesty, Queen Victoria the Good, as a mark of appreciation for Yoko's loyalty and devotedness to the British throne, and proclaimed her Supreme Ruler of the Kpa Mendes in the presence of an assembly of chiefs" (Yoko MS). The silver medal does indeed exist, as does the Mende tradition that Madam Yoko's "wealth" in dependents increased as a result of her role in the tax war.

All of her subjects, of course, did not remain loyal, her own town of Senehun being destroyed by vengeful Mende warriors. She moved to Moyamba, the new administrative headquarters nearby, and "sat down" on one of her subchiefs, a man of the Kaiyamba lineage. She arrived with a retinue of about 250 men and women, who would loyally serve her and form the core of her residential enclave (Ranson, 1968: 19). She centralized her rule by decreeing that all her subchiefs must build houses in her compound and reside there when she called them (Kandeh, 1969). She established a chapter of Sande at Moyamba (Kandeh, 1969) and may have had some role in establishing Wunde, the society of warriors

(Jaiah, 1970); what her relationship was with Poro is not known. She engaged in discreet little wars, enlarging the area under her direct control until she was the effective ruler of all the Kpa Mende (Fyfe, 1962: 604; Easmon, 1958: 168).

Madam Yoko may have died by her own hand, as Sir Harry Luke narrated, or "from the effect of poison through a mistake in the composition of some native medicine," as the *Intelligence Diary Ronietta District*, August 1906, stated (Ranson, 1968: 20). According to Ngolotamba Lamboi, Madam Yoko's classificatory grandson, she had a boundary dispute with Paramount Chief Beimba of Kakua Chiefdom. One of her subchiefs was to argue her case to the District Commissioner, but he failed to appear on time and the boundary was drawn to Chief Beimba's advantage, excluding from Kpa Mende territory the very town in Gbo Chiefdom where Yoko was born. "She felt she could not stand the shame ...and resolved not to live any longer to see another disgrace" (Abraham, 1971: 155–56).

Madam Yoko was succeeded by her younger brother, Lamboi, but within two years he became paralyzed, and ruled feebly until his death in 1917. By that time, their younger brother Goba was also dead. Lamboi's son, Kandeh, also died before being given the staff of office, allegedly "tricked by bad medicine" (Kandeh, 1969; Yoko MS). Two years later, Madam Yoko's Kpa Mende Confederacy was dissolved into 14 separate chiefdoms. The Kaiyamba lineage reasserted itself in Moyamba, and Madam Yoko lies in her lonely grave without descendants in the town to honor her memory.

Conclusion

Many of the political strategies Madam Yoko used were available to politically ambitious persons of both sexes. High office is more likely achieved by men and women who are members of an important lineage, maintain the support of patrilineal kin, and make new political ties through gifts, hospitality, and marriage. However, Mende women have particular advantages in being bearers of children and nurturing figures: the lingering affection that adults feel for women as supportive figures has a political dimension. Thus, one of Madam Yoko's subchiefs could explain his political allegiance to her by saying he looked upon her as a mother.

Although politically successful, Madam Yoko's life is the tragedy of a barren woman. She bore no children to guarantee her immortality. However, in life she possessed extraordinary womanly graces, which she exercised for political advantage. Those very womanly graces were recognized and valued by women as well as men, resulting in Yoko's ascendance as a leader in Sande, the women's secret society. Women as a group play a major role in creating wealth. They also enjoy a monopoly on producing children for their husbands' patrilineages. Sande has a monopoly on transforming girls into marriageable women, who may procreate and assume other wifely responsibilities. It was through Sande, an exclusively womanly institution, that Madam Yoko was perhaps most masterful in making political alliances, taking initiates as wards or quasi-wives, and then giving them out in a second-stage alliance.

In making her own conventional marriages, Yoko demonstrated that women are not necessarily passive pawns moved about in patrilineal-virilocal societies. She seemed to have exercised considerable initiative in dissolving her first marriage and choosing the subsequent men she would marry or take as consorts. While a wife, she managed to include her own kin and domestic slaves, her personal supporters, within her husbands' households. With grace and courage she earned the kind of respect that allowed her to enjoy the authority of head wife and to succeed her third husband in his chiefly office, vastly extending the area under her hegemony during a very stormy period of Sierra Leonean history.

Both oral tradition and written historical documents suggest that women in this ethnic area have enjoyed high office, as lineage heads, heads of secret societies, and chiefs, for centuries (Alldridge, 1901: 166, 181; Fyfe, 1962: 3, 19; Little, 1967: 195–96). A 1914 listing of paramount chiefs in Sierra Leone indicates 15 percent of the Mende chiefdoms ruled by women (Sierra Leone, 1970). In 1914 most women chiefs were described as strong figures, for example, "firm and just in her dealings with her people," or "a very shrewd and capable old woman" (Sierra Leone, 1914). Contemporary women paramount chiefs are equally prominent, and their political influence now extends into national and international arenas (Hoffer, 1972).

Some authors have attempted to explain away women chiefs by suggesting that they were chosen by their own people in order to obviate the vengeance of the British after the Hut Tax War (Little, 1967: 195), or that they are simply a creation of the colonial government, especially since women were viewed by the British as weak and easily manipulated (Abraham, 1971: 13). The historical record suggests otherwise, and Madam Yoko's case should raise the question of who was manipulating whom during the onset of British colonialism.

PEGGY R. SANDAY

Female Status in the Public Domain

In this cross-cultural analysis of female status, I have been guided by the need for an explanatory framework that includes both an explicit statement of relationships between phenomena and a specification of how these change as the relevant variables are altered. In the formulation that follows, I shall expand on a postulated model of the evolution of female status, described in detail elsewhere (Sanday, 1973). My emphasis will be on the ecological and demographic factors that influence a shift from a relative imbalance of power between males and females to a situation where power is more equally distributed between the sexes.

This model postulates that in the evolution of human culture social survival depends on the disproportionate expenditure of energy by males and females in three major activities: reproduction, defense, and subsistence. Since reproductive activity falls to the female, a constraint is imposed on the proportion of total female energy to be utilized in other activities. Such a constraint in turn increases the probability that the other two tasks draw more on the energy of males, thus placing men

This paper is an expanded and revised version of a paper published in the *American Anthropologist* (Sanday, 1973). This version constitutes further clarification of my thinking on the subject of female status cross-culturally. I am indebted to numerous persons who commented on the original version and whose criticisms forced me into conceptual clarification. Many of these people attended the meetings of the Society for Cross-Cultural Research (Philadelphia, Pennsylvania, February 1973), where I presented the present version. In particular I wish to thank Carol and Mel Ember, Ward Goodenough, Leigh Minturn, Albert Pepitone, Paul Rosenblatt, Alice Schlegel, and numerous graduate students in the Department of Anthropology at the University of Pennsylvania.

I also wish to acknowledge the aid of Rebecca Parfitt and William Morris, who spent many hours discussing with me the final theoretical model. Rebecca Parfitt also was extremely helpful and concise in her coding of many of the variables.

Finally I wish to acknowledge the intellectual debt I owe to many of the contributors to this volume. In particular, the papers by Louise Lamphere, Michelle Rosaldo, and Karen Sacks stimulated and supported many of the points I incorporate into the general theory. Michelle Rosaldo's editorial comments have also been extremely insightful.

in a strategic position to gain control of resources. The question of interest here concerns the conditions under which the distribution and allocation of male and female energy change sufficiently that females can move into one or more of the other task activities in such a way as to alter what was initially an imbalance of power favoring males. However, before continuing with a discussion of these conditions and how they effect a change in other variables that are posited to co-vary with relative sex status, we must discuss the operational definition of female status to be employed.

Female Status: Two Domains and Three Parameters

In developing an operational definition of female status, it is necessary to distinguish between the domestic and public domains and to decide whether to focus on the degree to which women are respected and revered in the domestic and public domains or to concentrate only on the degree to which women hold power and/or authority in one of these domains. Such considerations result in three possible, but not necessarily interrelated, parameters, which should be kept analytically distinct in the discussions of female status. Furthermore, the extent to which they are manifested in the domestic domain may be independent of their manifestation in the public domain.

The domestic domain includes activities performed within the realm of the localized family unit. The public domain includes political and economic activities that take place or have impact beyond the localized family unit and that relate to control of persons or control of things. The distinction between public and domestic realms, also drawn by Rosaldo and by Sacks (both this volume), is important, since high status in one domain might conceivably preclude high status in the other, in some societies.

M. G. Smith (1960: 18–19) defines power as "the ability to act effectively on persons or things, to take or secure favourable decisions which are not of right allocated to the individuals or their roles." Power, then, is de facto and not necessarily recognized. He defines authority as "the right to make a particular decision and to command obedience." In other words, authority is recognized and legitimized power. Rosaldo (this volume) also discusses female power and authority using Smith's definitions. Since most ethnographers have little or nothing to say explicitly about female power in the public domain, Smith's definition provides a useful operational indicator for making inferences. Furthermore, it is important to recognize in dealing with the subject of female status that although female authority *may* imply power (I shall not explore that question here), female power does not necessarily imply authority. Consequently, one must make inferences about the degree of female power in assessing female status.

The degree to which women are respected and revered is the parameter most ethnographers have in mind when they say that women have high status or subordinated status. Western women in their often highly valued roles as helpmate, sex object, the "driving force behind every successful man," etc., can be said to have relatively high status along this parameter. On the other hand, Nupe women, who occupy an economic position generally much better than that of their husbands but who are openly resented and feared by Nupe men (Nadel, 1960), would have to be defined as low in status according to this dimension alone. The same can be said of many African women who contribute heavily to the basic economy while male activities, according to LeVine (1970: 175), are much more prestigious. Brown (1970) makes a similar point when she notes that in one case high status may be inferred from deferential treatment, whereas in another high status may consist of an actual position of power over basic resources and important decisions. As she points out, the two need not coincide and should be considered separately. She describes in detail Iroquois women who were not accorded deferential treatment but who held considerable economic and political power. How deference relates to authority (does authority necessarily imply deference?) is another question we shall not get into here.

With these considerations in mind, female status is generally defined in terms of (1) the degree to which females have authority and/or power in the domestic and/or public domains; and (2) the degree to which females are accorded deferential treatment and are respected and revered in the domestic and/or public domains. An analysis of variation in female status and the causes of this variation in any one of these conceptual domains is a legitimate and interesting task. Even more interesting would be an analysis of the relationship between the domains. For example, it might be discovered that high female status in one domain precludes, or is antecedent to, high status in another domain.

In the empirical analysis of female status to be presented below, deferential treatment and respect will not be included in the operational definition of female status. The reason for this is that while power and authority may form a single continuum, deferential treatment may be either independent or negatively related to these parameters. Consequently, deferential treatment is excluded until this possibility can be empirically explored. *I shall concentrate exclusively on female power and authority in the public domain.* The domestic domain will be ex-

cluded for two reasons. First, to include both domains at this point
is likely to complicate matters, since it is conceivable that status in one
domain may preclude status in the other.[1] Second, at this time a cross-
cultural analysis of variation in female power and authority in the public domain is particularly appropriate in view of the current effort by
Western women to remove barriers that have traditionally confronted
them in the economic and political spheres. This effort has attracted
widespread speculation, mostly unsubstantiated, about the causes of the
status of women in general. A cross-cultural analysis of female public
power and authority brings to attention societies in which women have
achieved a relatively high status in the public domain, thereby con-
tradicting the popular belief that women have been universally excluded from this domain. Such an analysis also provides the only format
with which we can understand objectively the causes of variation in
female public status. This may give activist Western women further
insight into where to concentrate their efforts to bring about change in
the imbalance of power between males and females.

An Operational Definition of Female Status in the Public Domain

The general definition presented above is couched in terms of the
degree to which women have de facto or recognized decision-making
power that affects activities at the economic and/or political levels. I
have further specified this definition so that data could be collected from
a cross-cultural sample. In a pilot study of twelve societies (see Sanday,
1973), I selected four dimensions for coding female status in the public
domain. These are:

I. *Female material control.* Females have the ability to act effectively
on, to allocate, or to dispose of, things—land, produce, crafts, etc.—
beyond the domestic unit.

II. *Demand for female produce.* Female produce has a recognized
value either internally—beyond the localized family unit—or in an external market.

III. *Female political participation.* Females, even if only through a
few token representatives, may express opinions in a regular, official
procedure and may influence policy affecting people beyond the domestic unit.

IV. *Female solidarity groups devoted to female political or economic
interests.* Females group together in some regular way to protect or represent their interests, and are recognized and effectual in this activity.

[1] For a recent cross-cultural analysis of female domestic authority, see Schlegel
(1972).

TABLE 1

Scale of Female Status with Related Variables

(P = present; A = absent; ? = information not available or unclear)

Society	I Female material control	II Demand for female produce	III Female political partici- pation	IV Female solidarity groups	Scale score	Percentage of female contribu- tion to sub- sistence	Percentage of deities who are female
Yoruba	P	P	P	P	5	30	31.5
Iroquois	P	P	P	P	5	50	55.5
Samoans	?	P	P	P	5	50	53.1
Crow	P	P	P	A	4	29	40
Aymara	P	P	A	A	3	52	46.2
Tapirape	?	P	A	A	3	24	20
Rwala	P	?	A	A	3	10	0
Andamans	P	A	A	A	2	50	43.8
Tikopia	A	A	A	A	1	75	60a
Azande	A	?	A	A	1	59	33.3
Somali	A	A	A	A	1	45	40a
Toda	A	A	A	A	1	10	37.5

a Only 40 percent (Tikopia) and 20 percent (Somali) of female deities have general powers.

When the data were collected, it was discovered that, using Guttman scaling procedures, it was possible to order the indicators into a continuously scaled measure of female status. The scale and the societies of the pilot sample are presented in Table 1. The coefficient of reproducibility is .92. The high reproducibility coefficient suggests that each indicator can be seen as a point on a continuum of female status. This continuum is of the general form presented in Figure 1.

The fact that the indicators could be scaled suggests, for the pilot sample at least, that the antecedent of female political authority is some degree of economic power, i.e. ownership or control of strategic resources. Whether economic power, noted in indicator I of the scale, includes economic authority, i.e. the recognized right to act effectively on things, is unclear. In some societies, such as the Yoruba, women have a clear and recognized title to the produce they trade. In this sense the

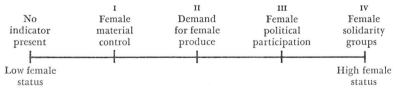

	I	II	III	IV
No indicator present	Female material control	Demand for female produce	Female political participation	Female solidarity groups
Low female status				High female status

Fig. 1. Scale of female status

Yoruba women can be said to have economic authority. In other societies women may have economic power but not authority. For example, among the Ibo (who were not included in the pilot sample) women made pots and traded, but the men controlled most of the income in the period before European contact (LeVine, 1970). After European contact the existence of certain other conditions aided Ibo women to mobilize their economic power and develop economic authority. The fact that female economic power precedes economic or political authority is not too surprising, since power over strategic resources has been frequently noted to be antecedent to or at least correlated with the development of economic and political authority.

The continuum of female status depicted in Figure 1 omits an important characteristic of political authority, i.e. the right to allocate or disburse political rights and power. This can be seen as a sixth step on the scale. It was excluded from the analysis because (it is conjectured) women do not seem to gain this right in many societies. If one accepts the assumption that female public status has evolved over time in response to a redistribution of male and female energy, then it would be expected that only a few societies would exhibit the sixth step on the scale. In the pilot sample, only the Iroquois show evidence of women's being accorded this right. As Brown notes (1970), Iroquois women had the authority to veto the nomination of the chiefs, could decide the fate of prisoners of war, could participate in the deliberations of the Council through their male speakers, and had a voice concerning warfare and treaties. Even among the Iroquois, although female power was socially recognized and institutionalized, female authority was exercised indirectly through women's power to veto and to withhold food from war parties. Female political authority in some areas of Africa has reached a more advanced state. According to Hoffer (1972), within the Mende/Sherbro area in 1970 there were eighty-one chiefdoms, ten of which were headed by women. In 1914 in the same ethnic area, there were eighty-four chiefdoms, ten of which were headed by women. For further examples of advanced female political authority, see Lebeuf (1963); and for an example of an effective and powerful female solidarity group, see Leis (this volume). The question of concern now is the conditions under which women move into the public sphere along the continuum of female status discussed above.

A Theory of Female Status in the Public Domain

The basic argument for the theory, presented in Figure 2, postulates that initially female energy is concentrated in the reproductive and

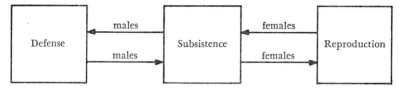

Fig. 2. The flow of male and female energy in three task activities

child-rearing sphere, whereas male energy is concentrated mainly in the subsistence sphere. Over time the presence of human predators causes men to move out of the subsistence sphere and into the defense sphere. Depending on the nature of the warfare, its prolongation, and its interference with male subsistence activities, females move into the subsistence sphere to replace the displaced male energy. Females remain in the subsistence sphere according to whether males continue in warfare activities or become involved in other activities resulting in prolonged male absence. Even if men move back into the subsistence sphere, some women may remain. Over time their number may grow as men periodically flow in and out of the subsistance sphere (see Lipman-Blumen, 1972, for an interesting discussion of this process in the United States). This process may in time give rise to a condition of balanced division of labor, i.e. both sexes contribute to subsistence activities. The importance of balanced division of labor in the development of female public status will be discussed in detail below.

This is a simplified model, which includes the assumption, mentioned earlier, that initially female energy was concentrated primarily in the reproductive child-rearing sphere. Another implicit assumption is that females do not develop public power and authority unless at least some of their energies are employed in productive activities. The empirical relationship between female production and female status in the pilot sample will be presented below. As will be seen, this is not a simple linear relationship.

The basic argument, then, focuses on male absence and female contribution to production. Male absence from the subsistence sphere forces women to enter this sphere if social survival is to be ensured. However, as noted elsewhere (Sanday, 1973), other conditions might also achieve the same result. Whereas defense or related activities increase the likelihood that females will enter the subsistence arena, this likelihood can increase independently when ecological conditions favor the successful utilization of female energy. In particular, when the mix between population density and the natural environment favors shifting agriculture or horticulture, women are more likely to engage in subsistence activi-

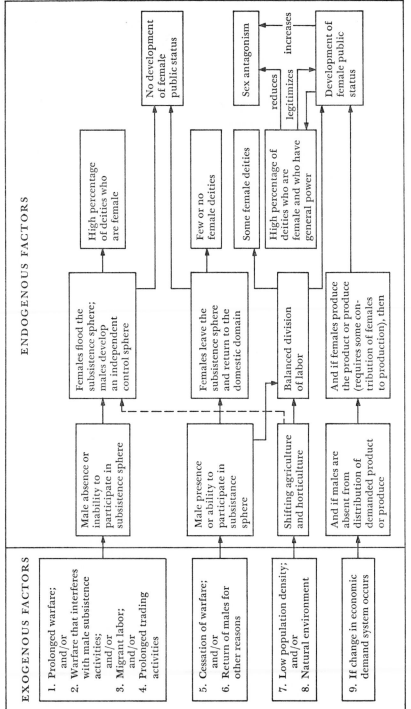

Fig. 3. Theory of female status in the public domain

ties. An interesting but unanswered question is whether this also frees men to engage in warfare or to develop an exclusively male control sphere.

Factors Affecting Female Contribution to Subsistence

The model of female status, further elaborated in Figure 3, rests heavily on female contribution to production as an intervening variable. In this section I shall undertake a summary of the empirical correlates of female contribution to subsistence. The hypothesized factors affecting female contribution to subsistence are presented in Fig. 3.

Using data drawn from the *Ethnographic Atlas* (see Sanday, 1973, for the details of this analysis), it was found that regional identification and type of agriculture explained most of the variance in percentage of female contribution to subsistence. Women contribute more to subsistence in Africa and the Insular Pacific and in shifting agriculture or horticultural societies. These findings, although they present some contradictory results for South America, support the hypothesized relationship between type of environment (see exogenous factors 7 and 8 in Figure 3) and female contribution to production. I have discussed the relationship between population density and natural environment and type of agriculture in an earlier paper (Sanday, 1973), drawing on the work of Boserup (1970).

Ample evidence indicates a relationship between the effect of a certain type of warfare and female productive labor. Ember and Ember (1971) find support for the hypothesis that men do more in subsistence than women unless a certain type of warfare prevents them. Epstein (1971: 11) discusses the increased utilization of women in the economies of the Communist-bloc countries caused by the huge wartime losses of manpower. In the Soviet Union, she notes that in spite of the wide base of female professionals, women are still not represented at the top of the Soviet professional and governmental hierarchy. The scale of female status presented here suggests that this is simply a matter of time and the development of female solidarity groups.

For the effect on female labor of other factors resulting in male absence and a drain of male labor, a study by LeVine is instructive. LeVine (1970: 175–77) discusses a pattern of labor migration that developed in colonial Africa, resulting in rural African men leaving home to work far away for a period of years. Many tasks performed by men were relegated to their wives and children. According to LeVine, the absence of the men loosened the control over their wives' activities, but it did not result in increased status for women. What has resulted, LeVine suggests, is increased hostility by mothers toward their children due to the frustrations of the excessive work burden. LeVine goes on to say that these women, and other African women who shoulder a heavy work load in the absence of men, find some emotional comfort in their subordinated status. I strongly disagree with this interpretation, and suggest instead that the frustration and hostility toward children is evidence that the women are not happy with their subordinated status. It is conceivable that the women in the societies LeVine refers to will assert their independence, with a consequent change in their status. LeVine's example, however, supports the contention that a drain on male energy will result in the redistribution of female energy. Ember and Ember (1971: 579) have also stressed the absence of males as a key determinant. In addition to their warfare example, they allude briefly to the necessity for men to be away on long trading trips in parts of Micronesia and Melanesia as another determinant.

Relationship Between Female Status and Female Contribution to Subsistence

The correlation between percentage contribution of women to subsistence and the scaled variable of female status in the pilot sample is negative ($r = -.16$). Plotting these two variables with data from Table 1 reveals a curvilinear relationship between these two factors (see Figure 4). This means that, when the percentage of female contribution to subsistence is either very high or very low, female status as measured by the scale depicted in Figure 1 is also low. In other words, when women contribute about as much as men, the value of the scaled variable is higher.

As would be expected from the graph presented in Figure 4, the correlation between female status and balanced division of labor by sex is high ($r = -.416$). The coefficient is negative because of the way the balanced division-of-labor variable was computed. The score for each society on this variable was determined by taking the absolute value of the difference from the overall mean percentage of female contribution to subsistence for the pilot sample. Thus a low value indicates more balance, and a high value imbalance. The correlation coefficient indicates, as does the graph in Figure 4, that the more balance there is in division of labor by sex, the higher the status score.

The overall mean percentage of female contribution to subsistence in the pilot sample is 40 percent. This is the same value found by Coppinger and Rosenblatt (1968) for a sample of sixty-nine societies, using

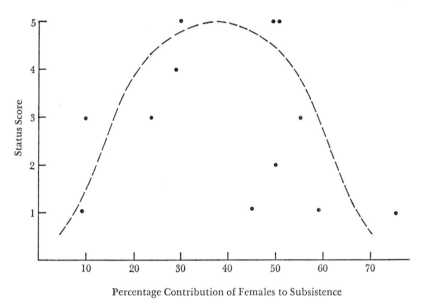

Fig. 4. Relationship between female status and female contribution to subsistence

a similar method for computing percentage of female contribution to subsistence. The fact that 40 percent is taken as representing balanced division of labor by sex is, according to these authors (p. 313), "a reasonable deviation from equal division considering that women must bear and nurse children." These authors found an association between balanced division of labor by sex and the absence of romantic love as a basis for marriage. They conjecture that the dependence of marriage partners on one another for subsistence is an important source of marital stability. They assume that some degree of marital stability is essential in reducing disruption, and that stable marriages need more than a private agreement between a man and a woman. Mutual dependence between spouses for subsistence goods is one source of stability. In the absence of such dependence, an alternative bond must develop. They hypothesize (p. 310) that "romantic love is such an alternative bond, that where subsistence dependence between spouses is strong, romantic love is unimportant as a basis of marriage, while where subsistence dependence between spouses is weak, romantic love is important as a basis of marriage."

The findings of the pilot study indicate that balanced division of

labor is also related to higher female status. This, and the results reported by Coppinger and Rosenblatt, raises two interesting questions. Is it
the presence of romantic love that impedes women's acquisition of
power and authority in the public domain, e.g. is romantic love a mechanism for keeping women in their place and happy with their lot? Or
does the equal participation of men and women in the subsistence arena
give women the impetus for moving into the public domain? It could
be that when men and women experience mutual dependence in the
subsistence arena, both are in a power position relative to each other,
i.e. either one can obstruct the other's actions by withholding something
the other needs. This fact may give men the experience of accepting
female power when it is exercised in other capacities.

The above argument does not explain why women seem to have a
relatively low status when they have a monopoly on the production of
subsistence goods. When women produce most or all of the subsistence
goods, it would be expected that they would have more power vis-à-vis
men. However, it may be the case in such situations that women are
far more dependent on men to meet nonsubsistence survival needs than
men are on women to meet subsistence needs. For example, if men are
engaged in warfare, women may depend on them for the protection of
the family unit. When such warfare ceases, men may develop an independent control sphere, and expressive or actual mechanisms may be
utilized to perpetuate female dependency. In the first case, romantic love
may be one of the expressive means by which women are trained to
maintain a subordinate stance and to be happy with such a position
relative to men. In the second case, women may be treated as slave
labor (as they are in the case of the Azande, to be discussed below) and
forcibly maintained in a subordinated position.

These are interesting speculations for which there is little empirical
support at present. Some of the above relationships are represented in
the flow diagram of Figure 3, which shows a number of avenues by which
women develop public status. It is clear from the above discussion that
contribution to production is a necessary but not sufficient condition.
An examination of some of the societies in the pilot sample supports
some of the above discussion and supplies further insights.

In societies where control and production are linked and a competitive market exists, female power is likely to develop *if* females are actively engaged in producing valued market goods. In societies where
control is based on a magical or religious title, female power is unlikely
to develop unless some exogenous influence (such as the introduction of
cash-cropping, famine, etc.) creates a new demand or results in a revalua-

tion of female produce. Such exogenous influences can result in the development of a new control sphere based primarily on who has access to the valued product rather than on a magical or religious title to it.

The Tikopian, Azande, and Somali women provide examples of cases where women contribute predominantly to subsistence activities but have no status. Firth (1939: 88) notes that whereas in modern European society control over the means of production is divorced from religious title to this control, in Tikopia production is controlled by chiefs whose political and economic influence rests on a religious basis. He also notes the absence of an external market, which means no external outlet for goods produced by women. Internally, the product of female labor is not valued as much as that of male labor, because the main tasks of women demand few technical aids and much hard work. In contrast, male tasks are much more diversified and require more technical assistance. Firth concludes that "the subordinate position of the women as property owners is then to some extent to be correlated with the type of technical equipment and system of production in vogue in Tikopia" (1939: 365).

Among the Azande, women are the main source of labor and are a symbol of wealth. Women are treated much like slaves and have traditionally been barred from the main source of power, which is through the exercise of magic. According to Evans-Pritchard (1937: 284), the exclusion of women from any dealings with the poison oracle has been the most evident symptom of their inferior social position and the means of maintaining them in this position. This situation has changed among the Azande as contact with Europeans has created a demand for some Azande crops. According to De Schlippe (1956: 145), under European rule women became emancipated, crops acquired cash value, war disappeared, hunting was reduced, and men were compelled to invest most of their effort in agriculture. It is interesting to note that when men moved into agricultural production they tended to favor the cash crops introduced by the Europeans, hence limiting the access of women to this new control sphere.

For Azande men, cash crops had a prestige value because of the hierarchical way of their introduction and because of their novelty (De Schlippe, 1956: 145). This, of course, partially limited the access of women to a new control sphere based primarily on production. Had the important cash crops among the Azande not had this prestige value, the status of Azande women might have changed drastically in a short period of time, as it did for the Afikpo Ibo women in eastern Nigeria. According to LeVine (1970: 178), before European contact Ibo women made pots, traded, and farmed, but the men controlled most of the income and performed the prestige activities of yam farming and slave trading. The mobility of Ibo women was limited because of the prevalence of warfare. With the cessation of warfare, mobility became possible and trading increased. At the same time cassava was introduced, which Ibo men regarded with disdain, preferring to farm their prestigeful and ritually important yams. The women were allowed to grow cassava between the yam heaps and to keep the profits for themselves. As time went on, according to LeVine (1970: 178):

This despised crop eliminated the annual famine before the yam harvest and attained a high and stable market value. The Afikpo women became capable of supporting themselves and their children without aid from their husbands, and nowadays they even rent land independently for cassava cultivation. Once a woman becomes self-supporting in this way, she can say, in the words of an elderly Afikpo woman, "What is man? I have my own money" (Ottenberg, 1959: 215). Afikpo husbands have found it increasingly difficult to keep their wives at home in their formerly subordinate position.

The Somali women were treated in much the same way as Azande women. The Somali regard their female children as stock, and in times of famine have sold them as slaves (Drake-Brockman, 1912: 137-38). Women were forced, under threat of physical violence from their husbands, to perform all the menial and heavy work and were allowed to tend sheep and goats. Somali men considered it beneath their dignity to tend anything but camels, cattle, and ponies—the most valuable economic assets of the Somali. Here again we see a case where women perform much of the labor but are denied access to the valued produce and are kept in a subordinate position by external threat.

The social contexts of the Iroquois, Yoruba, and Samoan women provide examples of the conditions under which women can achieve considerable economic and/or political power. Among the Iroquois the control of agricultural production was in the hands of a group of women in the village who formed a mutual aid society. Female control of agricultural production seems to have increased and been strengthened by the prolonged absences of males in warfare and trading activities (Noon, 1949). The literature on the Iroquois stresses the high position of women and their participation in political and religious activities. Women were able to influence decisions of the ruling council both directly and indirectly through the weight of public opinion. Since unanimity was necessary in decisions, any proposal unpopular with the women could be hindered by their disapproval. Women could also hinder or prevent the forming of a war party that lacked their approval by withholding supplies the warriors needed (Randle, 1951).

The Yoruba women are perhaps the most independent in Africa (Le-Vine, 1970: 179). Traditionally these women maintained an autonomous economic role and a higher degree of mobility than, for example, the Ibo women, who were prohibited from moving about freely because of warfare. This suggests that, although warfare may function to increase female participation in production, it may also inhibit the development of female power in some societies (although not in all, as the case of the Iroquois clearly shows). The role of Yoruba women as independent market traders is, and has long been, highly institutionalized. The women have organized trade guilds, which regulate the conditions and standards of the craft and protect the interests of the members. These are powerful organizations whose leaders play an important role in political activities. Such organizations in many African societies are examples of the very real authority exercised by women in African political systems (Lebeuf, 1963).

The status of Samoan women before European contact was not as high as it is reported by Keesing (1937) after European contact. The new status of women was an outgrowth of their organizations and functions in the traditional system (Keesing, 1934: 394). For example, there was an organization of the wives of chiefs and orators, which in modern Samoa developed into a female replica of the men's council, dealing with many matters other than those pertaining to women in earlier days (Keesing, 1937: 9). The traditional women's committees in western Samoa also laid the basis for the later women's *Mau* movement, which gave women a strong taste for politics.

Data on the traditional economic activities of Samoan women indicate that on an informal level women played as active a part as the men in controlling economic arrangements (Mead, 1928: 82). A woman's claim on her family's land rendered her as independent as her husband (Mead, 1928: 108). In agriculture the heaviest work was done by men and the lighter and more detailed work by women. There was little feeling about the relative prestige of men's and women's work. Fine mats, which have been called the Samoan currency, were made by women and were highly valued (Mead, 1930: 67–74). Thus, while traditional Samoan women did not seem to exercise the power that developed among Iroquois and Yoruba women, the basis for the later development of female power and authority seems to have existed.

Female Status, Sex Antagonism, and Female Deities

In developing a theory of female public status, my emphasis has been on ecological and economic factors and the efficient distribution of human energy. An alternative explanation might emphasize magico-religious means by which women gain and maintain title to control. For example, women might gain power and authority in societies where maternity is viewed as a sacred or magical function. As De Beauvoir (1953: 67) has said, this can occur in early agricultural communities where there is frequently an association between maternity and fertility of the soil. In these belief systems the earth is seen as belonging to women, thus giving them religious title to the land and its fruits. Such beliefs are to be found in many societies. Among the Iroquois, for example, the female virtues of food providing and the fertility and bounty of nature are the qualities most respected and revered. Only women's activities are celebrated in the ceremonial cycle. There are no festivals to celebrate hunting or war, though they probably existed in the past. Most of the ceremonies are thanksgiving for the fertility of the earth, especially for the crops, which are women's chief concern (Randle, 1951: 172).

The problem with this type of explanation is that it can be considered an effect and not a cause of female status. A belief system emphasizing maternity and fertility as sacred may function to legitimize female status that develops because of ecological and economic factors. There is ample evidence in the ethnographic material, discussed above, that a change in female status is associated with a change in the productive system. Where this has occurred, as with the Ibo, it is interesting to note that sex antagonism develops or increases. Perhaps sex antagonism develops in the absence of a belief system that legitimizes and sanctions the power of women. Sex antagonism might be reduced in such societies when a belief system develops in which female power is attributed to the natural functions of women.

In order to investigate further the relationship between the belief system and female public status, I made a study of the sex and domain of authority of the deities, personified natural forces, and folk heroes in each of the societies of the pilot sample. The number in each category having clearly defined and general powers over a group were counted for each society. The percentage of these who were female was computed, as well as the percentage who were female and had clearly defined general power over both males and females (as opposed to power over females only, or males only). The data are displayed in Table 1. These two variables were then correlated with the female status scale and percentage female contribution to subsistence. Whereas there is a high correlation between percentage of deities who are female and female contribution to subsistence ($r = .742$), there is no correlation between the percentage of female deities and female status ($r = .039$). The correlation between the percentage of female deities with general powers over both males and females and female status is low but positive (.300). The correlation between female deities with general powers and female contribution to subsistence is slightly higher ($r = .547$). These pilot results are intriguing and can be interpreted in different ways. Clearly, more work must be done in this area. The flow chart of Figure 3 suggests that the belief system is a reflection and dramatization of female activities in the subsistence domain and that it also may serve to legitimize a change in female public status.

Conclusion

There is no doubt from the data examined that there is a wide range of variation in female public status cross-culturally. In a few of the cases discussed, there is evidence that both men and women have power and authority in the public domain. However, in the majority of cases males clearly have higher public status. The question I have posed in this paper concerns the conditions under which the relative status of women changes in the direction of public equality. In answering this question I assumed that in the initial stages of human society—and probably throughout most of human history—defense, subsistence, and reproduction were necessary activities for social survival and that male energy was more likely to be expended in subsistence and defense while female energy was devoted primarily to reproduction and secondarily to subsistence. If this was the case, it would suggest that males were in a better position to gain both access to and control over strategic resources.

Figure 3 presents the factors that were hypothesized to influence a change in the balance of power between males and females. The predominant emphasis in this schema has been on male absence, ecological factors, and change in the system of demand for female goods. Any condition of prolonged male absence can result in females invading the subsistence sphere if social survival is to continue. Certain ecological conditions can have the same effect. When females move into the subsistence sphere, the flow diagram in Figure 3 suggests three possibilities: women may occupy this sphere temporarily while males are absent; they may become the predominant laborers and remain in this sphere; or they may continue to occupy this sphere in conjunction with males, and a condition of balanced division of labor may result. In the first two cases the data indicate that the public status of women does not change, whereas in the latter case the data indicate that women develop economic and political power. Where females invade the subsistence sphere and remain there, the evidence indicates that males develop an independent control sphere, with the result that women are treated as slave labor. The schema depicted in Figure 3 further suggests that increased demand for certain goods produced by women will also result in the development of economic rights that can lead to an overall change in status.

Finally, it was hypothesized that when females develop economic and political power, this will be legitimized over time through the expressive cultural system. The existence or development of female deities who have general powers can be seen as a means for recognizing and accepting female power. This also can serve to reduce sex antagonism, which seems to develop when the status of women changes in such a fashion as to threaten male power and authority.

This has been, by and large, a programmatic and pilot effort. Although empirical support has been found for some of the relationships represented in Figure 3, the overall model requires empirical testing with an adequate cross-cultural sample. Only then will the theory meet the objections raised by Murdock (1971: 19–20) concerning what passes as theory in anthropology. According to Murdock, anthropological theory "includes remarkably few propositions which meet the basic requirements of science, that is to say, which explicitly state relationships between phenomena, specify precisely how these change as relevant variables are altered, and support such statements with adequate validating evidence." It would be well to keep Murdock's criticisms of anthropological theory in mind when working in the area of relative sex status. Because this is an area prone to bias introduced by both ethnocentrism and sexcentrism, it is particularly important to seek the objectivity provided by the rigorous use of the scientific method.

KAREN SACKS

Engels Revisited: Women, the Organization of Production, and Private Property

This paper reexamines Engels's ideas on the bases of women's social position relative to that of men. Engels is almost alone in providing an account based on a materialist theory—one that sees women's position as varying from society to society, or epoch to epoch, according to the prevailing economic and political relationships of the society. Though he made a number of specific ethnographic errors,[1] I think his main ideas are correct, and they remain the best way of explaining data gathered since he wrote—namely ethnographic and historical data showing that women's social position has *not* always, everywhere, or in most respects been subordinate to that of men.

Since capitalism has dominated and transformed the social orders of most of the world's people, it is useful to look to the past, as Engels has done, through ethnographic and historical reconstruction, both to understand the present state of affairs and to help shape the future. Looking at noncapitalist ways of organizing economic and political relations and how these affected the relative positions of men and women provided Engels with an answer to why women were subordinate to men in capitalist society, and what political and economic changes were needed to end sexual inequality.

The Origin of the Family, Private Property and the State (1891) is more than an analysis of women's status. It is a contrast between nonclass and class societies. Set in an evolutionary framework, it shows how private property originated, how once on the scene it undermined an egalitarian tribal order, creating families as economic units, inequality

Judith K. Brown, Bridget O'Laughlin, Dorothy Remy, Jean Williams, and Soon Young Yoon, as well as both the editors, all contributed a great deal to this paper through their valuable suggestions and criticisms.

[1] I have excluded enumeration of these partly for lack of space, but also because they are substantively secondary and are more than amply dealt with by others.

of property ownership, and, finally, exploitative class societies. Embedded in this picture is a description of how women's social position declined as private property gained strength as an organizing principle for society. Woven into this is an analysis of why such property had the effect it did; specifically, how it transformed women's work organization and, more generally, the relationship of property to class and sex.

The first part of this paper pulls together some of Engels's key points on how the sexual egalitarianism of preclass societies was undermined by changes in women's work, and by the growth of families as important economic units. It is a selective and somewhat interpretive summary. A brief second part reinterprets Engels's terminology and framework in the context of nonclass societies. The third part presents some ethnographic data as historical reconstruction to illustrate Engels's emphasis on the importance of public labor for determining women's social status, and to modify his ideas about women being social adults *or* wifely dependents. The final part suggests why class societies have used the family to circumscribe and subordinate women.

Women in Engels's Theory: A Reconstruction

Engels presents a historical dynamic by which women are transformed from free and equal productive *members of society* to subordinate and dependent *wives* and wards. The growth of male-owned private property, with the family as the institution that appropriates and perpetuates it, is the cause of this transformation. First I shall summarize the way Engels saw this evolutionary process, and then clarify some of Engels's terms.

In the early stages of society, productive resources were owned communally by the tribe or clan. Food had to be collected and cooked daily. Production was for use only, that is, to meet people's subsistence needs. There was no surplus produced for exchange.[2] The group consisting of husband, wife, and dependent children was neither a productive unit nor one for performing housework—nor did it own property. Since Engels sees economic functions as key to the family, and since this group in no way was an economic unit, the family did not exist; it had not precipitated out of the larger household. The household, which was the basic social and economic unit, was communistic in that all food stores were

---

[2] Though Engels does not deal with this situation, people in many nonclass and noncapitalist societies do in fact produce for exchange. The question of how production for exchange in these societies differs from that in capitalist societies is a complex one. Perhaps the best discussion of the fundamental differences involved can be found in Sahlins (1971).

held in common and all work was done for the household rather than for individual members or couples. Women did the housework and ran these households. "In the old communistic household, which embraced numerous couples and their children, the administration of the household, entrusted to the women, was just as much a public, a socially necessary industry as the providing of food by the men" (Engels, 1891: 120).

At this stage the family, which Engels sees as a productive, consuming, and property-owning group, did not exist. Instead, the context of men's and women's life and labor was the tribe or clan. This was a communal property-owning group. Although individuals of both sexes owned tools and personal effects, on their death these passed to other members of their tribe or clan of the same sex, not necessarily to their own children. Decision making, both economic and political, involved the equal participation of all members, men and women. Both sexes were equal members of the group because both made crucial contributions to the economic life of the group.

Engels concluded that the absence of private property made men's productive work and women's household work of equal social significance. Men and women were simply involved in different stages of the production of the same *kinds* of goods—the production of subsistence. All production was of the same kind: production for use. People worked for the communal household or clan rather than for individuals. Since all work was for social use and all adults were social producers, all adults were equal members of the group.

Engels focused on the public rights of women in the early stages of society: participation in political decision making, and their collective right to depose a chief (for the Iroquois). These rights came from membership in the clan, which in turn was based on performance of public or social labor. He was also impressed with the high status of a wife relative to her husband. This he attributed to the solidarity and kinship among the women, the core of the household.

The material base for women's transformation from equal members of society to subordinate wives lay in the development of valuable productive resources, initially the domestication of large animals, as private property. For Engels, "private property" has a specific meaning. Only goods or resources with productive potential can be considered *property*. He was aware that people held personal goods individually. Though these are private, they are not property in the sense Engels means the word. In nonindustrial societies, the most important types of private property are domesticated animals and cultivated land. These are productive *resources*. Tools (productive means) are unimportant because the skills and materials for their manufacture are equally available to all. Engels is concerned with property that has productive potential. Other goods, for conspicuous consumption or display, are a result of economic and political inequality rather than a cause of it. When Engels speaks of private property, he is not referring to these goods.

Private property became possible in human history only when technological development and natural resources allowed a society to develop the skills needed to domesticate animals or to invest labor in land so that its productivity lasted for an appreciable length of time. Engels believed that enduring productivity led to enduring private ownership.

Engels's usage of "private" is broader than the way it is used under capitalism—where there are almost no restrictions on what the owner can do with the property. For Engels, private seems to mean property owned by an individual, or by a family where rights to manage it are vested in one of the owners. It also means that these goods can be disposed of with *some* leeway—that is, to acquire wives, clients, or service from others. Engels saw "gaining a livelihood" as always men's work, and the means of production as always owned by the user (with the stipulation that inheritance remained within the clan). From this, he reasoned that the earliest private productive property, which seemed to be domestic animals, must have been owned by men.[3]

Domesticated animals were assimilated into the older patterns of tool ownership; that is, they were privately owned. Yet animals were a qualitatively new kind of item: they met subsistence needs and they reproduced themselves—they were the first form of private property. The growth of private property shattered the communal political economy of the clan. The foundation for its egalitarianism had been collective ownership of productive property. Now that property was privately owned (by men), the family grew in importance and soon overshadowed the clan as the key economic and decision-making group. Unlike the clan, though, internal family structure was not egalitarian. Families contained propertyless dependents (all women and children, and some propertyless men).

But private property transformed the relations between men and women within the *household* only because it also radically changed the political and economic relations in the larger *society*.

[3] It is worth noting that Engels saw these new items (domesticated animals, cultivated land) as being assimilated into an already existing social context: the pattern of owning personal effects. The qualitatively different nature of these new "effects"— that they could reproduce themselves and their fruits—led to the destruction of the communal political and economic order that had created them. Engels does not attribute the development of private property to a greedy male nature.

The new wealth meant that there was a surplus of goods available for exchange between productive units. With time, production by men specifically for exchange purposes became more developed and expanded, and came to overshadow the household's production for use. Industrial capitalism has now reached the stage where production is almost exclusively social, outside the household, and for exchange, leaving women's work as private maintenance for *family* use.

As production for exchange eclipsed production for use, it changed the nature of the household, the significance of women's work within it, and consequently women's position. Women worked now for their husbands and families instead of for society. Their labor was a necessary but socially subordinate part of producing an exchangeable surplus. Women became wards, wives, and daughters instead of adult members of society.

Private property made its owner the ruler of the household. Women and other propertyless dependents worked to maintain and augment the household head's property, for he was now engaged in competitive production and exchange with other heads of households.

Families perpetuated themselves through time by the inheritance of property. Thus changes took place in the definition of children. From new members of a societal group, they became either private heirs or subordinate, dependent workers. This meant that women's reproductive labor, like their productive work, also underwent a transformation from social to private. People and property became intertwined, and each became part of the definition of the other.

With the further development of technology and accumulation of wealth, the property owners separated themselves from their subordinate kinsmen and allied with other property owners to preserve and defend their holdings against the claims of the nonpropertied. This marked the end of kinship-based *productive* groups and the beginning of class society and the state.

Engels's Theory and Nonclass Societies

To use Engels's concepts of social labor and production for exchange, I shall have to reinterpret them to be more in line with the ways nonclass societies are organized. Engels's usage of social or public labor in nonclass societies emphasizes work for and in the context of one's own corporate property-owning group. But marriage joins people from two groups; this generally means that at least one partner is not working for and in the context of his or her natal group. At the same time, he or she is not necessarily doing what Engels would call domestic work—work only for one's own household. Therefore, I shall stretch his concept of social labor to include any work done (singly or as part of a group) for use or appropriation by someone of another household. Some examples of social labor, illustrated in the next section, indicate the wide range of organizations it covers: participation in a cooperative work group, tributary labor for a chief, corvée, collective livestock raiding.

Production for exchange has to be expanded also. People do not spontaneously work to produce a surplus. There has to be some power forcing people to produce more than they themselves use. People in all societies give gifts, and gifts always put the recipient under an obligation to make a return. In a general way, as long as everyone has equal access to the means of subsistence, everyone has or can expect to have gifts by his own effort—and can thus make an equivalent return. But when the means of subsistence are privately and unequally held, a recipient is often unable to make an equivalent return in goods. He is then expected to return the favor with service: he becomes a loyal dependent or client-follower.

Both situations are instances of exchange. But only the second situation gives one of the parties the ability to harness the labor power of others for his own ends. This kind of situation is production for exchange: the production of goods used to gain control over the services of others. By contrast, production for use is simply producing goods to meet consumption needs.

Perhaps the beginnings of production for exchange lay in the use of wealth to gain loyal followers, and then needing to use the labor of one's followers to create still more wealth to keep their loyalty. In any case, production for exchange goes hand in hand with private property and political and economic inequality.

For example, there is wealth inequality and clientage in nonclass societies with large domesticated animals. Not only do these animals contribute to subsistence, but they are necessary for a man in order to marry and to have political standing in the society. Thus, in much of East Africa prior to imperialist rule, men obtained cattle from kinsmen or from service to a chief or other wealthy man, to whom they then owed loyalty in exchange for the cattle. The production of cattle is then production for exchange. Loyalty and service are given for livestock, and are used to augment the wealth and power of the benefactor, whether kinsman or not. Regardless of various people's overlapping rights and obligations to the livestock, these are private property, because there is some choice in how they will be allocated and because an individual is empowered to make that choice.

Though Engels has an integrated theory, at the risk of some distortion

I should like to separate two sets of ideas: (1) the immediate determinants or material bases of women's status—that social or public labor makes men or women adult citizens in the eyes of society and that men's ownership of private property establishes their dominance over women in the family and society; and (2) the evolutionary aspect—that women's status became solely subordinate and domestic with the development of male private property, production for exchange, and class society.

I shall discuss the immediate determinants of women's status by using illustrations from ethnography in the next part. This has the advantage of focusing first on the material bases of women's position. Even if Engels is right in a general way, that women are worse off in class than in nonclass societies, we still need to know what gives rise to this state of affairs. I do not believe that Engels's evolutionary explanation is valid as it stands. There is too much data showing that women are not the complete equals of men in most nonclass societies lacking private property. There are also many societies, with or without classes, where women do own and inherit property. Finally, I shall use some illustrations from class societies to suggest a different route to Engels's conclusions.

Women as Social Adults and Wives: Four African Societies

The following illustration is a reconstruction, mainly from ethnographies, of women's position in four African societies prior to the imposition of effective imperialist domination.[4] Using ethnographic reconstruction allows us to look at some of the variety in women's status in noncapitalist societies—nonclass as well as class—and to use the comparisons to illuminate Engels's ideas.

The Mbuti of Zaire can be characterized as a band society, with subsistence based on communal net hunting and gathering of vegetable food. In South Africa, the Lovedu were principally hoe agriculturalists, whereas the Pondo combined agriculture with livestock. Ganda, a class society in Uganda, also based subsistence on hoe agriculture.

If we place these societies on a continuum from egalitarian society to class society, our rankings can be seen to hold in three principal respects. First, the Mbuti and Lovedu have economies of production for use; the Pondo have the beginnings of production for exchange centered around cattle; and in Ganda production for exchange bulks quite large. Second, in Mbuti and Lovedu, both sexes perform social labor in a use economy,

---

4 Data come primarily from Krige and Krige (1943, Lovedu); Hunter (1936, Pondo); Turnbull (1965, Mbuti); and Roscoe (1966, Ganda). These societies were selected from the writings on East and South Africa primarily because the data on women were adequate and comparable. Thus many aspects—for example, concerning women in trade and marketing roles—though they are important, simply cannot be dealt with here.

and though this remains the organization of Pondo women's labor, Pondo men perform social labor at least in part in an exchange economy; whereas in Ganda women's work is individual domestic production for household use, while men work in groups, almost totally in production for exchange. Third, the Mbuti band owns the productive resources, whereas these are largely patrilineal family estates in Lovedu and Pondo; in Ganda the productive resources are in male hands, and less enmeshed in family obligations.

Among Mbuti, Lovedu, and Pondo, women's productive activities are social, and women have an adult social status. But in Ganda, where women's productive activities are domestic, the status of women is that of wife and ward only—despite the fact that women produce the bulk of the food. This suggests that Engels is right in seeing public or social labor as the basis for social adulthood.

But a more detailed look shows that women do not have to be characterized as *either* social adults *or* wifely wards. Rather, the data suggest that women can be both simultaneously. Women's status in a marital relationship seems to vary independently of their status in the larger society. But Engels seems correct in seeing the status of wife relative to husband as dependent on their relationships to the property of the household; that is, the spouse who owns the property rules the household.

Table 1 summarizes some indexes of women's status in society and in the family, and their relationship to women's organization of productive activities and to property ownership.[5] Essentially, Mbuti and Lovedu women are the equals of men, whereas Ganda women are subordinate and Pondo women fall somewhere between. The first five variables, which I have labeled social adulthood, involve egalitarian relations with people outside the household. A look at mutual aid relationships suggests that social adulthood is based on performing collective social labor. Lovedu men and women both have some sort of age groupings. These are mobilized to work for the district head and queen. For women at least, a neighborhood age group may take collective action against the group of a person who has offended one of its members. Pondo women of a neighborhood work together and cooperate in the performance of girls' initiation ceremonies, and women of the same household cooperate in arranging extramarital sexual affairs. Women's collective action is recognized by men when men collectively punish women and girls for what men deem to be sex offenses.

Self-representation in legal proceedings indicates that a woman is re-

<hr/>

[5] The variables and their categorization, rather than being determined in advance by a logical scheme, emerged as a result of comparing the positions of women in these four societies.

TABLE 1
*Women's Social and Domestic Status Compared with Men's
in Four African Societies*

Indexes of women's status	Discrimination against women's participation			
	Mbuti	Lovedu	Pondo	Ganda
SOCIAL				
Mutual aid	n.a.	none	none	active
Self-representation	none	none	none	active
Socializing opportunity	none	none	none	active
Extramarital sex	none	none	none	active
Divorce	none	none	none	active
Social disposal of wealth	none	none	active	active
Political office	none	none	active	active
Extra-domestic dispute settlement	none	none	active	active
Extra-domestic mediation with supernatural	none	none	active	active
DOMESTIC				
Wife's inheritance of marital estate	none	active	active	active
Wife's authority over domestic affairs	none	active	active	active
Wife as private reproducer (adultery compensation)	none	active	active	active
Menstrual and pregnancy restrictions	none	weak	weak	active

NOTE: Ownership of major productive resources: the band in Mbuti, the family in Lovedu and Pondo, and the individual in Ganda. Collective social production by women, as against that by men: equal in Mbuti and Lovedu, unequal in Pondo, and absent in Ganda.

garded as able to be wronged or to do wrong in the eyes of society, and is practiced among the Mbuti, Lovedu, and Pondo. A Ganda woman, by contrast, requires a male guardian (generally husband or father) to bring her case to court; the guardian is held responsible for her acts and receives compensation for wrongs done to her.

Though Mbuti, Lovedu, and Pondo men and women both participate in most of the same social activities, in the latter two societies young wives are kept busy at domestic work, which significantly restricts their ability to enjoy these events. But as older wives, as sisters visiting their own kinsmen, and as diviners, women attend social events as freely as do men. In Ganda, many of the social activities are patron- or state-oriented; women are excluded from these.

Although marital and social status are closely related, the ease of divorce for men versus women indicates their relative importance for each. In Ganda a husband can effectively end a marriage by simply ignoring his wife, but a woman must contend not only with her husband but with her brother, who as partial guardian generally acts to preserve the marriage.

Mbuti and Lovedu have a single standard regarding extramarital sexual affairs. Pondo women view their extramarital affairs as right and proper, but the men do not. A Ganda husband may kill his wife for real or suspected adultery, but a wife has little recourse against her husband. Men may use the courts to deal out severe punishment to their wives' lovers. In general, Ganda restricts extramarital sexual activity much more than do the other societies. Exceptions are made for high-ranking men who have affairs with peasant women, but men and women in the reverse situation are punished severely. Cohen's (1969) point seems borne out here, that restricted sexual activity serves to strengthen the marital bond at the expense of bonds that could serve as a basis for rebellion in class societies.

Being able to give and receive food and items of social exchange is the material basis for exercising political power. Engels suggests that real power develops only with production for exchange and private property. In societies without these—that is, in societies based on production for use—the performance of social labor gives a person the right to join with other adults in making political decisions and settling disputes. This is because political decision making and dispute settlement are responsibilities of adult members of an egalitarian society.

Among Mbuti and Lovedu both sexes give and receive food. Lovedu women give and receive cattle and may marry a wife with them; they become, in effect, husbands. But Pondo women, though they are social producers, cannot dispose of the most important exchange item: livestock. Perhaps the explanation lies in the nature of Pondo production for exchange. Women's agricultural work is for use; work is geared over the long and short run to the needs of the household. But men's organization for livestock raiding involves them in production for exchange; over the short run, warfare is geared more to the power need of a chief than to household needs; a chief keeps a following over the short run by having cattle to distribute. Over the long run, a chief keeps power by actually distributing cattle more or less widely. The chief owns the cattle captured in warfare, but sooner or later he distributes them among the warriors by virtue of their role in raiding. These livestock are the chief's to allocate. They are the most important item of exchange (in bridewealth, loans, and feasts) and of establishing long-term relationships (marriage and service). Because Pondo women do not participate in production for exchange (raiding), they cannot dispose of the property that establishes power relationships. Thus they do not hold overt political power.

Lovedu women hold political office, enter the decision-making arenas of the society, and predominate in officiating in religious rituals on be-half of their lineages. Ganda peasant women are barred from even the minimal access to political positions available to peasant men. Yet the mother and one sister of the king do hold important offices and exercise some power. This is predicated on their relationship to the king.

A wife's position vis-à-vis her husband is based on her ownership, or lack of it, of the marital estate. In Lovedu, Pondo, and Ganda, produc-tive resources are inherited patrilineally. Here, there is a contradiction, or opposition, in the fact that production is organized in a social or public way, but families or individuals appropriate and inherit the productive resources. A wife does not participate in the ownership of resources of her marital household. On the other hand, the Mbuti's appropriation for *use* by families seems to me qualitatively different from appropriation for inheritance and exchange, as in the other so-cieties. Mbuti resources are owned by the territorial band as a whole. Residence entitles a person to use these, and there is no inheritance. Thus, Mbuti husbands and wives have the same relationship to the band resources.

Lovedu, Pondo, and Ganda wives labor for their husband and his patrikin, but do not belong to the group that appropriates the product of their labor. Wives provide heirs, raise children, and do the bulk of the domestic work under the authority of the husband and his kin. They do not represent the household to outsiders. By contrast, Mbuti mar-riage carries no restrictions on a woman's authority over her work, chil-dren, or socializing. Her fertility cannot be said to be private, since her husband receives no compensation for her extramarital sexual relation-ships.

Menstrual and pregnancy restrictions on women's activities among Lovedu, Pondo, and Ganda seem to operate to separate women's repro-ductive functions from contact with the social production of exchange goods; that is, from contact with warriors, cattle, craft, and some med-ical practices. In these three societies children are potential heirs; they inherit property and continue the family line. Regardless of how wom-en's productive activities are organized, their reproductive potential is private. But among the Mbuti, where children are social members rather than private heirs, menstruation and pregnancy are not surrounded by any such restrictions. This contrast suggests that menstrual and preg-nancy restrictions are based on private property, and that they serve to symbolize a contradiction between social production of exchange goods and private or familial appropriation. Since men too are involved in the reproductive process and are subject to the same contradiction, logically they should—and actually they do—face analogous restrictions. Lovedu, Pondo, and Ganda men must separate sexual relations from their participation in social production for exchange. By contrast, Mbuti regard the collective hunt as an ideal time for sexual liaisons.

A final point remains. Though Ganda is a class society, I have not dealt with the differences between women of ruling families and women of peasant families. There are several privileges accorded to wives, sisters, and daughters of the king. Each category of ruling-class women shares some privilege with ruling-class men: freedom from productive labor for some wives; sexual freedom for sisters and daughters; political and economic power for the queen mother and sister. In these they are distinguished from peasants. But none of these women have all the privileges of men of their class. This seems to reflect the contradictory position of ruling-class women: they are of a privileged class but of a subordinate sex. I have not dealt with them in depth because their existence does not really change the generalizations made on the basis of peasant women. This should not be surprising if we recall Queen Victoria and her times in England. But it should make one wary of generalizations based on a few women holding prominent positions.

Though I have separated women's position as wives from their position as social beings, in reality the two are very much related. Wifely subservience reduces the ability of Lovedu and Pondo women to exercise their social prerogatives. They are held back from social activities to the extent that they work under the authority of the husband and his kin. Similarly, Pondo women may become diviners, and most diviners are women. This allows women opportunities for travel, socializing, and financial reward—but a woman may not be initiated to practice without her husband's consent.

Yet things can work the other way also. If a woman is socially regarded as an adult, this can limit the extent to which she can be subordinated as a wife. Thus, although a Pondo woman's fertility may be said to belong to her husband, and although he may claim compensation for her extramarital sexual affairs, this is a matter between men. A woman regards extramarital sexual relations as proper, and is assisted in arranging them by her husband's own kinswomen. Moreover, should a woman choose to end a marriage, or visit her own kin, there is little her husband can do to prevent it.

I have suggested, then, that there are two aspects to women's position —women as social adults, and women as wives—and that these can vary somewhat independently. What determines how, or whether, women are regarded as adults is not the same thing as what determines their positions vis-à-vis their husbands. Basically, women are social adults where they work collectively as part of a productive group larger than or separate from their domestic establishment. The meaning and status of "wife," though, depend on the nature of the family in much the way Engels suggests. Where the estate is familial, and the wife works for it but does not share in its ownership, she is in much the same relationship to her husband and his kin as is a worker to his boss. Where there are no private estates, or perhaps where the family estate is jointly owned, the *domestic* relationship is a more egalitarian one (Friedl, 1967). This last point is overstated, since the domestic and social spheres of life are not really independent. On the basis of the American experience, it is difficult to conceive of a completely egalitarian domestic relationship when only the male partner is regarded as fully adult beyond the bounds of the household.

Women in Class Societies: A Reinterpretation

When we note how the position of women declined from Mbuti and Lovedu to Ganda in this illustration, and since this is correlated with the domestication of women's work and the development of production for exchange and private property, it is tempting to conclude that Engels was right after all—that private property and production for exchange lead to women's domestication and subordination. Many anthropologists accept something like Engels's view of the relationship between private property and the growth of social inequality and classes. I too suspect that women in general stand in more equal relationship to men in nonclass societies than in class societies.

But I do not think that male property ownership is the basis for male supremacy in class societies. First, not all males own productive property. Second, in many class societies women as well as men own productive property—even in societies with a strong pattern of male dominance. In the latter case, a wife's ownership of property does give her a substantial amount of domestic power in relation to her husband (Friedl, 1967). But class societies result in a sharp dichotomy between the domestic and public spheres of life, and this domestic power is not translatable into social power or position in the public sphere. Moreover, in class societies the economic and political autonomy of a household is quite restricted. Thus, in necessary dealings in the public sector women are at a disadvantage. This probably militates against even domestic equality.

It seems likely, then, that in class societies the subordinate position of women derives not from domestic property relations but from something outside the household that denies women adult social status. The question then becomes, why do class societies have male public power and

ideals of male social dominance? For an explanation, the focus must
shift from the domestic to the societal level.

We have seen that public or social labor is the material basis for adult
social status. It follows that a society would have to exclude women
from public labor to deny them social adulthood for any length of time.
This seems to have been the case, at least for precapitalist agrarian states
of Eurasia (Boserup, 1970). Leaving aside for the moment the obvious
exception of industrial capitalism, what were the circumstances that may
have led class societies to exclude women from social production?

Class societies are exploitative, which means that many people must
work for the benefit of a few. Whereas tithes and taxes on domestically
produced goods can serve this end, even agrarian societies do not rely
exclusively or, I think, mainly on this form of production. Corvée for
public works (both sumptuary and productive), conscription and predatory war, and collective agricultural or wage work for the rulers—all
collective forms of social or public labor—are important productive activities in class societies. Although these may not necessarily bulk large
from the local viewpoint, they are crucial nationally for creating the
"surpluses" by which rulers and their states are maintained.

Though women may or may not engage in domestic agriculture, they
do not seem to participate in these large-scale forms of social production. It seems that class societies tend to socialize the work of men and
to domesticate that of women. This creates the material and organizational foundations for denying that women are adults, and allows ruling
classes to define them as wards of men.

But why would this happen in a class society? With the development
of socialized production for a ruling class, domestic production for subsistence becomes more precarious, forcing people into greater reliance
on production for exchange—laboring for the rulers in exchange for
their subsistence (alternatively, rulers can force people to work for them
as a condition of access to subsistence resources). Ruling classes select
men as social laborers partly because they are more mobile, but probably
more significantly because they can be more intensively exploited than
women, not having to nurse and rear children.

Clark (1968) provides rather gruesome data from seventeenth-century
England, a period *preceding* and setting the social conditions for later
industrialization. Peasants were being forced off the land and were swelling a class of rural, landless laborers. The idea of wages as something
paid for a task was not yet fully institutionalized. This belief contended
with the earlier notion that an employer was in some way obligated to
meet the subsistence needs of his workers. Yet payments were so low that
a landless family was barely able to survive. A man or woman without

children could survive, but prevailing remuneration did not allow for reproduction and rearing of the next generation of laborers. Indeed, they did not reproduce themselves. Clark shows that the laboring class grew in size only from constant new recruits from the peasantry. Women and children were deliberately excluded from wage work by employers, who felt an obligation to their workers but could not or would not bear the burden of supporting nonproductive dependents. In human terms the results were an abandonment of women and their early death, and in organizational terms a largely male public labor force.

Once such a dichotomy is made—women in domestic work for family use; men in social production for exchange—there is an organizational basis for a sexual divide-and-rule policy. Whether such policies are conscious or not, debates about motivation or conscious conspiracy are irrelevant here. The *effect* of state legal systems and other aspects of ideology developed mainly by ruling classes has been to convert differences between men and women in terms of their roles in production into a system of differential worth. Through their labor men are social adults; women are domestic wards.

Men are more directly exploited, and often collectively so—a situation where the possibility exists that they can act collectively to change it. Women's field of activity and major responsibility is restricted to the household, which neither produces nor owns the means of production for more than domestic subsistence—a level of organization at which little can be done to institute social change in a class society. This situation has several consequences. First, women are relegated to the bottom of a social pecking order (a *man's* home is his castle). Second, because of their isolation and exclusion from the marketplace, women can be used as a conservative force, unconsciously upholding the status quo in their commitment to the values represented by home, family, and children. Finally, the family is the sole institution with responsibility for consumption and maintenance of its members and for rearing children— the future generation of exchange workers. It is necessary labor if the system is to be perpetuated, but women are forced to perform it without compensation.

Modern capitalism has maintained this pattern of exploiting the private *domestic* labor of women, but since industrialization women have been heavily involved in public or wage labor. Meeting the heavy labor burden that capitalism places on the family remains socially women's responsibility. Responsibility for domestic work is one of the material bases for present barriers to women working for money and for placing them in a more exploitable position than men in the public labor force. As Benston shows (1969), this domestic work is not considered "real"

work because it has only private use value and no exchange value—
it is not public labor. Women's greater exploitability in the modern
wage labor force may even derive from a preindustrial adaptation to
being excluded from public labor (ironically, because women were *less*
exploitable in a prewage milieu). Only after they had been defined as
inadequate for public labor were the conditions right for industrial capitalism to discover women as a source of cheap labor.

In short, what I am suggesting is that intensive exploitation in social
production by and for ruling classes favored making this men's work.
In turn, ruling classes capitalized on the situation, legitimizing the division of labor by a thoroughgoing system of differential worth. In return for the loss of economic autonomy, they conferred on men exclusive
social adulthood and guardianship of women. Under these circumstances, even if women own property, the state intervenes to limit what
they can do with it publicly, and to subordinate the household to the
larger society. The key aspect, then, of women's position, especially in
class societies, is social adulthood, and this comes from participation in
social production.

This brief examination of the bases of women's domestic and social
status suggests some tentative conclusions about the kinds of economic
and social changes necessary for full sexual equality. Although property
ownership seems important for women's domestic position vis-à-vis a
husband, the exercise of domestic power, particularly in class societies,
is limited by whether or not women have adult status in the social sphere.
This in turn is determined by their participation in social production.
But the dichotomization of family and society, which is especially strong
in class societies, makes women responsible for the production of private
use value and makes men responsible for the production of exchange
value. The distinction between production for use and production for
exchange places a heavy responsibility on women to maintain themselves as well as exchange workers and to rear future exchange and maintenance workers. In this context wage work becomes an additional
burden and in no way changes women's responsibility for domestic work.
For full social equality, men's and women's work must be of the same
kind: the production of social use values. For this to happen, family and
society cannot remain separate *economic* spheres of life. Production, consumption, child rearing, and economic decision making all need to take
place in a single social sphere—something analogous to the Iroquois
gens as described by Engels, or the production brigades of contemporary
China. That is, what is now private family work must become public
work for women to become full social adults.

NANCY B. LEIS

Women in Groups: Ijaw Women's Associations

West Africa is noted for the independence of its women and for the associations that bring many of them together into groups serving a variety of purposes. The associations receiving the most attention in the literature are those with spectacular activities, such as the secret societies among the Mende and the market women's groups among the Yoruba. In each of these societies, women's maintaining these associations appears to have given them considerable power, and they can, to varying extents, even manipulate men or at least stand as virtual equals with them. It would be difficult for any anthropologist, male or female, to overlook the prominent role these organizations play in their societies.[1]

Some of the smaller village associations, in southern Nigeria particularly, have more diffuse functions, less impressive activities, and fewer accounts describing them. I think it safe to say that if it were not for the Aba Women's Riot in 1929 among the Ibo (Perham 1937: 206–17), we would have even fewer accounts. Ordinarily these small groups dealt only with the day-to-day concerns of women, but on this one occasion, when the Ibo women feared they were to be taxed for the first time, they rose up over a wide area and brought destruction not only to administrative headquarters but to themselves in their overly daring attacks. These events occasioned the British to send two women anthropologists to study the causes of the riot and to uncover the organizational base that permitted such spontaneity and solidarity among the women. Studies by Leith-Ross (1965) and Green (1947) resulted from this investigation.

Nowhere in this literature, however, is there an attempt to analyze

---

[1] Little (1951) has described the Poro and Sande societies for the Mende. There are several accounts of Yoruba market women's groups. For example, see Forde (1951) and Hodder (1962). A general description and bibliography of women's associations can be found in Lebeuf (1963).

what factors have allowed women's groups, whatever their functions, to develop in this area of Africa. The present study is such an attempt and will deal with one southern Nigerian society, the Ijaw of the Niger Delta,[2] where women are organized in the northern area into associations but in the southern area are not. This disparity permits us to employ the method of controlled comparison[3] to uncover those variables associated with the presence or absence of women's groups. As we shall see, the northern Ijaw are fairly typical in other ways of southern Nigerian societies, whereas the southern Ijaw depart just enough in some regards to provide the contrast that should make this approach fruitful.

Another purpose prompts this work, and indeed was the initial motivation to search out the underlying factors that might explain women's associations. I had read *Men in Groups* by Lionel Tiger and was both surprised and puzzled, surprised because he so readily proposes innate differences between the sexes to explain behavior, and puzzled because he himself has worked in West Africa and surely, I assumed, knew of the prevalence of women's groups there. In his book, he suggests that there is a biologically inherited propensity for men to form all-male groups, what he calls "male-bonding." Although he appears to recognize that women, though rarely, also form groups, he does not suggest that their appearance is the result of female-bonding. He promises us, in a footnote, yet another publication demonstrating that "all-female groups differ structurally from all-male groups, are generally less stable over time, and considerably less common for a variety of reasons" (1970: xiii). Thus women come together, we must assume, for reasons other than biologically inherited propensities. On this point, at least, Tiger is likely correct. It is not my purpose to explore the overall question of whether there are or are not sex-oriented bonds. What I hope to illustrate is that certain structural features, namely descent and inheritance systems, residence rules and polygyny, can and do operate to bring women together in groups—and groups that achieve considerable solidarity. We need not resort to the biological dimension to explain these groups. Do we for men's groups?

I shall be concerned here with two Ijaw villages in the Niger Delta. One of the villages, Patani, has several women's associations, which are patterned in much the same way as those of neighboring peoples on the

    [2] Research among the Ijaw was conducted from January 1958 to July 1959, and was supported by a Ford Foundation Foreign Area Training Fellowship.
    [3] Eggan (1954) used this term to describe studies in addition to his own in the American Southwest that demonstrated the development of social institutions within a limited area and brought together the cultural-process tradition of American anthropology with the social-structure approach of British social anthropology.

mainland, except that they reflect the segmentary organization of the town with its separate and virtually autonomous sections. Among these people, women not only regulate themselves but also see through decisions that affect nonmembers, including the men of the village, who demonstrate little interest in, or capacity for, acting collectively in any but their own kinship groups. In the other village, Korokorosei, women have no associations, and men are somewhat better able to work together in non-kin groups.

The two villages differ in other respects as well, despite the fact that they share an essentially similar culture. They have somewhat different social systems and different technologies, which reflect both ecological adaptations and varying contacts with neighboring groups. Korokorosei is isolated in the central part of the delta, whereas Patani is located to the north in close proximity to other groups. The question why the southern village has no associations and the northern community has a well-developed complex might be answered simply by reference to borrowing. So it may be. But I would suggest that certain aspects of their social systems allow for the easy adoption of this trait among the northern Ijaw and militate against its acceptance in southern Ijaw. By comparing the social systems of the two villages, we should be able to isolate those structural features that allow for the formation of women's associations, at least among the Ijaw, and perhaps even for other West African societies as well. If elements of structure can influence the appearance of women's groups and create a considerable sense of solidarity, a logically subsequent question is whether structure might not also have a good deal to say about men's groups. Mere "propensities," as Tiger argues, are hardly sufficient explanations in themselves.

I shall first describe the essential outline of the social organization of the two communities, emphasizing those features I see as most important for the development of the associations, and then analyze point by point the relevant correlations. The latter part of the paper deals with Patani women's activities and compares them with those of the Korokorosei women.

The Two Communities

The really major differences between the two communities are in the descent and inheritance rules and in the presence of a market in only one community. Several other differences, such as residence rules, land tenure, and the economic activities of women, relate directly to these variations. There are basic similarities, however, in the essential political structure and in some aspects of marriage, as well as in many other areas, such as the belief system, which do not concern us in this study. It would be difficult to say which community is more typical of the Ijaw in general, since these delta people are so diverse. Patani is atypical in its descent system, exhibiting patrilineality instead of the more common matrilaterality of the south and east, and Korokorosei is unusual because it has no market and its women do not trade.

Patani has approximately 2,000 inhabitants. Unlike other Ijaw, the people are patrilineal with residential patrilineages, a trait that may have come into being because of the community's proximity to other Nigerian groups emphasizing agnatic links. There are seven maximal lineages, called *polo*, each with its own history of origins in ancient villages farther to the south. Some of the polo in the town recognize kinship ties with one another, while others have closer ties with distant villages than with polo in Patani. The various polo are autonomous corporate groups owning farming land, which is first parceled into sections for the use of its numerous extended families, and then divided into plots, one plot per woman.

In the past, the polo was also the basic political unit; there was no village head or council to bring the villagers together, and all feuds and alliances were initiated only on the lineage level. In fact, two Patani polo once engaged in a feud, and resentment from that incident still lingers between them. In the 1930's, the British instituted a council and a court for the entire town. This court now hears most civil cases, but the newly formed council is rarely more than a debating society. Representatives from each of the sublineages come together only infrequently and have rarely been able to enact legislation that all of the townsmen would support. One of the council's most ambitious attempts was also one of the most telling examples of the divisiveness that still exists between some of the polo. The council had decided to lay claim, in the name of Patani, to a portion of land held at that time by a neighboring non-Ijaw group. However, it could not convince two polo to contribute financially to court costs, so that when it later won its case it denied access to the land to those who did not participate. The council also tried to mend an ancient quarrel between two other polo, but so far has been unsuccessful.

Men are still oriented very much toward their own kin groups, which of course bring them together through another kind of "biological propensity" than that to which Tiger refers. Some men have joined national political parties or local betterment leagues, but even here a man has a choice in terms of factions, which are as divisive and hostile to other similar groups as are some of the kinship groups. Only a few of the younger men are politicized enough to see the worth of such membership. The reliance of men on kin rather than non-kin groups is, as we shall see, quite in contrast with the group orientation of Patani women.

Korokorosei is a smaller village, with a population of 700, and is just as acephalous in its political structure. The basic units are ambilineal kin groups, sections of the village called *ware*, of which there are five. The ware are semicorporate, exogamous residence groups founded by the sons of the eponymous village ancestor. These groups have formed because men have a choice where they will reside after marriage. A man has the right to build and live in the section where his father lived and to affiliate with that group; but he also has the right to live among some of his uterine kinsmen, particularly his mother's mother, or, indeed, wherever any of his grandparents had lived. Any one ware, therefore, will be composed of men who actually have different kin ties with one another. The sections are corporate in the sense that they own fishing sites in common and act as a unit in communal work projects. The ware does not own farming land; individual tracts are inherited through uterine links.

In the political sense, the ware of Korokorosei operated very much as did the polo of Patani. Each ware was autonomous in settling disputes among its own members and in waging feuds with ware of other villages. There was no village head. The British attempted to effect the same changes toward wider regional affiliation, so that Korokorosei inhabitants now take their civil cases to a distant court and participate through representatives in a "clan council"—misnamed by the British—composed of several neighboring villages. Perhaps because of their smaller numbers and the ubiquitous kin ties throughout the village, the men have been somewhat more successful in achieving village-wide organization. All adult men participate in a village council, which, because it is ruled by consensus rather than the majority, only occasionally can enact legislation and begin communal projects. The real leaders in this council are rarely those elected to the position,[4] but rather two or three men who by their elementary education have become concerned with improving village life and are willing to take the abuse that invariably accompanies efforts to wield power. Although some of their schemes have failed, there are some notable successes at the village level. The

[4] Korokorosei was pressured by the regional government to elect a village head in the 1930's. At that time, the men chose an amenable man who never attempted to exercise authority by virtue of his office. He died only a few years later, but was not replaced until 1957, when the regional government again directed the village to name someone. Once more, a rather ineffectual person was elected, but this time the villagers assured his impotence by requiring him to take traditional and powerful oaths to the effect that he would do as they said. He was destined to be merely a figurehead who would only sign documents.

council passed and enforced a law that no one was to farm, fish, or do any labor in the forest on Sundays. Leaders were also able to persuade the regional government to locate a Standard VI school in the village (most villages of this small size had only Standard IV schools), and then, through the work and financial contributions of all the villagers, they organized the building of an attractive school compound with a concrete-block and pan-roofed schoolhouse, houses for the teachers, and a playing field. They even found the means to change some customs that the women particularly had come to feel were too harsh.

Unlike Patani, inheritance is matrilateral. Uterine links, however, are not utilized to form any important descent groups. A person might speak of his *nyighi ware* (mother's house), which refers to his or her uterine kinsmen, but this group is not corporate in any sense. A male inherits money, personal property, widows, and ritual office from his full brother, his mother's brother, or his sister's son. It is because of their inheritance rights that some men choose to affiliate with ware other than those where their fathers reside. A female inherits ritual office to certain female deities, her mother's property, and—most important—land her mother has farmed.

Rights to land, which are based as much on usufruct as on inheritance, become so involved that we can neither describe nor analyze them here. The important point is that a woman uses land her mother passes on to her. She also might use land her husband acquired from his mother, but in this case, neither she nor her husband can then transfer the right to farm it to their children. What complicates the picture so and creates a very unequal distribution of land among the inhabitants are the residence practices. A woman always changes residence on marriage, and if she comes from a distant village, she might be unable to use her mother's land. And her husband's mother's land might also be too far away for her to have access to it. This situation is quite different from that in Patani, where a woman farms land belonging to her husband's patrilineage and is assured of an adequate plot each year.

There are less significant and fewer differences in marriage practices. Women in both communities are incorporated into their husbands' residence groups for political purposes, although in most cases they retain very close ties, affective and jural, with their own kin and parents. They must contribute to funeral expenses and be willing to assist during illness and other emergencies. Women visit their parents frequently and may even return when they quarrel with their husbands. This closeness with kinsmen obtains if a woman is married by the so-called "small-dowry" system, by far the most prevalent form in the two areas. A "big-dowry wife,"[5] on the other hand, "belongs" to her husband and his kinship group, and loses all ties with her own family. In Korokorosei, this means that the children of such a union can inherit from their father and his matrikin. The incidence of such marriages here is low (about 7 percent), is practiced primarily for prestige purposes, and always involves nonlocal or non-Ijaw women. In Patani, the presence of such a marriage system would seem to indicate that the people were once matrilateral, since no different affiliation of the children results from patrilineality. No matter the form of marriage, a child affiliates with and inherits from his father. The only difference is in the distribution of a daughter's bridewealth on her marriage. Again, the incidence is low, but Patani females as well as non-Ijaw females might be married in this way.

Polygyny is also common in both villages, with over one-half of Korokorosei men having two or more wives, and just short of one-half in Patani. Although the relationship between co-wives differs somewhat in the two areas, equality among the wives is the general rule and certainly the expectation of women. A Patani man recognizes a senior wife, who has first choice in the distribution of land or food but no authority over her juniors; all Korokorosei wives, no matter the order of their seniority, expect equal treatment. Unlike wives in many other African groups, who live in their own huts, Ijaw wives have apartments within one large structure and are brought into much more frequent contact with their co-wives. A Patani man follows a prescribed order of sleeping with each of his wives, as does the Korokorosei husband, but the women differ in the scheduling of their domestic responsibilities to him. A Patani woman cooks and cares for her husband only when it is her turn to sleep with him. A Korokorosei woman must cook for her husband every day[6] and perform domestic tasks for him whenever he asks. As we shall

---

[5] The Ijaw term is *opu nana*, "big ownership," but has been rendered as "big dowry" by Ijaw who speak English, because a much larger bridewealth (£100 compared with £12 in Korokorosei) is involved. A token payment at the end of the negotiations, not necessarily the large sum, constitutes the actual transfer of the woman, however. Korokorosei inhabitants always acquire such wives from northern Ijaw or non-Ijaw groups at a very young age. Although some Patani women, usually those who had proved troublesome to their families in childhood, have been married by this system, most men acquire such wives from the Isoko or Kwale Ibo peoples to the north. In the past, women transferred through bloodwealth payments, daughters of male slaves, and redeemable pawns also became big-dowry wives. For a description of the intricacies of these forms of marriage in another Ijaw group, see Williamson (1962).

[6] This means that a man with two or more wives will have given to him two or more meals from which he must eat equally if he is to avoid accusations of favoritism. An account of the successes and failures in meeting the delicate balance of equality

see, the presence of associations in Patani assists a woman in coping with difficulties in her co-wife relationships. The Korokorosei woman must resolve her own problems.

Subsistence techniques have changed considerably in both areas over the last several decades. Men once participated much more fully in food production, but now Patani men have turned to urban occupations for lengthy periods, and Korokorosei men, most of whom remain in the village, produce and smuggle illicit gin. Women now do all the farming, and are expected to feed their children and their husbands virtually unaided.

Farming techniques in the two areas vary. A Korokorosei woman can grow only plantain, cocoyams, and cassava, because her farms are less fertile than those in Patani, where women grow water yams and groundnuts in addition. The farming season is also longer in the south and occupies women the entire year.[7] A Korokorosei grows only for household consumption, whereas the Patani farmer grows more than she herself uses and can plant certain crops specifically for sale. Women in both locations fish, in Patani seasonally and in Korokorosei the year round. These variations are due primarily to different ecological adaptations.

Another contrast, and an important one, is the orientation of Patani women to their market. Korokorosei has no market, nor is there one easily accessible. As with neighboring groups, Patani women usually earn some income through marketing their own produce or the sleeping mats they weave especially for sale. Most of these sales are made in the local market, although a few women also transport their goods to southern areas. Some women are part-time traders, dealing with foodstuffs purchased elsewhere to be sold in Patani or to the south, and still others trade full time in either foodstuffs, mats, or illicit gin. Full-time trading appears to be a new occupation and one not yet fully accepted as suitable for women, but marketing is expected of every farmer. In fact, for the

_____

would provide an almost total description of domestic life in an Ijaw village, and is one I shall attempt in a later publication.

[7] Although the two villages are only about twenty miles apart, they are located in different ecological zones. Korokorosei is just north of the mangrove and saltwater swamps of the coast and in a zone dominated by freshwater swamps and the many creeks and rivers that form the heart of the delta. The banks of the river are low, only about ten feet during the dry season, and most farmland is located on higher ground in the interior, where heavy tropical forests and numerous swamps make farming difficult. Patani is in the third zone closer to the mainland, where riverbanks are high, up to thirty or forty feet, and swamps less common. All farming is done on low, sloping riverbanks, which are covered by the annual Niger flood. These areas are easier and more productive to farm, since little clearing need be done in the shorter and less frequent periods when the soil must lie fallow. The Niger leaves a deposit of fertile silt on this land after the flood, thereby allowing intensive cultivation.

first year or two of her marriage, a woman can sell all of her farm produce because her mother-in-law provides her with food for her family. Whether she supplements her farming with some marketing or pursues a trading career, each Patani woman is entirely or almost entirely economically independent of her husband. Indeed, a few women see no need to remarry on divorce or widowhood.[8] The fact of economic independence manifests itself as an attitude simply of independence (Leis, 1964).

Not only do Korokorosei women rarely visit markets either to buy or sell; they do not know how to invest their small reserves of cash to obtain a profit. When a woman has more plantain or fish than she can immediately consume, she might sell it, but she then spends the money for cassava meal or for clothes rather than using it to purchase other items she might then sell, as the Patani woman does. Although a very few women have made frustrated attempts to begin trading, the sharp criticism of both men and other women has led virtually all of them to give up these projects. Women who travel are likely to be promiscuous, it is believed; and besides, farming, and farming alone, is suitable work for women. Interestingly, remnants of these same attitudes still exist in Patani.

Despite her inability to earn money, the woman in Korokorosei is just as alone in her responsibilities to feed her family as the Patani woman—perhaps more so, since her husband rarely gives her financial assistance. She meets these responsibilities with difficulty, but rarely with the sense that she is independent of her husband. She still needs his labor to clear the trees and brush from her farms and to provide her with a canoe and house. She cannot afford to hire help as the Patani woman does. Whether through widowhood or divorce, no Korokorosei woman remains unmarried for long.

Factors Allowing for Association

The most important factors allowing for associations in Patani but not in Korokorosei are the descent and residence rules that orient women toward their husbands' kin groups, polygyny, and their own economic independence.

[8] Full independence appears to have been reached by even more than those few women who have chosen, on widowhood, to remain unmarried. There are at least three cases in the town of women returning the bridewealth to their husbands out of their own resources, and then pursuing a very active trading career. One of these told me that she had received all she wanted from her marriage—children—and was no longer willing to tolerate the domestic demands of a husband who kept her from going and coming as she pleased.

The practice of virilocality takes women away from their natal residence groups and places them, as strangers, among people who have, by virtue of their birth, enduring ties with one another. These brides maintain a position of isolation within the kin groups, and the only persons with whom they have something in common, as a category, are other married women residing there. One link joins together one segment through consanguineal ties, and another joins the women through affinal ties. This trait is true for both Patani and Korokorosei. However, since the Patani woman only farms land belonging to her husband's patrilineage, since her children inherit from their father, and since authority over her and her children rests with the patrilineage, she has much more in common with other women of the residence group than that experienced by the Korokorosei woman. Her husband, in contrast, lives his entire life, in the town at least,[9] with his own kinsmen, and he gives them almost total loyalty. There were few non-kin groups he could join in the past,[10] and none at present that greatly dilute his kin-group orientation.

In southern Ijaw, a woman acquires farmland from her mother, whose land may be elsewhere. Her children inherit from and are under the control of her matrikin, especially her brother, who also live elsewhere. She is less integrated into the residence unit because the pull of kin ties and distant farms orients her toward other groups. But then, her husband also shares this trait. If he is living in his father's section of the village, he still maintains as close a relationship with his matrikin as his wife does with hers. At the same time, the men who live avunculocally do not completely sever their connections with their fathers. Both sexes, in other words, have diffuse loyalties. Korokorosei women are not in an especially separate category vis-à-vis the men, but the Patani women are.

As a result, for the Patani woman, being a member of a women's association is much more relevant. She has everything in common with the other women of her polo, and only a few commitments outside her residence unit. The same is true for her husband. Admittedly these struc-

---

[9] For at least two decades, men have been seeking temporary employment in the cities. Few of the men have enough education and training to get really high-paying jobs. They generally choose to stay away only until they have saved enough to acquire a wife or two and items for their own material comfort. On their return, they do little if any work, since their wives then take on the burden of feeding them and their children.

[10] The only association of any importance was a rather exclusive one, which initiated only men, and later their eldest sons, who had killed a leopard, or a man during war.

tural features may not be the "cause" of the associations, but their presence certainly sets up conditions orienting women toward one another. And indeed, Korokorosei women resisted attempts, made by the men, to organize them into groups with female leadership. We shall speak more of this later.

Polygyny is characteristic of both areas and therefore is not the feature that could effectively explain the presence of women's associations. Nonetheless, I maintain that polygyny plays some part because, in addition to providing more married women for the groups and thereby strengthening their position, polygyny lessens the possibility that women will experience a sense of closeness with men. Unlike Paulme, for example, who virtually laments the fact that polygyny keeps women from "conjugal intimacy" (1963: 9), I hold that the practice may actually serve to bring the women together by means of yet another attribute they share. And whereas I can agree with Fox when he points out that polygyny is "not necessarily about sex but about dominance" (quoted in Tiger, 1970: 271), I suggest that polygyny can nonetheless give women a considerable measure of independence. A polygynously married man must constantly be involved with wives; a polygynously married woman has some respite from husband.

What differences we find between the two communities in the institution of polygyny again relate back to the inheritance and residence systems. Patani co-wives are brought together on the farming land of the patrilineage. Each, because she has land equal to the other wives and the same potential in fulfilling her food-producing responsibilities, is not in competition for the financial assistance of her husband. Korokorosei women each go their own way in farming, some struggling to find at least one plot to work a year, and others comfortably situated with more than adequate landholdings. The poorer women ask their husbands for help. But notice, they have the need and the approach as individuals. They even cook for their husbands as individuals, and not as members of a group who take turns, as Patani co-wives do. Nor do Korokorosei co-wives ever join forces in registering some common complaint against their husband, as Patani women do.

Both Patani and Korokorosei women are the primary economic mainstays of their families, and both own and can use as they wish the products of their labor. Because of her marketing and trading, however, the Patani woman is better able to earn some income, which frees her from dependence on her husband's labor and financial assistance. On the foundation of the independence gained from polygyny, she can participate in activities and groups on her own and over which her husband exercises no control. The Korokorosei woman is restrained from any such independent activity. First of all, she cannot afford it, and second, she dare not flout her husband's authority for fear he will refuse to help her.

Patani Associations

I shall now turn to a description of the activities of the Patani women's associations and their achievement of solidarity as contrasted with the men's. There are seven such associations, with membership based on residence, as a married woman, in one or the other of the seven polo. The largest polo, Ekise, has the largest and most active association; most of the following will refer to its operation.

Before a woman can become a member of the association, she must first of all be married to a man of the polo (unmarried, divorced, or widowed daughters of polo residents are excluded), be living with him instead of with her own kin,[11] and then declare herself *ware anga*, i.e. capable of supporting a household and no longer dependent on her mother-in-law. Prior to this time, she is free to build up her economic assets through marketing and trading in anticipation of eventually being totally independent. When she is eligible, she must join the association, must attend its meetings, and must show up on time. The Ekise group, because it is large, even has "policewomen" who make rounds of the polo during meetings looking for stay-at-homes, and who have the authority to fine those who are late or absent without just reason. Meetings are scheduled on the afternoon of the big market, which is held every twelve days.

Leadership rests with elected officers whose main function is to call meetings, propose an informal agenda, and the like. Beyond that, they have no power and little authority. All decisions are reached by consensus of the members after lengthy and sometimes extremely emotional and tumultuous discussion. In short, no course of action may be taken unless virtually all the women agree.

Taking into account the number of activities of the Ekise association and the force with which its members implement decisions, we can correctly assume that the women, who number over a hundred, can frequently reach agreement. The group itself regularly performs several

---

[11] As in many African groups, marriage is a process, not an event, in this area. The stages are too numerous and complex to detail here, but in brief they involve the lengthy negotiations concerning the bridewealth, a period when a man visits and sleeps with his bride in her father's house, the residence of the bride with her natal kin when she undergoes clitoridechtomy during her first pregnancy, and finally various steps even after she has joined her husband. The entire process may require five or more years to complete.

functions. First of all, the women are informal mediators and, when called upon, hear minor cases between women or co-wives of the polo, and sometimes even between husband and wife. Sometimes they act as actual judges. Their opinion will be accepted in disputes over the boundary of garden plots, for example, and they can force a woman to uproot her yams if she has planted beyond her portion. They also make separate judgments against members who have violated some town-sanctioned laws and have already been taken to court for the offense. For example, a woman judged guilty of defaming another's character by unjustly calling her a witch or a slave, or of stealing in the marketplace, has to pay a fine to both her association and the court. In fact, where the judgments of the court and of the women's association differ, no further appeal is allowed beyond the association; if the women think a person guilty but the court does not, the women nonetheless demand their fine.

The associations also help, though perhaps unwittingly, to uphold some controls men have over women. Any wife who hears slander against her husband's kin group, commits adultery, or is even approached by a man must confess this to the ancestors of the extended family. Failure to make a public confession will anger the ancestors, who then might cause difficulty for her during childbirth or bring sickness or death to her children. Whenever a woman makes such a confession, her association levies against her the very largest fine it ever imposes. Their rationale is that adultery can cause innocent parties, the women's own children, to suffer; they are not, in taking this position, necessarily supporting the double standard.

The associations are also legislative bodies in the sense that they each pass their own laws, laws that can affect even non–association members, such as outlawing certain abusive language against a member, or purposely or accidentally disrobing a woman in public. One law mutually legislated by all the associations denies non-Ijaw women the right to sell certain items in the marketplace.[12] The women's right to pass these laws, or to fine for an infraction against either them or the generalized town laws, is unopposed and unquestioned by the men.

Not all of the activities of the associations are of a legal nature; the groups perform services as well. They periodically come together in work groups to clean up the polo and its waterside of refuse and tall grass. They dance with the daughters of the polo who are celebrating their clitoridechtomies and even sometimes arrange to wear identical

[12] Unlike the Yoruba and Ibo women's associations, the Patani associations do not control the market. No one does.

outfits for this occasion. Collections are made among members for contributions to funerals in their polo.

The service that brings the most attention to some associations is lending money. Through the fines they collect, the larger associations have considerable reserves of cash, which they are willing to lend to anyone whom they trust, especially if he or she has a sponsor who promises to refund their money in case of default. Loans are made for short periods —"two markets," or twenty-four days—or for up to a year, at an interest of 50 percent but sometimes reportedly up to 100 percent. Both men and women, in and outside of the polo, may ask for a loan. The profits from these transactions are used either to buy identical suits for the festival or, on a limited scale, to form a quasi-cooperative in, for example, the purchase of bags of salt to be shared. The smaller associations never acquire such large amounts of cash that they can lend it out, and therefore use it for drinks or a common purchase.

The cohesiveness of the association is demonstrated not only in the number of activities it is able to undertake successfully, but even more in the sanctions it employs. If a person refuses to accept its judgment, or fails to pay a debt, the women meet, again charging fines for absence or tardiness, to plan their strategy. They might, for example, choose to dance around a recalcitrant woman, sing taunting songs, and afterward refuse to have anything to do with her. Or, more usually, the group takes an indispensable item from her house, such as her cooking stand or mosquito net, and refuses to return it unless she relents. None of the woman's friends or co-wives, or even her husband, can support her position without risking similar treatment. When a debtor, who is usually a man, is in default of payment, the women may decide to meet at his house and hold him virtually captive there until he promises payment. Needless to say, these methods tend to give the association both a formidable and a respectable reputation in the town. I heard no reports of persons resisting the will of the association for very long.

Although the associations are separate units that rarely act together, Patani women once participated, through delegates, in an organization called the Western Ijaw Women's Union, which attempted to bring women together from a very large area. The group was organized about 1956 and was composed of representatives from most of the Ijaw subdistricts in the Western Region. As the Patani women understood it, its reasons for coming into being were to deal with affairs involving women of the region, most specifically to build a marketplace at the point where the Niger branches into the Forcados and Nun rivers. No one is sure—in fact, it is difficult to persuade a Patani woman even to speak of the union—what first motivated the women to form such a group. The minutes of the first meeting simply refer to a dispute some Ijaw women had with a group of non-Ijaw women.

The union met several times in 1956 and was involved in passing resolutions regulating such a wide range of activities—with which not only women but also men and non-Ijaw were concerned—that the minutes resemble a codification of many laws already in effect in the region. Some of the resolutions concerning women duplicated those already in effect in each of the polo associations, and others were attempts to prescribe the trading and other activities of women while outside the district. The women did not stop with their own affairs, however, and went on to formulate some completely new laws for the entire Western Ijaw District. They were attempting to legislate matters that each town decides independently, decisions that in any case are ordinarily made by men. For example, they proscribed certain economic activities of non-Ijaw men in the area and set up a sanitary code for all the villages. The attempt to regulate all the women was perhaps feasible, despite the fact that the women were accustomed to regulations only on the polo level. Legislating for towns and the entire district was another matter. That the women intended all their resolutions to have the effect of law is clear from the imposition of fines for infractions of them.

A detailed history of this organization is difficult to obtain in Patani, since the women prefer not to discuss something that has such unpleasant memories. When the organization was initiated, a few women admit, they all were enthusiastic because of the proposal for a new market close to Patani, which they hoped would attract traders from other areas. On the strength of this belief, they quickly raised money for the market through collections from the women every big market day, and turned their proceeds over to the union. Later, however, the union—some claim it was the president, the wife of a regional politician from another town —decided instead to build a wharf in Warri, a non-Ijaw mainland city. Patani women claim that they were not informed of this change until the wharf was built. In addition to being angered at the loss of a market they wanted, Patani women were further annoyed because few anticipated using the new wharf. The town's women since then have ceased to associate with the union and certainly do not adhere to any of its resolutions. The union itself appears to be moribund and, so far as I could learn, has never attempted to implement its many rulings. As one man in Patani expressed it, few men felt the union could last long, since the women were "taking themselves too seriously."

Incidents that took place during the rise and fall of the union illuminate the political behavior of Patani women. As exemplified in both the polo associations and the union, the women can be very effective when they plan a course of action; the rapidity with which they collected the money for the proposed market demonstrates this facility. When compared with the men, who are more individualistic and less inclined to give their loyalty to a large group (see Chodorow, this volume), women of the associations present a united front in attacking any project they are enthusiastic enough to initiate. That the women of the union were perhaps attempting to do too much may illustrate their naïveté about "modern politics" in the delta, but it also demonstrates that they have faith in their own power, a power that the Patani men recognize.

Large membership may prove to be a group's strength or its weakness. Neither the women in their associations nor the men in their councils can act unless almost all their members have been convinced of the proper course. Being able to achieve virtual unanimity facilitates their ability to accomplish their goals. The number of women in each polo association appears to be small enough to allow for viability, yet large enough to give them strength. The union, however, was very large, and could not reach unanimity; a simple majority carried the vote. When the union decided to do something the Patani women did not approve of, these women were unwilling to capitulate and therefore withdrew. That they do not reach decisions in their own associations by simple majority vote is, again, an aspect of their strength.

The Korokorosei Women's Council

Nothing at all that I have described for Patani has ever existed in Korokorosei. However, there was an abortive attempt on the part of men to organize the women, if not into associations, then at least into work groups based on ware residence and, more ambitiously, to set up a "council" that would have a role in regulating some of the women's activities. As with the defunct Women's Union of Patani, we can learn something about Korokorosei women in groups, or better, their resistance to groups, by reviewing the history of this attempt.

Two years before this study was made, a regional sanitation inspector, so the report goes, was concerned about the unkept grounds and houses in Korokorosei. He suggested, after learning that women were responsible for such delinquencies, that a women's council be selected to inspect the houses and ensure compliance with the law. The men were obviously intrigued by the idea of the council and, as it would appear from later reports, enthusiastically set out to create such an organization. They chose five women, one from each ware, who were noted for being outspoken and, hopefully, capable of withstanding criticism, and selected one of them as president. Note that the men initiated the entire operation and chose the women themselves, even though election, not appointment, governed their own selection of leaders.

Once chosen, the women pursued their task with an enthusiasm similar to that of the men. To facilitate the inspection, which somehow came to include the interior of houses and even women's bedrooms, the men enacted a village "law" that no one, either man or woman, was to "go to bush" on Sunday.[13] Rather, villagers were to remain at home to open their houses to the inspectors who initially were only to list the infractions of the "sanitary code." Fines were to be levied later if improvements were neglected, and a summons issued to appear in court if the fine was not paid.

The women councillors conducted two or three inspections before giving up the project. So far as anyone remembers, the inspectors never fined anyone for failing to clean up property, but they did cite several women for going to farm or to fish on Sundays, even on Sundays when no inspection was planned. When the women refused to pay their fines, they were taken to court, judged guilty, and made to pay court costs as well. The deep resentment that had been growing with each inspection then became manifest, and before long, women in the village began to insult the women councillors. They mocked their fine clothing, taunted them on their supposed behavior on trips away from the village, and, in a few instances, even fought with the inspectors. Women who had been taken to court refused to have anything to do with the persons, either men or women, responsible for their punishments. Although the councillors were women with strong personalities, most of them could not tolerate these abuses and simply refused to continue inspections.

The men's plans for the women councillors failed in yet another respect. In the work to be done in the school compound, the councillors were to supervise the women of their individual ware but were not to participate themselves. Not surprisingly, the village women would have none of this discrimination and, after only one work session, divided themselves into much smaller groups, without regard to ware affiliation, and forced the councillors, who no longer had ware groups to supervise, to work along with them. This incident points up two characteristics of Korokorosei women: they will not tolerate another woman having au-

[13] Requiring villagers to remain at home for specific purposes was already prevalent. Similar orders were issued whenever monetary contributions to village projects or taxes were to be collected.

thority over them, and they lack identification with women of their own ware.

The reasons the women's council failed were analyzed by some villagers, and are further suggested by values we have already seen in action. The male leaders were expecting from the women a type of behavior they themselves had great difficulty achieving in their own council. As described previously, individuality characterizes the political activities of men; authority is not readily accepted. Thus the men's anticipation of a different reaction from the women was unrealistic, a point the men now admit. It is possible that men were anticipating the same obedience they received as husbands; men should choose the women's leaders for them, tell them to cooperate, and "of course" the women would comply. If indeed these were their thoughts, they likely forgot, for one thing, that their wives were also co-wives and, as such, demanded strict equality.

This entire incident may be used to point up the value of equality among Korokorosei women and also their individual means for resisting intolerable directives from the men. I could cite, if space permitted, numerous other instances that would document these points. More significant for my thesis, however, is the fact that in no case did the women come together on their own, either to counter the men or to consider issues of common concern. The communal work groups were ware-oriented in the beginning and, for that time, perhaps a nascent form of the polo associations in Patani. But, as we have seen, the groups fractured into smaller cadres without reference to ware affiliation. Simply put, Korokorosei women do not come together in groups.

Summary

As should be apparent from the data and analysis above, the problem why only some Ijaw women have associations is not solved simply by reference to one important variable. If any one feature I have isolated as relevant to their formation were absent—virilocality, patrilineality, polygyny, or economic independence—Patani women might not be together in groups, or at least in groups with such solidarity and power. Similarly, merely achieving economic independence, for example, might not suffice to bring Korokorosei women together if they continued to be so strongly oriented toward their own kin, from whom they acquire land.

Among the Ijaw, and, I would venture, among other West African societies, the separation of women from their own kinsmen and incorporation as strangers into a kin group whose members have no other loyalties at least sets the stage for the formation of women's associations. But patrilineality and virilocality are much more common in Africa as a whole than are women's associations. Many societies in East and South Africa have these features. What these societies lack are permanent villages as found in West Africa, and, most important, a marketing and trading complex that would allow women to become economically independent. Markets exist in West-Central Africa, but women's participation in them is more limited than in West Africa. In addition, many of these societies are matrilineal and have a wide variety of residence rules. In other words, one or more features correlated with women's associations are absent in East, South, and Central Africa, while all of them are characteristic of many West African groups. I would suggest, therefore, that the combination of factors put forward to explain Patani women's associations are truly significant factors that would predict the presence or absence of women's groups elsewhere. Only a detailed cross-cultural study would test this hypothesis.

What can we say now of Tiger's approach? Although the women of Korokorosei may conform to his conception of women in groups, Patani women certainly do not. We have seen the considerable power and solidarity of their groups, and we have observed that their organization can be explained by reference to social structure. This one example alone scarcely destroys Tiger's thesis, but it represents an approach that might be more fruitful than one referring to biologically inherited propensities. How could a biologically based theory explain the West African women's associations? If we grant that women can form groups but that the groups are not caused by the innate propensities that create men's groups, we then have to grant that we are witnessing isomorphism within the same species—one kind of group generating from the biological system, the other from the social structure. Would the biologically based theory then take us to the next logical conclusion, that, because women are not dependent on innate propensities, they are therefore more "evolved" than men, and that they are consequently more adaptive? Montagu (1953) may have reached this point, but by a very different route.

Other theories that depend on innate qualities, whether they be termed "imperatives," "instinct," or what have you, purport to show the similarities between humans and animals. We have here a theory aimed at explaining the apparent differences between the sexes. Toward whichever point these theories are directed, to similarities or to differences, none of them, independently, can explain *both* the similarities and the differences. In the Ijaw case, concerning both men and women there is a complexity of contrasts and likenesses. Korokorosei men are somewhat more able to cooperate on non-kinship bases than are the men of Patani;

Patani women work well within their associations, whereas those in Korokorosei have never formed non-kin groups. In both cases, the lives of the women are very much separated from those of the men. Separateness is strong in the division of labor by sex, a feature we have come to expect with simpler technologies. However, as Shapiro points out, this division "could well have developed as an adaptive response," rather than as a manifestation of innate sexual differences (1971: 96). The separateness is also present in the residence rules and descent systems. A unilocal rule necessarily emphasizes one sex over the other, as indeed a unilineal system does. The virilocality and patrilineality of Patani are consistent with the formation of women's associations. Despite the virilocal preference in Korokorosei, their matrilaterality and ambilineality would seemingly militate against women's forming similar groups.

These structural features apply to both men and women and do not arise from innate sexual differences; to whatever extent sexual differences exist, their influence in matters of group formation is muted by the structural features of society. If men *or* women in groups are to be explained, the anthropologist would do well to spurn a theory about an instinct, a "herding" instinct, that operates in such a peculiarly selective way.

BETTE S. DENICH

Sex and Power in the Balkans

The story of a family can also portray the soul of a land. . . .
The story of any Montenegrin family is made up of traditions about the lives
of ancestors who distinguished themselves in some special way, most frequently
through heroism. These traditions, spiritually so close to one another, reach
back into the remote past, to the legendary founders of clan and tribes . . .
The life of my family . . . is typical in one respect: the men of several generations have died at the hands of Montenegrins, men of the same faith and
name. . . . Generation after generation, and the bloody chain was not broken.
The inherited fear and hatred of feuding clans was mightier than fear and
hatred of the enemy, the Turks. It seems to me that I was born with blood on
my eyes.

Thus begins the memoir of Milovan Djilas (1958: 3, 8), probably the
best known contemporary Montenegrin outside of Yugoslavia. I would
add one detail that Djilas takes for granted: the clans and tribes are
patrilineal, and the ancestors are all men. The other side of heroism is
death, as men carry out the repetitive cycles of blood and feud. In contrast to the memoir's predominant theme—the violent heroics of Montenegrin manhood—stands this brief glimpse of the author's mother (p.
183):

She devoted her whole being to that which she regarded as natural and inevitable—begetting and rearing children, being good to her husband, and
working slavishly. Apart from that no joy or thought existed for her . . . her
mind was hidden away somewhere deep, perhaps in those bygone ages from
which she, through her forbears, gained her simple and solid experience. . . .

An earlier version of this paper was presented at the 70th annual meeting of the
American Anthropological Association, New York, 1971. This analysis grows out of
observations on sexual roles and family organization made during field studies in
Yugoslavia. I gratefully acknowledge support for this research from a National Institute of Mental Health predoctoral fellowship and supplementary field grant (1965–66)
and a National Endowment for the Humanities Summer Fellowship (1972). I also wish
to thank Thomas Belmonte, Mario Bick, and Jack Ellenberg for their helpful suggestions at various stages in the writing of the paper.

In every moment of crisis for the family or for Father, her constant soul and simple and inexhaustible wisdom came forth.

The story of this family portrays the primary elements of a social structure that characterizes not only the small region of Montenegro but a considerable portion of the Balkan peninsula and, in variations, many other world areas. In the Montenegrin example is seen an extreme version of patrilocal, exogamous grouping with clear hierarchy along sexual lines, in which property and power are vested exclusively in men. The Balkan region has been peopled for millennia by pastoralists and plow agriculturists who have left a continuous record of patricentric organization. Documentation reaches back to ancient Greece, where women were lifelong jural minors without inheritance rights or any basis for autonomy. Passed from father's to husband's household, they were restricted to the domestic sphere and to the production of male heirs for their husbands' families and ancestral gods (Fustel de Coulanges, 1873). These ancient patterns are replicated today wherever social structures follow patrilineal principles, thus restricting women to functions of maintaining and perpetuating organizations that concentrate rights and power in men.

In the anthropological literature a similarity can be found among the forms of interpersonal relationship associated with patricentric organization in its world distribution (see Morgan, 1877; Goldschmidt and Kunkel, 1971). Patricentric organization establishes a framework of male priority and a master script for other familial roles that focuses on the stresses created by the subordination of women. Although these forms are widespread, cross-cultural comparison also shows that they are far from universal. The concentration of power in men cannot, therefore, be accepted as an inevitable result of biological difference, but must be viewed as a social form developing under specific circumstances. The analysis of Balkan social structures having clear sexual hierarchy is therefore significant as part of the comparative study of the circumstances and dynamics of differential sexual statuses.

Pastoralism, Agriculture, and Patricentrism

In the Balkan societies under consideration the smallest social units, households, are based upon males who are recruited by birth, generation after generation. In order to understand this organizational principle, we must consider its relation to the subsistence needs of these populations. Worldwide cross-cultural correlations demonstrate that the nature of basic subsistence activity and the sexual division of labor act together in demarcating strategic advantages for local group formation, tending to favor those forms that keep together the sex responsible for the most crucial tasks. Thus, nearly all matrilocal, matrilineal societies are found among horticulturists, where women are gardeners, and it is advantageous to maintain groups of kinswomen as the basic work force (see Schneider and Gough, 1951; Fox, 1967: 103–14). In contrast, both pastoralism and agriculture assign the primary herding and plowing tasks to men. The predominance of patrilocal residence among surviving pastoral and agricultural societies attests to the ecological adaptiveness of arrangements that keep together male kinsmen, maintaining continuity in their attachment to workmates and property (see Michaelson and Goldschmidt, 1971).

However, while acknowledging that patricentric organization has survival advantages under given conditions, it is crucial to distinguish between the concepts of "adaptation" and "functional integration." Although the selective advantages of male-centered forms can be understood in relation to particular ecological conditions, it does not follow that the other attendant structural features "fit" together with patricentrism to constitute an integrated whole, as the tradition of functional analysis would lead us to assume. One set of structural features may be in actual opposition to another, and the structure perpetuates its internal contradictions along with its adaptive advantages. Analyses of social structure in anthropology have generally overlooked built-in oppositions, and thus have failed to grasp the sources of endemic, unresolvable conflict (see Murphy, 1971). Because patrilineal structures correspond with the cultural assumptions of most anthropologists, they have been accepted as logically consistent, although the discrepancies in matrilineal organization have been acknowledged (cf. Richards, 1950). Accepting the ideological premises of patriliny, anthropological models focus upon male actors manipulating female objects so that the resultant "systems" operate smoothly, carrying out all their assigned functions.

My analysis derives from a different viewpoint, which, though accepting the demands of material survival as its baseline, does not assume the internal consistency of social systems and their ideological overtones. The values that justify sexual stratification can be understood as emanating not from consensus but from the conflict of opposing interests defined along sexual lines. The analysis investigates how external conditions define optimal courses of action in the area of survival, and proceeds to relate the resulting conditions of social existence to the ideological mechanisms that express the conflicts inherent in the established systems of sexual role and status.

In organizational terms, then, patricentrism is social structure in which the core residential and economic units consist of agnatically related men. However, there is an important difference between structures in which the core is connected only by vertical descent lines and those in which the agnatic core is broadened through horizontal links among kinsmen of the same generation. In the Balkans this distinction tends to correspond with that between agricultural peoples and the mountain dwellers, who rely heavily upon animal herding. The first situation, characteristic of agriculturists, occurs where males exclusively inherit the patrimonial estates and form autonomous households without wider corporate ties to other kinsmen. In contrast, the conditions in pastoral communities enforce the maintenance of corporate ties among brothers and with more distant collateral kinsmen. Although these organizational differences generally correspond to these modes of subsistence, it is necessary to caution that the causes are not exclusively ecological, but also involve the isolation of mountain herders from the authority of state systems, which have long intervened in the political affairs of agricultural villagers.

The formal structures in all these societies are based exclusively upon relations among male kinsmen. The only enduring social units are formed through the male descent line, and women are exchanged among these units to procreate future generations of males, leaving no enduring marks of their own existence in terms of the formal structure. Such systems can be diagramed neatly without any women at all: women serve merely as links between fathers and sons, and between male in-laws. Whether or not Lévi-Strauss's theory of woman-exchange is universal is open to debate, but it does provide an accurate model of kinship structures in the Balkan societies under consideration here. The statement that "in human society, it is the men who exchange the women and not vice-versa" (Lévi-Strauss, 1963: 45) may be paraphrased to read: the exchange of women leads to the formation of male groups, not groups acknowledging the equal participation of both sexes.

The size and extension of male groupings is a significant factor in determining the degree of sexual stratification in Balkan societies. Because the contrast in family forms generally corresponds to differences between pastoralists and agriculturists, the discussion is organized around a comparison between these types. The contrast has heuristic value in isolating variables that can also be applied to populations with mixed subsistence and intermediary familial forms. The Balkan area will be viewed with specific reference to the regions of Albania, Bulgaria, Greece, and Yugoslavia, known through readily available ethnographic literature and supplemented by the author's field observations in Yugoslavia. The available studies do not encompass the entire peninsula, but they do represent wider subareas.

Pastoralists and Man's Domain

The herdsmen of the Balkan mountains include several ethnicities, speaking different languages and dialects and adhering to three major religions. However, the ethnographic literature indicates remarkable similarity in their ecological adaptations and social structures, and in the ideological expressions of these structures. The societies included in this discussion are of Greek (Sarakatsani), Albanian, Vlach, and South Slavic (Montenegrin, Serbian, Moslem) ethnicities. The descriptions are in ethnographic present, but it is important to note that this does not always coincide with historical present. In all these cases, segmentary tribal structures have been incorporated into the national states within whose borders they fall, and indigenous patterns of action involving violence are now inhibited by national legal systems. However, it is too soon to relegate this description to historical past tense: forms of conflict continue in diminished scope, as do the basic features of household organization and rules of interpersonal and sexual behavior. The old order is fading and coexists today with new orders—but it is still there.

Men of the Balkan mountains are worthy subjects for the folk epics, in which they celebrate centuries of resistance against the Turks, as well as heroic feats against local rivals. Only the tiny land of Montenegro maintained legal independence through five centuries of Ottoman domination, though in the more mountainous regions of other provinces, where Turkish officials forbore direct rule or heavy taxation, the conquest was a modest burden. The heroic tradition is also expressed in the national costume of these regions, in which men are splendid figures, with midriffs bedecked in long sashes and assorted weaponry.

The work of transhumant pastoralism involves long treks between winter and summer pastures. It includes periods of isolation on lonely mountain peaks, herding and guarding the animals from raids by wolves, bears, and other shepherds. Flocks of sheep and goats are held in common by the males of a household, the numbers of generations varying with the phase of the domestic cycle in which a household finds itself at a given time. Although there is emphasis on maintaining joint households with collective property, fission occurs at regular intervals, with equal inheritance by all brothers of the generation that is dividing.

Grazing rights and pasturelands are collectively held by groups of households, connected by tribe and/or clan. Competition for these resources requires that herdsmen band together with allies to ward off actual attacks and discourage potential threats to their means of subsistence. The organizational solution to this problem has followed the pattern developed around the world by populations in analogous circumstances: patrilineally related groupings bonded through the dynamics of fusion against common external enemies (see Sahlins, 1961). Segments defined by patrilineal descent provide the most convenient basis for a permanent system of alliances among the men who watch and guard sheep. Among Montenegrins and Albanians, patrilineality defines a fully developed system of segmentary lineages and clans, whereas among the Greek tribes, a shallower system of agnatic grouping is operative (Campbell, 1964: 550–58).

In all of these societies the public face of each group vis-à-vis the external world represents its competitive posture toward potential rivals. Fighting, both defensive and offensive, is an exclusively male activity. Since all public arenas have the potentiality for combat, they are designated as male. The household's external environment is exclusively a male domain.

Among the Greek Sarakatsani, as described by Campbell (1964: 204), sheep theft, though rampant in the past, is now curbed by severe penalties imposed by the national government. Instead, grass is stolen by sneaking the flock onto another's territory by night. Successful theft of both sheep and grass is a source of high satisfaction to the thief, of grievance to the victim. The thief gains in wealth and prestige, while the victim is diminished in both. There is no moral sanction against stealing from unrelated persons, so that any dealings between unrelated groups are fraught with the continual possibility that one will take advantage of the other. To avoid being victimized, each group must keep its combative alliances in continual readiness and maintain a show of sufficient strength to discourage intruders.

Djilas describes similar rivalries in the Montenegro of his youth, shortly after World War I (1958: 114):

Down below, in the villages, tribal and clan divisions were already beginning to fade. The mountain, however, had been divided from earliest times. It was known to whom every peak and spring belonged, as well as the pastures and meadows. The tribes no longer fought over the valleys, but the shepherds still fought over their grazing lands, made up mocking jests and howled derisive songs at other camp settlements.

Amidst this generalized atmosphere of tension between groups of kinsmen, outbreaks of violence are frequent, for each man is obligated to defend his group against both physical and symbolic attack. The latter category includes a wide range of acts that diminish a group's reputation or honor. Response in kind is required for the sullied group to retain its "honor," which is really a symbolic screen for its power.[1] There are many levels of attack and defense, ranging from simple insult (including the joking insults described by Djilas) through fistfighting to homicide. In response to this ultimate form of violence, the blood feud developed as the institution that most clearly reveals the lines of agnatic solidarity: the agnatic core of the household, consisting of brothers and sons, bears responsibility for avenging the death of any of its members by killing the murderer. The rules for vengeance show some variation among different regions, but they are alike in placing the greatest responsibility on the most intimate agnates of the victim to uphold the honor of the lineage—i.e. their own reputations as fighters—by not allowing a murder to go unavenged. Only males participate in feuds, as perpetrators and as objects of vengeance. Hasluck (1954) describes collective vengeance in some regions of Albania, where a condition of "boiling blood" for twenty-four hours after a killing gave any man of the victim's tribe license to kill any man of the murderer's tribe. Blood feud was a major cause in the past for Serbian and Montenegrin men to emigrate to other regions of present-day Yugoslavia. Other men fortify themselves in their houses, unable to venture out for fear of avengers. Among the Albanian inhabitants of Yugoslavia, such house asylum is still widespread. Migration to avoid vengeance also still occurs. Campbell (1964) reports that several recent Sarakatsani murderers, when released from prison, moved to other places in Greece rather than face the threat of vengeance at home.

Although homicide is the ultimate challenge to an agnatic group, lesser verbal or physical challenges must also be met aggressively. When challenged, an individual shows his willingness to fight, although he may actually be grateful to those who jump in to prevent violence. Fights are occasions for demonstrations of solidarity among kinsmen, for calling potential alliances into action. The ideology of male group solidarity is internalized on the emotional level, provoking immediate response, as illustrated in the following incident in which an earlier fight between two individuals results in a second fight between their respective brothers: "In his own words, 'I suddenly saw him there, drinking and putting on airs. I remembered that his brother Vasili drew blood from my

[1] This concept of honor is obviously related to the honor-shame syndrome so widely noted in the Mediterranean area. The present analysis owes a portion of its inspiration to Schneider (1971), who first presented an interpretation of Mediterranean honor and shame in terms of resources and intergroup competition.

brother. I could not stand it.' The consequence for the other man was a head wound from a broken bottle before the two men were parted and expelled from the wedding" (Campbell, 1964: 198–99). This makes for a rather testy atmosphere wherever men from different kin groups are assembled. Otherwise festive events, such as weddings and village festivals, are frequently marred by violence, and even death is far from rare.

Concomitant with actual readiness for combat is a complex of more subtle prescriptions for male behavior that are deeply internalized through socialization. The public image of warrior courage is linked with a self-image of indomitable virility and elaborated ideologically in terms of the value codes of "honor." The public bearing of men is formidable, verging on a caricature of masculine qualities. In Yugoslavia men of pastoralist heritage walk tall and proud, asserting themselves conspicuously when advantageous. Simic (1969) equates this behavior with the machismo syndrome originally observed in Latin America. An examination of the survival problems of these populations presents a broader basis for understanding the sources of the prescriptions and ideals about proper masculine behavior. I am suggesting that the stance of masculine aggressiveness is essentially a defensive one serving to ward off potential threats to a group's fragile hold over its subsistence resources. This stance is articulated individually and collectively, for it is essential to recognize that what is at stake is the survival of families banded together agnatically in mutual protection. A group's power depends upon its unity, and any threat to this unity must be dealt with.

So far we have discussed the ways in which external threats are managed physically and ideologically; now we proceed to a discussion of internal threats.

Pastoralists and Woman's Place

Although the institutions of patrilineality, patrilocality, exogamy, and male inheritance neatly delimit, according to sex, memberships of local groups and access to rights over property and people, they conversely define *exclusion from* such rights according to sex. In Montenegro daughters are not even reckoned by fathers enumerating their children. This is consistent with a system in which a daughter's presence in the household is only temporary. Lines of exogamy are broadly drawn, so that custom and Orthodox religious law prohibit marriage between descendants of a common great-grandparent or any closer relative. Further prohibitions extend the net ever further, so that marriages usually ally previously unconnected households. Indeed, this becomes conscious design as fathers seek to maximize alliances with co–fathers-in-law.

Marriages are arranged by parents, celebrated with elaborate rituals and finalized by the bride's entry into her husband's household. Severed from her own natal group, in which she has no further rights, the bride joins a household consisting of a husband who is a virtual stranger, his male agnates, other in-married women with whom she has no consanguineal connections (prevented by exogamic prescriptions), and unmarried girls who are transitory members. The adult core of the domestic group thus consists of male agnates and unrelated in-married women. Whereas the males are born into a situation in which loyalty to the group coincides with their own interests as heirs and property holders, women marry into a group to which they have no equivalent basis for loyalty. Initially, there is not even sentimental attachment to any of the group's members, even to husbands. And yet the survival of the household depends upon the half of the adult membership that is composed of such women. *The basic dilemma of the agnatic group is to deal with the anomalous presence of those people who are in the group but not of it.*

Only as the mother of sons does a wife secure a place in the group, bound to it through a blood tie. Through influence on her husband and sons, a woman can establish an indirect power base of her own, but the particularism of her interests, focused upon men to whom she is directly tied, is a source of opposition within the larger circle of men. Eventually, as a mother-in-law she oversees the work of her sons' wives, turning these diverse women into a work force for the household. The survival of the group depends upon unified action by its male members in the public sphere; it depends also upon smooth functioning within the domestic sphere. The difference is that domestic functions are the province of those people lacking in inherent loyalty and solidarity—its attached women.

Agnatic solidarity requires control over these anomalous household members. Where a correspondence of interests does not exist as a basis for loyalty, negative sanctions are utilized to prevent behavior detrimental to the group. The individual interests of in-married women are subordinated to group needs, and a cooperative domestic unit is forged out of the diverse female members by inhibiting them from acting in accord with individual interests. Of course, the male members of the group are also inhibited from individual activity that would be divisive to the necessary solidarity, but as males they also share directly in the rewards accrued by the group in terms of prestige and self-esteem, where personal identity is so closely linked with group identity. However, the women are not in a structurally parallel situation. They can share only indirectly in these emotional rewards through the individual husbands and sons to whom they are attached. Although a woman's loyalty may develop naturally to these individual men, the examination of institutional mechanisms for controlling women indicates that coercion is necessary to reconcile the opposition between women's individual interests and the requirements for group survival.

The intensity of the dilemma presented by the presence of women within the male group is made clearer when we recognize the vital importance of the women to the household. Indeed, its survival depends just as crucially upon its in-married females as upon its males. The most essential function of women is, obviously, to serve as bearers of sons for the patriline. The fate of barren women is a sorry one, and the mother of daughters only is also in a difficult situation, without a permanent blood tie to the group and failing to provide her husband with direct heirs. Although the reproductive function is most important ideologically, the household's material survival also relies heavily upon the women's labor contribution. In all these societies women perform much of the most arduous labor. In addition to all work about the household, they do major agricultural work and carry the heavy burdens, such as firewood and water. Such tasks have been defined as demeaning to men, who are evidently ignorant of the concept "weaker sex." Hasluck (1954: 26) reports that Albanian women carry loads up to seventy pounds, if from a poor household without a donkey. Among the Sarakatsani, "Although men will lift heavy objects to secure them to a mule, they never carry burdens on their backs. However sick or feeble his wife or daughter, a man will never help her with the intolerable burden of heavy water barrels" (Campbell, 1964: 274). Sarakatsani women are even the builders of the dwelling huts. When not carrying out heavier tasks, Balkan women busy themselves with weaving and other handicrafts that are the prizes of folk art. A more delicate labor contribution is in child care, in which women are expected to socialize their sons along lines securing the future interests of the household.

Overcoming the natural diversity and rivalry among the women's interests is requisite to the accomplishment of day-to-day household tasks. These potentially divisive interests are subordinated to those of the group by keeping each wife under the authority of her husband and the other men. This authority is maintained through the elaboration of cultural forms that both directly and symbolically ensure the domination of the male-oriented group over its female members. The institutions of male domination take the forms of ritualized female deference and direct physical punishments for violating the rules of submission to the group. Public behavior is governed by a show of deference by women to their men, featuring such stylized performances as walking several paces behind their husbands, carrying whatever burdens need to be transported. If only one donkey is available the man rides while the woman walks behind. Among the Sarakatsani (Campbell, 1964: 152),

Publicly a husband addresses his wife in a stern, severe voice. Requests are commands, barked out in sharp phrases. It is important for a man's self-regard that other men should see that he is master in his own house. In public the wife is meek and modest, silent and submissive. She does not smile at him or laugh with him before strangers.

In Serbia ceremonial seating arrangements are by ranks, with males from elders through adolescents seated at the head of the table, with all women—beginning with the eldest—lined up below the lowest-ranking males. Within the household stylized behaviors also reiterate the theme of female subordination. In some South Slavic pastoral regions custom requires that a new daughter-in-law show respect by kissing the hands of all males in the household—including children (Erlich, 1966: 230–31). In Serbia women's subsidiary status is reenacted whenever there are guests: men serve as hosts, sitting and drinking with the guests, while the women prepare food and carry it to the table but do not sit with the guests. Sarakatsani men and women always eat separately, the men first eating their fill, the women taking the leftovers (Campbell, 1964: 151). Albanian men are served by women, who then eat separately in the kitchen with the children (Hasluck, 1954: 28–29). In many Yugoslavian regions women's degradation ceremonies include washing the feet of their husbands and fathers-in-law (Erlich, 1966: 232–34).

An ultimate manner of symbolizing the wife's status concerns her name. A two-way avoidance rule, subordinating conjugal to agnatic ties, prevents Serbian and Montenegrin husbands and wives from using each other's first names, in either reference or direct address. Albanians, Koutsovlachs, and Sarakatsani follow through to another step in structural logic in that the wife, after marriage, is known only by the possessive form of her husband's first name, thereby losing the separate social identity represented by her own first name (Hasluck, 1954: 33; Schein, 1971: 57; Campbell, 1964: 186). These various rules of female deference are ritualized expressions of the household authority structure, in which it is continually reiterated that women are under the jurisdiction of the permanent male cadre of the domestic group.

The punitive aspect of male domination occurs in response to women's behavior that threatens the group. The major focus for threat is in the area of sexual behavior, in which the question of control is most sharply posed, with its heaviest psychological concomitants. Marriage is contracted as an alliance between men, and the deal requires that the bride be a virgin. If it is discovered otherwise, it is a source of conflict, perhaps even blood feud, between the two groups. Durham reported the following (1928: 206):

> The "chastity" of the Montenegrin . . . consisted of old in the fact that he was given a wife when very young, and that he and any of his male relatives were liable to be shot if he tampered with any other woman. The betrothed girl, when handed over by her parents, had to be *intacta virgo*, and they were held responsible. . . . The girl, moreover, being already betrothed, was the property of her betrothed's family, and they would refuse to take "damaged goods," demand compensation, and a blood feud might follow. Tales were told of hapless girls being hunted out and left to starve; of being stripped and tied naked to a tree on the mountain; of being stoned or beaten.

Once the marriage takes place, fidelity is required from the wife. Death was formerly the ultimate penalty for the adulterous wife—the only question being whether it was her husband's or her own kinsmen's obligation to administer it (Campbell, 1964: 152; Durham, 1928: 206). Like blood-feud killings, such acts are now regarded as homicide by the national governments in which these peoples dwell. However, in Yugoslavia at least, murders of women by "jealous" husbands or lovers are commonplace, and they are punished by penal laws that impose relatively lenient sentences. In former times a lighter penalty for adultery in Montenegro was for the husband to cut off the wife's nose (Durham, 1928: 85). One of Erlich's informants in an Albanian village reported (1966: 324): "A husband leaves a faithless wife. During Turkish time, before the war, the husband had the right to cut off her nose, cut out her tongue, or cut off her hair."

Although there is an undoubted psychological component—"jealousy"—to this repressive control over women's sexuality, it plays a small part in explaining such severe sanctions. The explanation must be sought in structural terms: Why should women's sexuality be such an extreme focus for the exertion of male control? Why should the reactions against women's sexual freedom be so severe? There are two components to the control of women's sexuality—one practical, the other symbolic. On the practical side the tenuous bond between a woman and her husband's household would be further undermined by liaisons with other men. However, the more significant dimension of the severity of measures for sexual control over women stems from the symbolic importance of sex in the competitive social environment situation in which agnatic groups exist. The ability of a household's men to control its women is one of many indicators of its strength; accordingly, evidence of lack of control over women would indicate weakness and possibly reveal the men's vulnerability to other external challenges. One of Erlich's Montenegrin informants gave the following interpretation of adultery penalties in his region (1966: 324): "It is important for the unfaithfulness of a wife to remain a secret. If the husband catches the wife in the act, he is considered a coward if he does not kill the adulterer, and will be despised." In a similar vein Campbell makes the following observation about the Sarakatsani (1964: 152): "The act of disobedience by which she damages her husband most severely is adultery. . . . Adultery attacks the moral integrity and honor of the family and makes a *laughingstock* of its leader and head" (emphasis added). Inasmuch as the stance of the group's invulnerability, represented by its "honor," is crucial to its competitive situation with other groups, it is obvious that the stance of "laughingstock" would be very damaging to men attempting to play out their roles in the public arena.

In all these societies women not behaving in the properly submissive manner are liable to beating by their husbands. Campbell (1964: 152) observes that actual disobedience is rare among the Sarakatsani, but that the normal irritations between husband and wife are settled by the wife's receiving "a beating with a stick." Erlich's data on Yugoslavia in the 1930's show that wife beating was a regular practice in many regions of Yugoslavia. Some of her informants recognize that this practice is related to the structural features of extended families, as shown in the following comment (1966: 264):

A husband beats his wife only when the parents complain to the son about insults done them by their daughter-in-law. If a husband beats his wife in the presence of neighbors and children, it is considered that he has thereby gained a point to the advantage of his authority. A husband is the master of his wife and it is his right to beat her.

Although the husband is usually the direct administrator of punishment, the severity of these sanctions expresses the collective dominance of the agnatic household, rather than simply that of the individual husband over his wife. Maintenance of household unity requires that many sources of internal dissension be counteracted. The value of agnatic solidarity is contradicted by the reality of fission, which eventually divides the joint household among its component brothers. Inevitable rivalry between brothers must be suppressed to avoid fission that is too hasty or frequent.

In each of these societies the folk explanation for division of joint families rests on the women.[2] For example, the Sarakatsani (Campbell, 1964: 17) have two proverbs on the subject: "Women make the house and then destroy it"; and "Wives are like nuts from forty different walnut trees." This charge rests partially on the realistic assessment that each woman's interests lie primarily in the nuclear family segment based upon her husband and son, and that she does advance these interests in opposition to the rest of the collective. However, the explanation also serves as an ideological screen for another source of dissension: rivalry among the brothers themselves. Blame is deflected onto their wives, since the system can deal with dissension from women more easily than it can with disputes among its male members. All of these sources of dissension result in fragile household unity, maintained by suppression of disruptive behavior, particularly from those members least committed to the group as a whole—its wives.

Agriculturists

Ethnographic studies of agricultural communities in Bulgaria (Sanders, 1949), Greece (Friedl, 1962), and Yugoslavia (Erlich, 1966; Halpern, 1956; Hammel, 1968, 1972; Winner, 1971) describe social structures with the characteristics of peasant patricentrism delineated by Goldschmidt and Kunkel (1971). Emphasis upon the male line is clear, and along with it the formal authority of husbands over wives. But notably absent are extreme forms of actual and ritual subordination of women to men. Ethnographers speak of "partnership" between spouses and the sharing of participation in decision making. By comparing the social structures of agriculturists with those of the pastoralists, it should be possible to pinpoint features that determine the degree of inequality in sexual status and power.

In the agricultural communities, single-family households predominate. In Slovenia nuclear stem families are the traditional form; the other regions have had a past tradition of fraternal joint families, which have given way to the present nuclear households, with equal property division among male heirs. The joint family *zadruga* among Serbs and Croats would actually comprise a transitional type, with collective households stressing sexual hierarchy but without the extremes resulting from extra-household patrilineal organization. As the *zadruge* have given way to nuclear households, social organization in these regions

---

[2] Anthropologists have also accepted this explanation at face value. For example, Lockwood (1972: 59) reports that, among Bosnian Moslems, "Virtually every extended family household which divides does so regretfully and for the same reason—the incompatibility of its wives."

approaches that of regions with long-standing nuclear household traditions. Although inheritance is patrilineal, interlinking males through descending generations, there are no corporate patrilineal structures connecting males collaterally. In Serbia patriclans have ritual significance, but there are no collective obligations for male kinsmen vis-à-vis opposing groups, and no blood feuds. Each household manages its own basic resources, with title to land and other holdings enforced by state institutions, which eliminate the need for stable protective alliances against potentially rapacious neighbors. The unregulated intergroup conflict endemic among pastoralists is absent, and there is no pressure for households to maintain larger associations on the enduring basis of patrilineal kinship.

Patrilocality brings agricultural wives into their husbands' households. However, both stem family and divided inheritance provide for autonomous nuclear households where wives can take charge of domestic affairs without consideration for their husbands' agnates, who are also in separate households. The separation between public, male arenas and the women's household domain also characterizes agricultural communities. But the wife excluded from the coffeehouses is still queen of her own kitchen, rather than one who must defer even there to superiors among her husband's kinsmen. Women are expected to show deference to their husbands, but prescriptions for such behavior are much less elaborated than among the pastoralists.

Although sexual restrictions over women also are important in these agricultural communities, punishments are not draconian. Although an unmarried girl may suffer for sexual transgression, it does not involve her kinsmen in hostilities with her betrothed's agnates. Since the act is less grave in its collective consequences, punishments designed to prevent its occurrence are less severe. At worst, women bearing illegitimate children may be forced to leave the village (see Sanders, 1949: 83). More tolerant attitudes are held in areas with long-standing nuclear-household traditions. In Dalmatian coastal villages premarital sexual relations are permissible for engaged couples, limited only by any future difficulty the girl may have in marrying another man, once she is known to have been intimate with a fiancé (see Erlich, 1966: 155–56). Slovenian acceptance of women's premarital sexual relations has given these women a rather racy reputation in the more restrictive regions of Yugoslavia. Winner (1971: 202) reports that illegitimate children are traditionally accepted in Slovenian village households, and that "the occurrence of illegitimacy is looked upon as unfortunate but not tragic."

Similarly, adultery diminishes the honor of the cuckolded husband, but not the collective status of an entire kin group. Although the individual's reputation is at stake, there is no pressure upon a whole collective to restore its solidarity through retribution against the transgressor.

In contrast to collective domestic groups, nuclear households are spared the problem of maintaining a fragile unity among married agnates, which, as we have seen, leads to avoidance prescriptions between married couples and overall suppression of the conjugal relationship in favor of agnatic ones. In nuclear households husbands can turn to wives as partners—albeit junior ones—in running their family affairs.

In these agricultural communities the basic resource, land, is attached to male inheritance. Where dowries are important (e.g. Greece), wives do contribute property to their households, but the identifiable social unit is that defined by the husband's patrimony and residence. The male emphasis is formalized in the patrilineal inheritance of surnames, so that families are identified only by links through males. The question arises: how, in a formal sense, does this structure differ from the patrilineality of the pastoralists? First, there is no corporate relationship between patrilineally related households. Therefore, in the realities of interpersonal relationship there is no special bond that sharply distinguishes patrilateral from matrilateral kinsmen. Second, where patrilineal relationships lack instrumental functions, they are not elaborated as a framework for continuing relationships. Genealogies are not long remembered on either side, in contrast to the situation among Serbian, Montenegrin, and Albanian pastoralists, among whom (Hasluck, 1954: 33),

whereas the names of ancestors in the male line might be known for as many as twenty generations, those in the female line were forgotten after two or three. In the words of the Unwritten Law "a man has blood, and a woman kin," i.e. a man has a pedigree, and a woman her own relatives, and "a woman is anybody's daughter," i.e. comes from anywhere and has no pedigree.

Not having "pedigrees" or corporate groupings on either side, kinship relationships follow bilateral lines without a difference in kind between patrilateral and matrilateral kin.

Conclusion

The concentration of property, residence, and descent in the male line is sufficient to generate a structure in which each component household unit centers on males and articulates this focus in ritualized female deference and male dominance within the household, while public roles are reserved for the male bearers of formal title to the continuing elementary family units. When these conditions alone are present, as exemplified in Greek, Slovenian, Dalmatian coastal (see Erlich, 1966), and

Bulgarian agricultural villages, the subordinated status of women is mitigated by the de facto partnership between spouses, in which it is possible to argue that parallel spheres of influence exist—the wife's in the kitchen, the husband's in the village square.

However, when a threatening external social environment, in addition to these minimal conditions of patricentrism, requires solidarity among agnates beyond the range of the conjugal family, the conflicts inherent in any patricentric structure are magnified by the necessity to suppress all sources of internal divisiveness among the larger association of kinsmen. The formal structure, consisting of agnatically related males, does not include women at all, and would operate more neatly if women did not exist, since their interests do not match those of the unified males. Inasmuch as women do exist and are obviously necessary for group survival, the male groups have the problem of utilizing women for their necessary functions, while preventing them from weakening the group's position in its external struggles. There is no natural basis for loyalty from wives acquired from other groups, yet the group must depend upon women whose interests do not coincide with its own. The formal structure of the agnatic group is at variance with its internal realities; as men busy themselves dealing with the outside world, they depend upon women to keep things running smoothly at home. Keeping the behavior of women in line with group unity involves a problem of control, and the elaboration of coercive mechanisms shows that women are not by nature submissive, but must be prevented from acting in their individual interests. The ideological bifurcation of male and female qualities is exaggerated in proportion to the fragility of agnatic solidarity and the concomitant extent to which women are perceived as sources of dissension. Exaggerated values of male supremacy are linked with mechanisms of female suppression. The more omnipotent the males are construed to be, the more this omnipotence is threatened by ostensibly insignificant females.

Where male solidarity is of great importance, it is useful to find an ideological mask for the rivalries among males. As "the myths have thought themselves out in people's minds" (paraphrasing Lévi-Strauss), they have diverted the realities of conflict among the men themselves onto their attached women, where they may be dealt with in ways less subversive to the fundamental basis of the group. When brothers quarrel, the wives must be at fault and can receive proper punishment. The many sources of internal opposition are ideologically combined, and they are articulated in the elaboration of the male-female dichotomy, which both expresses the real opposition between males and females and serves as a screen to conceal the underlying oppositions among the males themselves. This conscious model is a simplification of reality that "is intended not to explain the phenomena but to perpetuate them" (Lévi-Strauss, 1963: 273).

The anomalous position of women within the male groups is defined by the structure itself; so defined, the contradiction cannot be overcome so long as the society perpetuates itself through the birth of men by women. The unresolvable contradiction is the source of institutions of coercion and repression that strain toward shaping the empirical reality along the lines of the ideological model by curtailing women's actions in their own self-interest and enforcing their participation in routines that perpetuate a structure in opposition to themselves. This is essentially the situation of any suppressed social class—but unlike Engels (1891; see also Sacks, this volume), I will not argue that women constitute a class; they are in a situation analogous to that of exploited classes, which, dependent upon structures that oppose their own interests, are compelled to act against themselves.

Inherent contradictions between the structure and reality of matrilineality have been recognized as constituting a "matrilineal puzzle," in the sense that the structure denies the importance of paternity, but reality is otherwise (Richards, 1950). Conversely, patrilineality has been accepted as the functionally neater arrangement. But as long as the contradictions in patrilineal structure are not recognized, the mechanisms for male superordination are not fully intelligible. I wish to suggest the existence of a "patrilineal paradox," in the sense that the structure denies the formal existence of women, while at the same time group survival depends upon them. The structure requires women's submission to group interests, but women are not by nature submissive—if they were, elaborate control mechanisms would not be necessary. The problem of the exogamous patrilineal group is to consolidate the interests of its wives so that they will work to the group's advantage instead of undermining its cohesion. Because there is no initial unity of interest between a wife and her husband's group, intersexual opposition is a keystone of the domestic group.

Epilogue

So long as no other causes can be shown for social institutions, explanations fall back on biology or destiny. Here I have presented some external material factors that have engendered the patrilineally oriented family structures of the Balkans. Such an approach not only lends intelligibility to previously mystifying practices, but also anticipates sources

TABLE 1
*Career Aspirations of Yugoslavian Rural-Urban
Migrants for Their Children*

Career aspiration	Sex of child	
	Female percentage (N=103)	Male percentage (N=110)
Professional careers		
(requiring university degrees)	40%	40%
Technicians		
(requiring secondary schools)	8	7
White-collar occupations		
(requiring secondary schools)	23	19
Skilled manual work		
(requiring secondary schools)	1	16
Teachers		
(requiring secondary schools)	10	4
Fine arts		
(usually requiring university degrees)	3	1
Marriage		
(actually married already)	2	—
"Let the child choose for him(her)self"	13	13
TOTAL	100%	100%

of change. Lacking space to develop the analysis, I shall present a bit of data from my research in Yugoslavia to demonstrate that behavior may alter rapidly in a changed context of material possibilities, and that response to new circumstances is more important in determining behavior than are ancient ideologies.

In the Užice region of Serbia, rural children were formerly trained for their adult lives as peasant householders and peasant wives. Although boys were sent to elementary school, girls were kept at home because schooling was considered irrelevant, even detrimental, to their performance as wives. There was distinct preference for male children to carry on the farm and the family name, and corresponding disappointment at the birth of daughters. Parents were obligated to provide for their daughters by placing them in marriage. With rapid industrialization after World War II, cities have swelled with recent in-migrants from rural areas (see Denich, 1970). Parental responsibilities still entail providing for children's future subsistence, but the means are now defined by an urban occupational structure in which occupations are not necessarily linked to male heirs, meaning that a continuing desire for male children is based upon sentiment rather than function. Urban families limit their offspring to the number they feel capable of educating properly: the two-child family is the norm, and few families exceed this number, whether or not they have sons. Parents define their responsibility in terms of preparing both children for economic self-sufficiency, regardless of sex.

The equivalence of parental aspirations for sons and daughters is shown by results of my interview with postwar rural-urban migrants in an industrializing town. Informants with children were asked what they desired their children to "become" when they grew up. Analysis of the responses (see Table 1) shows remarkably little differentiation in kinds of aspirations for boys and girls, despite the fact that these parents were themselves socialized according to the village traditions of dichotomized sex roles. Whereas girls were formerly prepared for dependence upon the economic base of male-dominated domestic groups, they are now consciously prepared for independence on the basis of their own urban occupations. Although the rural structure prescribed distinct and unequal statuses for males and females, the traditional ideology of inequality does not prevail in the urban context. At least in the important area of occupational status, biology is no longer destiny.

JOAN BAMBERGER

The Myth of Matriarchy: Why Men Rule in Primitive Society

There is little doubt that the public's interest in primitive matriarchies has been revived. Suddenly magazine articles and books appear attesting to a former Rule by Women, as well as to an archaic life-style presumed to differ radically from our own. Because no matriarchies persist anywhere at the present time, and because primary sources recounting them are totally lacking, both the existence and constitution of female-dominated societies can only be surmised. The absence of this documentation, however, has not been a deterrent to those scholars and popularists who view in the concept of primitive matriarchy a rationale for a new social order, one in which women can and should gain control of important political and economic roles.

Bachofen and Mother Right: Myth and History

The earliest and most erudite study of matriarchy was published in Stuttgart in 1861 by the Swiss jurist and classical scholar Johann Jakob Bachofen. His *Das Mutterrecht* (Mother right: an investigation of the religious and juridical character of matriarchy in the ancient world)[1] had an impact on nineteenth-century views on the evolution of early social institutions. Arguing from mainly poetic and frequently dubious historical sources (Hesiod, Pindar, Ovid, Virgil, Horace, the *Iliad* and the *Odyssey*, Herodotus, and Strabo),[2] Bachofen tried to establish as

The editors, Louise Lamphere and Michelle Rosaldo, deserve special thanks for their extremely useful criticisms of an earlier version of this paper. I would like to thank also Eugene Goodheart, Eva Hunt, and Robert A. Manners for their helpful comments on the final revision.

[1] Excerpts from *Das Mutterrecht* (1861) are available in translation in Ralph Mannheim, ed., *Myth, Religion and Mother Right* (Bachofen, 1967).

[2] The accuracy of these classical sources on matriarchy is questioned by Simon Pembroke (1967). He concludes a scholarly investigation of a number of Bachofen's Greek citations with the opinion that "What the Greeks knew about their past, and

moral and historical fact the primacy of "mother right," which he thought sprang from the natural and biological association of mother and child. Matriarchy, or the dominion of the mother "over family and state," according to Bachofen, was a later development generated by woman's profound dissatisfaction with the "unregulated sexuality" that man had forced upon her. A gradual series of modifications in the matriarchal family led to the institution of individual marriage and "the matrilinear transmission of property and names." This advanced stage of mother right was followed by a civil rule by women, which Bachofen called a "gynocracy." The rule by women was overthrown eventually by the "divine father principle," but not before mother right had clearly put its stamp on a state religion. Indeed, it was this sacred character of matriarchy, founded on the maternal generative mystery, that represented for Bachofen the bulk of his evidence in favor of ancient matriarchies.

In the same year that *Das Mutterrecht* appeared, another scholarly work was published that supported an opposing opinion, namely that patriarchy was "the primeval condition of the human race." Henry Sumner Maine's *Ancient Law* sought to establish, by the method of comparative jurisprudence, that all human groups were "originally organized on the patriarchal model" (1861: 119). Maine's argument rested on information contained in the Scriptures, in particular the early chapters of Genesis, and on Roman law. With the simultaneous publication of *Das Mutterrecht* and *Ancient Law* it may be said that the contest between the matriarchists and the patriarchists was launched in the intellectual circles of Western Europe. That neither side won a victory is owing to a paucity of evidence on both sides. The theory of matriarchy attracted such staunch supporters as John F. McLennan (another lawyer, who introduced a matriarchal hypothesis in 1865 independently of Bachofen; see Rivière's introduction to McLennan's *Primitive Marriage*, 1970), Lewis Henry Morgan (1877, whose influence on Friedrich Engels's *Origin of the Family, Private Property and the State* is well known), and Edward Burnett Tylor (1899). The patriarchal theory was defended with considerable skill in *The History of Human Marriage* by Edward Westermarck (1891), who successfully demonstrated that males could be dominant in both family and political affairs in societies with systems of matrilineal descent.

What is known about the past and present conditions of primitive

---

about their neighbors, turns out to be very little." I am indebted to Mary Lefkowitz of the Department of Classics, Wellesley College, for calling my attention to Pembroke's paper.

and early peoples does not augur well for any future discovery of a clear-cut and indisputable case of matriarchy. Patriarchal societies, however, seem to abound in fact as well as in theory, although admittedly there is still no certifiable way of documenting the political and jural relations of the earliest human societies. It is certain that if matriarchies ever existed, they do not now exist. Did they evolve perhaps long ago into patriarchies, as Bachofen supposed they did? This question, unanswered in history, once again raises interesting problems that today serve as foci for the contemporary women's movement. If anthropologists and scholars of classical jurisprudence no longer read Bachofen, the advocates of the current feminist movement do. They have rediscovered in his theory of mother right a scholarly precedent for the privileged position of females in primitive society.

Apart from the question of Bachofen's accuracy as a cultural historian, there is the question of the value and desirability of his moral defense of female rule. If I have read him correctly, Bachofen's matriarch is a far cry from today's liberated woman. Not surprisingly, she bears a closer resemblance to mid-Victorian conceptions of the perfect woman, "whose unblemished beauty, whose chastity and high-mindedness" inspired men to deeds of chivalry and bravery for her sake (Bachofen, 1967: 83). In his particular romanticization of womanhood, Bachofen was echoing his contemporary John Ruskin, who wrote that women, by virtue of their innate moral perfection, would exercise power "not within their households merely, but over all within their sphere" (quoted in Scanlon, 1973: 12), although this sphere was invariably exclusive of the male political arena. The Victorian vision of woman elevated her to the status of goddess, but it did little or nothing either to promote her independence or to offer her opportunities to fulfill herself outside the home. Bachofen was, it appears, no more enlightened than other Victorians in extolling the virtues of chaste love and monogamous and fruitful marriage.

Thus, in spite of all his so-called advanced notions about archaic matriarchies, Bachofen continued to promote through fiction and fancy a status quo that by now has become all too familiar. Motherhood, outliving mother right in its many guises, was brought firmly under the protective guardianship of father right, where it has flourished. It can only be said that Bachofen added little that was new to modern opinion concerning prehistoric social development. Not even the Amazons of classical reference, those single-minded, single-breasted warrior maidens, could account for an enduring political system in which women were the de facto rulers. The Amazons, for all their brave social and sexual innovations, were considered by Bachofen to represent an extremist group who, because they had a preference for working and living outside the acknowledged social system, were condemned to failure in their enterprise.

To give Bachofen credit, it must be realized that when *Das Mutterrecht* was first published, the city of Troy had not yet been excavated, and little, if anything, was known of the ancient Mediterranean world apart from what was recorded in the standard classical sources. Fully aware that such texts as the Homeric epics were not written as histories in the strictest sense, he nevertheless accepted these mythological accounts as a reliable reservoir of actual history. In thus mistaking myth for history, Bachofen committed what is even today a not uncommon error of judgment. But whatever Bachofen's confusions were, he did admit that the subject of his researches presented him with certain "difficulties." He saw that the absence of archaeological evidence meant that he could not support his mother right hypothesis with solid data, and he reminded the reader that "the most elementary spade work remains to be done, for the culture period to which mother right pertains has never been seriously studied. Thus we are entering virgin territory" (1967: 69).

Since the publication of *Das Mutterrecht* this "virgin territory" has been explored by a horde of archaeologists and social anthropologists. Their diligent searches into the prehistory of Mediterranean cultures as well as into the present conditions of primitive societies around the world have not uncovered a single undisputed case of matriarchy. Even the Iroquois, once a stronghold for "matriarchists," turn out to be matrilineal only,[3] although Iroquois society still comes the closest to representing Bachofen's ideal "gynocratic state," since Iroquois women played a decisive role in lineage and village politics. Yet in spite of the substantial power wielded by women, men were chosen consistently as political leaders. At most, the Iroquois today are considered a "quasi-matriarchy" (Wallace, 1971).

To have cast doubt, as I have just done, on the historical evidence for the Rule of Women is not the same thing as challenging the significance of the mythologies of matriarchy. The main issue would seem not to be

---

[3] Numerous cases have been recorded of societies in which the inheritance of lineage membership and property is transmitted legitimately only through females (matriliny). This system is understood to be quite different from that in which women have been purported to rule (matriarchy). Neither Cleopatra nor the queens of England were matriarchs in this narrowest sense, because their regimes were initiated by accidents of birth. In general, a female monarch has succeeded to the crown only when the requisite male heir was under age or when there was none.

whether women did or did not hold positions of political importance at some point in prehistory, or even whether they took up weapons and fought in battle as the Amazons allegedly did, but that there are myths claiming women did these things, which they now no longer do. This mythological status of primitive matriarchies poses as interesting a problem as any generated in the nineteenth century about the credibility or viability of matriarchy as a social system. Undoubtedly the false evolutionism and mistaken prehistory led to the obfuscation of any real contribution Bachofen might have made to the study of myth, since he did not consider that the "events" related by myths need not have a basis in historical fact.

Bachofen supports an erroneous view of myth as history throughout *Das Mutterrecht* by forceful assertion but without proof. "All the myths relating to our subject embody a memory of real events experienced by the human race. They represent not fictions but historical realities. The stories of the Amazons and Bellerophon are real and not poetic" (1967: 150–51). The relationship between myth and history is further distorted by Bachofen's use of mythical fragments rather than whole myths, and his frequent allusions to classical narrative texts assume a historicity never intended by their authors. Fragmentary references and disparate source materials combine to render weak the argument that myth is the equivalent of history.

Rather than replicating a historical reality, myth more accurately recounts a fragment of collective experience that necessarily exists outside time and space. Composed of a vast and complex series of actions, myth may become through repeated recitation a moral history of action while not in itself a detailed chronology of recorded events. Myth may be part of culture history in providing justification for a present and perhaps permanent reality by giving an invented "historical" explanation of how this reality was created.

No clearly defined rules exist for determining a "true" story as opposed to a fictional one when dealing with the oral literature of preliterate societies. Therefore, distinguishing historical from mythical events can often lead to confusion. The problem is greatly simplified when myths relate stories about talking animals and supernatural beings, since they can be more easily classed as myths, legends, or folktales than as histories. In accepting the Amazons and Bellerophon as historical personages, Bachofen did not observe this distinction. Instead he chose to build a history of human marital and legal practices upon the narrative experiences of mythical creatures, a tactic that twentieth-century anthropologists would reject as unsound. Present-day followers of Malinowski's "myth as social charter" theory (1926) prefer instead to view myth as spelling out, in symbolic terms, associations between social roles and institutions on the one hand and psychobiological aspects of the myth tellers on the other. This view regards myth as cultural history only insofar as a particular society makes use of its myths to replicate or reorder its social experience. Myths are rarely, if ever, verbatim histories, although they probably can be demonstrated to reinterpret certain crucial events in the growth and development of individual life cycles.

I propose to look at the myths of matriarchy as social charters in this essay. My strategy is first to present two constellations of myths about the Rule of Women that derive, not from the classical stock of Bachofen's numerous examples, but from recorded accounts of several South American Indian societies.[4] I then provide interpretations for these myths based on published ethnographic sources.

In South America, the most complete series of myths of the Rule of Women come from geographically and culturally distinct areas—from Tierra del Fuego at the extreme southeast tip of the continent, and from the tropical forests of the northwest Amazon and central Brazil. There have been a number of versions reported from other regions as well (see Métraux, 1943; Schaden, 1959). The myth itself has a venerable history in the annals of South American exploration. Variants of the myth were collected in the nineteenth and twentieth centuries by explorers, missionaries, and anthropologists who made their way along the rocky coasts and into the wild hinterlands of Tierra del Fuego, and by others who traversed the unknown waterways of the northwest Amazon territory.

Working in Tierra del Fuego in 1918–24, the Austrian-born anthropologist Father Martin Gusinde and his contemporary E. Lucas Bridges (born in 1874 in Tierra del Fuego), the son of an English missionary, collected several narrative accounts of the origins of the Yamana (Yaghan) and Selk'nam (Ona) male secret ceremonies. Both Gusinde and Bridges were accorded the unusual honor of admittance to these rituals as initiates, a fact that lends their reports on these extinct aboriginal Fuegian ceremonies a special authenticity.

---

[4] Although the discussion could be reinforced by many examples from other parts of the world, the South American bias reflects my own particular interest and training in central Brazil. I carried out ethnographic fieldwork in three villages of northern Kayapó (Gê) Indians in 1962 and 1963, and again briefly in 1966. For their encouragement and assistance in this research, I am grateful to the members of the Harvard–Central Brazil Research Project, directed by David Maybury-Lewis (Harvard) and Roberto Cardoso de Oliveira (University of Brasília).

Mythical Origins of Fuegian Male Ceremonies

Among the Yamana-Yaghan people the Kina is both a ceremony and an architectural structure. Called the Great Hut, or men's lodge, its membership is restricted to adult initiated males. On occasion a woman has been admitted to the Kina, but only after she satisfies the male members that she can be trusted with the Kina secrets. In 1922 Gusinde attended a ceremony in which one woman was singled out to receive this honor.

The following version of the Yamana origin myth of the Kina is shortened from Gusinde (1961: 1238–49):

> The chief goal of the group of men at their Kina is to remind the female population anew of their superiority and to make all the women definitely feel their greater power. . . . The women were the first to perform Kina. At that time the women had sole power; they gave orders to the men who were obedient, just as today the women obey the men. The men also sat in back at the stern, the women in front at the bow of the canoe. All the work in the hut was performed by the men, with the women giving orders. They took care of the children, tended the fire, and cleaned the skins. That is the way it was always to be.

The myth continues to relate how the women invented the Great Kina Hut "and everything that goes on in it," and then fooled the men into thinking that they were spirits. "They stepped out of the Great Hut . . . painted all over, with masks on their heads." The men did not recognize their wives, who, simulating the spirits, beat the earth with dried skins "so that it shook." Their yells, howls, and roars so frightened the men that they "hastened into their huts, and hid, full of fear." The women continued their dreadful performances, holding the men in "fear and submission" so that they should do all the work as the women had ordained.

One day the Sun-man, who supplied the women-spirits in the Kina hut with an abundance of game, while passing a lagoon overheard the voices of two girls. Being curious, he hid in the bushes and saw the girls "washing off painting that was characteristic of the 'spirits' when they appeared." They also were practicing imitations of the voice and manner of the daughters of the Sun, both prominent spirits in the Kina hut. Suddenly the Sun-man confronted them, insisting that the girls reveal to him "what goes on in the Kina hut." Finally they confessed to him: "It is the women themselves who paint themselves and put on masks; then they step out of the hut and show themselves to the men. There are no other spirits there. It is the women themselves who yell and howl;

in this way they frighten the men." The Sun-man then returned to the camp and exposed the fraudulent women. In revenge the men stormed the Kina hut, and a great battle ensued in which the women were either killed or transformed into animals, and "from that time on the men perform in the Kina hut; they do this in the same manner as the women before them." A new social order thus came to prevail among the Yamana. The women, once the proud owners of the Kina and its secrets, gave them up and became subordinate to the men.

Bridges (1948: 412–13) recounts the origin myth of the Selk'nam-Ona Hain, or ceremonial men's lodge, which is strikingly similar to the story of the Kina. The Kina and Hain ritual lodges appear to have had identical functions in the two cultures. They differed primarily in that the Hain was an exclusively male institution from which women were definitively barred.

In the days when all the forest was evergreen, before the parakeet painted the autumn leaves red with the colour from his breast, before the Giants wandered through the woods with their heads above the treetops; in the days when the Sun and Moon walked the earth as man and wife, and many of the great sleepy mountains were human beings: in those far-off days witchcraft was known only by the women of Ona-land. They kept their own particular Lodge, which no man dared approach. The girls, as they neared womanhood, were instructed in the magic arts, learning how to bring sickness and even death to all those who displeased them.

The men lived in abject fear and subjection. Certainly they had bows and arrows with which to supply the camp with meat, yet, they asked, what use were such weapons against witchcraft and sickness?

As this "tyranny of the women" became worse, the men decided to kill off all the women: "and there ensued a great massacre, from which not one woman escaped in human form." After this debacle the men were forced to wait to replace their wives until young girl children matured.

Meanwhile the question arose: How could men keep the upper hand now they had got it? One day, when these girl children reached maturity, they might band together and regain their old ascendancy. To forestall this, the men inaugurated a secret society of their own and banished forever the women's Lodge in which so many wicked plots had been hatched against them. No woman was allowed to come near the Hain on penalty of death. To make quite certain that this decree was respected by their women folk, the men invented a new branch of Ona demonology: a collection of strange beings—drawn partly from their own imaginations and partly from folklore and ancient legends—who would take visible shape by being impersonated by members of the Lodge and thus scare the women away from the secret councils of the Hain.

Given the geographic propinquity and cultural similarity of the Selk'-nam and Yamana peoples, the resemblance of their myths is not surprising. Both texts tell the same story: at the time of Creation the women ruled, keeping the men in subjection and fear until they discovered the source of female power and decided to wrench it from them. The myths are clearly misogynist, although, in this regard, the Selk'nam myth has the edge on the Yamana, if only because in it the women are described as loathesome witches, the harbingers of sickness and death. It is of some interest that Selk'nam and Yamana women are differentiated in the myths according to the degree of harm they are capable of inflicting on the subjugated males. In the Yamana version the women profit simply through a clever impersonation of the spirits, whereas in the Selk'nam version the women are instructed in the magical arts to be used against men.

The distinction between Yamana spiritual authority and Selk'nam power to inflict actual evil is ritual as well as mythological. Among the Yamana, for example, both sexes are processed through a lengthy initiation ritual called *ciexaus*, in which adolescents are taught the precepts of the tribe, whereas only the males among the Selk'nam go through the double *klóketen* initiation ceremony, from which women are barred. Occasionally, exceptional Yamana women are privileged members of the male Kina lodge, but this honor is never given to Selk'nam women. The origin myths of the Kina and Hain lodges emphasize a discrepant conceptualization of women by the two tribes, and the rituals reenacting the myths serve to maintain these distinctions.

In the Yamana myth the women invented the Kina hut and the ceremonial that took place in it. By their vivid performances and elaborate disguises the women managed to fool the men into thinking they were indeed fearsome spirits. In the Selk'nam myth the women were portrayed as witches who held the men in thrall by use of black magic. The Yamana women were clever spirit impersonators. They reigned by a ruse rather than by magical malpractice, as their Selk'nam neighbors did. Cleverness and reliability among the Yamana women were rewarded by an occasional invitation to join the men's lodge, but Selk'nam women could not qualify for a similar privilege. The myth of their past misbehavior is used over and over again to exclude them from the all-male initiation ritual. The utility of a myth that accounts for the origin of the men's lodge, separating men from women in action and in space, is easily demonstrated. As part of a cultural code distinguishing men from women in moral terms, the myth incorporates values that permit males a higher authority in social and political life. The myth, although it represents a time before the social order was established, fixes the invariance of that order.

The Tukanoan Myth of Jurupari

Masked dancers and men's lodges are not confined to Tierra del Fuego, but appear to be widespread throughout South America. Wherever they are discovered, however, these cultural manifestations of male authority represent restrictive measures invented to frighten and coerce women into socially acceptable behavior. Women (and children) are forbidden access to the men's lodges. They are kept ignorant of the manufacture and use of the spirit masks "on penalty of death." Among certain tribes of the northwest Amazon, and in central Brazil, sacred trumpets and flutes serve the same functions as the Fuegian masks. Knowledge of them is prohibited to women; and as in Tierra del Fuego, the origins of the sacred male paraphernalia are the subject matter of local myths. In particular, a complex ritual and myth cycle, known popularly as Jurupari (Yurupari), is common to a number of tribal peoples in the Vaupés region of the Colombian and Brazilian northwest Amazon.

The Jurupari myth and rite, in the many recorded variants, constitute part of a large inventory of cultural traits shared throughout the northern Amazon area by the Tukanoan-speaking Indians: the Tukano proper, the Desana, Uanano, and Cubeo, as well as the Witoto and Tukuna groups. Common shared elements include subsistence farming, with bitter manioc as the staple crop, the blowgun, bark cloth, the dugout canoe, pottery, large communal houses, patrilineal exogamous sibs, mythical ancestor cults, initiation rites, and sacred musical instruments. The myth of Jurupari relates the invention of these instruments, their ownership, and the ancient traditions associated with the playing of them.

One of the earliest and fullest accounts of the legend of Jurupari is that recorded by the Italian traveler Ermanno Stradelli in 1890. According to his narrative (Stradelli, 1964), Jurupari was considered the culture hero and lawmaker of the tribes of the upper Rio Negro. Born of a virgin girl-child who had become impregnated by the sap of a forbidden fruit, Jurupari almost at birth became the headman in a tribe of females whose men had died in an epidemic. It was Jurupari who subsequently taught his people that women should not be permitted to meddle in the affairs of men, or take part in the secret male rites when the sacred musical instruments were played. The woman who violates the prohibition stands condemned to death, and "any man who shows the instruments or reveals the secret laws to a woman" is obliged to kill himself, or be killed by his fellowmen.

The myth cycle is devoted to recounting numerous episodes in which women discover the men's hiding place for the sacred trumpets and observe the secret male ceremony, which they then make known to other women. The final episode of the myth ends on a singular note of despair. Jurupari, sent on a quest on behalf of the Sun (his father) for the perfect woman, appears to be without success:

"And what is the perfection that the Sun desires?"

"She must be patient, know how to keep a secret and not be curious," answers Jurupari (Stradelli, 1964: 66), who concludes: "No woman today exists on earth who combines these qualities. If a woman is patient, she does not keep secrets; if she keeps secrets, she is not patient; and all of them are curious, wishing to know everything and to experience everything."

Incomplete and less poetic versions of the Jurupari myth include Goldman's (1963: 193) relation of the origin of the Cubeo (Tukanoan, Colombia) sacred trumpets, which were part of an ancestral cult; and Murphy's (1958: 89–91) account of the Mundurucú (Tupian, central Brazil) myth, "The Invention of the Sacred Trumpets." Both the Cubeo and Mundurucú variants begin with ownership of the musical instruments in the hands of the women, who kept them hidden in the forests where they convened secretly to play them. In the Mundurucú myth, the women devoted so much time to playing the flutes that they eventually abandoned their husbands and their household duties. "The women, as possessors of the trumpets, had thereby gained ascendancy over the men. The men had to carry firewood and fetch water, and they also had to make [manioc bread]. . . . But the men still hunted and this angered them for it was necessary to feed meat to the trumpets. . . . So one of the men suggested that they take the trumpets from the women" (Murphy, 1958: 90). This they eventually did, forcing the women to return to the dwelling houses and to remain subservient to the men. Among the Cubeo, the culture hero Kúwai "took the trumpets from the women and gave them to the men, warning them never to allow the women to get them back" (Goldman, 1963: 193).

Nimuendajú (1952: 77–78), reporting on the Tukuna, who occupy the banks of the Solimões River on the Brazilian side of the Amazon basin, mentioned bark and wooden trumpets brought out under cover of darkness in the celebrations of girls' puberty ceremonies. The musical instruments were used to frighten women and children, who were forbidden to view them. A Tukuna text (Nimuendajú, 1952: 78) tells how a girl broke the rules and spied upon the flutes. In revenge she was killed and quartered. Her flesh was afterward smoked and made into mush for a village feast, to which both her mother and sister were summoned.

Another variant of the myth is that given by Reichel-Dolmatoff (1971:

169–70). The first Juruparí (Yuruparí) trumpet was manufactured by the praying mantis, who used the instrument to denounce the incestuous crime of the Sun Father, who had violated his prepubescent daughter. The myth continues:

Some time after the introduction of the flutes and the ceremonial playing of them ... some women followed the men when they went to the landing to hide the instruments. When the men had gone, the women took out the flutes to look at them; they took them into their hands and touched them with their fingers. But when they touched their own bodies with the hands that had been touching the flutes, suddenly hair grew on their pubis and under their armpits, places that previously had no hair. When the men returned to the landing, the women seduced them, and although they belonged to the same phratry, they cohabited with them. Only after supernatural punishments, which the myth does not describe, were the men able to establish order again. Since then the rules that are observed at present have been enforced.

It seems clear, even from the fragmentary forms given here, that the Juruparí myths and those of the Fuegian Hain and Kina lodges share a common set of themes that are their hallmark. First, the secret objects belonging to men (masks, trumpets, ritual lodges, songs, and the like) originally were invented by women and owned by them; or, if they originated with the men, their secrets were discovered by women, who contaminated their sacredness by viewing or touching them. Among the Desana, pollution resulted in the growth of body hair and in an incestuous union initiated by women who seduced the men of their own phratry. Punishment followed the forbidden sexual act. Among the Tukuna, and in Stradelli's version of Juruparí, the women were put to death for a lesser crime than that of incest. Spying on the sacred instruments was a death warrant for all violators of the prohibition. An obvious relationship is established in these myths between viewing, touching, and forbidden sex, although the association is a symbolic one and should perhaps be seen as part of a complex set of cultural laws establishing the proper set of behaviors expected between the sexes.

A second theme running through these myths is that a position of authority adheres to the possessors of tribal secrets, and that those who sit in authority, whether females or males, may also enjoy a life of relative leisure. The trumpets and lodges are the badges of this authority, permitting one sex to dominate the other. However begun, the myths invariably conclude with the men in power. Either the men have taken from the women the symbols of authority and have installed themselves as the rightful owners of the ceremony and its paraphernalia, or they invoke violent sanctions against the women who have dared to challenge male authority. In no versions do women win the battle for power.

Instead, they remain forever the subjects of male terrorism, hidden in their huts, fearing to look out on masked spirits and trumpeting ancestors. It is not clear from the published reports whether the women actually believe the tales told them by men, although the penalties brought to bear on women and children for infractions of the ceremonial injunctions seem to be real enough.[5]

The collected versions, not all of which have been cited here (see Lévi-Strauss, 1973: 271ff), of the South American myths of the Rule of Women establish guidelines for sexual behavior, at least in the minds of listeners. In Stradelli's account the desirable characteristics of the ideal woman are enumerated, whereas in the Tukuna fragment the punishment of the unhappy girl who spied on the trumpets is a cruel reminder of the rules of good conduct for women. In yet another version of the myth, a Tukano informant (Fulop, 1956: 341–66) insists that its true title is "Sexual Relations," a crucial piece of evidence that the anthropologist has relegated to a footnote. Reichel-Dolmatoff's Desana informant (1971: 171) tried to convey the same bit of information when he reported that "Yuruparí is not a person; it is a state—it is a warning not to commit incest and to marry only women from another group." Clearly, he meant to distinguish Juruparí, the culture hero, from the precepts of Juruparí, given as the founding principles of the social and sexual order and transmitted from generation to generation by recounting the myth and replaying the ceremony. The two aspects of Juruparí appear to be inseparable. Juruparí, depicted as the offspring of a virgin birth or as the son of the Sun, is made the vehicle through which the cosmic order becomes established. His laws are the laws of a tribal system that upholds a sacred convention wherein a separate set of values is maintained for men and for women. The laws stipulate that women are excluded from participation in important social and religious events because all females fall short of perfection as defined by the Sun Father and his earthly protagonist, Juruparí. Sexual differences, defined by and legislated in myth, are demonstrated in ceremony. To preserve these sexual distinctions in social life, supernatural sanctions are invoked. It appears to make little difference whether these penalties take the form of male spirits that make

---

[5] Women are punished throughout the Amazon area by gang rape for such misdemeanors as viewing sacred male paraphernalia. During my stay among the Gorotire Kayapó in 1962, a small girl attempted to peek under the palm frond costume of one of the ceremonial masked dancers. The incident took place at night, so the identity of the girl was never discovered, but a gun was fired to warn the village of the consequences of an infraction of the rules pertaining to sacred masks. The following morning male informants said that if they had been able to determine which little girl had violated the prohibition they surely would have killed her.

themselves known to women and children through eerie reverberations on sacred instruments or through the frightening masks worn by men, for the principle itself remains the same, in the northwest Amazon as in the southernmost reaches of Tierra del Fuego: men rule through the terror of a well-kept secret.

Myth and Social Roles

Each myth begins with a prior and chaotic era before the present social order was established, when women were supposed to have ruled over the land. It was said that the women originally created and owned the sacred lodges, trumpets, and masks. They sat in the seat of power, ruling without justice or mercy. Then the situation is suddenly reversed. In Tierra del Fuego the men discover by accident the real source of women's secret power. They plot to recover what they deem to be rightly theirs, and by fighting they succeed in banishing women from the men's lodges forever. In the northwest Amazon, Juruparí, the legendary culture hero of the Tukanoans, establishes sacred legislation in a lawless land of females. His laws proclaim that women are forbidden by threat of death to have knowledge of secret male activities. Everywhere women find themselves restricted in their actions and subordinated to rules set by men. This pattern of male dominance and female subordination is a consistent theme surfacing over and over again in South American myth and ceremony. The repetition of theme and circumstance cannot be entirely fortuitous, nor can it be claimed that they result from the vagaries of history, geography, or climate, for on these counts no two culture areas in South America are further apart. Principles other than historical connection or geographic contiguity therefore must account for the overwhelming likeness of myth and rite. But what principles are these, and can one know for certain that the same principles operate in the southernmost reaches of Tierra del Fuego as in the northwest Amazon territory?

Wherever the myth of the Rule of Women is discovered, there also exists a set of cultural rules and procedures for determining sexual dimorphism in social and cultural tasks. This opposition, separation, and general distinctiveness of male and female realms are hardly exclusive to the mythic order, for it is seen to pervade all aspects of human life. Every society to some extent divides its tasks according to sex. Obvious biological differences provide ready-made distinctions, and each society may interpret them differently according to principles that cannot be taken for granted but, rather, must be satisfactorily demonstrated in each particular instance. In some societies men make the pots and weave the baskets; in others women do. Who does them is not usually left to chance. The sexual division of labor is established by rules stipulated within each social group. Such rules are sex-related (and age-related), although not necessarily determined by either sex or age. Instead, social roles and tasks become associated with sex and age by an educational process of some kind, whether formal or informal. In preliterate societies the recitation of myth and the performance of ritual serve as educational processes.

In particular, initiations are recognizable educational institutes for those undergoing them. The transmission of cultural values, to boys in the form of esoteric lore, to girls in terms of lifelong prohibitions and restrictions on their behavior, constitutes the major focus of adolescent initiations in tropical South America. Boys are taught proper adult behavior, and sometimes certain male skills and esoteric knowledge. Young adolescent males learn as part of the initiation process that men, not women, rule in their society, although this fact may well contradict other expectations prevalent in childhood domestic experience. As the male offspring of female-supervised households, young boys need to be reeducated with regard to their future social and political roles, and initiation serves this function. The most acute severance of the mother-child bond for both members of the dyad is experienced at the outset of the initiation, when the young initiates are physically removed from their natal households. At the conclusion of the initiation period the boys are introduced ceremonially to the society of adult men, which is a public demonstration of their accession to adult status.

This regrouping of adolescent boys with adult males is prefigured in some societies in myths foretelling the demise of female power and the concomitant rise of male privilege. The myth of the Rule of Women in its many variants may be regarded as a replay of these crucial transitional stages in the life cycle of an individual male. In both sets of South American myths, for example, final accession to the adult male role is gained by capturing the symbols of power (masks and sacred trumpets) from the women. In this battle of the sexes women are consistently portrayed as the perennial losers of their male children to the men's lodges. Male rights and privileges are documented and justified in myth and in ritual. By contrast, female influence and authority are totally absent from these symbolic expressions.

Male initiation ceremonies dramatize the breaking away of adolescent boys from female-dominated households. Among the uxorilocal Kayapó of the Gê language family of central Brazil, to cite the example I know best, boys between the ages of twelve and sixteen are led in ritual procession from their maternal households and installed in the men's house after a protracted and elaborate ceremony that takes several months to complete. During the initiation period Kayapó boys are sent into the forest each day under the guardianship of ceremonial companions to learn forest lore and the techniques of stalking game. After the completion of their initiation ceremony, the young men reside in the men's house until they marry and establish residence for themselves in their wives' houses. At the men's house they are taught male occupations: hunting, basketry, and the manufacture of weapons and ornaments, as well as such male secrets as the identity of the ceremonial masked dancers.

The Kayapó share with their neighbors the Mundurucú a male ideology frequently expressed in the ritual humiliation of women. As far as I can determine, no myth of the Rule of Women has been recorded for the Kayapó, but such aggressive male activities as gang rape and enforced ritual intercourse for young girls, which takes place in the men's house, represent the kinds of punishments women are continually threatened with in the mythologies of the northwest Amazon. The Kayapó, it could be said, "act out" their fantasies, and thus have little use for the myth, except for the fact that the punitive element in Kayapó male sexual activity appears to be amply demonstrated in other Kayapó myths concerning problems in male-female relationships. It is only for our purposes that the crucial myth is lacking. Any number of other Kayapó myths might be substituted to make the same point.

Kayapó girls' initiation rites are not as elaborate as those held for boys. In fact, the girls' ceremony I witnessed took no more than fifteen minutes to perform, unlike the ceremony for boys, which lasted the better part of three months. Village participation is not a requirement for the girls' initiation as it is for the boys', and indeed, the abbreviated ritual performed for girls does not stress upheaval of the old domestic order or emergence of a new adult regime. Instead, the brief ceremony celebrates a woman's physical maturation, her fertility and future child-bearing role.

In the Tukuna initiation ceremony, as described by Nimuendajú (1952), male symbols of power are used to frighten the young girl. Ancestral trumpets are played for her edification, but she is not instructed in their secret lore. The Tukuna ceremony, more elaborate than that of the Kayapó, is directly related to the functions of the girl's pubescent body. Female ceremonies the world over are closely associated with body rituals. They emphasize in dramatic form the biological specialization of women.

Similar concerns with female reproductive distinctions are nowhere in evidence in the myths chosen for consideration here. Perhaps it is not immediately obvious to the tribal peoples of South America that the only or even rightful place of women is at the hearth because of her child-bearing capacity. Certainly the mythical message used to bind women to their household duties in aboriginal South America stresses moral laxity and an abuse of power rather than any physical weakness or disability on the part of women. If the dictates of biology were carefully adhered to, women might well find themselves still in the seat of power, for it is obvious that the biological functions of females are necessary for the continuity of any human group. No male occupation, however exalted, can compensate for the unique ability of the female to conceive, bear, and nurse the young of the species. This important contribution of women to group survival is celebrated in female puberty ritual but overlooked in myth. Why should this be so?

It appears from this cursory study of a handful of South American myths that women frequently are subjected to harsh outside controls because of their putative immorality—or at least this is my reading of male-informed mythologies. And so it seems from myth that less tangible forces than biology were brought to bear on the subversion of the female sex role. When, for example, woman was told that she behaved like a child and, like other children, was kept uninitiated (in the full masculine sense), or when she was compared to an animal, and on this ground became the unwilling victim of a male ideology, she had forfeited her right to rule. The case against her was made out to be a moral one, divorced from the biology that might have given her sex priority under other circumstances.

Whether or not women actually behaved in the manner of the charges recorded in myth is not an issue in understanding the insistent message of the myth. What is at issue is the ideological thrust of the argument made in the myth of the Rule of Women, and the justification it offers for male dominance through the evocation of a vision of a catastrophic alternative—a society dominated by women. The myth, in its reiteration that women did not know how to handle power when in possession of it, reaffirms dogmatically the inferiority of their present position.

Whatever the justification for it, the sacred male order laid down in myth and reenacted in ritual continues unchallenged in many societies throughout the world. One may surmise from this state of affairs that the Rule of Men proceeds unchanged because women, its potential challengers, have been trapped for so long in a closed system that they are unable to perceive how otherwise they might break down the successful methods used to inculcate in them an ideology of moral failure. Such feelings, I have suggested, at least for South American societies, are reinforced by the strong arm of a male religion.

Myth and rituals have been misinterpreted as persistent reminders that women once had, and then lost, the seat of power. This loss accrued to them through inappropriate conduct. In Tierra del Fuego the women tricked the men into performing both male and female chores; and in the northwest Amazon they committed the crime of incest. The myths constantly reiterate that women did not know how to handle power when they had it. The loss is thereby justified so long as women choose to accept the myth. The Rule of Women, instead of heralding a promising future, harks back to a past darkened by repeated failures. If, in fact, women are ever going to rule, they must rid themselves of the myth that states they have been proved unworthy of leadership roles.

The final version of woman that emerges from these myths is that she represents chaos and misrule through trickery and unbridled sexuality. This is the inverse of Bachofen's view of pre-Hellenic womanhood, which he symbolized as a mystical, pure, and uncorrupted Mother Goddess. The contrast between mid-Victorian notions of the ideal woman (they are not those of ancient Greece, as Bachofen supposed) and the primitive view, which places woman on the social and cultural level of children, is not as great as it appears. The elevation of woman to deity on the one hand, and the downgrading of her to child or chattel on the other, produce the same result. Such visions will not bring her any closer to attaining male socioeconomic and political status, for as long as she is content to remain either goddess or child, she cannot be expected to shoulder her share of community burdens as the coequal of man. The myth of matriarchy is but the tool used to keep woman bound to her place. To free her, we need to destroy the myth.

The Mastery of Work and the Mystery of Sex
in a Guatemalan Village

Comparative studies of social structure demonstrate that peasant societies display a prevailing tendency toward economic and social segregation of the sexes, accompanied by male dominance (Wolf, 1966; Michaelson and Goldschmidt, 1971). However, the nature of the distinctive female subculture, which is a corollary of such segregation, has received relatively little attention. Nor is this surprising in view of the characteristic reserve of peasant women in the presence of strangers, especially men, and the fact that women's domestic activities do not lend themselves readily to formal analysis (Rosaldo, this volume).

The fact of a standard status gap between the sexes leaves unanswered a number of questions. How do women construe their position vis-à-vis men? Do they see themselves as more subordinate to men in one sphere and less in another? What are women's sources of satisfaction and self-esteem? Their fears and defenses? What are their ideas of the body and its boundaries? What, in short, are their self-concepts?

Self-concepts, as Goffman (1956), among others, has shown, are developed and enacted in a social matrix and reflect cultural definitions of social roles and situations. Ideas about the body are an important component of self-concept and can provide important clues to a fuller understanding not only of the individual but of the social order as well. In anthropology, Bateson and Mead provided an innovative model for viewing the body as a metaphor for culture in Bali (1942), and more recently Douglas makes the consonance between the human body and the social group the pivot of her symbolic analysis (1966, 1970). Colby includes cultural beliefs about the body in characterizing the major psychological orientations of Mesoamerican Indians (1967).

Since women's roles are intimately linked to biological processes and experiences (Ortner, this volume), ideas about the body figure prominently in the self-concepts of women. They figure in women's ideas of their limitations and their powers, and provide the analyst with a framework for understanding how women conceptualize their situation in society. In this essay, body concepts relating to women's work and to sex and reproduction are used to illuminate how the women of San Pedro la Laguna see themselves and their world.

San Pedro is one of a dozen settlements on the shores of Lake Atitlán in the southwestern highlands of Guatemala. Virtually all of its inhabitants are Indians, speaking Zutuhil, a variant of the Maya-Quiché family of languages. Many of the men and a few of the women also speak Spanish. A population of approximately 2,000 people occupied 400 households in 1941 when my husband and I lived in San Pedro for twelve months. At the time we left in January 1942, we had no plans to return. As it happened, however, we did return for periods of several months at a time in 1956, and again on four occasions during the decade of the 1960's to observe changes (Paul and Paul, 1963; Paul, 1968).

The following account reflects the situation in San Pedro as we first encountered it. This was before there was a road to the outside world, before water was piped in, and before diesel-powered mills were available for grinding corn. These innovations have affected some daily routines, but the changes in women's lives have not been fundamental. Most women continue to marry men of their own town, joining the household of the husband's family at first; and they continue performing the tasks traditionally assigned to women. Despite the presence of corn mills, women still regrind the corn by hand before making tortillas. Use of the present tense in the following exposition is to be understood as referring to the "ethnographic present" as of 1941.

The Mastery of Work

As in other Mesoamerican communities, the sense of village identity is strong (Tax, 1937), but women have an identity as *Pedranas* (women of San Pedro) apart from that of the men. An element of their self-concept is the reputation Pedranas enjoy among *ladinos* (non-Indians) for their beauty. This, combined with the wealth of San Pedro relative to other Lake Atitlán communities, gives Pedranas a sense of themselves as "aristocrats" compared with the women of neighboring towns. Pedranas make it a point of pride that they never go to the fields to help their husbands or fetch firewood like women of neighboring San Juan la Laguna, whom they deprecate as "manly-women." They never carry burdens long distances to markets like the women of Chichicastenango. They see themselves as industrious weavers who do not "sit and gossip all day in the market like the shameless women of Santiago Atitlán." Elsewhere Indian women on the roads, in the markets, or at domestic tasks sling their infants on their backs. Never away from home for long, Pedranas always carry their babies on the arm like ladino women.

Like aristocratic women elsewhere, Pedranas are more segregated and their life space is more circumscribed than that of many of their neighbors. Yet they work as hard as other Indian women of the Maya highlands. In the households of the richer families (those owning more land), the women often work harder because there are hired field hands to feed in addition to the members of the family.

Women hold no civic offices in San Pedro and they play only a minor role in the religious organization of *cofradías* (lay brotherhoods). Nor are they concerned with the growing of corn, the staff of life in Mesoamerica. The courthouse in the town's center, the cofradía chapels with their altars and images of Catholic saints, the cornfields on the hillsides beyond the town, these constitute man's domain. A woman ventures into the courthouse only when she is a plaintiff in a suit or when she is summoned as defendant or witness. Women feel less comfortable than men in the public streets. On an errand to buy meat or matches, or to visit a sick relative, or crossing the town square to light a candle in church, a woman moves hurriedly, almost furtively, her face half hidden in the shawl she always wears in public. A woman may exchange polite greetings with a man who is not a close relative, but she runs the risk of arousing suspicion and even provoking a domestic quarrel. By day a woman out on the street may risk her reputation, but a woman seen walking the streets at night is likely to be taken for a witch, bent on snatching the soul of a sick person, or threatening the masculinity of an unwary male.

Women's domain. If Pedrano women feel ill at ease in public and if they appear as impassive spectators in a crowd watching a religious procession or a group of masked dancers during a fiesta, they are altogether self-confident and at ease in their own familiar precincts. These are the house and patio, the pathways leading to the lake below the town, and the stretch of lakeshore where women congregate to wash clothes, bathe, and fetch water. In their own domain women talk and joke with great animation, expressing mirth, surprise, incredulity, and indignation, and laugh easily at any slip of the tongue or double entendre. In their own families by day, when men are absent in the fields, mature women can be commanding and authoritative with younger children and younger women. As Slater reminds us, "The more the male imprisons the female in the home and takes himself elsewhere, the more powerful is the female within the home" (1968: 8). That the Pedrano male fears the retaliation of the female is evidenced by such rules of avoidance as those surrounding men's and women's implements.

Men and women have tools appropriate to their sex and their tasks, and the lines must not be crossed. Every man has his hoe and machete for working the fields and cutting firewood and his tumpline for carrying burdens on his back. If a woman steps over her husband's hoe, the implement will break or her husband's masculinity will be weakened, or her unborn male child will be changed to female. Every woman has her water jar, her backstrap stick loom, and her grinding stones; every housewife has her hearth. A man must not touch the grinding stone or the hearth stones lest he lose his strength and become *manso* (impotent).

Consisting of three large stones set in a corner of the packed-earth floor of the one-room house, the hearth supports the cooking pots and the griddle on which tortillas are toasted. The hearth and its fire are the heart and shrine of woman's domain and must be treated with special care. It is a sin to discard the hearthstones once they have been put in place. One of the three stones is known as the grandmother stone, and it is a sin even to move this sacred stone. The umbilical cord of a baby girl should be placed under the grandmother stone so that the girl will stay at home when she is grown. A boy's umbilical cord is hung in a granary so that he will work well in the fields.

Although it is a woman's task to fetch water for household use, there are occasions when young men also must carry water from the lake—as part of their duties during a year of service in one of the cofradías, for instance—but they always use distinctively different jars, carrying them on their backs with a tumpline rather than on their heads. To avoid ridicule, men who must fetch water try to do so in the early hours of the dawn or after nightfall.

Women's tasks and the work ethic. The typing of sex roles starts almost immediately after a child is born. On the eighth day following a birth, the midwife bathes the infant with a protective infusion of rue. After the bath she places the sticks of a loom over the head of the infant girl so that she will be a good worker and learn the tasks appropriate to her sex. The infant girl's ears are then pierced for earrings and she is dressed like a miniature woman in tiny blouse and skirt.

In their economic roles, men and women are complementary partners; each performs essential tasks and is considered indispensable to the other. Women rise before their husbands at three or four in the morning and spend several hours on their knees grinding and regrinding the soaked corn for tortillas. They make several trips daily up and down steep paths to the lake to wash clothes on the rocks and to replenish the household water supply. They spend long hours weaving on backstrap looms. Between times they nurse babies and feed the chickens, turkeys, and pigs.

Despite the long hours and the physical difficulty of their work, women generally do not regard themselves as drudges, or their tasks as menial ones. For the most part, they face the endless round of daily duties with an air of purposeful good spirits. It is not uncommon to hear women humming or singing as they grind or weave. The gratifications of work appear to arise from three main sources: the ethical value of work, the sense of competence, and the symbolic value of women's products.

Labor, in fact, is the badge by which the Indian has been set off from the ladino since the Spaniards came to Guatemala in 1524 under the leadership of Pedro de Alvarado. Both Indians and ladinos believe that Indians have a greater innate capacity for working hard and tolerating pain than do ladinos. Work is a necessity but it is also a moral imperative in the Pedrano value system. Myriad beliefs support the view that work is virtuous and sloth sinful. A woman should never succumb to fatigue or bodily distress except under the most extreme conditions. To lie down in the middle of the day because one is tired or has a menstrual cramp is to invite a truly serious illness. A woman who fails to clean her grinding stone or tie her loom promptly will be punished with a difficult delivery and a lazy child.

Although Pedranos believe that one's destiny is ultimately predetermined by the divinities, they also believe, as did the ancient Maya, that the body can be shaped by correct manipulation and instruction. Thus training for endurance and hard work begins early. Soon after the child is born, mothers start to mold the child's body and make it strong for the tasks it will perform. A mother wraps the body of a newborn infant tightly, with arms at the sides and legs stretched out, so the child will grow up with straight, strong limbs. Parents tie their babies into miniature homemade chairs "to make their backs strong" and provide special pens to hasten learning when a child begins to walk.

The sense of competence.[1] Female tasks in San Pedro not only are arduous but require a high degree of motor skills ranging from the refined wrist and finger movement required for weaving and making tortillas to the control and balance of the whole body. Analyses that emphasize women's roles and statuses vis-à-vis the dominant males in peasant cultures tend to overlook women's skills, as well as the psycho-

[1] People everywhere may, from early childhood, develop a sense of competence associated with their productive tasks, but it seems that cultural elaboration upon women's productive skills is particularly likely in those peasant societies where women are processors rather than primary producers of foodstuffs (Michelle Rosaldo, personal communication). In such situations, a woman's competence as a processor has the direct consequence of increasing the value of raw products acquired by men. Therefore, it is not surprising that we find in peasant societies, in particular, a strong appreciation of women's skill in cooking, sewing, weaving, and the like.

logical and cultural meanings of their work. The attentive observer cannot fail to admire the ease and dexterity with which the Pedrano woman executes every task. She glides gracefully up and down the paths to the lake balancing a heavy pottery water jar on her head. She pats and twirls corn dough into perfect tortillas with the motions of a skilled craftswoman. And she weaves handsome textiles with fingers deftly shuttling the woof back and forth across the warp.

For most girls, learning these skills is a gradual process, embedded in a context of close personal relations with their mothers and sisters (Chodorow, this volume). Little girls imitate their mothers, modeling their play on the familiar tasks of everyday life. A three-year-old girl bends intently over her own body, her big toe used to anchor a make-believe loom fashioned from a corn leaf by her seven-year-old sister. Two little girls rub fiercely at bits of rag stretched over stones in the patio, pretending to wash clothes. In posture and seriousness they are already miniatures of their mothers.

Thus training for adult skills begins as play, when there is strong motivation for exploration, activity, and manipulation of the environment and pleasure in feelings of mastery and a sense of industry (White, 1959). The young girl is motivated by the normal drive to acquire increasing control over the environment and by the satisfaction such growing ability confers. The culture strongly reinforces the sense of mastery and industry in both males and females while discouraging exploratory impulses in the females. One woman reports that when her sister was only seven she could already do the grinding for tortillas and would burst into tears if her mother did not give her corn to grind in the morning. Work can also become addictive. Older women continue to weave long after it is necessary despite the pains of arthritis and rheumatism, because, in the words of one woman, "I cannot sit around doing nothing and I enjoy weaving."

The feelings of competence and efficacy concomitant with the development of a woman's skills are reenforced by cultural norms that recognize the quality of women's products. Thus, Pedranos take great pride in the tortillas their women make, comparing them favorably with the grosser tortillas made by women in other towns. When a Pedrana produces tortillas that are heavier and more misshapen than the local high standards demand, they are derisively compared with those made in the highland town of Nahuala, from which Pedranos draw many of their hired field hands. And of the few inept Pedranas whose tortillas "always come out burned with a pocket full of smoke, like a blister," they say, "this is because they laugh at their own farts." A tortilla must be not only filling to the stomach but pleasing to the eye; it must demonstrate the deftness of its maker's touch.

The drive to acquire competence is strong in the young, but in adults it can give way to monotony once the mastery of skills is achieved. But in the case of the Pedrana, several factors operate to overcome monotony: the rhythm of daily work, the social context of women's work, and the periodicity of fiestas. A woman's daily tasks are more varied than a man's, and trips to the lake offer a welcome change of scenery and a postural change from hours spent on the knees, weaving or grinding corn with heavy, stone rolling pins. Pedrano girls and women take great pains washing and dressing their glossy black hair. In a culture that denies women most other forms of narcissistic or erotic enjoyment, bathing and hair grooming are among the few permitted kinesthetic pleasures.

But the attractions of the lakeshore must not detain females from their less alluring tasks. To this end, the culture provides strong sanctions in the form of supernatural punishment. The most common consequence of dallying too long at the lake are reported cases of disappearing pregnancies or fetal deaths. Older women tell of a huge female deity living at the bottom of the lake who comes to the surface when no one is present. "One day when old Manuela stayed at the lake all day washing her clothes," they recount, "this lady of the lake came out of the water and scolded her, saying 'All day I have waited for you to leave so that I can come out and wash my clothes; why don't you go home and take care of the house and do your work?' Suddenly Manuela felt her mouth swell up and a minute later all her teeth began to fall out."

At the lake women meet neighbors with whom they can exchange fresh gossip and air complaints against an overdemanding mother-in-law or competitive sisters-in-law. And at home women rarely want for company since they are surrounded by children and other housewives within earshot across the patio. There is no pattern of casual or social visiting, but births and deaths among relatives and neighbors offer frequent opportunities for sociability. To prepare large quantities of ceremonial food on occasions of birth or death and especially during fiestas, groups of young women and girls stay up all night grinding corn while older women cook special foods. The work is demanding, but the banter and excitement of such occasions are recalled and rehearsed long after the aching muscles are forgotten.

Fiestas occur no less than once a month. Fiesta time feeds all the senses. The streets are full of people in bright new clothing following the procession of the saints, watching masked dancers, sampling sweet snacks offered by vendors. There is color; music of the marimba, drum, and reed flute; exploding rockets; the smell of incense and candles; and other delights. Most women participate only as spectators, but just being part of the throng is sheer joy.

The symbolic value of women's products. Women derive satisfaction not only from a realization that work is virtuous and from a feeling of mastering their physical environment, but also from the knowledge that the products of their labor are socially valued. Men's work in the corn fields has symbolic as well as material significance. This is well recognized in the literature. Less recognized, however, is the fact that women's products too have symbolic as well as utilitarian significance.

Excellence of weaving is admired by men, as well as by the women, who weave and embroider most of the family's clothing, and there is great demand in other Indian towns for the colorful shirts woven by Pedranas. The introduction of a greater variety of colored yarns into Guatemala and the increase in tourism have stimulated even greater variations in color and pattern. There is considerable scope for innovation and individual expression within a stylistic pattern, affording the individual weaver aesthetic and creative gratifications; in addition, the weaving is a source of cash income.

Clothing has high symbolic value among all the Indians of the highlands, serving as a link to tradition, a source of social approval, and a badge of village identity. The Indians of each village can be recognized by their distinctive costume. New clothing is essential for the major fiestas, and the poorest families will sell their labor for cash in order to buy yarn; if necessary they will even go to the coastal plantations to work for the cash. Just as the incense, music, dancing, and candles are thought to be offerings to please the ancestors and Christian saints, so too Pedranos don new clothing to please their spiritual patrons while they satisfy their own need for color in an otherwise routine existence.

In contrast to the production of foodstuffs by men, the conversion of these products to food generally receives insufficient attention in the literature. Of all male and female activities, those surrounding corn consume the most time and assume the greatest importance. Once the corn is brought home in net bags on the backs of men and boys, it comes under the management of the women, and the processing—shelling, soaking, grinding, and cooking—is no less critical than the planting, weeding, and harvesting.

In her cooking as in her weaving, the Pedrano woman is dealing with a prized commodity. More than just the dietary mainstay, corn commands special respect, unlike cash crops such as chickpeas and coffee. It is enriched by manifold meanings dating from the time the ancient civilization of the Maya grew to greatness on the base of corn, with its symbolic proliferation in art, myth, and religion. Corn remains a central focus of the culture, with all of its sacred freighting of the past. To defile corn by intercourse in the field, even on the part of husband and wife, for example, is to invite death, which can be averted only by eating some of the offended earth.

Fantasied fears of being eaten by strangers and by fierce animals suggest an unconscious association between eating and aggression, and oral impulses are constrained by strong cultural curbs (Paul, 1950). As distinguished from snacks such as fruit, candy, and soft drinks, food in general and corn in particular are regarded with reverence. Moderation and privacy surround the satisfaction of hunger. All meals are marked by formal etiquette and an atmosphere of restraint. For the Pedranos food in its cooked form symbolizes the social nature of humans, differentiating them from animals. Stories are told that long ago people were changed into animals when they ate raw corn. By converting corn into cooked foods, women perform a vital humanizing function in San Pedro as elsewhere (Ortner, this volume).

For men, as for women, the arduousness of toil is ameliorated by the moral value of hard work, the satisfaction of skillful performance, and the importance of their products. But the specific nature of their respective tasks sets women's work apart from men's in several respects. On a daily basis women's work is more varied and less lonely. Moreover, the rewards of a project completed are more certain and more immediate. Success in the cornfield is subject to many hazards and is long postponed, in contrast to the greater control women can exert over the outcome of their work and the daily evidence of completed tasks.

The Mystery of Sex

The Pedrano woman perceives her body in two lights. As a productive instrument it is under her control, but as a reproductive vehicle it is controlled by other forces. Whereas husband and wife are united by a bond of corn in a cooperative economic relationship, their asymmetrical sexual relationship generates an atmosphere of distrust in which the male is seen as an aggressor planting semen in the body of a passive victim. The influences of the ancient Maya and the Spanish friars have combined to produce an attitude that makes each sex think that the other is dangerous and that intercourse is sinful (Colby, 1967: 423; Mendelson, 1967: 406–8).

A double standard prevails, however. Sexual relations are legitimately enjoyed only by men, and men and women both agree that men are potential aggressors and women out of customary bounds are fair game. Women who seem to enjoy sex are suspected of infidelity or of being witches, and it is considered immoral for a wife to assume any posture in sexual embrace other than the supine and passive position. Although adultery is theoretically sinful for both sexes, men are expected to take advantage of an available opportunity. It is the woman who is held responsible for philandering, especially if she strays too far beyond her customary precincts. Thus one widow who manages her own fields, a rare activity in San Pedro, always borrows a neighbor's child to accompany her so that, in the words of an informant, "she will not be raped or be called a whore by other women."

Boys learn early about sexual exploits and the art of being manly from older youths in informal neighborhood groups, which they join at about age twelve and in which they remain until after they marry. Sexual adventures provide proof of manliness as well as an element of attractive risk and excitement. Sex is a game that some men play with other men's wives if they can seduce them, with the rare woman willing to have intercourse for money, and perhaps rarer still, with a woman found unaccompanied in the fields.

In the Pedrano view, men are naturally more hedonistic than women. Two opposing temperamental types express the cultural norms: men are appropriately *k'an* (aggressive, assertive, irascible), while women are ideally *nakanik* (mild, docile, submissive). Pedranos, like other Maya Indians, value moderation and fear excesses of emotion, which they believe can lead to illness or misfortune, but persons who represent extremes of the type appropriate to their gender are not unduly censured. A woman who is extremely nakanik may only arouse the sympathy of other women if her reticence prevents her from leaving the house at all. A man who is very k'an may be disliked and feared but he is usually accorded respect, particularly if he has wealth or supernatural power. But display of temperament or behavior inappropriate to one's sex is cause for ridicule or divorce. Thus meek men who let themselves be managed by their wives are derided and referred to as nakanik.

The concept of blood strength is fundamental to the concept of temperament. Men, in general, are said to have stronger blood than women. Women who are k'an are believed to have strong blood, probably as the result of an intrauterine sex change from male to female due to an infraction of some taboo by their mothers. Women who are barren are thought to have stronger blood than their husbands. Of one young woman of twenty, barren despite three marriages, it is said, "She boasts of being able to take on twenty men in one night. She is stronger than any man. They say only a burro could beget a child with her." Of another childless woman, neighbors say, "She has no children because she has intercourse all night with her husband," the implication being that she enjoys it. Both of these anomalous women are reputed to be witches.

From early childhood girls are trained to be modest. Although boy toddlers may be permitted to appear without pants in the patio or on the street, little girls by the age of two or three learn to feel shame and to keep pulling their skirts demurely over their knees and to drape tiny shawls over their heads. Little girls are discouraged from touching their own genitals, and children of any age are beaten if they are caught indulging in sex play of any kind. Girls grow up in a female world in which older women carefully keep secret the facts of female physiology. To become a woman in San Pedro, a girl is inducted into the mysteries of menstruation, intercourse, and childbirth at the appropriate time.

Menstruation and courtship. Menstruation comes as a shock to most girls at thirteen or fourteen. When a girl suddenly finds herself bleeding and comes crying to her mother, she is given an old rag as protection and told to expect such bleeding each month. She may also be told that if she stops menstruating she might "swell up and die." No further explanation is given her by her mother except for the warning never to divulge the secret of her bleeding to any male and never to let any male see her bloody rag or catch her washing it. Because a girl's blood is "hot" when she is menstruating, she is told not to look directly at infants, turkey chicks, or sprouting beans lest these sicken and die.

There are no groups for girls corresponding to the adolescent boys' groups and no legitimate channels of sex education for girls. Most women regard it as immoral to tell unmarried girls about sex or reproduction, and even the few mothers who might like to do so are restrained by their own shame and embarrassment.

Despite crowded sleeping arrangements, most girls reach adolescence in a state of semi-ignorance. But a great deal of curiosity and fascination with sex is expressed between age mates who regularly go in twos or threes to the lake for water. On these occasions adolescent girls, whispering and giggling, exchange forbidden information, as well as fantasies and misinformation.

Despite the precautions of their mothers, young girls are sometimes subject to advances by men. Girls do not report such episodes to their mothers for fear of punishment. Some encounters with men remain on the joking level and provide only titillation, but in other instances a girl can experience intense shame and guilt, particularly when the man who makes a grab for her genitals is a relative or a village dignitary. Such encounters only rarely result in actual rape, but they become known among girls, making young women feel vulnerable just when their interest in the other sex is most intense. It is not surprising that girls keep to the narrow paths where the traditional public forms of stylized courtship ensure safety and minimal physical contact, along with sweet promises and soothing words. Traditional courtship is a romantic drama that has little relationship to the problematics of marriage or sex. The drama takes place each afternoon at the lakeshore, where the young men, returned from the fields, station themselves to wait for the girls to ascend from the lake with full water jars on their heads. The young man detains the girl by grasping her wrist from behind and addresses her in rehearsed phrases learned from his companions. Courtship is the high point of a girl's life, beginning when she is thirteen or fourteen. She has every motivation to prolong the pleasures of courtship. By deferring consent she also exerts power over men, a rare privilege for an adolescent girl. A man may court only one girl at a time but a girl may have several suitors simultaneously, each awaiting his turn as the girl ascends. Elderly women nostalgically boast of the hours it took them to reach home with their water jars because of the number of suitors who detained them along the way.

Eventually the girl is persuaded to marry, usually between the ages of fifteen and seventeen. She is given a choice by the youth she favors. He offers to have his parents petition hers in the lengthy traditional way, or to steal her away from her parents one night as she goes outside on a pretext (Paul and Paul, 1963).

Intercourse. Whether the girl arrives at her new home by elopement or by parental arrangement, typically she suffers fear and loneliness. Her first night in alien surroundings with her husband, a virtual stranger despite courtship on the water paths, is more often a nightmare than a dream come true. Most girls have been shielded from the facts about sexual intercourse, if not from the mixed aura of anxiety and fascination that surrounds the subject.

In the presence of other members of the boy's family, the young couple hardly exchanges a word; outside of the stylized courtship situation they hardly know how to communicate with each other even when they are alone. The girl may know nothing about the mechanics of sexual intercourse. A new wife may spend her first night sitting up in bed crying. Sometimes a mother-in-law has to intervene to quiet the shrieks of protest of the young bride lest she bring shame on the family. And when newly married women reproach their mothers for not having warned them about sexual intercourse, they are only told that it is something women must endure. In the words of one older woman, "all men are like dogs."

Menstruation is mysterious and frightening at first, but a girl has usually seen blood before, from cuts and wounds. But to be mounted and penetrated by a man who heretofore has only held her wrist is experienced by a young woman as a traumatic violation of a privacy heavily guarded even from her own touch or sight until this moment. From early childhood she has never been without her skirt, even when bathing in the lake.

A girl of fourteen reports that her newly married female cousin advises her never to marry. The cousin says she wants to run away to the coast because her husband insists on intercourse every night. "Don't tell your mother," she warns, "because she will tell my mother, who will beat me for telling you. The first night he didn't do anything, but the second night he woke me up from a sound sleep saying, 'give me a little bit.' I wondered why he was asking me for something and answered that I wasn't eating anything. He said, 'No, it's not food, it's something else, you know what.' I didn't know what he was talking about and I began to cry. He hit me, grabbed my hands, and climbed on top of me. And not only once, but he wants it three times every night. It's terrible; he is very big and it hurts a lot." The younger girl, saying that her cousin tells her all men do this, hopefully concludes, "perhaps there are some men who don't; don't you think so?"

Young men exchange sexual information and they associate sexual exploits with masculinity in the Spanish romantic tradition, but girls have no such preparation for or associations with sexual intercourse. For the girl courtship has been without sexual overtones. Sexual pleasure in terms of biological survival is adaptive, but it is not essential for both sexes to experience pleasure. The culture of San Pedro assigns pleasure to the male and reproduction to the female. However, although San Pedro women, as Catholics, pay for the sin of Eve by renouncing sexual pleasure, they also inherit from their Maya ancestry a measure of supernatural power connected with fertility, as explained below.

Childbirth. The birth of the first baby is perhaps the most important status transition for a young woman in San Pedro, where most marriages take place informally without benefit of ceremony. Giving birth provides proof of her fertility, improves her standing in her husband's household and among older women generally, and reknits ties with her family if these have been ruptured by her flight from home. But young women do not look forward to the birth of their first baby because they are not supposed to know that they are pregnant.

The mystery that cloaked menstruation and intercourse continues throughout the first pregnancy. A conspiracy of secrecy prevents a young woman from knowing about, or acknowledging awareness of, her first pregnancy until she is ready to give birth. Until that point she and everyone around her maintain the fiction that the periodic visits of the midwife are only "to cure her illness" and restore menstruation.

Pregnancy is a dangerous time for the expectant mother and child. The family midwife is summoned as soon as the mother-in-law, experienced in these matters, judges that the girl is pregnant. The midwife, following an ancient Mesoamerican practice, periodically massages the girl's abdomen and, as the pregnancy advances, manipulates the fetus through the abdominal wall, if necessary, to ensure a normal presentation.

The midwife assumes responsibility for her patient and is aware of the special dangers to which the woman and fetus are susceptible. The life of the fetus can be imperiled by the envy of jealous or malevolent neighbors, by anger or any other abnormal emotional state of the mother, by failure of the mother to have her food cravings satisfied, or by misconduct of the mother in her duties and obligations as daughter, wife, or daughter-in-law.

The nature deities of the ancient Maya pantheon have receded into relative obscurity; nevertheless pregnant women remain particularly subject to the harmful influences of personified natural phenomena. It is dangerous for pregnant women to venture out of the house at midday when the sun is at zenith, to look at the moon when it is full or in eclipse, or to point at the rainbow, represented in current lore as a colored serpent with a human head. Failure to observe such precautions can result in a defective or crippled child. Should a pregnant woman venture out during a thunderstorm, her child will be born with clubfeet and claimed by the rain gods as their helper.

Not only is a pregnant woman subject to misfortune; she can endanger others. It is thought that during pregnancy blood accumulates that is normally discharged and replaced by "clean" blood. In pregnancy, as in menstruation, the woman's blood is "hot" or "strong" and her direct gaze can cause babies and young plants or animals to sicken and die.

All of these hazards are known to midwives and older women, but the woman having her first baby is told only what she should and should not do, without any explanation. The mother-in-law may increase her surveillance and management, perhaps augmenting the tension already existing between the two women. Whatever the true state of their presumed ignorance and innocence, pregnant women realize that their situation is not the normal one, although no limitations are put on their work until the very end of pregnancy. The young wife cannot speak of her mounting anxiety to her husband, or to anyone else. She may have an inkling of what is happening to her, but lacking any explanation for her "swelling" and fetal movements she feels possessed by strange and awesome powers.

Childbirth is a private affair, with only the midwife, the young husband, his parents, and possibly the parents of the wife in attendance. Children of the household are always sent to the homes of relatives and later told only that a baby has been bought from a foreigner. Although women experience severe pain in labor, especially during the first delivery, they are admonished to suppress their cries lest neighbors hear them. Adolescent girls never admit knowing that their own mothers are pregnant. Since women's clothing is bulky and swellings are a familiar syndrome, pregnancy can pass unnoticed by the uninitiated.

The woman is supported by her husband from behind as she squats to deliver her child. Trained to accept the authority of older women, she tries to obey the instructions of the midwife, a woman she regards with respect and some awe. But silent apprehension, compounded by an aura of conspiracy on the part of the older women around her, usually results in tightening of the muscles when they should be relaxed, thus prolonging the delivery of the first child.

Native ideas of a woman's body as the scene of organs that can become disorderly and move around, or even leave the body altogether, give cause for great anxiety. When a woman is seized by *cólera* (a paroxysm of suppressed rage), her heart is said to be "rising up to the throat and trying to escape." During childbirth, the uterus is believed to descend and there is danger that it will come out. This would result in the death of the woman. Therefore, "the midwife must know how to raise it back up into place and it is for this reason that she binds the woman's abdomen with a sash after childbirth." There is a great concern that the placenta will rise up and attach itself to the woman's heart, causing her death.

Midwives resort to various empirical and magical methods to hasten delivery of the baby and ejection of the afterbirth. The midwife owes her obstetrical skill and her right to officiate at childbirth to a super-

natural mandate. One must be born with the "power" to become a midwife, signaled by the presence of a "cap" at the time she is born. A potential midwife who fails to exercise her mandate when she reaches
adulthood runs the risk of dying from a lingering disease.

A midwife is not like other women. To practice her profession she
must behave in ways that are proscribed for ordinary women. She must
walk all over the town and outskirts at any hour of the day or night
to see her patients. She must visit the homes under the most intimate
and private circumstances, and finally she must have intimate contact
with other women's sexual organs. Furthermore, if she were an ordinary woman she could not risk coming in contact with the "hot" blood
and other magically dangerous substances that issue with the infant at
birth.

Each midwife herself suffers a chronic and severe illness that is only
cured when she has been validated by a local native priest-diviner who
sponsors her. She learns the arts of midwifery from the spirits of dead
midwives, the supernatural patronesses of childbirth, who appear in
her dreams and place in her path the tangible proof of her divine
power—scissors or a penknife for cutting the umbilical cord, and a
conch shell or strangely shaped bone, stone, or figurine having magic
power to cure sterility. Midwives have mystical experiences with supernatural patrons who inhabit local hills and volcanoes. As a sacred professional in the service of higher authorities, the midwife must not
charge fees. At the same time, she must accept graciously each patient's
gift, no matter how small. The midwife is a ritual specialist, as well as
an obstetrical expert, serving as intermediary between the pregnant
woman and supernatural patronesses of childbirth.

These patronesses are the spirits of dead midwives and a host of
Catholic female saints, who preside over the delivery and over the eight-
day period of enforced bed rest for the new mother. On the eighth day
the midwife sanctifies the house by spreading incense into the four cor-
ners, bathes and swaddles the infant, exorcises the evil spirits by whip-
ping the hammock that will serve as the infant's daytime cradle, and
washes the mother's hair semipublicly in the patio. This ceremonial act,
restoring the mother to normal status, also marks the final stage of in-
duction into the mysteries of womanhood.

The mystic power of women. After experiencing menstruation and
intercourse, the girl becomes a woman by crossing the sacred threshold
of childbirth. Through her pain and suffering the young woman is entitled to share the esoteric sex knowledge that experienced women see
as a source of mystic power, which resides in all women and can be

used by desperate wives or by witches to break the strength of unruly husbands.

What purposes does it serve to mystify menstruation, intercourse, and childbirth? The mystery surrounding these phenomena can appear to support the ascendancy of men over women, of older women over younger, of parents over children. But in terms of the Pedrano world view, the mystification of biological processes contributes, not to a sense of powerlessness on the part of women, but rather to a sense of participation in the mystic powers of the universe. The ancient pre-Columbian gods of nature were dual in their attributes; they were both death-dealing and life-giving, like the natural phenomena they personified. Some of this dualism still characterizes the Pedrano outlook. Because of the miraculous nature of their biological processes, women are more attuned than men to cosmic rhythms.

A girl's first experience with menstruation and intercourse generates fear and a sense of helplessness. But this feeling is transmuted into an attitude of awe and wonder with the birth of a baby, an attitude heightened by the ministrations of the midwife and her sacred connection with supernaturals who can confer the gift of life or withhold it. With the birth of her first child, the young woman is no longer estranged from her own body; she is now aware that her body is the seat of magical powers.

Childbirth is the final rite admitting a girl to womanhood. In her new status she is privileged to know that women's bodies are the locus of destructive as well as life-giving powers. She learns that all women, not just witches, have a secret weapon to be used illegitimately as a desperate last resort to defend themselves against incorrigibly mean or aggressive husbands. Men are aware of the power that resides in women's sexual organs, fearing that they can be robbed of their virility and rendered manso. This is why a woman must not step over a recumbent male or over one of his implements. Women in San Pedro say that in the town of Totonicapan the women sleep with their skirts off but that no wife in San Pedro would risk her husband's anger by doing the same.

All Pedranos know that some women of the town are witches. They are born "rolled up in a ball" (in the unbroken amniotic sac) and cannot escape their destiny. The few women so identified by general gossip live as semipariahs, marrying men from out of town. Before a witch changes into her animal counterpart by doing four somersaults, she shakes her skirt over her husband to make him manso and to make sure he remains asleep while she goes out at night to do her evil work.

A woman learns that menstrual blood is particularly damaging to a man's virility and that during menstruation she must avoid intercourse with her husband. An older woman complains: "It is very bad for a man to have intercourse with his wife when she has her 'flower' because a long thing like a rope inside the woman descends and beats him when he enters her. And when a woman, to protect her husband, doesn't want to 'talk' with him he will scold and sometimes even take her to court or kick her out of the house, saying perhaps she doesn't like him anymore, or perhaps she has a lover. Men are such curs, they want it all day and all night too. It costs men nothing, but women have all the pains." But women generally manage to avoid intercourse by pleading a stomachache or headache. No wife would tell her husband she menstruates.

Men, so women say, think that any woman who menstruates is a witch and that only a witch will use her menstrual blood to emasculate a man. But women know that menstrual blood is one of their own ultimate weapons against intractable husbands. "Many men have eaten their beans with the blood of their wives and didn't know it." Should a man discover a bloody rag, especially if it is one of his own kerchiefs, he will take his wife to the local courthouse and accuse her of being a witch. When their husbands confront them with reports about the evil deeds of another woman, to avert suspicion and to protect the secrecy of women's magical power, wives will deny that they menstruate or know about such magic, replying that the woman in question must be a witch.

Women's lives are more restricted than men's and men dominate women in sexual relations, but the cultural assignment of mystic powers to female sexuality gives women a symbolic weapon with which to counter the power of males. Women do not belong to informal neighborhood groups in San Pedro, nor do they have formal organizations to enhance their status, but all women who have been initiated into the female mysteries feel a sense of kinship with other women of San Pedro. Although men control the civil and ceremonial offices, it is the women who are in closer touch, directly through their own bodies and indirectly through the midwife-cum-priestess, with the cosmic forces controlling life itself.

Conclusion

This paper has explored areas of feminine culture in a Mesoamerican Indian society that have been underreported. I have shown that, just as men are masters of their sphere of work, women are masters of theirs; that the tedium of women's daily toil is relieved by gratifications derived from the conviction that work is a virtue, from the sense of competence that skill confers, and from the symbolic and social importance of the products of women's work.

In matters of sex, however, the relationship between men and women is much more asymmetric, and marked by mutual distrust and anxiety. In work women command their bodies, but in sex their bodies are commanded not only by men but by mysterious powers that periodically cause bleeding and gestation. Barriers of shame leave the maturing female unprepared for the crises of first menstruation, her wedding night, and the birth of her first baby. But each experience admits her by stages to the inner arcanum of female secrets, which unites her with other mature members of her sex.

Colby states: "The main feature of Mesoamerican self-concepts is a very weak body-boundary image. This is of two kinds: the belief that impulses emanating from within the body (e.g. inner rage or sexual passion) can be contained or controlled only with difficulty, and the belief that defense against threats coming toward or into the body from the outside (e.g. witchcraft or the magical intrusion of destructive objects) is inadequate" (1967: 427).

Colby's evidence for the image of a permeable body boundary is more acceptable than the one-sided connotations conveyed by the negative terms "weak" and "inadequate." As this paper has shown, with reference to the work sphere, women's sense of physical mastery and perception of their bodies as skilled instruments require inclusion of the concept of competence in the self-concept equation. In relation to reproduction, the image of a permeable body boundary reflects more accurately the dual nature of such permeability in native conception. It implies not only vulnerability to dangers but a sense of union with transcendent powers that are the source of life as well as death.

BRIDGET O'LAUGHLIN

Mediation of Contradiction: Why Mbum Women Do Not Eat Chicken

The inferior status of women in most if not all societies has often been related to the natural division of labor within the family. Sexual asymmetry is thus said to be rooted in the reproductive activities of women as bearers and nourishers of children, even though the degree and expression of asymmetry vary widely among different societies. In order to understand the force of reproductive constraints on the definition of women's positions, it is therefore important to consider in detail and in particular cases the actual relations of determinance between biological reproduction, the sexual division of labor, and sexual hierarchies.

The purpose of this paper, then, is to describe the basis of sexual asymmetry in one African society, that of the Mbum Kpau of southwestern Tchad.[1] I hope to show that the dominance of men in Mbum society is based primarily on their control of the forces and means of reproduction (women and surplus), rather than on any technologically defined or natural division of labor. The ideology of the Mbum Kpau, however, defines the nature of woman in such a way that certain tasks, incapacities, and prohibitions associated with inferior status are regarded as inextricably linked to the reproductive activities of women, over which they themselves have only limited control. That which is arbitrary and contradictory (a reflection of women's subordination to men) is defined as biologically determined: eating chicken, for instance, is forbidden to women under pain of reproductive failure.[2]

---

[1] The fieldwork upon which this paper is based was carried out in the subprefecture of Baïbokoum, Republic of Tchad, from December 1969 through September 1971. The research was supported by the Foreign Area Fellowship Program and Yale University.

[2] This prohibition of chicken to women is common in Equatorial Africa, and is discussed in several of Mary Douglas's papers on the Lele. When I lived as a teacher in Cameroun, I dined quite often with the families of young professionals and government officials. Although there was great variety in the menu and presentation of these

The Problem: Sexual Asymmetry in Food Prohibitions

Among the Mbum Kpau, women eat neither chicken nor goat for fear of pain and death in childbirth, the bearing of abnormal or unhealthy children, or even sterility.[3] No such prohibitions apply to men today, although the elders say that in their youth no man ate these meats either until his first child was able to walk.[4] Men do not have to enforce the prohibition of goat and chicken, for women themselves usually refuse with horror to eat either. Nowadays a few young girls will eat chicken on the sly before initiation or marriage, and a few women will eat goat when they are too old for childbearing, but most women still follow the required abstinences. Knowing that I ate forbidden foods, women would loudly pity me my childlessness and carefully verify the ingredients of any meat dishes I served them.

Respect of the food prohibitions is not difficult to understand, for sterility or failure to bear living children is a major tragedy for a Mbum Kpau woman. Sterility embitters the relationship between husband and wife, and may cause a young woman to lie sleepless, brooding and weeping, through the nights of her menstrual period. After a number of childless years or plural marriages (for sterile women marry often), the term *maatu*, sterile woman, is finally publicly applied as a characterization of a woman; the use of the epithet continues long after a woman has passed childbearing age. Male sterility is culturally recognized and distinguished from impotence, but even though it is said to be linked to "crazy" or "foolish" behavior, it is not related to moral violations, as is that of women.

The prohibition of goat and chicken to women is not important in everyday life, for both animals are usually killed and consumed only on special occasions. Yet in such culturally special contexts, the prohibition serves to distinguish sexual differences and sexual ranking. When food is prepared for a hoeing party, for example, a chicken dish is usually served to the men while the women are given fish and greens, even though during the hoeing men and women work together in a single group. Although senior women as well as men may be sacrificers, only

---

meals, the initial course was almost invariably a chicken dish, of which all the women present took portions. For a woman to eat chicken in this situation is a signal of advanced education and "modern" orientations.

[3] Mbum women also do not eat any kind of eggs or partridge or other game birds. They avoid eating snakes for fear of bringing forth snakelike children. During pregnancy they also avoid certain foods, such as bony-headed fish and the meat of antelopes with twisted horns, for fear of physical deformation of the child in the womb.

[4] I saw young men laugh in disbelief when the elders spoke of observing these prohibitions out of respect for their fathers and the ancestors.

men may consume the major sacrifices consisting of chicken and goat. The chicken and goat prohibition therefore serves both to recognize implicitly and to define explicitly the subordination of women.

Absolute eating prohibitions for women are not the only forms of sexual skewing in the food consumption patterns of the Mbum Kpau. The distribution of certain preferred foods—porridge of white flour, meat, and beer—is also sexually imbalanced, with men consuming a disproportionate share. Men expect to have meat sauces to go with their porridge, and will sometimes refuse to eat sauces made of greens or other vegetables, which are said to be women's food.[5] Men and women normally eat their meals separately, and the women always place the largest morsels of meat in the men's bowls. "Good" wives are also supposed to serve only light porridge (prepared from the flour of the inner kernel of millet) to their husbands. Similarly, whenever beer is served, within the village or at a work party, the first and largest amounts are always offered to the senior men present.

As these examples illustrate, masculine privilege in food consumption is expressed almost entirely within the class of "prestige" foods—white porridge, beer, and meat, particularly chicken and goat.[6] To understand why this is so and, more important, why chicken and goat should be distinguished as a special class with an absolute prohibition, it is necessary to describe how these goods are produced and distributed within the Mbum economy.

Sex-Role Ascriptions in the Technical Relations of Production

The Mbum Kpau are primarily shifting cultivators,[7] but also practice hunting and gathering, livestock raising, and craft production. Settled in small village communities, consisting of one or more patrilineally organized wards, the Mbum Kpau inhabit a region of low population density.[8] Both men and women are responsible for clearing and cultivating their own plots, although a man may help his wife cut down large

[5] When mothers complained to me about their children's refusal of vegetables, I puzzled over the air of pride with which the complaint was made, until I realized that all the children referred to were male.

[6] In fact, records of everyday individual consumption indicate that women consume at least as much prepared food (porridge and sauce) as men. Men supplement their diets with greater proportions of raw manioc and peanuts dug in the fields, wild fruit, and small birds and rodents caught and roasted in the bush.

[7] The principal crops cultivated in swidden fields include cotton (the cash crop), millet, sorghum, manioc, sesame, and peanuts. Gardens within the village are intensively cultivated in corn, sweet potatoes, and variety of vegetables.

[8] The population density for the prefecture of Logone Oriental as a whole is 8.4 per square kilometer (*Enquête Démographique au Tchad*, 1964). The density in the Kpau canton is probably somewhat less.

trees on her clearing. Both men and women reap the grain at harvest time, but if beer is brewed, men do most of the threshing while women sweep and winnow. Women hoe and harvest supplementary plots of vegetables and oil seeds more frequently than men do, while men alone cultivate small plots of jute. Despite these and other minor differences in crops cultivated, there is very little sexual differentiation in either task assignment or intensity of labor in Mbum agricultural practices.

Sexual ascription of roles is more common in hunting and gathering, which, although of minimal importance in allocations of labor time, still provide a significant supplement to Mbum subsistence. Men hunt with nets, dogs, and spears, set snares for small game and birds, and fish with nets, hook and line, weirs, and traps. Women participate in the great net hunts only as porters, but they kill small game near the village during the fire hunts, dig crabs, and dam pools for scoop fishing. Throughout the year, women also gather greens, flowers, fruits, and mushrooms from the bush for sauces, and in times of food shortage they dig wild tubers and collect oil seeds. Men may gather when traveling or working in the bush, but only occasionally do they bring food home to their wives or mothers.

Dogs, goats, and chickens, the most commonly raised livestock, require only a minimal amount of care, for they are usually left to scavenge or graze around the village. Only men keep dogs, but goats and chickens are raised by men and women. Livestock are not kept for consumption, but so, it is said, that they may become many. Thus, dogs should not be eaten at all, and goats and chickens should be used only for sacrifices, work parties, celebrations, gifts, payment of fines, bridewealth—all non-subsistence requirements of the household.[9]

In the forms of production summarized above—livestock raising, cultivation, hunting, and gathering—the contributions of both sexes are nearly equal, in terms of subsistence derived as well as input of labor time. Further, the intensity of labor of pregnant or nursing women is only slightly less than that of men in their age group. Perhaps more important is the fact that sexual ascription of productive roles is minimal in cultivation and livestock raising, though only men hunt large game. The importance of man the hunter in Mbum society was undoubtedly greater in the past, when large game such as lion, panther, buffalo, and wild boar was still abundant, and prior to the colonial occupation, when men might be warriors, hunters of men.

[9] This does not mean that the meat of livestock does not contribute to general subsistence; in fact only a small number of mature male livestock are maintained in the community.

In addition to direct forms of production of goods, there are other kinds of labor activities in the economy of the Mbum Kpau that entail the transformation of a product into another, more usable or more desired, form. These secondary forms of production include craft manufacture, food preparation, and trade.

There is little sexual division of labor in the provision of materials for manufacturing a craft item; both men and women cut grass and reeds, dig clay, cut down small trees, and grow calabashes. Specific craft skills, by contrast, are sexually differentiated. Women fashion pots and engrave calabashes, while men carve wood, cast metals, weave mats and baskets, dress skins, and construct houses. No man would make a pot or engrave a calabash unless he were a transvestite, but women frequently perform certain craft operations of men, such as twining rope, carving a pestle, binding grass for a roof, or making bricks. Complex craft operations are assigned by age as well as sex: one must be old and furnished with special medicines to make a very large pot, to hollow out a mortar, or to weave the joint of a granary wall.

Food is prepared almost entirely by women. Most men use pots for cooking only when preparing a sacrificial chicken, or when boiling game scraps for the dog's share of the catch.[10] Men and boys also frequently roast manioc, peanuts, and corn over an open fire in the fields, and they spit-roast fresh game or birds. Men who live alone without wives sometimes prepare their own meals, but because of the shame of doing women's work they cook only inside the house. They may also fetch water and sweep their own courts, but they will never pound or grind grain, nor will they make beer or oil or render salt (essential in a tasty cuisine). In fact, most unmarried men manage to eat the greater part of their meals with close kin, and they are often heard begging women to pound flour, brew beer, or make oil for them.

Another form of transformation of product is trade. The Mbum Kpau have no marketplace, but women barter small amounts of subsistence goods in kind and sell beer within the village. Young men and boys are occasional vendors, hawking small items for cash, but senior men never vend, and seldom enter into barter transactions for small amounts of goods. They do, however, frequently establish exchange friendships with elders in other communities, friendships entailing long-term prestations and counterprestations of millet, livestock, and cash. Women also establish such friendships, either with men or with other women, but the scale

10 Women are supposedly ignorant of the fact that in the initiation camps away from the village boys do not subsist entirely on the meals their mothers send them; they also pound flour and prepare food themselves.

of the transaction is likely to be small and the duration of the relationship short.

It would appear that the sexual division of labor is more strictly defined in the processes of transformation of products centering in the household than it is in simple production. Women cannot make certain essential items such as houses, granaries, hoes, and mortars, just as men cannot make pots, pound flour, brew and sell beer, or render salt. This greater rigidity in sexual definition of roles cannot be associated with any increased importance of biologically determined differences in strength and aptitude between men and women.[11] In most aspects of Mbum production, with the possible exception of hunting and warfare, the slight sexual division of labor is culturally, not biologically, determined.

Up to this point, we have considered the organization of production in the Mbum economy only in relation to the division of labor within various work processes. The economic subordination of women to men was shown to be not technologically determined, for within production as a whole there are few sexually assigned roles outside of the domestic sphere, and the contributions of both sexes are quite equitable. To discover the primary expression of male dominance it is therefore necessary to turn from technology to the organization of production.

Sexual Inequality in the Social Relations of Production

Mbum production is organized by a series of multifunctional and overlapping units of labor cooperation and resource pooling: the individual, the household, the granary group, the compound, the ward, and the lineage. Within each group, authority over both resources and products is vested in the senior male. The head of a granary group that produces and stores its millet together, for example, distributes equal shares of grain to the wives of the group for consumption and allocates millet for special purposes such as work groups or exchange.

Similarly, within the household, which is the basic unit of cotton cultivation, a man controls the cash revenues of his wives and unmarried sons. The elders of localized lineage segments likewise control bridewealth, medicines, nets, and musical instruments held commonly by the lineage, and they supervise certain cooperative work groups. Although widows and divorcees past childbearing age may become heads of their

11 Unmarried women, for instance, quite often do the heavy work of cutting turf, mixing mud, and molding bricks, but they feel incapable of constructing an even wall. Consequently women must depend on the assistance of men for the physically light work of bricklaying and mortaring.

own households, only senior men control significant amounts of resources through their authority in extended units of production. Sexual asymmetry in the distribution of the means and forces of production can be most easily demonstrated by a review of the control of resources in the different aspects of Mbum production.

Control of land and instruments of production. Within hoe agriculture, land and instruments of production are held by both men and women. Jural rights to use of land for cultivation are obtained through residence in the community: no individuals or descent groups have special rights or claims to cultivable land. Each cultivator owns a hoe, and sometimes an axe. Seed is held by the individual cultivator for most crops except millet, which is allocated by the head of the granary group.

Although rights to cultivable land for swiddens are neither individually nor collectively held, certain land areas are associated with specific patrilineages. The elders of these lineages have ritual responsibility for the areas, and are entitled to small portions of all large game killed on these lands. Game caught by dogs or nets is taken by the owner of the instrument: dogs are individually owned by men, whereas nets may be owned by individuals (including women) or lineages. Women do not own spears, but often borrow them from their spouses or male kin. Women may raise domestic animals for exchange, sacrifice, or sponsorship of work groups, even though they cannot consume the meat of chickens or goats.

The stock of tools required for Mbum craft production is small and multifunctional. Hoes, axes, and knives are used in potting, wood carving, and weaving, as well as in agriculture, and may be individually owned by either sex. A woman cannot own the forge and anvil of the smith, but then neither in any real sense can a man, for the tools of the blacksmith are commonly owned by a segment of the patrilineage. Most kitchen utensils are owned only by women, although most men have a few pots for storage and preparation of medicines.

Juridically, access to the basic means of production among the Mbum Kpau is thus not sexually defined; yet the actual distribution of tools and breeding animals is markedly skewed in favor of men. Only a few women in fact own hunting nets, axes, or large numbers of goats. Women are also unlikely to control large amounts of surplus seed grain, since only unmarried women may be heads of granary groups, and then only of small groups. Women never attain positions of authority within their own lineages that would give them control over the nets, tools, musical instruments, medicines, and livestock held commonly by the group. Although there are no fixed rules of inheritance of individual property, women rarely inherit from their fathers, whereas men often inherit from both parents.

Egalitarian rules of property assignment in the jural superstructures[12] of the Mbum Kpau do not, then, reflect real relations of production, which are marked by considerable sexual (and age) asymmetry. Sexual asymmetry in the distribution of the means of production is a function of the locus of authority in senior males for all extended units of production. This rule of authority is also expressed in rules of exogamy and virilocal residence: at marriage women must leave their own lineages and the households of their fathers to join the households and granary groups of their husbands.

Control of labor. Control of labor in the process of production, like control of the means of production, belongs preeminently to men. Within a lineage, members cooperate in terms of an ideology of generalized reciprocity, cultivating their plots together at beer parties and sharing their craft skills. Theoretically women remain members of the lineages of their fathers even after marriage, thus maintaining their rights to cooperative and craft labor, but with a rule of virilocal residence they are seldom in a position to claim these rights. Instead women must depend almost entirely on their husbands and children for shared labor. If a woman's husband cannot carve a decent hoe handle for her, for instance, she must buy one herself, although her husband's was probably carved gratis by one of his patrilineal kin.[13] Similarly a woman's cooperative labor transactions outside of her own household are usually reciprocal; her husband, in contrast, may recruit many days of unreciprocated labor from his junior patrilineal kin. Consequently, although both men and women may sponsor cooperative work groups, men (particularly senior men) recruit many more days of surplus labor than do women.

Men are thus able to recruit more labor than women can in contexts in which access to labor is determined largely by co-residence with the patrilineage. In addition, senior men, as heads of extended-family gra-

---

12 The model of overdetermined social structure employed in this paper has been best described by Marx (1970: 20): "In the social production of their existence, men inevitably enter into definite relations which are independent of their will, namely relations of production appropriate to a given stage in the development of their material forces of production. The totality of these relations of production constitutes the economic structure of society, the real foundation, on which arises a legal and political superstructure and to which correspond definite forms of social consciousness."

13 A recently widowed woman in a distant village once sent word in mid-rainy season to her brother, my neighbor, requesting that he carve a hoe handle quickly and send it to her. She had broken hers, had no money to buy another, and could find no one among her affines who would give her one.

nary groups, are able to allocate labor recruited outside of their own households. The technology of the Mbum Kpau is simple, requiring a limited stock of tools, and land is freely obtainable through residence in a community with a shifting path of swidden sites. The primary determinant of variation in levels of production and possible accumulation is consequently the input of labor.[14] Sexual asymmetry in appropriation of surplus labor is therefore the strongest indication thus far of the subordinate status of women within the Mbum economy.

The superior position of men in control of labor as well as of the means of production has been shown to be related both to residence rules after marriage and to the locus of senior male authority within all extended production groups. There is a contradiction between the technical and social relations of production: senior men, as heads of large granary groups and lineage elders, are able to control part of the labor and surplus product of their sons and junior siblings as well as of their wives. An analysis of sexual asymmetry in relations of production thus leads inevitably in this case to a close consideration of two problems— rules of marriage and accumulation of surplus.

A discussion of the organization of production among the Mbum Kpau is, in other words, incomplete without a description of the organization of reproduction. A number of anthropologists,[15] working in the Marxist tradition inspired by Althusser, have in fact suggested that the dominance of male elders in African societies may usually be based on their control of the forces of reproduction—surplus product and labor, rights in women, and bridewealth. Structures of reproduction thus provide the link between economic infrastructure and politico-judicial superstructures. It is finally here, in a discussion of reproduction, that the metaphorical connection between women, goats, and chickens becomes clear and the meaning of the eating prohibition understood.

Reproduction of Conditions and Relations of Production

As Marx (1964: 82–83) has indicated, a mode of production must provide not only a set of productive processes but also the conditions of

[14] The importance of relating the efficiency of swidden cultivation to total yield per unit of labor rather than to total yield per unit of area has been noted by Conklin (1954) among others.

[15] Since the translation of *Pre-Capitalist Economic Formations* (Marx 1964), scholars working within the Marxist tradition have become more aware of Marx's recognition of alternative historical processes of social evolution, as exemplified by his interest in Germanic and Asiatic modes of production. For a review of research relating to the formulation of African modes of production, see Terray (1969), Berthoud (1969–70), Dupré and Rey (1969), and Willame (1971). The distinctiveness of certain forms of

its reproduction. Three aspects of reproduction can be analytically isolated: reproduction of the means of production, reproduction of the
labor force, and reproduction of the relations of production (Althusser,
1971: 128).

Reproduction of the means of production. Land (soil, flora, fauna),
simple tools, breeding animals, and seed are reproduced in the processes
of production. As shifting cultivators and hunters, the Mbum make little
attempt to renew the land or its cover: composting or other methods of
soil improvement are not used, and female game animals are not spared
in the hunt. Accordingly, maintenance of the land has traditionally required constant shifting of cultivation and, eventually, residence sites.
In livestock raising, female breeding animals are carefully tended and
cared for in hatching or birth, but no effort is made to improve the stock.

Much of the stock of tools and equipment required for Mbum production can be manufactured and repaired by craftsmen within the
community. Yet many important tools, such as knives, axe heads, spear
points, and hoe blades, must be obtained from an increasingly rare village smith or from the "Arab" blacksmiths in the nearest town. Even
prior to the modern scrap-iron era, the Mbum Kpau did not mine or
smelt ore, but were dependent on trade with the neighboring Laka for
the provision of iron. Livestock, grain, and sometimes slaves were exchanged for lumps of crude iron ore, which circulated as a medium of
exchange (in bridewealth transactions, and for the sale of grain, beer,
livestock, medicines, and titles), and were forged by local smiths into
iron implements.

Maintenance of a stock of implements as well as of a supply of seed
grain has thus among the Mbum long been dependent on the accumulation of surplus through production beyond subsistence requirements.
Control of this surplus product is vested almost entirely in senior males,
through the mode of organization of units of production. The conditions of reproduction of the means of production among the Mbum
Kpau consist, therefore, in the accumulation of surplus by senior males.
Prestige foods—beer, white porridge, chicken and goat—are an expression of the existence of this surplus, and the skewing in the consumption of these foods toward senior men is an expression of their control.
In time of famine or even severe food shortage, beer is seldom brewed,
men eat red porridge as well as white, and livestock are exchanged for
grain.

African social organization has been noted in another context by Kathleen Gough
(1971: 111) in her description of certain patrilineal kinship systems that separate rights
in a woman as sexual partner and domestic worker from the rights in her as genetrix.

Reproduction of labor. The second form of reproduction essential to the existence of a particular mode of production is that of the labor force. The reproduction of labor demands not only biological reproduction but also the socialization of individuals into their productive roles. Given the crucial importance of labor relative to the means of production in the Mbum economy, one would expect that control over the reproduction of labor would entail great authority within the society. In fact this is so; yet it is here that one encounters a central contradiction of this system: women have primary responsibility for both biological reproduction and socialization of children, but control over reproductive rights in women of the lineage, and authority derived from that control, are vested entirely in male elders.

Among the Mbum Kpau, it is biologically necessary not only that women bear children but also that they nurse them for at least two years. During this period, a woman should not have intercourse with her husband for fear of pregnancy, but as soon as the child walks steadily and appears healthy, the mother is likely to conceive again immediately. Childbirth is considered both painful and dangerous; in fact, the mortality rates for mothers and infants in childbirth are high. Yet no form of contraception is practiced, for women wish to bear as many children as they can. This means that the strength of women during much of their youth is impaired and their mobility limited through continual childbearing and nursing.

Children sleep in the houses of their mothers until they are about six years old, and usually go to the fields with the women during the day. Women assume all responsibility for feeding their children and for nursing them in time of illness. Mbum men, however, also spend much time with young children: bathing them, fondling them, telling them stories in the village in the evening, and even taking charge of the small boys in the fields during the day. After the age of six, most socialization is performed by older siblings in same-sex play groups. At the time of male initiation, senior men assert their authority over socialization and attempt to purge all that is woman-like in the boys.

Male initiation is an implicit recognition by men of the power women have over the socialization of both male and female children, but it is also a denial of this power. Women become identified with the biological reproduction and nurture of the community, whereas men are identified with its moral reproduction. Although both men and women may be healers and diviners, women take on the nurturing roles of midwife, nurse, and mourner in opposition to the roles of men, who hobnob with the ancestors as judges, musicians, and buriers of the dead.

Thus, although women are responsible for the biological reproduction of the labor force and a considerable part of its socialization as well, they have neither the moral nor the political authority that this responsibility would seem to imply. This lack of authority must be related to rules of exogamy, virilocal residence, and patrilineal descent, through which women bear children for groups other than their own. The prerequisite of biological reproduction therefore becomes the alienation of women from their own reproduction: reproductive rights in women must be exchanged between patrilineal groups invariably controlled by senior males.

The word "alienation" is perhaps too strong a term, for Mbum women in fact have a considerable amount of control over their choice of a husband, although they will usually yield to the firm opposition of their parents or elder brothers. The termination of a marriage also occurs most often at the initiative of the wife, who takes down her water jars from their pedestals, packs her cooking utensils, and leaves her husband's compound in a tirade of insults. It is considered shameful and even dangerous for a man to drive his wife away by taking down her water jars, or even to quit his wife's mat for a night because of a quarrel. Yet while women maintain control over the transfer of their uxorial rights in marriage, the exchange of their *reproductive* rights is controlled by men, particularly by the elders.

When a woman becomes pregnant before marriage, a small fine (*lari mbOl*) must be paid by the man she designates as the father of her unborn child. The fine consists of a cash payment and at least one chicken, which will be sacrificed by the girl's patrilineage. A small share is also given to the patrilineage of the girl's mother for the sacrifice of the chicken. The patrilineage of the man who pays this fine receives rights to the child, whether or not a marriage occurs.[16] When a woman marries, the *lari mbOl* is paid (if it has not already been paid), though payment is sometimes delayed until after the first pregnancy.

After the birth of several children, a much larger payment of bridewealth (*lari ūī*) should be given by the patrilineage of the husband to that of the wife. In turn, a small share of the bridewealth should be given by the wife's lineage to her mother's sister for her personal use (*lari tu pam*, "nipple or colostrum money"). If the bridewealth is not given, then all rights to the bridewealth of the daughters of the marriage will be retained by the patrilineage of the wife. Reproductive

---

16 However, a "raising" fee must be paid to the mother's father if a child born out of wedlock goes to live with his father's patrilineage. This notion of precondition should not be read as a rejection or distortion of infrastructural overdetermination.

rights in women thus include not only rights to children but also rights to bridewealth: the first are obtained by the transfer of the *lari mbOl* and the second by transfer of the *lari ũĩ*. For about the last twenty years the bridewealth payment has been made entirely in cash and livestock, but it previously consisted of livestock and the lumps of crude iron from which tools and weapons were forged.

With the cultivation of cotton as a cash crop, most young men can now provide the *lari mbOl* themselves, but they still depend on their elders for provision of the *lari ũĩ* out of the cash hoards they control in the name of the lineage segment. These hoards are accumulated by the elders through the collection of fines and revenues of initiation, the sale of beer and surplus grain (including the surplus product of women and junior male members of granary groups), the conversion of livestock, the provision of medicines, and especially the receipt of bridewealth for women of the patrilineage. The control by the lineage elders over the reproductive rights in bridewealth of the women of the group thus consolidates their authority over sons and junior siblings, who are dependent on their elders for the payment of bridewealth and fines.

Substitution of a bridewealth token for a woman liberates the lineage from immediate dependence on the reproductive success of its women for its own existence and for the reproduction of its constituent granary groups and households. If not enough women are born in one generation to provide wives-in-exchange for their brothers, then surplus product can be converted into tokens of bridewealth exchangeable for a woman. Conversely, despite moral sanctions against use of bridewealth for subsistence, in times of emergency bridewealth may be exchanged for tools, livestock, and seed. The bridewealth system thus links the reproduction of labor with the reproduction of the means of production, and at the same time reinforces the authority of senior men over women and juniors. It is the control of bridewealth, the first expression of the power of the elders, that merges superstructures of lineage authority with infrastructural relations of production.

The alienation of women from aspects of their own powers of reproduction in the Mbum system of bridewealth exchange is therefore a precondition of the basic infrastructural contradiction—the alienation of women and juniors from their own surplus product.[17] The contra-

17 A Marxist framework (questions, categories, and causality) facilitates analysis of the structures of any society—capitalist or precapitalist—but this is not to say that an analysis of Mbum society should replicate Marx's analysis of capitalism. Although all periods of production have certain common features, "not only is production particular production, but it is invariably only a definite social corpus, a social subject, that is engaged in a wider or narrower totality of productive spheres" (Marx, 1970:

diction inherent in the exchange of bridewealth and rights in women by lineage elders is perhaps even more stubbornly irreconcilable than is the infrastructural contradiction between technical and social relations of production: in time a number of junior males will move through the life cycle to the status of elder, just as widows and divorcees may eventually head their own production units; but as permanent jural minors within the lineage, women will never attain authority over the fruits of their own reproduction.

Reproduction of the relations of production. The irreconcilability of the contradiction inherent in the particular forms of sexual asymmetry in Mbum society brings us to the final forms of reproduction required for the continued existence of a social formation: reproduction of its relations of production. In order to reproduce a system of social relations of production that either contains or is grounded in contradiction, the society must mediate these contradictions within politico-juridical superstructures and/or ideological representations. So it is here that we finally begin to understand, at least partially, why Mbum women do not eat chicken.

Superstructures of lineage authority and rules of succession and inheritance generally express and reinforce the same relations of senior male dominance established in the organization of units of production. Similarly, positions of political authority within the village can never be held by those who have not passed through men's initiation, and are never held by junior men. Nevertheless, senior women who are widowed or divorced may come to have considerable influence as peacemakers in the community, particularly if they are also skilled healers, midwives, or diviners. In the arbitration of disputes by the elders, in canton and regional courts as well as within the community, women may bring complaints and speak for themselves; they need not have men represent them.

Though there are relatively few politico-juridical superstructures that exclude women or relegate them to an inferior position (the Mbum Kpau generally have no specialized political structures), at the level of ideology there are myriad expressions of sexual distinction and affirma-

---

191). Accordingly, it is entirely possible, as in the Mbum case, that superstructural relations may function in the establishment of relations of production. Marx himself invoked the idea of preconditions in his analysis of precapitalist economic formations: "The primitive forms of property necessarily dissolve into the relation of property to the different objective elements conditioning production; they are the economic basis of different forms of community, and in turn presuppose specific forms of community. These forms are significantly modified once labour itself is placed among the *objective conditions of production* (as in slavery and serfdom)" (Marx, 1964: 101).

tions of male dominance.[18] Perhaps ideological elaborations in mediating sexual contradictions in Mbum social relations could be expected even if complex hierarchical political structures were present. In societies where women are responsible for most socialization in early childhood, women themselves reproduce sexual role structures and ideologies of sexual inequality. Accordingly, it is Mbum women who teach their children that little boys cannot stand vegetables and that women are foolish and quarrelsome.

Within the mesh of ideological elaborations of male dominance, accepted to some extent by women as well as men, the force of the prohibitions on consumption of goats and chickens by women becomes clearer. Women are in some ways like chickens and goats—animals domesticated by men and kept primarily for reproduction, not to be consumed but to multiply through breeding to bring wealth to their owners through exchange.[19]

As a form of surplus product, by definition not intended for subsistence, livestock are linked to the process of reproduction of the means of production, just as women are linked to the processes of reproduction of labor. This structural equivalence between livestock and women is explicitly recognized by including livestock in bridewealth payments. And bridewealth, as we have previously seen, is that link between the reproduction of labor and the reproduction of the means of production upon which the dominance of senior men is based. Women, then, are barred

18 Ideological expressions of sexual asymmetry are so numerous that only a few are mentioned here. Maleness is equated with being strong, durable, and aggressive, while femininity is associated with being silly, passive, and transient. There is a proverb that says: "The things of men go forward, forward; the things of women go backward, backward." When a mother hen flies to defend her chicks, it is said that she is "coming out and doing the man." The right hand, the eating hand, is the side of men, and the left hand, the fouled hand, the side of women. The term used to designate an old man is an honorific, while the term used for an old woman is insulting if used in her presence. The ancestors are referred to as "the fathers," although it is said that when a sacrifice is large, the spirits of women may sometimes crouch alongside their brothers to be given a small share of the food.

19 In this paper I have stressed the basis of the chicken/woman metaphor in structures of production and reproduction, but the metaphor may also express other representations of sexual asymmetry. Mary Douglas (1966), for example, has related the prohibition of Lele women's eating chicken to the problem of category mixing: chickens are animals living in the village, just like women and children.

Nor is the metaphorical relationship between women and chickens exhausted by the simile of the domesticated animal, for there are other prohibitions forbidding game birds and eggs to women on pain of sterility. A further expression of the woman/egg relation occurs in childbirth among the Mbum: "When the water breaks, the women cry out: 'The chicken egg has shattered.'" This paper is not, however, an attempt to fully interpret a symbolic system, but is only intended to demonstrate how one particular set of ideological representations may serve to mediate contradictions.

from the consumption of that which is both metaphorically like and structurally equivalent to them, just as they are barred from control of the fruits of their own reproduction (bridewealth as well as children).

The prohibition on chicken and goat, taken by itself, is no more than a supportive reflection of the sexual asymmetry in Mbum social relations, marking sexual distance in ritually important situations such as beer parties and sacrifices, and subordinating women to male privilege. The real strength of the prohibition, however, is in its reputed means of enforcement: the retribution of reproductive failure—sterility, and pain or death in childbirth. Moral guilt is assigned to women for that which makes them vulnerable to male dominance.[20] Reproduction of a set of social relations in contradiction is ideologically merged with reproduction of labor: that which is arbitrary and culturally determined is morally linked to that which is biologically necessary, that women successfully bear children.

It thus appears that the prohibition of chicken and goat to Mbum women is a further instance of the often noted metaphorical connection between marriage rules and food taboos (see Lévi-Strauss, 1963b). However, the marriage rule metaphorically stated as a food prohibition does not describe a pattern of exchange of women, but instead defines the underlying subordination of women inherent in systems where women become relations between groups of men. A causal link is metaphorically established between an expression of sexual asymmetry in social relations (i.e. that women not eat foods reserved for men), and that which reproduces people themselves. When Mbum women do not eat chicken, there is an illusive ideological mediation of the contradiction implicit in the alienation of women from aspects of their own powers of reproduction.

Conclusions

That symbolic expression of sexual asymmetry should be rooted in biological reproduction is not surprising, for differing reproductive systems are, after all, the basic physiological difference between men and women. The conversion from difference to asymmetry must, however, be socially motivated, that is, explained by reference to social practice. Since degrees and expressions of sexual asymmetry vary so widely in different societies, one must look at particular cases in order to see how

---

[20] For a structurally similar prohibition, compare the result of Eve's eating of the forbidden fruit of a domesticated tree: "I will make great your distress in child-bearing; in pain shall you bring forth children; for your husband shall be your longing, though he have dominion over you" (Genesis 3: 16).

the "natural division of labor" is socially and ideologically extended into relations of sexual inequality.

In the Mbum Kpau case, as in a number of other African societies, it is not biological constraint on technical relations but rather the linking of biological reproduction to infrastructural relations of production that is the basis of social asymmetry, defined by both sex and relative age. Marriage and economy in Mbum society are not then separate parallel systems of communication sharing common deep structures and linked only by metonymical transformations (see Lévi-Strauss, 1963a); they are instead part of a single system of social production. The functional interdependence of the two systems supports structures of social asymmetry in the dominance of senior males, but this is not to say that structure is therefore either harmonic and free of contradiction or a direct reflection of the division of labor. Quite the contrary, for many aspects of Mbum superstructure and ideology (the male initiation cycle, residence rules, the ancestral cult, food prohibitions, etc.) are concerned with the enforcement of senior male dominance and mediation of infrastructural contradiction. Consciousness can be no measure of contradiction, since, as in the instance described in this paper, women themselves may live out the representation of their own inferiority.

To find the basis of sexual asymmetry in the social rather than technical relations of production in the Mbum case is not to embrace a psycho-physiological explanation for the nearly universal subordination of women to men. For societies exist in history, power breeds power, and the reproduction of a particular set of social relations of production can be both condition and consequence of social reproduction.

One can easily imagine (but not so easily reconstruct scientifically) a stage of the development of the material forces of production in which female vulnerability during childbearing and extended nursing may have led to the establishment of male control of the forces of production. Yet such quests for origin—whether fanciful or scientific—are often essentially mythical: in arguments from genesis, explanation of inequality in the present social order may become apology. The more important question is how, given a more advanced technological order (perhaps that of the Mbum Kpau and certainly that of the industrial West), such structures of male dominance are reproduced. Here the Mbum material is particularly rich as an illustration of the ways in which functional interdependence of infrastructure and superstructure and ideological mediation of contradiction support disharmonic social orders.

Finally, since ideology is allusion to underlying reality as well as illusion (Althusser, 1971: 162), interpretation of representations of sexual asymmetry may provide clues to the anthropologist attempting to determine the functional position of women's subordination in a particular society. In the Mbum case, for example, the metaphorical equivalence of women and livestock in the food prohibition represents both an illusion—the natural necessity of male privilege—and an allusion to the rooting of basic social relations of production in the bridewealth system. So it would seem that a comparable analysis of competitive rituals of beauty (or even of a language of social science that describes women as commodities) might provide some insight into the place of sexual asymmetry in a society that so tenaciously treats relations between persons as relations between things.

References Cited

References Cited

Rosaldo and Lamphere: Introduction

Ardener, Edwin. 1971. "Belief and the Problem of Women," in J. S. La Fontaine, ed., The Interpretation of Ritual, Essays in Honour of A. I. Richards. London.

Bachofen, J. J. 1861. Das Mutterrecht. Stuttgart.

Bailey, F. G. 1969. Stratagems and Spoils. New York.

Bardwick, Judith M. 1971. The Psychology of Women: A Study of Bio-Cultural Conflicts. New York.

Barth, Fredrik. 1959. Political Leadership Among Swat Pathans. London School of Economics, Monograph 19.

Chiñas, Beverly L. 1973. The Isthmus Zapotecs: Women's Roles in Cultural Context. New York.

Davis, Elizabeth Gould. 1972. The First Sex. Baltimore.

De Beauvoir, Simone. 1953. The Second Sex. New York. Originally published in French in 1949.

Fernea, Elizabeth Warnock. 1965. Guests of the Sheik: An Ethnography of an Iraqi Village. Garden City, N.Y.

Firth, Raymond. 1962. Essays in Social Organization and Values. London School of Economics, Monograph 28.

Geertz, Clifford. 1962. "The Growth of Culture and the Evolution of Mind," in J. Scher, ed., Theories of Mind. New York.

Goodale, Jane C. 1971. Tiwi Wives. Seattle.

Hutt, Corinne. 1972. Males and Females. Middlesex, Eng.

Kaberry, Phyllis M. 1939. Aboriginal Women, Sacred and Profane. London.
———— 1952. Women of the Grassfields. London.

Kreuz, Leo, Robert Rose, and J. Richard Jennings. 1972. "Psychological Stress Results in Suppression of Androgen Activity," Archives of General Psychiatry, 26: 479–82.

Landes, Ruth. 1938. The Ojibwa Woman. Part I: Youth. New York: Columbia University Contributions to Anthropology, vol. 31.
———— 1947. The City of Women: Negro Women Cult Leaders of Bahia, Brazil. New York.

Leach, Edmund. 1954. Political Systems of Highland Burma. Boston.

Leacock, Eleanor B. 1972. "Introduction" to Origin of the Family, Private Property and the State, by F. Engels. New York.

Leith-Ross, Sylvia. 1965. African Women. New York.

Linton, Sally. 1973. "Woman the Gatherer: Male Bias in Anthropology," in Sue-Ellen Jacobs, Women in Perspective: A Guide for Cross-Cultural Studies. Urbana, Ill.

Maccoby, Eleanor, ed. 1966. The Development of Sex Differences. Stanford, Calif.

Maccoby, Eleanor, and Carol N. Jacklin. 1974. The Psychology of Sex Differences. Stanford, Calif., forthcoming.

Money, John, and Anke A. Ehrhardt. 1972. Man and Woman, Boy and Girl. Baltimore.

Morgan, Elaine. 1972. The Descent of Woman. New York.

Morgan, Lewis Henry. 1851. League of the Hodenosaunee, Iroquois. Rochester, N.Y.

———— 1877. Ancient Society. New York.

Paulme, Denise, ed. 1963. Women of Tropical Africa. Berkeley, Calif.

Rowell, Thelma. 1972. The Social Behavior of Monkeys. Middlesex, Eng.

Schlegel, Alice. 1972. Male Dominance and Female Autonomy: Domestic Authority in Matrilineal Societies. New Haven.

Strathern, Marilyn. 1972. Women in Between: Female Roles in a Male World: Mount Hagen, New Guinea. New York.

Sweet, Louise. 1967. "Appearance and Reality: Status and Roles of Women in Mediterranean Societies," *Anthropological Quarterly*, 40 (entire issue).

Tanner, Nancy, and Adrienne Zihlman. n.d. "Becoming Human: A Model for the Reconstruction of Early Human Social Life." Unpublished manuscript.

Washburn, Sherwood L., and C. S. Lancaster. 1968. "The Evolution of Hunting," in Richard B. Lee and Irven DeVore, eds., Man the Hunter. Chicago.

Webster, Paula, and Esther Newton. 1972. "Matriarchy: Puzzle and Paradigm." Paper presented at the 71st Annual Meeting of the American Anthropological Association, Toronto.

Wolf, Margery. 1972. Women and the Family in Rural Taiwan. Stanford, Calif.

Rosaldo: A Theoretical Overview

Bachofen, J. J. 1967. Myth, Religion and Mother Right. Selected Writings. Ralph Mannheim, trans. Bollingen Series, 84. Princeton, N.J.

Bardwick, Judith M. 1971. Psychology of Women: A Study of Bio-Cultural Conflicts. New York.

Barry, Herbert, M. K. Bacon, and I. L. Child. 1957. "A Cross-Cultural Survey of Some Sex Differences in Socialization," *Journal of Abnormal and Social Psychology*, 55: 327–32.

Bateson, Gregory. 1958. Naven. Stanford, Calif.

Bettelheim, Bruno. 1954. Symbolic Wounds: Puberty Rites and the Envious Male. New York.

Bloch, Maurice. 1971. Placing the Dead. London.

Brown, Judith K. 1970a. "Economic Organization and the Position of Women Among the Iroquois," *Ethnohistory*, 17 (3–4): 151–67.

———— 1970b. "A Note on the Division of Labor by Sex," *American Anthropologist*, 72: 1073–78.

Campbell, J. K. 1964. Honor, Family and Patronage. Oxford.

Cancian, Francesca. n.d. What Are Norms? Chicago. Forthcoming.

Chodorow, Nancy. 1971. "Being and Doing," in Vivian Gornick and B. K. Moran, eds., Women in Sexist Society. New York.

Collier, Jane F. 1973. Law and Social Change in Zinacantan. Stanford, Calif.

Davis, Elizabeth Gould. 1972. The First Sex. Baltimore.

Deacon, A. Bernard. 1934. Malekula: A Vanishing People. London.

De Beauvoir, Simone. 1953. The Second Sex. New York. Originally published in French in 1949.

Douglas, Mary. 1966. Purity and Danger. New York.

Durkheim, Emile. 1964. The Division of Labor in Society, trans. George Simpson. New York. Originally published in French in 1911.

Ellman, Mary. 1968. Thinking About Women. New York.

Engels, Friedrich. 1891. The Origin of the Family, Private Property and the State, 4th ed. Moscow.

Felstiner, Mary. 1973. Personal communication.

Fernea, Elizabeth. 1965. Guests of the Sheik: An Ethnography of an Iraqi Village. Garden City, N.Y.

Fortune, Rio. 1932. Sorcerers of Dobu. London.

Harper, E. B. 1969. "Fear and the Status of Women," *Southwestern Journal of Anthropology*, 25: 81–95.

Hogbin, Ian. 1970. The Island of Menstruating Men. Scranton, Pa.

Kaberry, Phyllis. 1939. Aboriginal Women, Sacred and Profane. London.

Keenan, Elinor. 1974. "Norm-Makers, Norm-Breakers: Uses of Speech by Men and Women in a Malagasy Community," in R. Bauman and J. Sherzer, eds., Explorations in the Ethnography of Speaking. Cambridge, Eng. (In press.)

Krige, E. Jenson, and J. D. Krige. 1943. The Realm of a Rain Queen. London.

Landes, Ruth. 1971. The Ojibwa Woman. New York.

Lebeuf, Annie. 1963. "The Role of Women in the Political Organization of African Societies," in Denise Paulme, ed., Women of Tropical Africa. Berkeley, Calif. Originally published in French in 1960.

Lee, Richard B. 1968. "What Hunters Do for a Living, or How to Make Out on Scarce Resources," in Richard B. Lee and Irven DeVore, eds., Man the Hunter, pp. 30–48. Chicago.

Lévi-Strauss, Claude. 1949. Les structures élémentaires de la parenté. Paris.

Lewin, Ellen, J. Collier, M. Rosaldo, and J. Fjellman. 1971. "Power Strategies and Sex Roles." Paper presented at the 70th Annual Meeting of the American Anthropological Association. New York.

Lewis, I. M. 1971. Ecstatic Religion. London.

Liebow, Elliot. 1967. Tally's Corner. Boston.

Linton, Sally. 1973. "Woman the Gatherer: Male Bias in Anthropology," in Sue-Ellen Jacobs, Women in Perspective: A Guide for Cross-Cultural Studies. Urbana, Ill.

Little, Kenneth. 1951. The Mende of Sierra Leone—A West African People in Transition. London.

Lloyd, P. C. 1965. "The Yoruba of Nigeria," in James L. Gibbs, ed., Peoples of Africa, pp. 547–82. New York.

Mead, Margaret. 1935. Sex and Temperament in Three Primitive Societies. London.

——— 1949. Male and Female. New York.

——— 1971. The Mountain Arapesh. New York. Originally published in 1938.

Meggit, M. J. 1964. "Male-Female Relationships in the Highlands of Australian New Guinea," *American Anthropologist*, 66 (4, part II): 204–24.

———— 1965. "The Mae Enga of the Western Highlands," in Lawrence P. and M. J. Meggit, eds., Gods, Ghosts and Men in Melanesia. Oxford.

Murdock, George P. 1934. Our Primitive Contemporaries. New York.

Murphy, Robert. 1959. "Social Structure and Sex Antagonism," *Southwestern Journal of Anthropology*, 15.

———— 1964. "Social Distance and the Weil," *American Anthropologist*, 66: 1257–74.

Nadel, S. F. 1952. "Witchcraft in Four Societies: An Essay in Comparison," *American Anthropologist*, 54.

Parsons, Talcott. 1964. Social Structure and Personality. New York.

Parsons, Talcott, and Edward Shils, eds. 1951. Toward a General Theory of Social Action. Cambridge, Mass.

Paulme, Denise. 1963. "Introduction," in Denise Paulme, ed., Women of Tropical Africa. Berkeley, Calif. Originally published in French in 1960.

Schneider, David. 1968. American Kinship: A Cultural Account. Englewood Cliffs, N.J.

Shapiro, Judith. 1970. "Yamomamo Women: How the Other Half Lives." Paper presented at the 69th Annual Meeting of the American Anthropological Association, San Diego.

Simmel, Georg. 1955. Conflict and the Web of Group Affiliations, trans. Kurt Wolff and Reinhard Bendix. New York. Originally published in German in 1922–23.

Smith, Michael G. 1960. Government in Zazau. London.

Tiger, Lionel. 1969. Men in Groups. New York.

Turnbull, Colin. 1961. The Forest People. New York.

Weber, Max. 1947. The Theory of Social and Economic Organization, trans. and ed. Talcott Parsons. New York.

Wolf, Margery. 1972. Women and the Family in Rural Taiwan. Stanford, Calif.

Zborowski, Mary, and Elizabeth Herzog. 1955. Life Is with People. New York.

Zelditch, Morris. 1955. "Role Differentiation in the Nuclear Family," in T. Parsons and R. Bales, eds., Family, Socialization and Interaction Process, pp. 307–52. New York.

———— 1964. "Cross-Cultural Analysis of Family Structure," in H. T. Christensen, ed., Handbook of Marriage and the Family, pp. 462–500. Chicago.

Chodorow: Family Structure and Feminine Personality

Ariès, Philippe. 1962. Centuries of Childhood: A Social History of Family Life. New York.

Bakan, David. 1966. The Duality of Human Existence: Isolation and Communion in Western Man. Boston.

———— 1968. Disease, Pain, and Sacrifice: Toward a Psychology of Suffering. Boston.

Balint, Alice. 1954. The Early Years of Life: A Psychoanalytic Study. New York.

Barry, Herbert, M. K. Bacon, and I. L. Child. 1957. "A Cross-Cultural Survey of Some Sex Differences in Socialization," *Journal of Abnormal and Social Psychology*, 55: 327–32.

Bettelheim, Bruno. 1954. Symbolic Wounds: Puberty Rites and the Envious Male. New York.

Bibring, Grete. 1953. "On the 'Passing of the Oedipus Complex' in a Matriarchal Family Setting," in Rudolph M. Lowenstein, ed., Drives, Affects and Behavior: Essays in Honor of Marie Bonaparte. New York, pp. 278–84.

Brunswick, Ruth Mack. 1940. "The Preoedipal Phase of the Libido Development," in Robert Fliess, ed., pp. 231–53.

Burton, Roger V., and John W. M. Whiting. 1961. "The Absent Father and Cross-Sex Identity," Merrill-Palmer Quarterly of Behavior and Development, 7, no. 2: 85–95.

Carlson, Rae. 1971. "Sex Differences in Ego Functioning: Exploratory Studies of Agency and Communion," Journal of Consulting and Clinical Psychology, 37: 267–77.

Chodorow, Nancy. 1971. "Being and Doing. A Cross-Cultural Examination of the Socialization of Males and Females," in Vivian Gornick and B. K. Moran, eds., Woman in Sexist Society: Studies in Power and Powerlessness. New York.

Cohen, Rosalie A. 1969. "Conceptual Styles, Culture Conflict, and Nonverbal Tests of Intelligence," American Anthropologist, 71: 828–56.

Deutsch, Helene. 1925. "The Psychology of Woman in Relation to the Functions of Reproduction," in Robert Fliess, ed., pp. 165–79.

——— 1930. "The Significance of Masochism in the Mental Life of Women," in Robert Fliess, ed., pp. 195–207.

——— 1932. "On Female Homosexuality," in Robert Fliess, ed., pp. 208–30.

——— 1944, 1945. Psychology of Women, Vols. I, II. New York.

Durkheim, Emile. 1897. Suicide. New York, 1968.

Erikson, Erik H. 1964. Insight and Responsibility. New York.

——— 1965. "Womanhood and the Inner Space," in Robert Jay Lifton, ed., The Woman in America. Cambridge, Mass.

Fairbairn, W. Ronald D. 1952. An Object-Relations Theory of the Personality. New York.

Fliess, Robert. 1948. "Female and Preoedipal Sexuality: A Historical Survey," in Robert Fliess, ed., pp. 159–64.

——— 1961. Ego and Body Ego: Contributions to Their Psychoanalytic Psychology. New York, 1970.

Fliess, Robert, ed. 1969. The Psychoanalytic Reader: An Anthology of Essential Papers with Critical Introductions. New York. Originally published in 1948.

Freedman, David. 1961. "On Women Who Hate Their Husbands," in Hendrik M. Ruitenbeek, ed., pp. 221–37.

Freud, Sigmund. 1925. "Some Psychological Consequences of the Anatomical Distinction Between the Sexes," in James Strachey, ed., The Standard Edition of the Complete Psychological Works of Sigmund Freud, Vol. XIX. London, pp. 248–58.

——— 1931. "Female Sexuality," in Ruitenbeek, ed., pp. 88–105.

——— 1933. "Femininity," in New Introductory Lectures in Psychoanalysis. New York, 1961, pp. 112–35.

Geertz, Hildred. 1961. The Javanese Family: A Study of Kinship and Socialization. New York.

Guntrip, Harry. 1961. Personality Structure and Human Interaction: The Developing Synthesis of Psycho-Dynamic Theory. New York.

Gutmann, David. 1965. "Women and the Conception of Ego Strength," *Merrill-Palmer Quarterly of Behavior and Development*, 2: 229–40.

Harper, Edward B. 1969. "Fear and the Status of Women," *Southwestern Journal of Anthropology*, 25: 81–95.

Jay, Robert R. 1969. Javanese Villagers: Social Relations in Rural Modjokuto. Cambridge, Mass.

Jones, Ernest. 1927. "The Early Development of Female Sexuality," in Ruitenbeek, ed., pp. 21–35.

Klein, Melanie, and Joan Rivière. 1937. Love, Hate and Reparation. New York, 1964.

Kohlberg, Lawrence. 1966. "A Cognitive-Developmental Analysis of Children's Sex-Role Concepts and Attitudes," in Eleanor E. Maccoby, ed., The Development of Sex Differences. Stanford, Calif., pp. 82–173.

Komarovsky, Mirra. 1962. Blue-Collar Marriage. New York, 1967.

Lampl-de Groot, J. 1927. "The Evolution of the Oedipus Complex in Women," in Robert Fliess, ed., pp. 180–94.

LeVine, Robert A. 1971a. "The Psychoanalytic Study of Lives in Natural Social Settings," *Human Development*, 14: 100–109.

——— 1971b. "Re-thinking Psychoanalytic Anthropology." Paper presented at the Institute on Psychoanalytic Anthropology, 70th Annual Meeting of the American Anthropological Association, New York.

Mead, Margaret. 1935. Sex and Temperament in Three Primitive Societies. New York, 1963.

——— 1949. Male and Female: A Study of Sexes in a Changing World. New York, 1968.

Millman, Marcia. 1972. "Tragedy and Exchange: Metaphoric Understandings of Interpersonal Relationships." Ph.D. dissertation, Department of Sociology, Brandeis University.

Minturn, Leigh, and John T. Hitchcock. 1963. "The Rajputs of Khalapur, India," in Beatrice B. Whiting, ed., Six Cultures: Studies in Child Rearing. New York.

Mitscherlich, Alexander. 1963. Society Without the Father. New York, 1970.

Parsons, Talcott. 1964. Social Structure and Personality. New York.

Parsons, Talcott, and Robert F. Bales. 1955. Family, Socialization and Interaction Process. New York.

Ruitenbeek, Hendrik M., ed. 1966. Psychoanalysis and Female Sexuality. New Haven.

Siegel, James T. 1969. The Rope of God. Berkeley, Calif.

Slater, Philip E. 1961. "Toward a Dualistic Theory of Identification," *Merrill-Palmer Quarterly of Behavior and Development*, 7: 113–26.

——— 1968. The Glory of Hera: Greek Mythology and the Greek Family. Boston.

——— 1970. The Pursuit of Loneliness: American Culture at the Breaking Point. Boston.

Tanner, Nancy. 1971. "Matrifocality in Indonesia and Among Black Americans." Paper presented at the 70th Annual Meeting of the American Anthropological Association, New York.

Tax, Meredith. 1970. Woman and Her Mind: The Story of Daily Life. Boston.

Thompson, Clara. 1943. " 'Penis Envy' in Women," in Ruitenbeek, ed., pp. 246–51.

Whiting, John W. M. 1959. "Sorcery, Sin, and the Superego: A Cross-Cultural Study of Some Mechanisms of Social Control," in Clellan S. Ford, ed., Cross-Cultural Approaches: Readings in Comparative Research. New Haven, 1967, pp. 147–68.

Whiting, John W. M., Richard Kluckhohn, and Albert Anthony. 1958. "The Function of Male Initiation Rites at Puberty," in Eleanor E. Maccoby, T. M. Newcomb, and E. L. Hartley, eds., Readings in Social Psychology. New York, pp. 359–70.

Winch, Robert F. 1962. Identification and Its Familial Determinants. New York.

Young, Michael, and Peter Willmott. 1957. Family and Kinship in East London. London, 1966.

Ortner: Is Female to Male as Nature Is to Culture?

Bakan, David. 1966. The Duality of Human Existence. Boston.

Carlson, Rae. 1971. "Sex Differences in Ego Functioning: Exploratory Studies of Agency and Communion," *Journal of Consulting and Clinical Psychology*, 37: 267–77.

De Beauvoir, Simone. 1953. The Second Sex. New York. Originally published in French in 1949.

Ingham, John M. 1971. "Are the Sirionó Raw or Cooked?" *American Anthropologist*, 73: 1092–99.

Lévi-Strauss, Claude. 1969a. The Elementary Structures of Kinship. Trans. J. H. Bell and J. R. von Sturmer; ed. R. Needham. Boston.

———— 1969b. The Raw and the Cooked. Trans. J. and D. Weightman. New York.

Lowie, Robert. 1956. The Crow Indians. New York. Originally published in 1935.

Ortner, Sherry B. 1973. "Sherpa Purity," *American Anthropologist*, 75: 49–63.

———— n.d. "Purification Beliefs and Practices," *Encyclopaedia Britannica*, forthcoming.

Pitt-Rivers, Julian. 1961. People of the Sierra. Chicago.

Siu, R. G. H. 1968. The Man of Many Qualities. Cambridge, Mass.

Ullman, Stephen. 1963. "Semantic Universals," in Joseph H. Greenberg, ed., Universals of Language. Cambridge, Mass.

Collier: Women in Politics

Bailey, Frederick G. 1969. Stratagems and Spoils. New York.

Barth, Fredrik. 1959. Political Leadership Among Swat Pathans. London School of Economics, Monograph 19.

———— 1966. Models of Social Organization. Royal Anthropological Institute, Occasional Papers 23.

Buchler, Ira, and Hugu Nutini, eds. 1970. Game Theory in the Behavioral Sciences. Pittsburgh, Pa.

Campbell, John K. 1964. Honour, Family and Patronage: A Study of Institutions and Moral Values in a Greek Mountain Community. London.

Clark, Terry N. 1968. "The Concept of Power," in T. Clark, ed., Community Structure and Decision-Making: Comparative Analyses. San Francisco.

Cohen, Ronald. 1971. Dominance and Defiance, a Study of Marital Instability in an Islamic Society. Anthropological Studies No. 6, American Anthropological Association, Washington, D.C.

Collier, Jane F. 1973. Law and Social Change in Zinacantan. Stanford, California.

Dahrendorf, Ralf. 1968. "On the Origin of Inequality among Men," in R. Dahrendorf, Essays in the Theory of Society. Stanford, California.

Evans-Pritchard, E. E. 1963. The Position of Women in Primitive Societies and Other Essays in Social Anthropology. New York.

Fallers, Lloyd A. 1969. Law Without Precedent: Legal Ideas in Action in the Courts of Colonial Busoga. Chicago.

Firth, Raymond. 1951. Elements of Social Organization. London.

Fox, Robin. 1967. Kinship and Marriage: An Anthropological Perspective. Baltimore.

Gibbs, James L., Jr. 1963. "Marital Instability among the Kpelle: Towards a Theory of Epainogamy," *American Anthropologist*, 65: 552–73.

Gluckman, Max. 1965. Politics, Law and Ritual in Tribal Society. Chicago.

Gough, Kathleen. 1971. "Nuer Kinship: A Re-examination," in T. O. Beidelman, ed., The Translation of Culture. London.

Michaelson, Evalyn Jacobson, and Walter Goldschmidt. 1971. "Female Roles and Male Dominance Among Peasants," *Southwestern Journal of Anthropology*, 27: 330–53.

Runciman, W. G. 1968. "Class, Status and Power" in J. A. Jackson, ed., Social Stratification. London.

Schneider, David. 1961. Introductory essay in D. M. Schneider and Kathleen Gough, eds., Matrilineal Kinship. Berkeley, California.

Turner, Victor. 1957. Schism and Continuity in an African Society: A Study of Ndembu Village Life. Manchester, Eng.

Whitten, Norman E., Jr., and Dorothea S. Whitten. 1972. "Social Strategies and Social Relationships," *Annual Review of Anthropology*, 1973.

Wolf, Margery. 1972. Women and the Family in Rural Taiwan. Stanford, California.

Lamphere: Women in Domestic Groups

Aberle, D. F. 1961. "The Navaho," in David Schneider and Kathleen Gough, eds., Matrilineal Kinship. Berkeley, Calif.

Bailey, F. G. 1969. Stratagems and Spoils. New York.

Barth, Fredrik. 1959. Political Leadership Among Swat Pathans. London School of Economics, Monograph 19.

Billingsley, Andrew. 1968. Black Families in White America. Englewood Cliffs, N.J.

Bott, Elizabeth, ed. 1968. Family and Social Network. London.

Briggs, Jean. 1970. Never in Anger. Cambridge, Mass.

Clignet, Remi. 1970. Many Wives, Many Powers. Evanston, Ill.

Cohen, Ronald. 1971. Dominance and Defiance, a Study of Marital Instability in an Islamic Society. Anthropological Studies no. 6, American Anthropological Association, Washington, D.C.

Damas, D. 1968. "The Diversity of Eskimo Societies," in Richard B. Lee and Irven DeVore, eds., Man the Hunter. Chicago.

Fortes, Meyer, ed. 1949. Social Structure: Studies Presented to A. R. Radcliffe-Brown. New York.

——— 1950. "Kinship and Marriage Among the Ashanti," in A. R. Radcliffe-Brown and Daryll Forde, eds., African Systems of Kinship and Marriage. New York.

Fortes, Meyer, and E. E. Evans-Pritchard, eds. 1940. African Political Systems. New York.

Friedl, Ernestine. 1967. "The Position of Women: Appearance and Reality," *Anthropological Quarterly*, 40: 97–108.

Gluckman, Max. 1950. "Kinship and Marriage Among the Lozi of Northern Rhodesia and the Zulu of Natal," in A. R. Radcliffe-Brown and Daryll Forde, eds., African Systems of Kinship and Marriage. New York.

Goldschmidt, Walter, and Evalyn Jacobson Kunkel. 1971. "The Structure of the Peasant Family," *American Anthropologist*, 73: 1058–76.

Goody, J., ed. 1958. The Developmental Cycle of Domestic Groups. Cambridge Papers in Social Anthropology no. 1. London.

Hoebel, E. A. 1954. The Law of Primitive Man. New York.

Ladner, Joyce. 1971. Tomorrow's Tomorrow: The Black Woman. New York.

Ladner, Joyce, ed. 1973. The Death of White Sociology. New York.

Lamphere, Louise. 1971. "The Navajo Cultural System: An Analysis of Concepts of Cooperation and Autonomy and Their Relation to Gossip and Witchcraft," in Keith Basso and Morris Opler, eds., Apachean Culture History and Ethnology. Tucson, Ariz.

——— 1974. To Run After Them: Cultural and Social Bases of Cooperation in a Navajo Community. Tucson, Ariz., forthcoming.

Leach, Edmund. 1954. Political Systems of Highland Burma. Reprinted Boston, 1964.

——— 1955. "Polyandry, Inheritance, and the Definition of Marriage," *Man* 55: 182–86.

Lee, Richard. 1968. "What Hunters Do for a Living or How to Make Out on Scarce Resources," in Richard B. Lee and Irven DeVore, eds., Man the Hunter. Chicago.

——— 1972. "!Kung Spatial Organization: An Ecological and Historical Perspective," *Human Ecology*, 1, no. 2: 125–47.

Liebow, Elliot. 1967. Tally's Corner, Boston.

Marshall, Gloria. 1964. "Women, Trade, and the Yoruba Family." Unpublished Ph.D. dissertation, Columbia University.

Marshall, Lorna. 1959. "Marriage among the !Kung Bushman," *Africa*, 29, no. 4: 335–65.

——— 1960. "!Kung Bushman Bands," *Africa*, 30, no. 4: 325–54. Reprinted in R. Cohen and J. Middleton, eds., Comparative Political Systems. New York.

Michaelson, Evalyn Jacobson, and Walter Goldschmidt. 1971. "Female Roles and Male Dominance Among Peasants," *Southwestern Journal of Anthropology*, 27: 330–52.

Minturn, Leigh, and John T. Hitchcock. 1966. The Rajputs of Khalapur, India. Six Cultures Series, Vol. III. New York.

Parsons, Talcott. 1963a. "On the Concept of Power," *Proceedings of the American Philosophical Society*, 107: 232–62.

———— 1963b. "On the Concept of Influence," *Public Opinion Quarterly*, 27: 37–62.

Radcliffe-Brown, A. R. 1950. "Introduction," in A. R. Radcliffe-Brown and Daryll Forde, eds., African Systems of Kinship and Marriage. New York.

Rainwater, Lee, and William Yancey, eds. 1967. The Moynihan Report and the Politics of Controversy. Cambridge, Mass.

Schneider, David, and Kathleen Gough. 1961. Matrilineal Kinship. Berkeley, Calif.

Spencer, Robert F., Jesse D. Jennings, et al. 1965. The Native Americans. New York.

Stack, Carol. 1972. "Kindred and Exchange Networks in a Black Community." Unpublished Ph.D. dissertation, University of Illinois.

Tiger, Lionel. 1969. Men in Groups. New York.

Weber, Max. 1947. The Theory of Social and Economic Organization. Trans. by A. M. Henderson and Talcott Parsons. New York.

Witherspoon, Gary. 1970. "A New Look at Navajo Social Organization," *American Anthropologist*, 70: 55–65.

Wolf, Margery. 1968. The House of Lim. New York.

———— 1972. Women and the Family in Rural Taiwan. Stanford, Calif.

Young, Michael, and Peter Willmott. 1957. Family and Kinship in East London. London.

Stack: Sex Roles and Survival Strategies

Abrahams, Roger. 1963. Deep Down in the Jungle. Hatboro, Pa.

Bernard, Jessie. 1966. Marriage and Family Among Negroes. Englewood Cliffs, N.J.

Buchler, Ira R., and Henry A. Selby. 1968. Kinship and Social Organization: An Introduction to Theory and Method. New York.

Fortes, Meyer, 1958. "Introduction," in Jack Goody, ed., The Developmental Cycle in Domestic Groups. Cambridge, Eng.

Gonzalez, Nancie. 1965. "The Consanguineal Household and Matrifocality," *American Anthropologist*, 67: 1541–49.

———— 1969. Black Carib Household Structure: A Study of Migration and Modernization. Seattle.

———— 1970. "Toward a Definition of Matrifocality," in N. E. Whitten and J. F. Szwed, eds., Afro-American Anthropology: Contemporary Perspectives. New York.

Hannerz, Ulf. 1969. Soulside: Inquiries into Ghetto Culture and Community. New York.

Ladner, Joyce. 1971. Tomorrow's Tomorrow: The Black Woman. Garden City, N.Y.

Liebow, Elliot. 1967. Tally's Corner. Boston.

Moynihan, Daniel Patrick. 1965. The Negro Family: The Case for National Action. Prepared for the Office of Policy Planning and Research of the Department of Labor, Washington, D.C.

Otterbein, Keith F. 1970. "The Developmental Cycle of the Andros Household: A Diachronic Analysis," *American Anthropologist*, 72: 1412–19.

Rainwater, Lee. 1966. "Crucible of Identity: The Negro Lower-Class Family," *Daedalus*, 95 (2): 172–216.

Smith, Raymond. 1970. "The Nuclear Family in Afro-American Kinship," *Journal of Comparative Family Studies*, 1 (1): 55–70.

Stack, Carol B. 1970. "The Kindred of Viola Jackson: Residence and Family Organization of an Urban Black American Family," in N. E. Whitten and J. F. Szwed, eds., Afro-American Anthropology: Contemporary Perspectives. New York.

——— 1972. "Black Kindreds: Parenthood and Personal Kindreds Among Blacks Supported by Welfare," *Journal of Comparative Family Studies*, 3 (2): 194–206.

——— 1974. All Our Kin: Strategies for Survival in a Black Community. New York.

Valentine, Charles. 1970. "Blackston: Progress Report on a Community Study in Urban Afro-America." Mimeo. Washington University, St. Louis.

Tanner: Matrifocality

Bell, Carol. 1971. "A Re-evaluation of the Matrifocal Family in Latin America and the Caribbean." Unpublished manuscript.

Dewey, Alice. 1962. Peasant Marketing in Java. New York.

Epstein, Cynthia Fuchs. 1973. "Black and Female: The Double Whammy," *Psychology Today*, August.

Geertz, Clifford. 1963. Agricultural Involution: The Processes of Ecological Change in Indonesia. Berkeley, Calif.

Geertz, Hildred. 1961. The Javanese Family: A Study of Kinship and Socialization. New York.

Glazer, Nathan, and Daniel P. Moynihan. 1963. Beyond the Melting Pot. Cambridge, Mass.

Gonzalez, Nancie L. 1969. Black Carib Household Structure. A Study of Migration and Modernization. Seattle.

——— 1970. "Toward a Definition of Matrifocality," in Norman E. Whitten, Jr., and John F. Szwed, eds., Afro-American Anthropology: Contemporary Perspectives. New York.

Green, M. M. 1947. Ibo Village Affairs. New York.

Henderson, Helen. 1969. "Ritual Roles of Women in Onitsha Ibo Society." Ph.D. dissertation, University of California, Berkeley.

Henderson, Richard N. 1967. "Onitsha Ibo Kinship Terminology: A Formal Analysis and Its Functional Applications," *Southwestern Journal of Anthropology*, 23: 15–51.

——— 1972. The King in Every Man: Evolutionary Trends in Onitsha Ibo Society and Culture. New Haven.

Herskovits, Melville J. 1941. The Myth of the Negro Past. New York.

——— 1967. Dahomey, An Ancient West African Kingdom. 2 vols. (Originally published in 1938.) Evanston, Ill.

Iljas Pajakumbuh. n.d. Hikajat si Umbuik Mudo dengan Puti Galang Banjak. C.V. Pustaka Indonesia. Bukittinggi.

Jack, Lenus, Jr. 1973. "Kinship and Residential Propinquity: A Study of the Black Extended Family in New Orleans." IXth International Congress of Anthropological and Ethnological Sciences. Chicago.

Johns, Anthony H., ed. and trans. 1958. Rantjak di Labueh: A Minangkabau Kaba. Cornell Modern Indonesia Project. Ithaca, N.Y.

Kunstadter, Peter. 1963. "A Survey of the Consanguine or Matrifocal Family," *American Anthropologist*, 65: 56–66.

Ladner, Joyce A. 1971. Tomorrow's Tomorrow: The Black Woman. Garden City, N.Y.

Lebeuf, Annie M. D. 1963. "The Role of Women in the Political Organization of African Societies," in Denise Paulme, ed., Women in Tropical Africa. Berkeley, Calif.

Lewis, Diane K. 1973. "The Black Family: Socialization and Sex Roles." Unpublished manuscript.

Moynihan, Daniel P. 1965. The Negro Family: The Case for National Action. U.S. Department of Labor, Washington, D.C.

Ottenberg, Simon. 1959. "Ibo Receptivity to Change," in William R. Bascom and Melville J. Herskovits, eds., Continuity and Change in African Cultures. Chicago.

Randolph, Richard R. 1964. "The 'Matrifocal Family' as a Comparative Category," *American Anthropologist*, 66: 628–31.

Schneider, David. 1968. Review of the Moynihan Report and the Politics of Controversy, by Lee Rainwater and William L. Yancey, *Bulletin of the Atomic Scientists*, March.

Schneider, David M., and Raymond T. Smith. 1973. Class Differences and Sex Roles in American Kinship and Family Structure. Englewood Cliffs, N.J.

Shimkin, Demitri B., Gloria J. Louie, and Dennis A. Frate. 1973. "The Black Extended Family: A Basic Rural Institution and a Mechanism of Urban Adaptation." Unpublished manuscript.

Siegel, James. 1969. The Rope of God. Berkeley, Calif.

Smith, Raymond T. 1956. The Negro Family in British Guiana. London.

———— 1970."The Nuclear Family in Afro-American Kinship," *Journal of Comparative Family Studies*, 1: 55–70.

———— 1973. "The Matrifocal Family," in Jack Goody, ed., The Character of Kinship. Cambridge, Eng.

Snouck-Hurgronje, C. 1906. The Achenese. Trans. A. W. S. O'Sullivan. 2 vols. Leiden.

Stack, Carol B. 1970. "The Kindred of Viola Jackson: Residence and Family Organization of an Urban Black American Family," in Norman E. Whitten, Jr., and John F. Szwed, eds., Afro-American Anthropology: Contemporary Perspectives. New York.

———— 1971. "Parenthood and Personal Kinship Networks Among Blacks 'On Aid.'" Paper presented at the 70th Annual Meeting of the American Anthropological Association. New York.

———— 1973."Who Raises Black Children: Transactions of Child Givers and Child Receivers." IXth International Congress of Anthropological and Ethnological Sciences. Chicago.

Tanner, Nancy. 1969. "Disputing and Dispute Settlement Among the Minangkabau of Indonesia," *Indonesia*, 8: 21–67.

———— 1970. "Disputes and the Genesis of Legal Principles: Examples from Minangkabau," *Southwestern Journal of Anthropology*, 23: 375–401.

———— 1971. "Matrifocality in Indonesia and Among Black Americans." Paper presented at the 70th Annual Meeting of the American Anthropological Association. New York.

——— 1972. "Minangkabau," in Frank Le Barr, ed., *Ethnic Groups of Insular Southeast Asia*, Human Relations Area Files Press. New Haven.

Tulis St. Sati, ed. 1963. Tjerita si Umbut Muda. Djakarta.

Uchendu, Victor C. 1965. The Igbo of Southeast Nigeria. New York.

Valentine, Charles A. 1968. Culture and Poverty. Chicago.

Young, Virginia Heyer. 1970. "Family and Childhood in a Southern Negro Community," *American Anthropologist*, 72: 269–88.

Wolf: Chinese Women

Crook, Isabel, and David Crook. 1959. Revolution in a Chinese Village: Ten Mile Inn. London.

Elliott, Alan J. A. 1955. Chinese Spirit Medium Cults in Singapore. Monographs on Social Anthropology, No. 14 (new series), Department of Anthropology, London School of Economics. London.

Hinton, William. 1968. Fanshen: A Documentary of Revolution in a Chinese Village. New York.

Hsu, Francis L. K. 1948. Under the Ancestors' Shadow: Chinese Culture and Personality. New York.

Johnston, R. F. 1910. Lion and Dragon in Northern China. New York.

Levy, Marion J., Jr. 1949. The Family Revolution in Modern China. Cambridge, Mass.

Myrdal, Jan. 1964. Report from a Chinese Village. London.

Smith, Arthur H. 1899. Village Life in China. New York.

Wolf, Arthur P. 1973. Marriage and Adoption in Northern Taiwan. (In press.)

Yang, C. K. 1959. The Chinese Family in the Communist Revolution. Cambridge, Mass.

Yang, Martin C. 1945. A Chinese Village: Taitou, Shantung Province. New York.

Zen, Sophia H. Chen. 1931. "China's Changing Culture," *Pacific Affairs*, 4: 1072–78.

Hoffer: Madam Yoko

Abraham, Arthur. 1971. "The Rise of Traditional Leadership Among the Mende: A Study in the Acquisition of Political Power." M.A. thesis, Fourah Bay College, Freetown, Sierra Leone.

Alldridge, T. J. 1901. The Sherbro and Its Hinterland. London.

Great Britain. 1875. Parliamentary Papers. Continuation of Command Paper 1343 of 1875, part I, nos. 51 and 52. London.

Caulker Manuscript. 1908. *Sierra Leone Studies*, o.s. nos. 4, 6, 7. Original copy in Sierra Leone Government Archives, Freetown.

Denzer, LaRay. 1971. "Sierra Leone—Bai Bureh," in Michael Crowder, ed., West African Resistance: The Military Response to Colonial Occupation. New York.

Dow, Thomas E., Jr. 1971. "Fertility and Family Planning in Sierra Leone," *Studies in Family Planning*, 8: 153–65.

Easmon, M. C. F. 1958. "Madam Yoko: Ruler of the Mendi Confederacy," *Sierra Leone Studies*, n.s. no. 11: 165–68.

Fyfe, Christopher. 1962. A History of Sierra Leone. London.
——— 1964. Sierra Leone Inheritance. London.
Hoffer, Carol P. 1971. "Acquisition and Exercise of Political Power by a Woman Paramount Chief of the Sherbro People." Ph.D. dissertation, Bryn Mawr College. Ann Arbor, Mich.
——— 1972. "Mende and Sherbro Women in High Office," *Canadian Journal of African Studies*, 6 (2): 151–64.
——— 1973. "Bundu Society: Female Solidarity in a Political Context." Paper presented at the Ninth International Congress of Anthropological and Ethnological Sciences, Chicago.
Jaiah, David. 1970. Personal communication. Moyamba, Sierra Leone.
Jambai, A. E. 1970. Personal communication. District Officer, Moyamba District, Sierra Leone.
Kandeh, Hannah. 1969. Personal communication. Moyamba, Sierra Leone.
Kup, Peter. 1962. A History of Sierra Leone, 1400–1787. London.
Leigh, W. W. 1969. Personal communication. Moyamba, Sierra Leone.
Little, Kenneth. 1967. The Mende of Sierra Leone. London.
Luke, Sir Harry. 1953. Cities and Men: An Autobiography, vol. I. London.
Mannah-Kpaka, J. K. 1953. "Memoirs of the 1898 Rising," *Sierra Leone Studies*, m.s., no. 1: 28–39.
Margai, Milton, A. S. 1948. "Welfare Work in a Secret Society," *African Affairs*, 47: 227–30.
Ranson, Brian H. A. 1968. A Sociological Study of Moyamba Town, Sierra Leone. Zaria.
Sierra Leone, Government Archives, Freetown (unless otherwise indicated):
  1878–82. Governor's Aborigines Letterbook.
  1882–86. Aborigines Department Letterbook.
  1886–87. Aborigines Department Letterbook.
  1887–89. Aborigines Department Letterbook.
  1889–98. (Confidential) Native Affairs Department Letterbook.
  1890. Aborigines Department Letterbook.
  1895–96. Native Affairs Department Letterbook.
  1914. List of Paramount Chiefs, Their Chiefdoms, Characters, and Sub-Chiefs. Sierra Leone Collection, Fourah Bay College, Typescript.
  1970. Provinces Handbook, 1969/70. Ministry of Interior. Mimeo.
Sierra Leone. 1899. Report by Her Majesty's Commissioner and Correspondence on the Subject of the Insurrection in the Sierra Leone Protectorate, 1898 (Chalmers Report). London.
Yoko MS. n.d. Original with D. L. Sumner, Shenge, Sierra Leone.

Sanday: Female Status in the Public Domain

Boserup, Ester. 1970. Women's Role in Economic Development. New York.
Brown, Judith K. 1970. "Economic Organization and the Position of Women Among the Iroquois," *Ethnohistory*, 17 (3–4): 151–67.
Coppinger, Robert M., and Paul C. Rosenblatt. 1968. "Romantic Love and Subsistence Dependence of Spouses," *Southwestern Journal of Anthropology*, 24: 310–19.
De Beauvoir, Simone. 1953. The Second Sex. New York. Originally published in French in 1949.

De Schlippe, Pierre. 1956. Shifting Cultivation in Africa: Azande System of Agriculture. London.

Drake-Brockman, Ralph E. 1912. British Somaliland. London.

Ember, Melvin, and Carol R. Ember. 1971. "The Conditions Favoring Matrilocal Versus Patrilocal Residence," *American Anthropologist*, 73: 571–94.

Epstein, Cynthia Fuchs. 1971. Woman's Place. Berkeley, Calif.

Evans-Pritchard, Edward E. 1937. Witchcraft, Oracles and Magic Among the Azande. New York.

Firth, Raymond. 1939. Primitive Polynesian Economy. London.

Hoffer, Carol. 1972. "Mende and Sherbro Women in High Office," *Canadian Journal of African Studies*, 6: 151–64.

Keesing, Felix M. 1934. Modern Samoa: Its Government and Changing Life. London.

——— 1937. "The Taupo System of Samoa," *Oceania*, 8: 1–14.

Lebeuf, Annie M. D. 1963. "The Role of Women in the Political Organization of African Societies," in Denise Paulme, ed., Women of Tropical Africa. Berkeley, Calif.

LeVine, Robert A. 1970. "Sex Roles and Economic Change in Africa," in John Middleton, ed., Black Africa. London.

Lipman-Blumen, Jean. 1972. "Role De-Differentiation as a System Response to Crisis: Occupational and Political Roles of Women," *Sociological Inquiry*, 43: 105–29.

Mead, Margaret. 1928. Coming of Age in Samoa: A Psychological Study of Primitive Youth for Western Civilization. New York.

——— 1930. "Social Organization of Manua," Bernice P. Bishop Museum Bulletin 76, Hawaii.

Murdock, George P. 1971. "Anthropology's Mythology: The Huxley Memorial Lecture 1971," *Proceedings of the Royal Anthropological Institute of Great Britain and Ireland for 1971*, pp. 17–24.

Nadel, S. F. 1960. "Witchcraft in Four African Societies: An Essay in Comparison," in S. Ottenberg and P. Ottenberg, eds., Cultures and Societies of Africa. New York.

Noon, John A. 1949. "Law and Government of the Grand River Iroquois," Viking Fund Publications in Anthropology, No. 12, New York.

Ottenberg, P. V. 1959. "The Changing Economic Position of Women Among the Afikpo Ibo," in W. R. Bascom and M. J. Herskovits, eds., Continuity and Change in African Cultures. Chicago.

Randle, M. C. 1951. "Iroquois Women, Then—Now," in *Symposium on Local Diversity in Iroquois Culture*, Bureau of American Ethnology, Bulletin 149, Washington, D.C.

Sanday, Peggy R. 1973. "Toward a Theory of the Status of Women," *American Anthropologist*, 75: 1682–1700.

Schlegel, Alice. 1972. Male Dominance and Female Autonomy: Domestic Authority in Matrilineal Societies. New Haven.

Smith, Michael G. 1960. Government in Zazau. London.

Sacks: Engels Revisited

Benston, Margaret. 1969. "The Political Economy of Women's Liberation," *Monthly Review*, 21: 13–27.

Boserup, Ester. 1970. Women's Role in Economic Development. New York.
Clark, Alice. 1968. Working Life of Women in the Seventeenth Century. London.
Cohen, Yehudi. 1969. "Ends and Means in Political Control: State Organization and the Punishment of Adultery, Incest and the Violation of Celibacy," *American Anthropologist*, 71: 658–88.
Engels, Friedrich. 1891. The Origin of the Family, Private Property and the State, 4th ed. Moscow.
Friedl, Ernestine. 1967. "The Position of Women: Appearance and Reality," *Anthropological Quarterly*, 40: 97–108.
Hunter, Monica. 1936. Reaction to Conquest. London.
Krige, E. J., and J. D. Krige. 1943. Realm of a Rain Queen. London.
Roscoe, John. 1966. The Baganda. New York.
Sacks, Karen. 1971. "Economic Bases of Sexual Equality: A Comparative Study of Four African Societies." Ph.D. dissertation, University of Michigan.
Sahlins, Marshall. 1971. Stone Age Economics. Chicago.
Turnbull, Colin. 1965. Wayward Servants. New York.

Leis: Women in Groups

Eggan, Fred. 1954. "Social Anthropology and the Method of Controlled Comparison," *American Anthropologist*, 56: 743–63.
Forde, Daryll. 1951. "The Yoruba-speaking Peoples of South-Western Nigeria," in D. Forde, ed., Ethnographic Survey of Africa. London.
Green, M. M. 1947. Ibo Village Affairs. London.
Hodder, B. W. 1962. "The Yoruba Rural Market," in Paul Bohannan and George Dalton, Markets in Africa. Evanston, Ill.
Lebeuf, Annie M. D. 1963. "The Role of Women in the Political Organization of African Societies," in Denise Paulme, ed., Women of Tropical Africa. Berkeley, Calif.
Leis, Nancy B. 1964. "Economic Independence and Ijaw Women: a Comparative Study of Two Communities in the Niger Delta." Unpublished Ph.D. dissertation, Northwestern University.
Leith-Ross, Sylvia. 1965. African Women. New York.
Little, Kenneth. 1951. The Mende of Sierra Leone. London.
Montagu, Ashley. 1953. The Natural Superiority of Women. New York.
Paulme, Denise, ed. 1963. Women of Tropical Africa. Berkeley, Calif.
Perham, Margery. 1937. Native Administration in Nigeria. London.
Shapiro, Judith. 1971. Review of The Imperial Animal, by Lionel Tiger and Robin Fox. *Natural History*, October.
Tiger, Lionel. 1969. Men in Groups. New York.
Williamson, Kay. 1962. "Changes in the Marriage System of the Okrika Ijo," *Africa*, 32: 53–61.

Denich: Sex and Power in the Balkans

Campbell, J. K. 1964. Honour, Family, and Patronage. New York.
Denich, Bette S. 1970. "Social Mobility and Industrialization in a Yugoslav Town." Ph.D. dissertation, University of California, Berkeley.
Djilas, Milovan. 1958. Land Without Justice. New York.
Durham, M. E. 1928. Some Tribal Origins, Laws and Customs of the Balkans. London.

Engels, Friedrich. 1891. The Origin of the Family, Private Property and the State. 4th ed. Moscow.

Erlich, Vera S. 1966. Family in Transition: A Study of Three Hundred Yugoslav Villages. Princeton, N.J.

Fox, Robin. 1967. Kinship and Marriage. London.

Friedl, Ernestine. 1962. Vasilika: A Village in Modern Greece. New York.

Fustel de Coulanges, N. D. 1873. The Ancient City. Garden City, N.Y.

Goldschmidt, Walter, and Evalyn J. Kunkel. 1971. "The Structure of the Peasant Family," *American Anthropologist*, 73: 1058–76.

Halpern, Joel. 1956. A Serbian Village. New York.

Hammel, Eugene A. 1968. Alternate Social Structures and Ritual Relations in the Balkans. Englewood Cliffs, N.J.

——— 1972. "The Zadruga as Process," in Peter Laslett, ed., Household and Family in Past Time. Cambridge, Eng.

Hasluck, Margaret. 1954. The Unwritten Law in Albania. Cambridge, Eng.

Lévi-Strauss, Claude. 1963. Structural Anthropology. New York.

Lockwood, William. 1972. "Converts and Consanguinity: The Social Organization of Moslem Slavs in Western Bosnia," *Ethnology*, 11: 55–79.

Michaelson, Evalyn J., and Walter Goldschmidt. 1971. "Female Roles and Male Dominance Among Peasants," *Southwestern Journal of Anthropology*, 27: 330–52.

Morgan, Lewis Henry. 1877. Ancient Society. New York.

Murphy, Robert F. 1971. The Dialectics of Social Life. New York.

Richards, Audrey. 1950. "Some Types of Family Structure Among the Central Bantu," in A. R. Radcliffe-Brown and D. Forde, eds., African Systems of Kinship and Marriage. London.

Sahlins, Marshall. 1961. "The Segmentary Lineage: An Organization of Predatory Expansion," *American Anthropologist*, 63: 322–43.

Sanders, Irwin. 1949. Balkan Village. Lexington, Ky.

Schein, Muriel. 1971. "Only on Sundays," *Natural History*, 80, 4: 52–61.

Schneider, David, and Kathleen Gough. 1961. Matrilineal Kinship. Berkeley, Calif.

Schneider, Jane. 1971. "Of Vigilance and Virgins: Honor, Shame, and Access to Resources in Mediterranean Society," *Ethnology*, 10: 1–24.

Simic, Andrei. 1969. "Management of the Male Image in Yugoslavia," *Anthropological Quarterly*, 42: 89–101.

Winner, Irene. 1971. A Slovenian Village. Providence, R.I.

Bamberger: The Myth of Matriarchy

Bachofen, J. J. 1967. Myth, Religion and Mother Right. Selected Writings. Ralph Mannheim, trans. Bollingen Series, 84. Princeton, N.J.

Bridges, E. Lucas. 1948. Uttermost Part of the Earth. New York.

Fulop, Marcos. 1956. Aspectos de la cultura Tukana: Mitología. *Revista Colombiana de Antropología* (Bogotá), 5: 337–73.

Goldman, Irving. 1963. The Cubeo. Indians of the Northwest Amazon. Illinois Studies in Anthropology, 2. Urbana.

Gusinde, Martin. 1961. The Yamana. The Life and Thought of the Water Nomads of Cape Horn. 5 vols. Originally published in 1937. Frieda Schütze, trans. Human Relations Area File. New Haven.

Lévi-Strauss, Claude. 1973. From Honey to Ashes. Introduction to a Science of Mythology, vol. 2. Originally published in 1966. John and Doreen Weightman, trans. New York.

Maine, Henry Sumner. 1861. Ancient Law: Its Connection with the Early History of Society and Its Relation to Modern Ideas. Boston.

McLennan, John F. 1970. Primitive Marriage: An Inquiry into the Origin of the Form of Capture in Marriage Ceremonies. Peter Rivière, ed. Originally published in 1865. Chicago.

Malinowski, Bronislaw. 1926. Myth in Primitive Psychology. New York.

Métraux, Alfred. 1943. "A Myth of the Chamoco Indians and Its Social Significance," *Journal of American Folklore*, 56: 113–19.

Morgan, Lewis Henry. 1877. Ancient Society. New York.

Murphy, Robert F. 1958. Mundurucú Religion. University of California Publications in American Archaeology and Ethnoolgy, 49. Berkeley.

Nimuendajú, Curt. 1952. The Tukuna. University of California Publications in American Archaeology and Ethnology, 45. Berkeley.

Pembroke, Simon. 1967. "Women in Charge: The Function of Alternatives in Early Greek Tradition and the Ancient Idea of Matriarchy," *Journal of the Warburg and Courtauld Institutes*, 30: 1–35.

Reichel-Dolmatoff, Gerardo. 1971. Amazonian Cosmos: The Sexual and Religious Symbolism of the Tukano Indians. Chicago.

Scanlon, Leone. 1973. "Essays on the Effect of Feminism and Socialism upon the Literature of 1880–1914." Unpublished Ph.D. dissertation, Brandeis University.

Schaden, Egon. 1959. A Mitologia Heróica de Tribos Indígenas do Brasil. Rio de Janeiro.

Stradelli, Ermanno. 1964. La Leggenda del Jurupary. Caderno 4, Instituto Cultural Italo-Brasileiro. Originally published in 1890. São Paulo.

Tylor, E. B. 1899. "On a Method of Investigating the Development of Institutions, Applied to Laws of Marriage and Descent," *Journal of the Royal Anthropological Institute*, 18: 245–69.

Wallace, Anthony F. C. 1971. "Handsome Lake and the Decline of the Iroquois Matriarchate," in F. L. K. Hsu, ed., Kinship and Culture. Chicago.

Westermarck, Edward A. 1891. The History of Human Marriage. 3 vols. 5th ed. London.

Paul: Work and Sex in a Guatemalan Village

Bateson, Gregory, and Margaret Mead. 1942. Balinese Character. New York.

Colby, Benjamin J. 1967. "Psychological Orientations," in Handbook of Middle American Indians, pp. 416–31. Vol. 6, Social Anthropology, ed. M. Nash. Austin, Tex.

Douglas, Mary. 1966. Purity and Danger. New York.

——— 1970. Natural Symbols. London.

Goffman, Erving. 1956. The Presentation of Self in Everyday Life. Garden City, N.Y.

Mendelson, Michael E. 1967. "Ritual and Mythology," in Handbook of Middle American Indians, pp. 392–415. Vol. 6, Social Anthropology, ed. M. Nash. Austin, Tex.

Michaelson, Evalyn Jacobson, and Walter Goldschmidt. 1971. "Female Roles and Male Dominance Among Peasants," *Southwestern Journal of Anthropology*, 27: 330–52.

Paul, Benjamin D. 1950. "Symbolic Sibling Rivalry in a Guatemalan Indian Village," *American Anthropologist*, 52: 205–18. (Reprinted in C. K. Kluckhohn and H. A. Murray, eds., Personality in Nature, Society, and Culture, pp. 321–33. New York, 1953.)

———— 1968. "San Pedro la Laguna [a case of culture change, in Spanish]. Los Pueblos del Lago Atitlán," *Seminario de Integración Social Guatemalteca*, 23: 93–158.

Paul, Lois, and Benjamin D. Paul. 1963. "Changing Marriage Patterns in a Highland Guatemalan Community," *Southwestern Journal of Anthropology*, 19: 131–48.

Slater, Philip E. 1968. The Glory of Hera. Boston.

Tax, Sol. 1937. "The Municipios of the Midwestern Highlands of Guatemala," *American Anthropologist*, 39: 423–44.

White, Robert W. 1959. "Motivation Reconsidered: The Concept of Competence," *Psychological Review*, 66: 297–333.

Wolf, Eric R. 1966. Peasants. Englewood Cliffs, N.J.

O'Laughlin: Mediation of Contradiction

Althusser, L. 1971. Lenin and Philosophy. Translated from the French by Ben Brewster. New York and London.

Berthoud, G. 1969–70. "La validité des concepts de multicentricité et de sphères d'échanges," *Archives suisses d'anthropologie générale*, 34: 35–64.

Conklin, Harold. 1954. "An Ethnoecological Approach to Shifting Agriculture," *Transactions of the New York Academy of Sciences*, 17: 133–42.

Douglas, Mary. 1966. Purity and Danger. London.

Dupré, G., and P-Ph. Rey. 1969. "Reflexions sur la pertinence d'une théorie de l'histoire des échanges," *Cahiers internationaux de sociologie*, 46: 133–62.

Gough, Kathleen. 1971. "Nuer Kinship: A Re-examination," in T. O. Beidelman, ed., The Translation of Culture. London.

Lévi-Strauss, Claude. 1963a. Structural Anthropology. Translated from the French by Claire Jacobson and Brooke Grundfest Schoepf. New York.

———— 1963b. Totemism. Translated from the French by Rodney Needham. Boston.

Marx, Karl. 1964. Pre-Capitalist Economic Formations. Translated from the German (1953 edition) by Jack Cohen. New York.

———— 1970. A Contribution to the Critique of Political Economy. Translated from the German by S. W. Ryazanskaya and edited by Maurice Dobb. New York.

Terray, Emmanuel. 1969. Le Marxisme devant les sociétés primitives. Paris.

Willame, J-C. 1971. "Recherches sur les modes de production cynégétique et lignager," *L'Homme et la société*, 19: 101–19.

Index

Index